Jacob B. Shook

Shook's Guide for Swine, Poultry and Stock Breeders

Jacob B. Shook

Shook's Guide for Swine, Poultry and Stock Breeders

ISBN/EAN: 9783337330088

Printed in Europe, USA, Canada, Australia, Japan

Cover: Foto ©Lupo / pixelio.de

More available books at **www.hansebooks.com**

SHOOK'S GUIDE

FOR

SWINE, POULTRY,

AND

STOCK BREEDERS.

BEING A

CAREFULLY COMPILED HISTORY

OF THE

ORIGIN, DEVELOPMENT AND PRESENT CONDITION

OF THE

SWINE, POULTRY, SHEEP,

CATTLE AND HORSES

OF AMERICA,

AS WELL AS FULL INSTRUCTIONS FOR BREEDING, REARING AND
MANAGEMENT OF THE SAME.

TOGETHER WITH

A VAST AMOUNT OF VALUABLE MISCELLANEOUS INFORMATION
FOR STOCKMEN, AND A PRACTICAL TREATISE ON

HOG CHOLERA—SWINE FEVER.

AND THE VARIOUS DISEASES OF DOMESTIC ANIMALS, AND THE PROPER TREATMENT
FOR THE SAME.

By J. B. SHOOK

CIRCLEVILLE, OHIO:
UNION-HERALD BOOK AND JOB PRINTING HOUSE.
1885.

Entered according to Act of Congress, in the year 1885,

By J. B. SHOOK,

In the Office of the Librarian of Congress, at Washington, D. C.

TO THE

AMERICAN FARMERS AND STOCK BREEDERS,

I RESPECTFULLY DEDICATE

THIS WORK.

Devoted to their Interest and Service.

PREFACE.

The object of the author in offering this work to the public is to furnish to American stockmen a concise and reliable treatise on the breeding and rearing of domestic animals.

In this work, especial attention has been given to the diseases of swine and poultry, as the experience of the author has shown him that such diseases as Hog Cholera—Swine Fever, and the various diseases of Poultry and the proper treatment for the same, are less understood than ailments of other animals and their treatment.

Believing that no disease exists for which nature has failed to supply the proper remedy, the author, many years since, began the study of these diseases, and the success which has attended his treatment of the same has fully confirmed his theory that domestication should not be allowed to change the physical condition of swine, and that artificial means should be employed to supply what nature requires. Intelligently acting upon this belief, the author has completely demolished many old theories, and a simple, practical and efficient course of treatment has superceded the ignorant methods formerly employed.

The increasing demand for information concerning domestic animals, their diseases and treatment, renders a work of this kind indispensable as a book of reference.

The opportunity which the author has had to gather information by reading and observation, as well as his years of practice in breeding and handling stock, and in treating their diseases, enable him to compile a work, which, in his judgment, will fully meet the requirements of the American stockmen.

The author, in this work, has given to the public not only his own ideas, but has in many instances furnished the remedies used, as well as the modes of treatment practiced by some of the most learned veterinarians and scientists in the land.

The ideas it contains are couched in plain, simple language, and all technical terms have been avoided, so far as possible, thus peculiarly adapting it to the wants of the farmer and stock breeder.

It has been condensed into the smallest possible space, and the contents so arranged that any subject can be found at a glance, and the information wanted easily obtained.

In a work of this kind, more perhaps than anywhere else, applies the often quoted remark of Dr. Johnson: "Books that you may carry to the fire, and hold reading in your hand, are most useful after all. A man will often look at them, and be tempted to go on, when he would have been frightened at books of a large size, and of a more erudite appearance."

For the protection of the public, as well as the reputation of the author, this work will be sold by subscription, by responsible agents who deal directly with the publishers, and who will be furnished with the proper credentials. As none but men of character will be employed, persons buying can confidently rely upon the authenticity of the book published.

CONTENTS.

CHAPTER I.

HISTORY OF SWINE IN EARLY DAYS.

The first introduction of Swine into America.—Their characteristics.—Mode of living, and their health.—How they became benefactors.—Their improvement and health.—The germ theory. . . . 6

CHAPTER II.

IMPROVED SWINE.

The first improvement of swine.—Names of the different breeds.—Magie, or Poland China.—Chester White.—Durock, or Jersey Red.—Berkshire.—Victoria.—Yorkshire.—Suffolk and Essex.—Their origin and characteristics. 9
The Chinese hog and his effects upon other breeds. 17
What breed of hogs to use. 19

CHAPTER III.

SWINE BREEDING.

Swine breeding a science.—How to select the breeders.—
Selecting Sows. 22
The boar. 24
How to judge pigs. 25
Breeding time. 27
One litter a year better than two. . . . 28

Exceptions to the general rule. . . 30
Fall pigs, and how to winter them. . . . 32
Make them comfortable.—Age of pigs best suited for clover. 33
Old view not correct. 34
A case of cooking that pays. . . 36

CHAPTER IV.

THE BOAR, BROOD SOWS, PIGS, AND HOW TO CARE FOR THEM.

The boar and his care. 38
   The brood sows.—When to put them up. . . 39
   When and how to feed them. . . . 41
   Notes worth mentioning. 42
   Teach the young pigs to eat. . . . 43
   Keep them from robbing each other. . . 44
   Treatment of suckling pigs. . . . 46
   Weaning time. 50
   The time to castrate pigs.—Save the sows. . 51
   Care of pigs after being weaned. . . . 52
   Good things repeated. 53

CHAPTER V.

FATTENING SWINE.

The most profitable age to fatten swine.—Farmers A and B's experince. 56
   Mixed husbandry. 59
   Times have changed. 61
   How and when to feed fat hogs, and their food. 62
   Neglect of farmers or feeders. . . . 64

How much pork will a bushel of corn make? . 66
Feeding hogs for a special purpose. . 70
Professor Saborn's experiments. . . 73

CHAPTER VI.

PURE BRED SWINE.

Pedigreed swine. 74
  A good time to buy pure bred swine. . . 77
  Show pens.—That fine pig and its care. 79
  Don't go too much on the color. . . 81
  Where to keep the young boar. . . . 82
  Breeding swine for breeding purposes. . . 82
  This business demands a good profit. . . 84
  When to breed the sows. . . . 85
  Take care of the brood sows and pigs. . . 87
  Fitting swine for exhibition or sale. . 88

CHAPTER VII.

SELECTIONS OF SUBJECTS.

Improved and scrub stock. . . . 90
  Fixing the characteristics of a breed of hogs. 93
  An illustration how to form a breed. . . 95
  In and in-breeding. 97
  Merit pedigree and color. 97
  Roots, vegetables, grass etc., for swine. . . 99
  Ringing hogs. 106
  Stock catcher. 108
  Our hogs as to trichinæ. 110
  Trichinæ in pork, by Dr. Detmers. . . . 115
  How hogs are killed. 117

CHAPTER VIII.

BUTCHERING AND CURING THE MEAT.

Preparing to Butcher	120
Rack to hang hogs on	121
A regular system of killing and cleaning hogs	122
Cutting up the hogs	124
Preparing the lard and sausage	126
Preparing and curing meats	126
A dry salt and quick sugar cure	128
Brine for pork or beef	129

CHAPTER IX.

HOUSES AND TROUGHS FOR SWINE.

Hog houses or pens are necessary	131
Building designs	134, 137 and 140
A bath box for hogs	139
Movable pig house	142
Troughs for hogs	146

CHAPTER X.

PREVAILING CAUSES OF SWINE DISEASE.

Cholera—Swine Fever---Its causes	148
Certain breeds cholera proof	149
Common errors in feeding	150
Wheat stubble pasture	150
Confinement, bad food and water	152
Straw stacks, manure heaps and barns	153
Cholera—Swine fever in its infectious or contagious character	155
Danger arising from streams or pools	156
Danger in exposure of the dead hogs	156

Periods between exposure and its attacks . 157

CHAPTER XI.

INVESTIGATIONS OF SWINE DISEASE BY THE GOVERNMENT.

Investigations . . 159
  Reattacks of cholera 161
  How cholera—swine fever effects the lungs. 161
  When the death rates increase . . 162
  Intestine and lung worms . . . 163
  Opponents of the germ theory . . 164
  Extracts by Prof. James Law 165 to 170
  Theoretical and practical ideas . . . 171

CHAPTER XII.

TREATISE ON DISEASED HOGS.

Introduction . . . . 174 to 176
  Cholera—Swine fever . . . 176
  Observe its causes . . . 177
  When medicine fails 178
  Sort the hogs 179
  Exercise and air 180
  Grade the sick 181
  When to feed 182
  How to prepare the feed . , . 183
  Length of time it takes to cure sick hogs . . 184
  As a preventative . . . 185
  When hogs are coughing 186
  For pigs or hogs with scours . . 186
  How to drench . . 187
  Injections . . . 188
  External applications . 189

Rheumatism liniment 190
Tonic powder, see recipe or . 191
Treatment of sows with pig 192
Objections to pens . . 193
Directions for medicine repeated 194
Medicine for poultry . . 195
Caution as to drugs . 195
Incurable cases . . . 195
Why my treatment is a success . 197
For further information see Special Notes.
Practical explanation of hog cholera-swine fever 457-60

CHAPTER XIII.

LOCAL DISEASES AND THEIR TREATMENT—REMARKS.

Local diseases—thumps . . 199
   Pneumonia—lung fever . . 200
   Sore throat—diptheria . . 200
   Kidney disease 201
   Blind staggers—founder and rheumatism 202
   Snuffles and Piles . . . 203
   Intestine worms . . . 204
   Sweating pigs and scours 204
   Blood poison, scrofula . . . 205
   Mange 205
   Lice 206
   Frosted hogs 207
   Black teeth 208
   Prevention is better than cure . . . 209
   Hints as to feeding 210
   Special notes as to my formula for swine . . 211
   Remarks as to my treatment . . . 212

Offers for a cure for hog cholera 214
My methods of disposing of my treatment 214 and 216
My propositions 215
How my medicines are prepared . . 215

CHAPTER XIV.

PROFITABLE POULTRY RAISING.

Poultry Raising . . . 221 to 227
   Light Brahmas 227
   The old blue hen 228
   Plymouth Rocks 229
   American Dominicks . . . 230
   Poultry investments . . . 230
   Careful selections 232
   Cull the flock 233
   Incubators 235
   How to feed fowls 236
   Nest for hens 239
   Poultry in the garden 241
   Sunflower seed 242
   Poultry houses 242
   Eggs—how to preserve them . . 245
   Eggs—their weight 246
   Vermin—Lice 246
   Ducks—their houses 249
   Geese—their treatment . . . 251
   Turkeys 252
   Diseased Poultry 254
   How to tell when sick . . . 255
   Cholera 255
   Roup 258

CHAPTER XV.

TREATISE ON SHEEP HUSBANDRY.

Sheep husbandry	261
Why wool growers do not fail	262
Forage consumed by sheep	265
Information as to breeding	265
Coupling season	267
Selecting a ram	268
Ewes—when to breed them	268
Lambs—their care	269
Castration—methods	269
Weaning Lambs	270
Mutton breeds	270
Cotswolds, Southdowns and Hamshiredowns	271
Merino	272
What constitutes a good sheep	273
How to breed up	274
Suggestions as to feed and care	275
Things to be remembered	278

CHAPTER XVI.

THE AMERICAN CATTLE INDUSTRY.

Cattle industry	283
Shorthorns	284
Herefords, Polled Angus and Galloways	288
Holstein and Jerseys	291
Ayrshires—Noted cows and steers	292
The monster steer	296
How to select breeders	297
Controlling influence	298

Handling stock	299
Breeding from show herds	300
Science of inbreeding	301
Stock raising profitable	303
Growing of feeding cattle	305
Water for stock	309
Bull and his care	310
Cows and calves—their care	311
Improper milking	313
Removing calves	314
First year of calves	315
Age heifers should calve	317
Unruly milkers	319

CHAPTER XVII.

MODERN METHODS OF DAIRYING.

Dairying for profit	321
The best dairy cattle	322
How to judge a cow	324
How to buy a cow	326
Stabling cows	327
Ventilation not necessary	330
Bedding more necessary—How to feed and milk	331
How to produce milk	333
Making butter	334
Packing butter	337

CHAPTER XVIII.

THE DIFFERENT BREEDS OF HORSES AND THEIR CHARACTERISTICS.

The ancient horse . . . 341
  The Canadian Kanuck . . 342
  The thoroughbred . 344
  The American trotter . 348
  The founder of trotters 349
  Prominent sons and grandsons of Imp. Messenger 350
  Rysdyks Hambletonian . . . 351
  Imported Bellfounder . . . 353
  Mambrino Chief . . . 354
  Mambrino Hambletonian . 355
  The Morgan Family 356
  The Bashas, Clay and Patchers . . 357
  Messenger Durock and the pacing element . 358
  The Draft Families 361

CHAPTER XIX.

THE BREEDING OF HORSES A SCIENCE.

The art or science of breeding . . . 365
  Rules for breeding 366
  Errors in breeding 368
  Speed an essential point . . . 369
  A Standard-bred trotter—popular sires of trotters 370
  Trotting records of 2:14 or less . . . 375
  Pacing records of 2:14 or less . . . 376
  Fastest records trotting or pacing all distances—all ways going 377

Breeding draft horses 380
Pacers and saddle horses . . . 385
General purpose horse 387

CHAPTER XX.

GENERAL INFORMATION UPON THE HORSE.

Management of stallion 389
   His feed and care 390
   His education 391
   When to try mares 392
   Uncertain breeders 393
   Number of mares served 394
   Stallion's age, its effect upon his get—Care of
     mares and colts 396
   Rules to be observed 397
   Their care after foaling 399
   Weaning time 400
   When to castrate colts 401
   Care of horses 402
   Value of grooming 404
   Shoeing horses . . . . 405 to 408
   Education of horses 408
   Things to remember . . . 409
   Careful training of horses 410
   Timidity in a horse 413
   To avoid accidents 414

CHAPTER XXI.

VETERINARY DEPARTMENT FOR HORSES.

Introduction 417
   How to observe diseases 418

Colic—spasmodic and flatulent . . 419
Botts, dysentry and scours . . . 420
Inflammation of lungs 421
Over exertion and profuse staleing . . 422
Colds and distemper . . . 423
Epizootic and pinkeye 424
Heaves, glanders and brain fever . 425
Fistula and poll evil 426
Spavins—thoroughpins—ringbone and curbs 427
Cribbing—windsucking and lampass . . 428
Scratches and grease-heel . . . 428
Thrush—foot dressing—injured feet . . 429
Founder and sweeney . . . 430
Sprained tendons—swelled legs—surfeit and mange 431
Hide-bound—galls or boils and wolf teeth . 432
Valuable eye wash . . . 433
Cataract liniment—cooling lotion—leg or body wash 434
Foot oil—removing callouses—thrush recipe and May apple liniment . . . 435
Corrosive liniment—worm powder—fever powder and cough powder . . . 436
Condition powder—cleansing powder and Dexter liniment 437
Healing powder—how to produce prespiration—strained stifle or whirlbone—to stop flow of joint water—capped hocks—canker—sore mouth or tongue, and sweating liniment . . 438
Tonic preparation—care of tail and mane and parturition-giving birth 439
Diseases or injuries of colts 441
Wounds or cuts 442

CHAPTER XXII.

VETERINARY DEPARTMENT FOR CATTLE AND SHEEP.

Sore eyes and Scotch powder 443
   Hoven and milk fever, or garget . 444
   Abortion with cows 446
   Cow pox and choke . . . 447
   Egat, smut poison or murrain . . . 448
   Black leg 449
   Foot and mouth disease and pleuro-pneumonia . 451
   Hide-bound urinary trouble . . 452
   Scours with calves or lambs and grub in sheep 452
   Maggots and scab 453
   Foot rot with sheep 454

CARD.

This book, if carefully read and studied, will be found a practical educator for the general farmer or those interested in stock. It will not only learn them how to plainly treat all the fatal diseases to which our domestic animals are now subject, but also, to intelligently discuss any subject pertaining to all our improved domestic animals, as to where and how the breeds originated and their characteristics, which are subject of greats importance to those contemplating or already engaged in handling stock of any kind. For by being well educated in this line, as well as any other, any one can often save some serious mistakes.

If a man empties his purse into his head no man can take it away from him. An investment in knowledge always pays the best interest. FRANKLIN.

THE

ORIGIN AND DEVELOPMENT

OF

AMERICAN SWINE,

FROM 1609 TO 1885.

A TREATISE ON THE BREEDING, REARING AND FATTENING OF SWINE, WITH INFORMATION AS TO THE BEST METHODS OF BUTCHERING, CUTTING AND CURING THE MEAT, TOGETHER WITH A REVIEW OF THE PREVAILING CAUSES OF THE VARIOUS DISEASES TO WHICH THEY ARE SUBJECT, AND THE MOST EFFECTIVE MODERN TREATMENT THEREFOR.

CHAPTER I.

HISTORY OF SWINE IN EARLY DAYS.

THE FIRST IMPORTATION OF SWINE.—THEIR CHARACTERISTICS.—MODE OF LIVING AND THEIR HEALTH.—HOW THEY BECAME BENEFACTORS.—THEIR IMPROVEMENT AND HEALTH.—THE GERM THEORY.

THE FIRST IMPORTATION OF SWINE.

THE first swine in America, according to history, were brought by Columbus in 1493, then by De Soto to Florida in 1538, and then in 1609 some were brought to Virginia, direct from England. The congeniality of the climate favoring their rapid increase, and from being so worthless that no one cared to possess or use them, or from some other cause, in less than twenty years they had so increased about Jamestown as to be a public nuisance, and to have made it necessary to fence the settlement against them. Other lots of hogs were afterwards brought to the colonies from Europe, and later to the states. They were seldom bred with much care, and in some localities became almost as troublesome as they had been at Jamestown in 1627; for, as history goes to show, very strict laws were in force in a great many places as to killing them.

As the tide of emigration moved westward, the hog went with it as one of the means of food supply in the new settlements. There is no record of those early times to show that civilization had as yet taken hold of "His Lordship," the American hog, in any great degree. On the contrary, we find that, as of old, he often went wild when opportunities for doing so were offered him. As late as 1828, according to history, large numbers roamed the wild woods of Ohio and Indiana, far from all human dwellings, where they grew very fat upon the abundance of oak and beech mast, and in some parts, where great numbers were allowed to run almost wild about the settlements, a triangular yoke was placed around the neck, to keep them from breaking through the fences.

HOW THEY BECAME BENEFACTORS.

In the problem of subduing the great territories of unimproved lands west of the Allegheny mountains, the hog was destined to become an important factor. The immense forests and heavy mast, the fertile valleys along the rivers and streams, and the broad, rich prairies of the uplands between, produced corn in the greatest abundance. One of the most ready means of disposing of these vast crops was the feeding of them to hogs and then driving them to market, and as late as the year 1840 they were gathered together in large droves from the forests and feed lots of Ohio and driven to Philadelphia, Pa., or packed and then shipped upon flat-boats to New Orleans. Efforts were made from time to time to improve the feeding capacity of the breed by the introduction of better feeding stock from the Eastern Hemisphere, chiefly from Europe, and the success of those efforts have been that we have exceeded the weight of the old elm peeler at one-half the age : but as to what effect this improvement has had upon the health and constitution of the hog, we have seen.

My object in repeating, in the way of an introduction,

this often told story of when and how the hog was first introduced into America, and the way he was raised and fattened in those days, is to once more recall to the mind that for about three hundred and fifty years under such treatment, such a thing as hog disease was entirely unknown. It was only when we began to improve and civilize the hog that he became subject to all the ills and ailments known to civilization, and sickened and died. When they were allowed to roam at large over the wild wood and prairie, and develop more slowly, building up the bone and muscular system first, before being fed upon corn, disease of any kind was unknown to them.

BLOOD, CONFINEMENT AND CORN.

It was only when the improvement of swine was begun, and after considerable progress in that line had been made, then by confining them, thus depriving them of the wild range and the roots and herbs that nature supplied and instinct taught them to hunt, without being supplied with any artificial substitute to take their place, and the constant exclusive feeding of corn from the time the pig will eat it until he is taken to market, that they became diseased. While none of us might be willing to go back to the old fashioned hog to once more have health among our swine, yet I wish to offer the suggestion that this alone should prove to any breeder or feeder of swine, that the way to raise them is as near like nature as possible. Also, against the constant confinement of swine in any form, for I believe it produces many of the ills to which hog flesh is heir. Corn may be the principal food, but along with it should be fed shorts, oats, oil cake, milk or slops of any kind, vegetables, weeds or grass, and plenty of exercise in the pure air, with "fresh water and clean mud."

The first and the most important object to the breeder or feeder is the health and constitutional vigor of his stock, and in the way I have indicated, it can be best secured.

"It is of the utmost importance to successful swine breeding and fattening, that attention should be given to the development of growth as well as fat. It is of so much importance and yet is so largely neglected, that we deem it prudent to refer to it frequently. The swine of this country have been greatly injured by our very prevalent system of feeding by the crowding and forcing process to which they have long been subjected."

THE GERM THEORY.

"If the very generally accepted theory of disease is correct, such a course can but result in making the hog an easy prey to disease. The parasitic or germ theory depends upon the system, human or animal, being vulnerable to the attacks of the parasites or germs. If the system is perfectly strong in every part, disease cannot find a lodgment in it. In general, parasites do not seek a particular organ because they prefer that organ, but because it is weak enough to allow their depredations. There is no part of the skin that they would not attack, if it were vulnerable, and the blood were in such condition as to favor their depredations. But the skin is able to resist, and hence they seek the weaker membranes and muscular tissues. It is, perhaps, impossible for us to keep our animals or ourselves in such strict accordance with the laws of nature as to prevent sickness, and hence disease and death from disease are in the world and are more or less active. But we can and should live up to the knowledge that we have. We know that if a child's bones are weak, it may not only lead to deformity, but that the child is not vigorous. That is just as true with the animal, though it may not show it as plainly as would the child. If a hog has never been furnished with material with which to build up its bony and muscular system, it is practically in a diseased condition all the time. If the same state of affairs existed with an animal of less vigorous digestion, it would go to pieces and become a wreck at once. But the hog's digestive apparatus will often keep working very successfully, while its system is a perfect bubble, ready to collapse at any moment. But no one should be surprised to find any or all of the organs of such a hog refusing to perform their offices at any time. Hence such an animal is constantly exposed to disease. Cholera, in some of its forms, breaks out in a herd and sweeps through the community, and in most cases the learned veterinarian, or those whose services are sought, attributes the difficulty, in all probability, at once to uncleanly surroundings. But, as we have frequently had occasion to know, he is astonished when he arrives at the farm where the disease exists, to find everything as neat as a pin, and is dumfounded, and knows not to what cause to attribute the disease. As said before, our hogs, or other animals, may live in violation of the laws of nature, without our knowledge, and hence sicken or die under apparently the most intelligent treatment. But there can be no question at all that in the vast majority of cases in which the cholera appears, where the surroundings are cleanly, the cause is too much corn and a consequent unequal development of the system. Our unlimited supply of corn in this country has not been an unmixed blessing. It is so plentiful with us that we feed it in ruinous excess, even when we are not prompted to make a hog before the animal has ceased to be a pig, and there are millions of dollars lost every year through the sickness and death of animals that have been stuffed with this compartively unnourishing, but fat producing and heat creating food. Fat, except in limited quantities, is not growth or an element of strength. It is a disease—unquestionably a disease—because it is wholly useless, and not only that, but a burden. Whatever is useless in the economy of nature, is at variance with nature, and excessive fat is as useless as a wen on an animal, so far as the needs of the system go.

Now the constant exclusive feeding of corn from the time the pig will eat it until it is taken to the market, under our very bad system—as we think—of fattening hogs the first year, is a direct effort to create a diseased condition. It makes fat and nothing else. The bones and the muscles are not nourished, and they cannot be forced to maturity, except to a limited extent. They may be said to be forced when the animal is fed all the bone and muscle forming food that it will assimilate, as distinguished from starving it, but there must be time allowed it for full development. The process cannot be hastened, except in a limited degree. But we can force fat whenever we wish to. We can fatten the pig, or fatten the hog."

CHAPTER II.

Improved Swine.

THE FIRST IMPROVEMENT OF SWINE.—NAMES OF THE DIFFERENT BREEDS.—THEIR CHARACTERISTICS.—THE CHINESE HOG.—HIS EFFECTS UPON OTHER BREEDS.—WHAT BREED OF HOGS TO USE.

THE FIRST IMPROVEMENT OF SWINE.

In the early history of swine-breeding in the Miami Valley in Ohio (for it was here, beyond doubt, that the first and greatest efforts were made to improve our swine), it is clear from the best authority that there were two breeds, the Russia and the Byfield.

In 1816 the Shakers, of Union village, Warren county, Ohio, purchased at Philadelphia, Pa., one boar and three sows, pure China, called Big China hogs. The Shakers and other judicious breeders of Warren and Butler counties continued to use the breeds at command, and produced by repeated crosses a hog of exceedingly fine qualities for that period, known as the Warren county hog. This condition of the breeds continued until sometime between 1835 and 1840, when the Berkshires and Irish Graziers were introduced. Some claim that the Berkshires were introduced first, and others the Irish Graziers. But let that be as it will, positive proof shows that these two breeds of hogs were crossed upon the hogs already produced by the cross of the China, Russia and Byfield.

This crossing of breeds continued for some time, until the breeders of swine in the Miami valley settled down to the conviction that the basis of a good breed of hogs had been established, and stimulated by the success, they have aimed to improve what they have been so successful in forming. All defective points or qualities have, as far as possible, been corrected or improved by care. Thus we have a breed thoroughly established, which can be relied upon for the production of like qualities and character in progeny. This breed of swine was formerly known as the Magie, or Butler county hog—having derived that name from David Magie, of Butler county, Ohio, who was one of the leading men in introducing this hog into the heavy feeding districts of the world—but was afterward named by the Swine Breeders' Association, Poland-China. The best specimens of this improved breed, Poland-China, have good length, short, broad backs, straight on both lines, deep sides, very broad, full square hams and shoulders, drooping ears, short heads, slightly dish-faced, broad between the eyes, with a good coat of hair, and are of a dark, or spotted color. They are hardy, vigorous and prolific. Their chief excellencies consist in their quiet disposition, and their susceptibility of being well fattened at any age, large growth when desirable, and a great amount of flesh laid on in proportion to the food consumed. They sometimes dress three hundred and fifty pounds when no older than ten or twelve months, and if kept until two or three years old, will often dress from six to nine hundred pounds ; and as a machine to turn corn into pork they have but few equals.

THE CHESTER WHITE.

The Chester White is a native of Chester county,

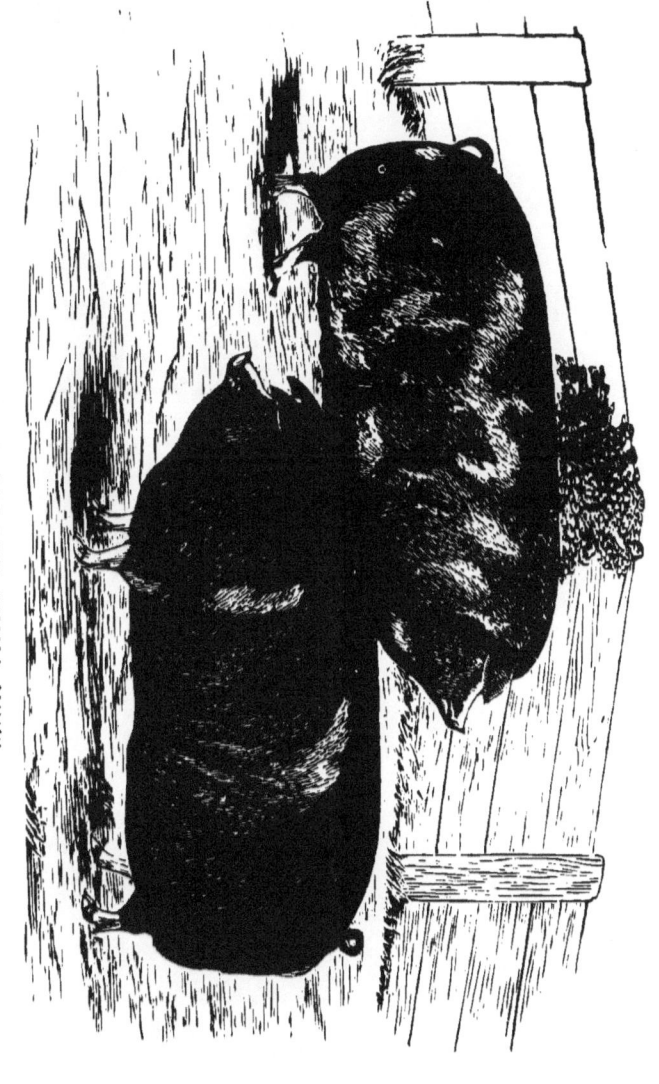

MAGIE, OR POLAND CHINA HOGS.

Pennsylvania, where the breed originated. The first improvement in that county, according to history, was an introduction of a pair of white pigs from Bedfordshire, England, about 1820. They were crossed with the common breeds of the locality, and by careful breeding and selections of the best progeny, and judicious crossing to improve points, the well formed, large, easily fattened, and pure white hog, known as the Chester White, has resulted. All hogs called Chester Whites are not of that breed. There are other characteristics besides color to be estimated in the true type. Some object to this breed as being too coarse in bone and texture of flesh; but if they are of the true improved type, they are no coarser in bone or flesh than the other large breeds, and at any age obtain as great or greater size. But owing to their being white, they have never become as popular as the darker breeds; but this prejudice is fast disappearing, and they are becoming more popular. Of all breeds of swine, they are the most prolific breeders and best sucklers, and as now bred are splendid feeders. When crossed with any other breed of hogs the results are good, and there is no other breed that marks their progeny better than the Chester White. Owing to this, many spurious animals have been sold for breeding purposes that were not pure bred.

THE DUROCK, OR JERSEY RED.

According to history, the origin of this breed is not positively known, they having been bred in England as well as this country for a great many years. In England they are known as the Tamworth hog, and in some parts of America as the Red Berkshire; but having been bred in New Jersey for more than fifty years, that is claimed as their home, and from this they received the name, Jersey Reds. But in 1884 they were named Durocks. They vary in color from a dark to a sandy red, like the Poland China, are docile and easily kept fat at any age, and in general make-up resemble that hog very much. The ear has been the most objectionable feature, being very large; but judicious breeding has refined them in this and some other respects, and they now are considered one of the best grazing and feeding breeds in the world, and always bring the top price in the pork market. They are prolific and hardy, with the best constitution, and when matured become very heavy, often weighing from six hundred to one thousand pounds; but their average weight, at any age, is about that of the Poland China.

THE BERKSHIRE.

The earliest account we have of the Berkshire hog is, that he is believed to have sprung from the old or native English hog, and the county of Berks, in the south of England, is credited as his home. He has been known from time immemorial. Here he underwent those changes in form and feeding capacity, that the Poland China,

Chester White and other improved breeds did in their native homes: and from here he went forth to other parts of the United Kingdom, and throughout the civilized world. The high estimation in which he is held is shown by the frequent mention of his use as a means of improving other swine. He is credited with being used to improve almost every popular breed of swine known. This has been a fashionable breed for farmers of this country, there having been much speculative fever in the past, and a great many, imported and native-bred, have been sold throughout America at fabulous prices. The color is black, with white on feet, face, tip of tail, and an occasional splash of white on arm; a small spot of white on any other portion of the body is not accepted as evidence of impurity of blood, yet the color is generally uniform and markings the same. He is dish-faced, with small neat head, short neck, thin, erect ears, broad, short back, deep sides and well rounded hams, small bone, but strong, and of the best quality. He is very thin-haired, but a breed of great muscular power and vitality, with strong digestive powers, very hardy, a quick maturer, and when ten or twelve months old usually weighes about three hundred pounds. As a rustler he has but few equals, and is therefore an economical breed to turn the produce of the farm into marketable flesh. The pigs are smart and active at birth, fatten readily at any age, and produce the finest quality of pork. They are not so large as the Poland-China, Chester White or Durock, but are superior to them in quality of flesh, it being finer and better marbled, and the best meat for home use.

THE VICTORIA.

This breed of swine was originated in Lake county,

Indiana, by Mr. G. W. Davis, and was formed by the crossing of four distinct breeds of hogs, viz.: Poland-China, Chester White, Berkshire and Suffolk. They are very fine of bone and quality, and are good hogs for crossing on the large breeds, as they possess great power of transmitting their color and fine quality, when bred to other breeds. They are white in color, with occasional dark spots in the skin, and have a good coat of hair; stand very firm on their feet, and have an excellent constitution. They have small, neat heads, dish-face, thin ears, short legs, broad, straight backs, strong bone, deep sides, and excellent hams. The quality of their meat cannot be surpassed, even by the Berkshire or Essex. They are as hardy as any of the black breeds, good grazers, quick maturers, and fatten readily at any age. When twelve or fourteen months old they will weigh three hundred and fifty or four hundred pounds. They are prolific, and good sucklers and mothers, and the pigs are very hardy.

THE YORKSHIRE,

Like the Berkshire, is a foreign breed, but not so prevalent in this country as other breeds. They are a white hog, with a good coat of hair, firm skin, and hardy constitution. They are of good length, with short legs, and very dish-faced, positive in their crossings, are prolific breeders, and fatten readily, and no doubt it would be an improvement to have more of them introduced in most parts of America.

THE SUFFOLK.

This breed is not so great a favorite with the farmer, nor so frequently met with. Popular opinion is, that they are delicate in constitution, and not so valuable to cross with other breeds. They are small, thin-haired, with tender skin, but this may be the result of errors in breeding, and might be obviated, as has been done, with other more popular breeds. They are a quiet hog, and fatten very readily. For a hog for the small farmer, gardener or mechanic to fatten for his own use, he has no superior Any one contemplating buying this breed of hogs for breeding purposes should use some care, as they are scarcer than most breeds in their pure state.

THE ESSEX.

The Essex hog, like the Berkshire, is of English blood, and its general characteristics are about the same. In color it is black, without any white markings, and is heavy-haired. It is smaller, and this has prevented its general introduction, as the American farmer demands a larger machine, in the form of a hog, to consume his corn. The flesh of the Essex, like the Berkshire, is well marbled, the lean and fat being intermixed, and of the most excellent quality. The sows are good sucklers, but the pigs are delicate in infancy, and must have good attention for a few days to prevent loss, or at least such is the general opinion.

THE CHINESE HOG.

"No influence, aside from those of selection and nutrition, has been so powerful in effecting improvement in our breeds of swine as that of the infusion of the blood of the Chinese variety. In fact it is, perhaps, not claiming too much for the influence of this cross to assert, that it has formed the basis for all our modern improved breeds of swine. Its influence has transformed the long-legged, elephantine-eared, coarse-boned, gigantic hog of old England into the heavy-jowled, short-legged, compact, early-maturing Berkshire, Essex, Poland-China, Small Yorkshire, and Suffolk of to-day. Almost every litter dropped from sows of any of our improved breeds contains a living witness to the prepotency of this blood, in the shape of one or more members of the family that shows a decided tendency to revert to the original Chinese type.

How long the Chinese hog has held the type which, since our knowledge of the domestic animals of that country began, we know he has retained without any preceptible modification, is, and always will continue to be, matter of mere conjecture. Its civilization, such as it is, is older than that of any other country of which we have any knowledge, and it is quite likely that its breed of swine ante-dates, in its origin, that of any other race of domestic animals known to Europe or America.

The distinguishing characteristic of the Chinese hog is the facility with which he converts everything he eats into fat. From the time he is a week old, until the day of his death, the Chinese pig or hog is fat. If kept in the same pen with others, even of our best varieties, and with feed barely sufficient to sustain life in them, the Chinese pig is fat; and when slaughtered, no matter at what age, the butcher finds him a mass of fat.

The early workers for the improvement of the swine of the British Islands were not slow in discovering the vast superiority of the Chinese hog in this respect over their own native breeds, and the cross was early resorted to and extensively used. The purely-bred, or imported China hogs, were found to be ill adapted to the climate of the British Islands or the United States, and their flesh was not prized because of the superabundance of fat; but improvement, effected by crossing them upon the coarser breeds of England, made them marketable, and none of the various foreign crosses introduced by English breeders have left so marked an impress upon the stock of that country.

The shape of the Chinese hog is peculiar; the body is long; legs short, back long and swaying toward the centre, the belly nearly touching the ground; jowls very heavy; ears rather small, standing out from the head, but not drooping; head and nose short, and very broad between the eyes; neck short; color white or black, or a mixture of both, but usually the white predominating. As before remarked, every breeder of improved swine may occasionally see among any of the modern breed, no matter how purely bred, specimens that very nearly approach the Chinese type—and which, from the very earliest days of their pighood, manifest the characteristic tendency of their Chinese ancestry to become fat, no matter how they may be kept—a silent but constant attestation of the influence of the Chinese blood coming down through many generations, but ever tending to re-assert itself, and revert to its original type."

WHAT BREED OF HOGS TO USE.

In deciding this question every person must be governed by the location. There is no one breed of hogs adapted to all sections of the country or situations. The diversity of crops and methods of feeding make this more noticeable, and as long as we overlook the facts, the more will we attempt to discover a better animal than those we have, which, fortunately, is not necessary. In the East, where the hog is given the range of a pasture, or in the South, where the forests are used for ranges, and corn is scarcer and higher than in the West, the smaller improved breeds, such as the Berkshire, Essex, Yorkshire, or Suffolk, would most likely prove the most valuable, as they are quick maturers and do not require so much feed. But in the West the system is somewhat different, for the hog is used as a means of converting the products of the farm into produce that is more profitable and easier transported.

CORN THE MAIN CROP.

In some sections corn is the great staple to the exclusion of all other crops, and it is often the case that it can not be grown profitably, and sold in that shape. What the Western farmer most desires, is a hog that is hardy; to grow to a large size; that is easily fattened at any age, and is adapted to the climate, for his object is to feed his corn and sell the pork. For this purpose the larger breeds, such as the Poland-China, Durock, Chester White, Berkshire, or Victoria, are the best adapted. There is not a great deal of difference now in the different breeds, except in the single matter of color. All the breeders of the various sorts of swine have had the same points in view, and have bred to the same form until they have been brought to substantially the same thing, except, as I have said, in the matter of color. If you put a few white spots on the model Berkshire of to-day he will make a pretty fair Poland-China, barring the erect ears. If you take all the white hairs from him and give him black ones instead, he will be a good Essex pig; and if you change all his hair to white, he will make a good Suffolk, Yorkshire, or Victoria. You can make any sort of a hog you want in five years of crossing and selection. Our breeders have all been coming toward one point for a long time, and consequently, they have all substantially reached about the same place.

CHAPTER III.

Swine Breeding.

SWINE BREEDING A SCIENCE.—HOW TO SELECT BREEDERS.—SELECTING SOWS.—THE BOAR AND HIS CARE.—THE TIME TO BREED.—EXCEPTIONS TO THE RULE.—CUSTOM AMONG HEAVY BREEDERS.—ONE LITTER A YEAR BETTER THAN TWO.—FALL PIGS AND HOW TO WINTER THEM.—MIXED HUSBANDRY.

SWINE BREEDING A SCIENCE.

At the present age the breeding of swine, like the breeding of all other domestic animals, has become a science, and for various reasons it is not every person that can make it a success. The first element of success is a love for the business. There is no instruction or rule of any kind that can be given which every one can or will follow: but for the benefit of those who may wish to learn from the experience of others, I will endeavor to give a few plain points as gathered by experience and observation as how to select breeders, to raise the best feeders and to avoid diseases of all kinds to a great extent.

To be successful in raising swine, there are several points on which the breeder should be very particular when selecting the stock from which his future herd and profits are to come, as a mistake at that juncture may deprive him of all chances of success, and eventually drive him out of the business in poverty and disgust.

The first and most essential thing to be considered, is the health and thrift of swine; therefore, in order to secure this, we must first look to the breeding animals. We should breed only from well-bred, well-matured, thrifty, healthy stock, remembering that like begets like, and if the good qualities are transmitted, the evil ones are sure to be.

SELECTING SOWS.

In the selection of sows, it will depend entirely upon what is expected of them. If it is desired to produce hogs for pork, instead of to sell for breeding purposes, it is neither necessary nor desirable that the sows be of any pure breed; but they should be good animals individually, and be known to be from good ancestors on both sides, about whose health, vigor, growthiness and prolificacy there has been no question. Always select the largest, most growthy and best sows for breeders. The main points are length, depth and bone. They should be animals which, when well grown, will be of good size; big enough and roomy enough to hold and develop within themselves a reasonable litter of lusty, well-formed pigs. As to bone, it is not the size, so much as the quality, that is wanted. A good, clean, bony leg, with a hog, as well as with any other animal, is far better than a fleshy one. In selecting either sows or boars, notice closely whether they show a tendency to weakness in the ankles and feet. Some hogs stand up as squarely on their feet as a horse, while others are extremely faulty in this respect, and sometimes before half grown are so broken down that they get about with great difficulty, and when fat and heavy can not stand up long enough to walk a short distance, and, consequently, have to be provided with conveyance whenever they are ready to be taken off the farm. "The model hog of any kind should not be so modeled that, when fat, its legs will not carry it to market, let that be one mile or fifty."

Breeding from stock too young is not only injurious, but dangerous; and as to what age young sows should be before breding, I would say from eight to nine months old is young enough. A great many breeders prefer to have them older, upon the theory that if bred too young it retards their growth. They never develop as well as when bred older. Their true value as breeders can not well be known until they have been bred two or three times; then they will be in their prime, and the best can be retained for still further and better service, and the unprofitable ones sent to fulfill their destiny.

Among all breeds of swine there are families that are shy breeders, have small litters and give but little milk. Such should be shunned, as they are a source of much aggravation and profanity. While some sows have from twelve to sixteen pigs, I never saw one that could give anything near enough milk for that number after they were a few days old, and I have come to the conclusion that a sow that has and raises well from seven to ten pigs, three times in two years, is a prize to her owner which he can afford to cherish and nourish abundantly. Occasionally one does a little better, and a great many do as well, but millions fall far short of it.

As to the age to which sows can be kept profitably, that depends upon how valuable they may be. Most breeders prefer to put them off the third or fourth year, as then they are liable to become very heavy and sometimes feeble or treacherous; and unless very valuable they had better be fed off, and replaced with good young ones, for the following reasons: First, an old and feeble sow will not raise any more nor any better pigs than a good young sow will, and if she is treacherous in any way, her progeny is liable to inherit it. Second, when her pigs are weaned, in a great many cases, she cannot be bred to have pigs again, at the proper time, much sooner than one of her daughters; and then the risk and expense of keeping her are so much greater.

THE BOAR.

As so much value depends upon the male, at the head of a herd, great care should be taken in selecting a boar. As the labor of a lifetime, or the expense of a great deal of money and time in getting together a herd of good sows may be vitiated by a week's use of an inferior boar, it is important that he should not be selected at random. He should be purely bred of whatever stock the party prefers, and not only a first-class individual himself, but have a pedigree showing unmistakably that his parents, grand-parents and great-grand-parents were of the same character. The pedigree is simply a certificate of character, and unless it shows good character it is of no practical value. It should back up the pig, but if the pig fails to back up the pedigree as well, there is probably something wrong in one or the other. "Hands off" would, in that case, be good advice. He should be a healthy, robust fellow, and of such form that, when fat, he would be about the model of such hogs as it is desired to raise. The generally accepted idea among experienced breeders is, that the male should be somewhat more blocky and compact than the female, on the theory that the offsprings in outward form resemble the sire more than the dam.

The boar should be medium in length, of great width and depth, back straight and strong, legs the same, but not too heavily boned, and should stand up well on his toes; neck and head short, dish-faced, ears, hair and tail fine, features masculine, hams deep and well turned, ribs well sprung, being good in the shoulder and girth, as that denotes vigor and constitution (color is of the least importance). When wanted for service he should be at least from eight to ten months old. How long he should be kept for service, as in the sow, depends upon his value as a breeder. He would have to be at least two years old before anything could be determined. If then he begins to prove a valuable sire, he should be kept as long as possible, which, with good care, may be until he is five years old, or longer if he still retains his health and vigor.

HOW THE ENGLISH JUDGE PIGS.

"The following dialogue, which occurred at a recent English exhibition of stock, will perhaps illustrate some of the points which should be looked for in a good pig for breeding purposes, and also show how differently an old hand and an amateur set to work. The first class is that for young boars, of which there were seven. After these are let out of the pen for inspection it is remarked by

A. Some fine young boars here, especially that one with the beautifully turned-up short snout, wide shoulders, thin coat, and delicate skin.

B. Do you think so? It is not quite my style of animal; I like one with a nose of fair length, the lower jaw sprung or bent (not straight), head wide between the ears, a small, keen eye, muscular neck, shoulders slightly upright, but not open or splayed on the top, ribs well sprung, deep in flanks for and aft, loin wide, hips well apart, hind-quarters long and deep, all covered with a fair quantity of not too fine hair and skin, and placed on legs well outside the body. You are then certain to get masculine character and good constitution, as well as the largest weights of meat where it is worth most per pound.

A. Yes! but look at the beautiful head and quality of the further pig.

B. I admit that your favorite does appear to have what sometimes goes by the name of quality, i. e., fine hair, thin skin, and delicacy of appearance generally; this is to me a proof of effeminacy in a male animal. The young boar you admire, as well as one or two others in the class, has no muscle or lean meat, and no middle; he is slack in the loin, and the fore-legs are either bent or both appear to come out of the same place; the tail is also set low on a light ham.

A. I must frankly say that these boars are not so good behind and through the middle as they should be, but I am told the most difficult point to obtain in show pigs is a good head.

B. But what earthly use is a head such as you require when it is nearly always accompanied by a light neck and hind-quarters. The end of all breeding pigs and their produce is the slaughter-house, and, to judge a pig properly, you must first ask yourself or a bacon-curer which part of the pig's carcass is the most valuable. My simple plan is to divide the carcass into three nearly equal portions. Take the head to the shoulder, the shoulder to the hip, and the hip to the tail, and the pig with the best middle and hind-quarters is far the most valuable. Thus, for argument, a dead pig is worth 56s. per cwt., or 6d. per lb. No. 1 part, or that with the head, will be worth to a bacon curer 4d. per lb.: and the second part, the hindquarter, at 6d. per lb.; and the middle, or third part, would be valued at 8d. per lb. These little facts I always keep in mind when acting as judge of pigs. Of course, I do not ignore the useful points which fanciers assert the various breeds should possess, but I try very hard to get the utility points as well, which include in a boar every appearance of being useful as a sire, and with sows that all of them above fifteen months old have not only bred pigs but reared them. This latter is especially necessary, as many of the sows whose lives are spent in the forcing and show-yard pens are useless as brood sows."—*Farm, Field and Stockman.*

Rule: A male hog should be vigorous and compact, void of any extreme coarse or delicate points, sows more coarse and roomy, and both of a kind disposition. This rule will hold good in any breed of hogs, and when breeding for any purpose, either breeders or feeders. To take this advice, and some more with it, I would still say, "never select, of either sex, the chubby pig of a small litter from a small sow reared in a small pen for a breeder. It is betting against success, and giving luck the biggest kind of odds."

BREEDING TIME.

The time to breed sows, so as to have them farrow at the most profitable time, is a question that has to be governed altogether by circumstances. The general rule is. that December is the best month to breed in, then the pigs will come in April, or about the time of new grass. This is considered the best time for the general crop of pigs to come, so that the sows, after weaning their pigs, can have the summer and fall in which to regain their strength and vigor before bred for the next year, unless rebred soon again for a fall litter, which is not always considered best.

There are exceptions, of course, to this rule. First: The location will have to be considered; in some localities pigs farrowed in February or March would do as well as if farrowed in May in other localities. It is thought best not to have them come so early, as they are liable to be lost or stunted by the cold before they have learned to eat well, or can have the benefit of new grass. Second: If pigs are designed specially for exhibition, the time for them to come should be governed by the date of the show, and the age required by the premium list. Third: In feeding for some particular market, the time to reach it must be considered in connection with the facilities likely to be at hand for keeping and feeding for the purpose in view.

IN THE HEAVY FEEDING DISTRICTS.

In the heavy hog feeding districts many breeders of large experience are satisfied to get one good litter a year from each sow, for, by this means, they can have them come in April or May, and by good care, turn them off in February, weighing from two hundred and fifty to three hundred pounds. This they consider the most profitable way of feeding, as hogs, up to that age and weight, take on pounds much faster than they do after that time, and then the risks are so much less. In feeding off these young hogs, very often their dams are fed off with them, especially the old or inferior breeders, and some choice young sows are retained in their place.

ONE LITTER A YEAR BETTER THAN TWO.

"Many breeders of large experience in raising pigs are

satisfied to get one good litter a year from each sow. A first-rate litter, strong and thrifty, is considered more profitable than two of second-rate quality. This is assuming that by the two-litter plan the pigs are necessarily inferior, and there is good reason for supposing this to be the fact.

If a sow produces two litters each year it follows that during two-thirds of the time the energies of her system are directed to the growth of these litters before farrowing. This leaves only four months of the year in which to suckle the two litters; or only the length of time usually allowed for one. It sometimes happens that sows are bred soon after they have farrowed and are thus required to carry one litter while suckling another, but this always results in the diminished thrift and value of one litter or the other, and often in the injury of both, as well as of the sow herself.

If two litters are to be had within the year, the spring litter will come so early that the little pigs are liable to be lost or stunted by the cold before they have learned to feed well, or can have the benefit of new grass. The fall litter, necessarily coming late, will also suffer from the cold of early winter after they are weaned. Even with the best care the growth of fall pigs is retarded by the cold weather and their being compelled to rely on dry feed at an age when the addition of grass and clover to their diet is so much needed for their best development.

Good shelter and regular attendance, with generous feeding, will go far towards keeping them in a thrifty condition: but this adds to the cost of rearing, and is made to count against fall litters, except under special circumstances or conditions which may at times make it profitable to rear fall or winter pigs.

By the two-litter plan the sow does not have the needed time in which to recover fully from that wear and tear on her system which is inseparable from the proper rearing by her of a litter of healthy, fast-growing pigs.

There are cases in which it is advisable or unavoidable that sows farrow at some other season than from about the first of March to the middle of April, or about the time of new grass; but as a rule the general crop of young pigs should come at this time, so that the sows, after weaning their pigs, can have the summer and fall in which to regain their strength and vigor before being bred for the next year.

EXCEPTIONS TO THE GENERAL RULE.

If pigs are designed specially for exhibition the time for them to come should be governed by the date of the show and the age required by the premium list.

Whether to be fed for sale to the local butcher or for shipment to the great pork-packing centers, the particular market to be reached must be considered in connection with the facilities likely to be at hand for keeping and feeding for the purpose had in view.

If it is intended to rear sow pigs to be retained or sold for breeding purposes, there can be no better time to have them come than in the spring, as recommended for the general crop. This gives them the whole summer on grass, and if with this they are allowed a little mill feed daily, made into swill, and after harvest turned on the wheat stubble, or fed on oats and rye, they will make the best possible growth, and be ready to receive the boar in January or February. They will then throw their first litters early in May or June following, or when they are a little over one year old. As it is not generally deemed advisable to save as breeders pigs from the first litter of a young sow, the fact that these May or June pigs would be too young to be bred for spring pigs the next year would not be considered any disadvantage. And yet, if particularly well bred and valuable as breeding stock, they may be retained and served in time to drop their first litters in July or August, or when twelve to fourteen months old.

In the rearing of young boars for breeding purposes it sometimes happens that there is a demand in the fall for boars that are nearly a year old. When such demand is likely to occur it is well to provide for it by having a few litters of fall pigs. The extra expense of keeping them through the winter may be more than realized by the good prices they will command the following season. The chief demand, however, for young boars, is for those of very early spring litters. Here again some additional risk and care are required, but with well-bred stock which can be relied on to prove its good breeding the prices to be had for such young boars will justify the extra care given them.

A sow that is cross or bad to handle at farrowing time should be bred so as to have pigs in mild weather. When near her time she can be turned into a woods or other pasture and permitted to take care of herself. After her pigs are a few days old she will not be so cross, and if then approached with a little corn or other feed a few times she will soon become manageable, and can then be taken to the barn-yard, or where the other sows and their pigs are kept. We would not like to have many of the savage kind of sows to deal with, but it sometimes pays well to humor a sow, valuable for the stock that is in her, by keeping away from her at farrowing time. Having her pigs to come in mild weather is the surest way of having her save them, but even then it is generally a "hit and miss" case.

It is sometimes claimed that sows, in order to become good milkers, should be bred when quite young—say at six or eight months old—so that they may have their first litters at ten or twelve months of age. But oft-repeated trial does not support the claim. Improvement in this direction is best secured by the careful selection of breeding stock, and by feeding when young and growing, with a view to the development of milking qualities in the young sows."—Phil. Thrifton in the Breeders' Gazette.

FALL PIGS AND HOW TO WINTER THEM.

"There are so many failures made in the wintering of small pigs that many farmers claim it does not pay to raise them. Now, if one of this large class would say 'It does not pay me to raise fall pigs,' I would not call his statement in question. The fault is in the man and not in the pigs. The writer finds it profitable to raise enough fall pigs to have a car load of extra good hogs by the time they are twelve or fourteen months old. Simply because fall litters are not as easily kept, and are more liable to disease, as usually kept, than spring litters, does not settle the question of profits.

If the corn crop of the farm is sufficient to make one hundred good porkers, the risk of the business will be lessened by having about one-third of them come in the early fall and two-thirds in early spring. Every one knows that liability to disease increases as the numbers increase. Then, too, there are not needed on the farm so many pens and feeding floors. The risk of swine-raising has become so great within a few years, that we do well to use every precaution to prevent outbreaks of disease, as it is more easily prevented than controlled. We can keep the quarters clean and comfortable for forty, and have the grazing lots kept fresh and free from mud and bare places, where if we had twice or three times that number we would surely fail if caught in a wet, disagreeable spell of weather.

MAKE THEM COMFORTABLE.

Unless the farmer plans to make the fall litters comfortable from November to May, when they should be ready to turn to clover, he will not likely make it pay to handle fall litters. Comfort and suitable feed they must have.

The fall pigs which are to live on dry corn and ice-water from December to May will invite disease; and I would be disappointed if by such keep a large per cent did not die, and the survivors have coughs and a staring coat. If that is the keep the fall pigs must have, then I will agree that I want no fall pigs. But the day has come when we can not afford to raise any kind of hogs on dry corn and cold water. The men who limit their hogs and pigs to the corn and water diet are the ones who make heavy losses in the business. If we have learned anything about the management of swine, it is that the health of the herd must be the first consideration, and that can not be secured without due regard to sanitary law.

BEST FOR CLOVER.

The pigs which come in spring have not sufficiently strong digestion by the middle of May to go into the clover field and make profitable growth on clover alone, as have the pigs farrowed the September or October previous. The spring pigs, to be ready for market by the December or January following, must have grain every day, with the clover or grass to bring them to the butcher before the year closes. The fall pigs, if turned on clover in May, in good order, will make rapid growth until the clover becomes woody, in August or September. By this time the roasting ears are formed, and we begin to cut up the corn and feed stalk and all on the clover fields. The corn is green and is all eaten, if fed in moderation, until the stalks harden. The change from clover to grain is thus most gradual, and we find the pigs often ready for market by November, and to weigh over three hundred pounds at ten or twelve months, four months of which time they have had no grain. This period of clover feeding has greatly reduced the average monthly expense of keep, and has enabled us to convert clover into pork to an extent which would be impossible with that number of spring pigs.

OLD VIEW NOT CORRECT.

'But fall pigs don't do any good,' I have often heard farmers say, and once thought an old farmer's opinion on that point was so valuable that it was hardly worth while to test its correctness by experiment. Having, however, tested the matter, I conclude that, with the dry corn and ice-water diet, and muddy feed lots, and dirty, damp, cold beds, 'fall pigs don't do any good.' If, however, September pigs are provided with good sleeping quarters, with clean bedding, good ventilation, without the wind whistling through, they can sleep comfortably and find escape in the daytime from storm and chilling winds. Then, if instead of rooting and wading in the mud, belly deep, for their feed, they have a board or stone floor to eat on, they can eat with comfort. And if, in connection with this house and feeding floor, they can have the range of a grass lot they will spend hours here every day, unless it is very stormy, grazing.

NOT CORN ALONE.

Now, their feed must not be corn alone. With it and the grass lot they will do well if the winter is open, so they can every day get grass and plenty of exercise; but if the winter is a hard one, and they are shut from the grazing by snow or intense cold, they will soon show constipation and a feverish condition, and by March the chances are they will look rough and come out in the morning coughing; and it is a cough that none of the so-called remedies will cure so long as the corn and ice-water diet continues.

To avoid any check in growth by such deranged condition we had better meet the demands of nature. If instead of the rich carbonaceous diet we modify it by reducing the amount of corn and substituting bran and oil-cake meal we have a ration which will not provoke constipation and feverishness while the pigs are deprived of grass and exercise. But these are not enough. We want a less-concentrated food. We get this cheaply by mixing corn-meal, bran and oil-cake meal with clover hay run through the cutting-box. If the meal and mill feed be mixed with the chaffed clover and moistened and fed in a trough there will be no waste, and better pay for the feed consumed than in any other way the writer has ever tried. It will insure more growth and better health than corn, or corn and bran, or mill feed, without the clover.

PLENTY OF DRINK AND GOOD.

But pigs will not do their best for us without plenty of

drink. How to secure that long bothered me; for young pigs will not drink as much ice-cold slop or water as they need to keep them in good condition. A trough full of ice does not make any fat or bone.

KEEPING SLOP WARM.

A cheap device for keeping slop warm is: Take a coal-oil barrel, put it inside of a box and pack with cut straw or saw-dust. Have a lid to close down tight. An old coffee-sack or piece of blanket or carpet laid over the barrel before putting on the lid of the barrel and closing down the lid of the box, will keep in the heat.

A CASE OF COOKING THAT PAYS.

We make the barrel full of cooked feed. If kept covered it will keep warm until fed out. It is made as thick as mush or cream, and one bucket of the feed mixed with a bucket of water from the well makes a tepid mess which pigs enjoy, and will eat up clean, and go off happy to bed or to rambling about the grass lot.

Here is a case where it pays well to cook feed for stock, and it is the only use of cooked feed the writer has ever found profitable.

With this jacket around the slop barrel the hot dish-water, and all waste hot water of the kitchen or laundry, can be utilized to the comfort and health of the pigs. The chill ought to be taken off of any drink given to the pigs in freezing weather if we would get best results for care and feed.

This device may seem small to the farmer who handles pigs and swine by the hundred, but as the bulk of the pork of the country is made by the farmers who handle a few hogs, the hints here given will meet their case."—L. N. Bohman in the Breeders' Gazette.

MIXED HUSBANDRY.

Now here we have the experience of two prominent writers and breeders, one favoring one litter a year, coming in the spring, and the other favoring two litters a year. My experience and observations have been, that mixed husbandry in swine breeding, as well as mixed husbandry in farming, is the true method for the general farmer; therefore, I would be in favor of Mr. Bohman's system of breeding, and raise some pigs each fall instead of having them all come in the spring. Of course they will need some attention, but there are few but what can give them all the attention they need, if they will.

The device to keep swill warm, as given by Mr. Bohman, is good, and where you have but a few pigs and do not want to use that, I have found it very convenient, at times, to fill a large iron pot with milk or good slops, evening and morning, and heat it on the cook-stove to boiling heat, in this stir bran or ground grain of any kind to give it a body, then cool it to blood heat. This will make feed enongh for twenty or more pigs, and for which they will be very thankful, and prove it by their fine appearance. Those who have never tried this should try it once, and see how much better their pigs will do than if confined to dry corn and cold water. Give a sow and pigs, or a dozen pigs, a good, warm bucket of slop twice a day, and see how much faster they will gain than if compelled to drink ice-water.

CHAPTER IV.

The Boar, Brood Sows, Pigs, and How to Care For Them.

THE BOAR AND HIS CARE.—THE BROOD SOWS.—WHEN TO PUT THEM UP.—WHERE TO PUT THEM.—WHEN TO FEED THEM.—THIS MAY NOT SUIT SOME.—HOW THEY SHOULD BE FED.—NOTES WORTH MENTIONING.—TEACH YOUNG PIGS TO EAT.—KEEP THEM FROM ROBBING EACH OTHER.—TREATMENT OF SUCKING PIGS.—WEANING TIME.—TIME TO CASTRATE PIGS.—SAVE THE SOWS.—THEIR CARE AFTER BEING WEANED.—GOOD THINGS REPEATED.

THE BOAR—HIS CARE.

As the boar is one-half the herd and he is expected to impress his qualities with surety on his progeny, he should be kept quiet, and in a strong and healthy condition all the time. Knowing this, there is no place better to keep him than a good grass lot, well fenced, with shade and shelter, and away from other hogs. Here he will have a chance for exercising and grazing, and is not so liable to become restless and breachy. As for his food, that should be a mixture of mill feed and corn, or oats and corn, and in such quantity as will keep him in a nice thrifty condition, but not too fat when wanted for service. He should be well supplied at all times with fresh water, and frequently with a mess of good slops, etc., when wanted for service. It is always best to turn the sows in the lot to him, as by this means he can be kept more quiet. Never turn but one in at a time, and only allow one service: this is considered as good as two or more, and the additional services only exhaust the hog. Then turn the sow out and put her away where he cannot see her; by this means you will always have a good and quiet hog. There are two old customs that are practiced all over the country, that the owner of a good hog will find it to his advantage to abolish. First: Turning the boar out with a lot of brimming sows and letting him go. Second: Loaning him to everybody else for the same purpose.

BROOD SOWS.

A great many breeders of swine seem to think brood sows require but little attention when not suckling pigs. This is a mistake, for the health and thrift of the pigs depend entirely upon the health and thrift of the sows while caring for and suckling them; therefore, too much attention can not be given them. They should be in a healthy, thrifty condition when bred, and receive such attention after that as to keep them in a thriving condition. Their feed should be a mixture of corn, mill feed, oats, roots, etc., with plenty of exersise in a grass or wood lot. They should be kept separate from other stock especially, some six weeks before farrowing time, and provided with a clean, dry, warm place to sleep, so that they will not pile up and injure one another, for this is the cause of more pigs being lost at or before farrowing time than any other thing, and can be nearly always avoided with a little care and attention.

WHEN TO PUT THEM UP.

Some two weeks before farrowing time, each sow

should be put into suitable quarters (the season of the year being taken into consideration), so that she may become acquainted with the place before farrowing; if not, they are liable to become very restless. They should not have too much material furnished them, out of which to construct a nest, as they are liable to overdo the thing when they can; but a sow should be allowed to make her own nest, as she can make it better than you can for her. Let them do as they please; worrying them makes them feverish and nervous. When I say too much bedding should not be furnished them, I do not mean an armful of straw is enough for a large sow to make a bed, especially in cold weather, but there is no need of her having an excessive amount of loose material when confined in small quarters. Their bed should be prepared in a place where it and its surroundings can be kept clean and dry. It should never be allowed to become wet, musty or foul, and no dust should be allowed to accumulate, as dust on young pigs is very injurious to them, and a very small injury to young pigs may prevent a week's growth, as well as to insure disease. At all seasons they should have a shelter above them. If the weather is warm this is about all that is necessary. If in the winter or early spring, they should be sheltered from the wind and storms. There is not much danger of getting their quarters too warm. After giving birth the sow will be weak, circulation and all the vital functions reduced, and the bodily heat will be lowered in proportion. Nor will it be too warm for the pigs. Their mothers' body has been a warm home, and they fully realize that this is a cold and heartless world when first they make its acquaintance. At the critical hour leave the sow completely alone, and disturb her just as little as possible after that time.

WHEN TO FEED THEM.

Do not feed or slop her until she gets up and hunts for food or drink. She is weak and nervous, and very much afraid some one will hurt her babies. If one goes " poking their nose " around they will get her excited, and she will probably step or lay on some of her pigs. The best treatment that can be given her at this time is to leave her alone. One of the greatest troubles in raising pigs is, to prevent the sows from laying on them and killing them. This is the reason why they should not be fed or disturbed until they get up in search of food. As long as they remain quiet and do not stir around the pigs are safe, unless there is too much bedding. When a pig may get outside of the nest, and not being able or wise enough to get back again, it may perish from cold or hunger. But if disturbed or given food, they will certainly get up to eat it, or get excited, and then they will lie down again, and very likely on a pig or two. Whereas, this advice may not suit those who are engaged in the breeding of fine hogs, who may want to be present upon all occasions at the critical hour, to give the sow and pigs such assistance as they may need, and who, most always, have their sows so tame or kind that they will permit such attention. Yet they will find that it will win "nine times out of ten." All a sow wants is a suitable place to farrow, and be let alone.

HOW THEY SHOULD BE FED.

From the time the sows are put up, their feed should be increased gradually, until up to the full feed, but should be of a loose and laxative kind. Milk, house-slop, bran, oil-meal, ground barley, rye or oats, and but little corn in any way, until the pigs are a week old. Corn is too heating, and is liable to cause fever and constipation, and is not as good to produce milk as other food. An abundance of milk for the first eight or ten weeks of the young pigs' existence is the best preparation they can have to fit them for profitable growth in after life. Therefore the sows should be supplied with a milk-producing food, regularly three times a day, all they will eat. How ever well she may be fed, if the pigs thrive as they should, their capacity for taking all the milk will always excede the ability of the sow to furnish it, even when she is placed under the most favorable circumstances.

NOTES WORTH MENTIONING.

First: Great care should be taken in using slops from the house, not allowing vinegar, salty brine, or much sour buttermilk to be poured into the swill, as a pig is a delicate, tender animal when young, and great care should be taken that the food of the sow be sweet and sound. Any violent change of food given the sow, or her drinking sour or salty swills, will effect the pigs much more than the sow.

Second: Sometimes a sow refuses to own her pigs or let them suck, and if some means are not used to bring her to terms, the pigs will die for want of nourishment. The American Stock Book says: "The sow can be brought to terms by pouring a mixture of ten to twenty grains of spirits of camphor with one to three of tincture of opium into the ear. The sow will immediately lie down on the side of the ear to which the application was made, and remain quiet for several hours in this position without interfering with the pigs, and on recovery from the stupor will have lost her irritability in regard to them.

The experiment has been tried in Germany hundreds of times, according to one of the agricultural journals, without any injurious effects." This may be worth trying, in order to save a good litter of pigs, but if she needed doctoring more than once for this reason, I would send her to the fattening pen as soon as possible. Some sows are "natural born fools," and the sooner they are gotten rid of the better.

Third: Occasionally sows lose part of their pigs from cold weather or some other cause, and it is necessary to put two litters together, in order to breed one of the sows again. This can be done very easily, when there is only two or three days difference in their ages, and can often be done when there is a week's difference. Put the pigs in the nest with the sow, then sprinkle her with warm water, with a small amount of whisky or coal-oil in it; let it run down off of her on the pigs, and she can not tell them apart. Their instinct for knowing their young is principally by the scent. Very often a sow can be made to own her own pigs the same way.

TEACH THE YOUNG PIGS TO EAT.

It is always best to teach the young pigs to eat by themselves as soon as possible. This is all the more important if the sow happens to be bred again soon after farrowing.

If, then, they have been taught to depend largely on feed given them, instead of on the milk of the sow alone, they may safely be taken from the sow when they are eight weeks old. But if the sow has not been bred, it will be much better to leave them suck until twelve or fourteen weeks old; or, in other words, until the sow weans them herself. When the pigs are about three or four weeks old, a small trough should be placed in some convenient place near the bed, where only the pigs can get at it, and it should be supplied regularly three times a day with some good, sweet feed. Sweet milk, good house-slop, midlings, oil-meal and boiled potatoes make the best feed until they get older, when oats, rye, barley and corn can be added, which should be either ground or soaked, as it is easier digested. It is best not to feed too much at a time, but to feed often and regular. Do not neglect the sows, but feed them regular, and all they will eat until the pigs are weaned.

KEEP THE PIGS FROM ROBBING EACH OTHER.

"One of the most important points in the management of sucking pigs is to prevent the robbing of young litters by those that are older. Unless timely and proper measures are taken, this is almost as certain to occur as that the appetites of young pigs will grow with the growth of the pigs themselves. As an easy way of satisfying this increasing appetite the older litters soon acquire the habit, if opportunity offers, of driving the younger from their dams and taking their milk themselves. Plundering and foraging are the first traits of lively character shown by young pigs. The present good is all they care for; and when litters of different ages are allowed to run together, no amount of extra feeding will prevent the older and stronger from taking the milk intended for the younger. The only way, therefore, to have all do well is to keep the litters apart while young. After they are five or six weeks old, if thriving well and following their dam with that earnest, well-to-do and saucy air usual with hearty, good-feeding pigs, there is less danger of their being imposed upon by older ones. A litter of vigorous, high-feeling pigs will whip out in a moment any that would dare to intrude upon their rights as sucklers. The habit of robbing comes only by degrees, and, as a rule, it is only the younger litters, which have not yet begun to enjoy fully their happy lot in life, or such as have never been of strong and hearty growth, that are liable to suffer from the impositions of older comrades. The young and weak can not be expected to grow and do well unless protected in a way that will insure to them the milk of their dams. The separation of the litters will not only accomplish this, but will make it possible to keep the larger pigs from getting an undue share of any choice feed that may at times be had for distribution.

The keeping of the litters apart is some trouble, to be sure, but let any one try the experiment for a few weeks and he will find it time and care well invested. If, as they grow older and learn to eat by themselves, they are well and regularly fed, the owner will feel well repaid for the extra attention given, by the increased growth and thrift of the little pigs. To the farmer's boy, who likes fun, there is pay of another kind, viz., in the entertainment to be had from an occasional innocent and gallant little pig-fight. When two litters, after being kept in this way for a time, as strangers to each other, are brought together, by letting the older into the premises occupied by the younger, it will amuse almost any one to see the dust fly in the regular pitched battle which is sure to take place. One not used to seeing these encounters will be surprised also to find the smaller pigs the victors, unless the difference in weight is nearly as two to one against them, and then, when the fight is over, how proudly the little fellows stand on their ground while the big strangers scamper away. These little battles are not, of course, suggested as a necessary part of the rearing or training of the pigs, nor are they mentioned here to encourage the boys in this kind of sport. But, however they may occur, whether from accident or design, they show that young pigs, which have been well kept, are generally able to defend themselves."—Phil. Thrifton.

TREATMENT OF SUCKING PIGS.

"Sows with large litters begin to feel the tax made on them to furnish milk so frequently and abundantly as a healthy litter will demand at three to four weeks. By this time if she does not furnish them nourishment enough, the little fellows try to eat what they see the dam eat. Her food is not always of the kind best suited to their stomachs.

It may here be said that in all our management of the pig, our first aim should be to not injure the stomach or digestive powers. His value as a pork-producer depends solely on his power to assimilate food. He is the machine by which we wish to convert grass and grain into pork, and the value of the machine depends wholly on the amount of feed it can assimilate, or the amount of feed it can regularly digest each day. We want to keep that stomach in condition to work every day, lose no time, and increase its daily capacity for work. We wish to treat the digestive apparatus of the pig rationally as we do our trotting colts. We begin to train them by degrees; give them light work, and be careful that their bone or tendon or strength are never overtaxed, yet all regularly exercised and strengthened. The law of physiology is, use strengthens, but disease weakens any of the animal functions. But like all nature's laws it is limited. When we overtax any member weariness notifies us that we are near the limit of endurance. The young can not endure the long-continued effort of the more mature.

This power to digest is as important to develop in the pig as the power to trot in the colt. As the trotting quality can be bred into and developed in the colt, so the power to readily digest and assimilate a large quantity of food has been bred into and can be developed in the pig. We can ruin the chances of the best bred and most promising colt by one month's or one week's over-training. So one week's over-feeding our young pig may ruin his chances of making as profitable a porker as he was capable of making with wise and judicious feeding.

The day has passed when farmers can afford to let the sow and pigs shift for themselves. They have not the great forests and wood-pastures, with abundance of mast, and tender juicy roots, and grubs, and tid-bits among the leaves, to satisfy their hunger with; nor the cool shade, pure water from the spring and brook for drinking and bathing, and the abundant leaves for clean beds. Man has destroyed all these, and we must now anticipate the wants of the pig which were, under the old regime, met in the woods. Then the sow and pigs could roam till the master wanted them for bacon; and if they grew slowly, they were costing nothing for feed or care, and he could afford to let them live until they were two or three years old. But now all this is changed. The hog must adapt himself to the civilized conditions, and the owner must provide everything for him, that they may live and help one another.

The owner who makes pork-raising profitable must meet the wants of that machine. As soon as the sow fails to furnish enough milk, she must be fed to keep up the flow to her fullest capacity, and then this must be supplemented with something as near like it in digestibility and ability to form bone, fibre, force and fat in a harmonious way. We must not feed that pig merely to make him fat. If we do, we shall do it at the expense of bone and force, and we shall too late learn that our pigs fatten, but do not grow to meet our expectations. While the ability of a pig or steer to lay on fat is desirable and a thing to strive for, we must not have it in excess, or we soon reduce the size of our pigs to that of the Chinese.

Nor must we take the other extreme and compel the sow or pigs to root or die, and compel them to pick up a living by constant labor and hunting. If we do we shall have a lean, long-legged, long-nosed, restless set of brutes that will never be still long enough to lay on flesh, but will spend all the feed consumed in furnishing force and not flesh. We have a laboring animal and not a flesh-producer. The feed has been wasted. It must be evident that the matter of feeding and caring for the sow and pigs during the time of suckling will give character to the litter, and decide largely what kind of hogs they are to make. The writer assumes that our greatest profit in producing pork and beef comes from early maturity, and he also believes that the greatest profit in pork production can not be reached without a generous aud watchful care of the sow and pigs before weaning.

As soon as the pigs begin to tax the sow they should have provided a side-table, where they can slip in and lunch often. At first it should consist of sweet milk, and if this can be had it is the safest feed for pigs and calves. But where it can not be had, we must approximate to it as closely as possible. The grain of wheat supplies the elements of growth of fibre, fat and bone, and we can furnish a slop made of middlings and oil-cake meal which is most easily digested, and which distends and strengthens the stomach. It is better than dry corn or corn-meal for sucking pigs. My own experience is that corn-meal alone is neither the most economical nor best suited for development of the pig. If it must be fed to young pigs, better results come by mixing it with cut clover or grass.

The side-table for the pigs will need to be replenished often. If one is trying to make the most of his litter of pigs and keep them in good form, and hair and skin glowing with health, he will do well to feed five times a day, rather than two or three, though he gives no more feed in the five times than in the two or three. A small quantity of shelled corn, soaked in pure water twelve to twenty-four hours, when pigs demand more than the sow can furnish, is a handy and useful ration. Corn and oats, half and half, ground fine, is an excellent feed. But when we are feeding grain to pigs at three months old or under, we must take great care that they have a run to grass, and that the grain rations are not so heavy as to make the pig hog fat. He can most profitably be kept plump and thrifty, but not fat and lazy. Health is of first importance now."—L. N. Bohman.

WEANING TIME.

In order to wean the pigs, some discretion and care should be used, as too sudden a change is not always good for either sows or pigs, especially if weaned at an early age. If the sows have been bred while the pigs are suckling, which can be done the fifth day after farrowing, if so desired, or where they are expected to be bred soon again, the pigs can be weaned at six or eight weeks of age. Where this is expected, it is all the more necessary to teach the pigs to eat as soon as possible, by giving them some milk and other feed in a trough to themselves, so that in weaning them, the change is not so sudden. Put them in a pen, or what is better, a grass lot, and if where they can not see the sow, all the better; then feed them well three times a day, with every kind of sweet food: good mill feed, ground oats or barley, milk, etc., is what they want, and if the weather is cold, do not forget to warm their feed. If necessary, turn the sow into them once a day, for a few days, until her flow of milk is decreased. Continue to feed the pigs well, increasing their feed as their ability increases to consume it. And as to age, there is no material difference between "pighood and hoghood," except to increase the amount and strength of the feed.

The Breeders' Live Stock Journal says: "The mistake is often made of feeding young pigs on food that is purely fattening, which gives the pigs a short dumpy form which can not be made to stretch out and grow into a large thrifty hog afterwards. If the little pigs are thus fed and crowded with fattening food in their early life, they will grow into little round dumps of fat, with no substantial frame or foundation to back it. They will be stunted, and show the effects of this kind of food ever afterwards."

If they are not intended to be fed right along, their feed, at any time or age, should not be checked or changed too sudden, but fed once a day, and the amount gradually decreased until the change is made.

This effect can be produced by confining pigs too close, and feeding corn in any form very heavy, or by the combinations of fat producing food, such as corn, oil-cake, sugar beets, etc. But where they are allowed plenty of range, and a variety of food, this effect is seldom produced.

THE TIME TO CASTRATE PIGS.

All the pigs that are intended for feeders should be handled just before being weaned, as they do much better while young and following the sow than they do after they get older, and in case of death, caused by the operation, the loss is less. At six or eight weeks of age is considered the best time to handle them, and, as to "signs," the weather should be clear and warm. If any of them are showing sickness, or the swine plague is raging in the neighborhood, I would say, wait until they are well, or the plague has abated, as investigation has shown that a hog with a wound or open sore will contract the disease quicker than one without.

SAVE THE SOWS.

I have made it a practice for several years, and observed others do the same, not to handle the female pigs, for the following reasons: First: If they are to be fed off at a young age, they will do fully as well open as if spayed, for they are not liable to brim very often, and if necessary, they can be bred four or six weeks before turning them off, and they will then gain in weight very fast.

Second: When they are to be kept until a year or more old, before being fattened, they can just as well raise a litter of pigs as run idle, and when they may not make quite as good growth in doing so, the pigs would more than offset the loss. Third: There is, with most breeders, an unnecessary expense attached to the spaying of sows, in procuring some competent person to do the work; and then the loss is always greater by death with sows than with the male pigs. Furthermore, by leaving them go, some very fine brood sows are obtained that would otherwise be lost.

THEIR CARE AFTER BEING WEANED.

As to the care of the pigs after being weaned, that will depend entirely on what is expected of them. If they are expected to be fed off at nine or ten months of age, and weigh two hundred and fifty or three hundred pounds, they will have to be fed some grain and swills, and kept all summer on grass. But as every farmer can not do this, it is very important that they should not be taken off of feed too sudden, and made to depend upon grass alone, especially where the grass is so poor they can hardly find a living. Their feed should be gradually reduced, and continued for a few days after they are turned out, and then if they are not expected to be fed any more during the summer, they should have plenty of good grass. A mixture of grasses is better than clover. In July, before new corn is fit to cut up and feed, if the pasture fails and a better one is not to be obtained, it is best to mow some good, tender grass every day, and feed it to them. They will eat this greedily, and do as well on it as running on pasture. As soon as new corn is fit to cut up and feed, stalk and ear, on grass, it should be done, giving but a small amount at first, and gradually increasing up to full feed.

GOOD THINGS REPEATED.

"A brood sow should be a good milker. However good in other respects, if deficient in this, she should hardly be retained as a breeder. An abundance of milk for the first eight or ten weeks of their existence is the best preparation young pigs can have to fit them for profitable growth in after life. It is not always possible to decide with certainty whether or not a young sow will prove to be a good milker; but as with cows, so with pigs, we may learn from observation and trial to know in some degree, judging from their general appearance, what to expect. Much will depend upon the dam and grandam in this regard. Milking qualities in swine are as surely transmissible to progeny as in cattle. Thus it is true of swine as of cattle, that this trait may be greatly improved by retaining only good milkers for breeders, as well as by feeding them when young, with a view to their development as milk-producers, rather than as fat-producers. For this reason spring and early summer litters are usually the best from which to select young brood sows. They can be kept through the summer almost entirely on grass, which, if abundant and in variety, will make them grow nicely, and, at the same time, the exercise required in grazing will keep them in good health and thrift. By the time the cold weather comes on, and corn is to be fed, they will have become nearly old and large enough for service. But even after this, continued care should be taken that too much corn, or other fat producing food, should not be given them. We must, however, bear in mind that at this period all animals naturally lay up fat, which afterwards goes to enrich the milk. Hence, while they should not be allowed to become over-fat, they should yet be so fed as to supply this demand of nature, and to retain the general health and vigor of the system. In the winter time there is not much danger of getting them too fat, and they should be fed very liberal.

FARROWING TIME.

When they have dropped their first litter, the most they will need for the first five or eight days will be cooling drinks, and very little rich food, scalded, and then thinned. Ship stuff, with cold water, is the best feed for ten days or two weeks. The richness of the food may be gradually increased, great care being taken not to feed too much at the start, but gradually increaseing the amount until they have been brought up to full feed, which should be given regularly, at least three times a day, until the pigs have reached that age, and learned to eat and depend more upon their feed than the milk of the dam.

WEANING TIME.

"The weaning of young pigs at any age should be done gradually, and with care. If, for a while, they are kept from the sow a part of each day, they will the more quickly take to feeding on their own account. By thus preventing them from sucking the sow regularly, and at the same time lessening her supplies of milk-producing feed, her milk will diminish. By the end of the first week, under this treatment, the pigs may be taken away entirely, except, perhaps, one or two of the smallest, which may be allowed to go to her occasionally for a day or so longer.

Special care in feeding at so young an age is, of course, required. They should be fed regularly and not less than five times each day. Corn and oat-meal, in equal proportions, cooked together and then thinned with skimmed milk, make an excellent diet for them. Wheat bran and middlings, the latter particularly, may also be used with the corn-meal. Oats is the best and safest of the grains to be given whole or without cooking at this age. When older, other grains can be used. Peas, ground with corn or oats, or mixed with middlings, and all cooked together, can be used to good advantage; also cooked potatoes. The latter should be well mashed and thoroughly mixed with cooked meal, and the entire ration then thinned with skimmed milk. If cooked potatoes, only partly broken up, are fed in bulk with the meal, the pigs are apt to gulp them down too fast and thus over-load their stomachs. Then they gag, leave the trough sick, and throw up part of what they have eaten. They sometimes do this also with other feed, when given them in bulk, particularly if they have been allowed to become very hungry. If their feed be reduced to a liquid state, there is less danger in this way; and then, having drank to their satisfaction, threshed oats or other grain may be given them to crack and eat at more leisurely.

Oil-meal, in the proportion of one part to six parts of corn-meal, is recommended as good for young pigs. Barley and rye-meal are also good. Variety in diet is advisable, yet no great or sudden change should be made in the feeding of pigs so young. Give them at each feeding only so much as they will eat at the time, and see that they have a clean and dry place to sleep, and at all times a grass lot for exercising."

CHAPTER V.

FATTENING SWINE.

THE MOST PROFITABLE AGE TO FATTEN SWINE.—FARMERS A AND B'S EXPERIENCE.—MIXED HUSBANDRY.—TIMES HAVE CHANGED.—HOW TO FEED FATTENING HOGS, AND THEIR FOOD.—WHEN TO COMMENCE FEEDING CORN.—WINTER FEEDING.—NEGLECT OF FARMERS OR FEEDERS.—HOW MUCH PORK WILL A BUSHEL OF CORN MAKE?—DOES COOKED FOOD PAY?—FEEDING HOGS FOR A SPECIAL PURPOSE.

THE MOST PROFITABLE AGE TO FATTEN SWINE.

As to what age is the most profitable to fatten swine, there is a vast difference in opinion, and it is something that, very often, has to be governed, to a great extent, by situation; whereas, one person who may be so situated that they can afford to keep their hogs until somewhat matured before fattening them, another person may find that practice quite to their disadvantage, as the following discussions show:

FARMER A'S EXPERIENCE.

I am in favor of the matured hog as a feeder. My experience for many years in the raising and feeding of hogs is, that a hog from twelve to eighteen months old is the most profitable one to feed. I breed my sows to farrow by the first of May, or about the time grass starts, then the loss of pigs is light on account of cold weather, and the sows will not require so much care, in order to raise them. They seldom need to be put up at that time of the year on account of the weather if they have a suitable range, and will, as a rule, save as many pigs. Then with a little care and plenty of feed and grass, the pigs can be weaned in eight weeks, and the sows re-bred. I then give the pigs good attention for two or three weeks, in order to get them well started; after that they will do well on grass with very little feed. I will admit that they do not grow as fast as if well cared for and well fed, but they are more healthy, and the expense of so much feed and care is saved. Besides I get my second crop, and do not have to carry my sows a year for one litter, which I claim will not pay any feeder. And while the early fattener is raising his pigs, at the highest possible expense, upon the most costly foods during their whole life, and carrying his sows a whole year in order to get one litter, I keep my one litter growing in a comparatively inexpensive way, and building up my hogs every day to resist disease more successfully than the mushroom development can possibly do. This has been my practice for many years, and I claim it is the only true way of raising swine. I do not feed my young hogs very heavy the first year, but keep them until they have fully developed, and have a frame strong in every part, which they will have done by the second fall, as they will then be a year or more old. They are then ready to take on fat rapidly. Now, as soon as the corn is in condition to feed, I commence to cut it up and feed it to them, and they begin to respond grandly at once, and will take on fat so much more rapidly than a young hog, and with less risk as to disease. By proceeding in this manner they obtain a better weight and demand a better price in the market."

FARMER B IS IN FAVOR OF THE PIG,

And says: "No man can afford to keep a hog over winter, unless he keeps it for breeding purposes, and I firmly believe just what I say. No man can afford to do that which brings him less money than something else he can do, for his neighbor will do the other thing, and then he can not compete with his neighbor. No man can afford to persistently lose money when by so doing he can get no future returns. Therefore, no man can afford to winter hogs for other than breeding purposes. Whether a hog is kept one year or ten years, it is most profitable to have it farrowed in the early spring. The pig farrowed in the spring requires very little food, other than its mother's milk, till grass comes. After that it will grow fast and keep fat on good pasture, if it has the skimmed milk and other slops from the house for a few weeks after it goes to grass. I have tried this so often, and have so frequently seen others do it, that I know positively that it can be done. The past year my hogs were in extra good condition for market at any time after the first of June, and all the food they got was, as stated before, an abundance of blue grass, timothy and clover pasture. This was all they had until the middle of September, when the grass began to fail. By that time they weighed not far from one hundred and seventy-five pounds. Then I commenced to feed corn, and fed it largely for three months, when my hogs would weigh three hundred and twenty-five pounds. I know that many will smile at the idea of the common farmer making his nine or ten months old hogs, or pigs, if it pleases you better, weigh three hundred and twenty-five pounds. But I know it can be done, for I have tried it too often with the same results, to be mistaken. You can not do it with scrubs; you must have good hogs; you can not do it with good hogs if you neglect them; they must be well cared for. The market now demands a hog weighing about three hundred and fifty pounds, and a spring pig fed and treated as I have indicated, is what the market wants, and it will, therefore, bring the highest price. And last, but not least, it is true, that the longer a hog is kept the greater the likelihood of loss from disease or accident, and this is another argument in opposition to wintering hogs."

MIXED HUSBANDRY.

Here we have the experience of two breeders and feeders, both claiming that they have tried their system thoroughly, and both believeing they are right. Experience and observation teaches me that mixed husbandry is the true system of farming for the majority of farmers, and the same rule will hold good in swine husbandry, but can only be governed by the situation. Some may have an abundance of cheap pasture land or forest to let their hogs run in, and by so doing, can keep them until a year or more old, at a small expense, compared to what other farmers can, who live upon high-priced land and have to keep their hogs more confined. In the former case A's system would, no doubt, do, but it is a system that but few farmers in the older states could adopt at a profit; for I am satisfied, as a rule, where there is anything except a very light expense in keeping the hogs, no one can afford to keep a hog much longer than one year, except for breeding purposes. A's system of breeding, so as to get two litters a year, is very good with his system of feeding, for the spring pigs can be raised with very little expense, until late in the fall, when they would have acquired such age and size, as to bear heavy feeding, and if well fed and cared for until the following summer, should have obtained a good marketable weight, when I would consider it far more profitable to sell them than to feed them longer, and take the heavy attendant risks. For one year with another, there is more disease during the late summer and fall than any other time of the year, and the markets are better than later, when the heavy bulk of hogs are on the market. As for the fall pigs, they will have to be well cared for all winter, and until grass comes, if anything is expected of them; they could then be turned on grass until new corn is fit to feed, when they should be fed off as soon as possible, for I do not believe in keeping a hog, or any other feeding animal, one day longer than it takes to fit it for the market. There are instances where money is made by holding on for a while for a rise in the market; but that is only speculating, and the chances are, two to one, you lose. One is, the market will decline, and the other is, death. And this is where B has one advantage: He believes in forcing his pigs, by giving them as much feed and care in nine or ten months as A would his in fourteen months or longer, and thereby have as good hogs, and save the risks of death and interest on the money for six months, which is quite an item in his favor. But then he can only turn off one lot of hogs in a year, and have to carry his sows a whole year for one litter of pigs, or else breed young sows all the time; which, in either case, would offset his gain. Therefore I am in favor of two litters a year, or at least three litters in two years, and pushing them right along, never keeping them one day longer than I can help.

TIMES HAVE CHANGED.

"A few years ago the most fashionable weight for a market hog was greater than now. Hogs of three and four hundred pounds gross weight were considered the best for market, and were the favorites among the farmers. The farmer demanded a breed that would produce even heavier weight than this. The man who had the biggest hogs for market was credited with having the best lot. If a man had a considerable number which would average about four hundred pounds, it was noised about the neighborhood that this man had a superior lot of hogs, and he was spoken of as a good hog raiser. But this is now all changed. The market demand is for a hog weighing somewhere between two hundred and three hundred pounds, and the nearer it is to the middle ground between these the better, while it is just such a hog which has grown most fashionable among the farmers. The hog of medium weight is the popular market animal, because consumers have learned that such an animal yields meat of the best quality, and they have grown more discriminating and critical. Medium weight hogs not only cut in pieces of the best size, but the flavor of the flesh is superior; hence the consumer demands a two hundred and fifty pound hog. Packers have favored this demand of consumers, because the medium weight hog is the one most easily cured. While the packing was all done in winter, large hogs could be cured without much trouble or loss. But now the packing is continued throughout the year, and for summer packing hogs of less than three hundred pounds weight are demanded. The demand of consumers and packers should lead the farmers to produce medium weight hogs; but this result has been hastened by the discovery on the part of the farmers that such hogs were more profitable than those weighing about four hundred pounds. A hog which would attain to the latter weight had to be kept until eighteen to twenty months old, and therefore had to be fed throughout one winter and through part of the second. This made expensive pork, and greatly increased the danger of disease. Farmers come to figure more closely the cost of production, and found that the cheapest pork was produced by growing and fattening a pig at the same time, till it was nine or ten months old, by which process it could be made at that age to weigh from two hundred to three hundred pounds. Thus all circumstances have conspired to make the hog of this weight the popular one."—Canada Breeder.

HOW TO FEED FATTENING HOGS, AND THEIR FOOD.

With this, as with the age of swine, there is a vast difference of opinion. As for the food for them, corn occupies the first place.

Dr. Stetson says: "It makes no difference to us where or when this grain originated, or who first found out its use for feeding and fattening hogs—no doubt he found it out himself, as he has the habit of helping himself to any thing good to eat, providing he can always reach it—but that corn was intended for the hog, and the hog for corn, is an opinion generally accepted."

The only difference of opinion is, how shall we feed it? When the time has come to fatten the hogs, especially in the fall, some prefer to put them up in a pen or small lot, so as to keep them quiet, and keep corn by them all the time, and think by this means they will take on flesh faster, while others prefer to turn them into the corn field and let them feed themselves. Both are old and unprofitable ways of feeding, and should be abandoned, for they are not only wasteful and show bad husbandry, but are the causes of the death of more hogs than any other methods of feeding. The true method of feeding hogs any place to insure health, which will always insure thrift and fat, is to feed them two or three times a day, and only what they will eat up clean at each feed.

WHEN TO COMMENCE FEEDING CORN.

It is best to commence feeding corn upon grass, so as to not make the change of feed too suddenly, and great care should be taken not to feed too much at the start, but gradually increase their feed until you have got them up to full feed, then feed regularly, and no more than they will eat. This gives their food a chance to digest between feeds; where, if they are kept eating all the time, their food passes off only partially digested. The most profitable time to commence feeding on grass is, as soon as the grass begins to get tough, or to depreciate. About then the roasting ears have formed, and if the corn is cut up and fed, stalk and all, on the grass, the hogs will eat stalk and ear for a while, and by the time the stalk and grain are hard, and it is desired to bring the hogs up to fuller feed, they will be ready to assimilate greater quantities of corn. This method of feeding not only utilizes feed, but prevents shrinkage during drouth and keeps the hogs in prime condition. So there is no loss of flesh or derangement of the system. The change from scant grass feed to a gorge of new corn is too sudden. The vast amount of starch taken into the stomach can not be assimilated, and it either ferments or passes off undigested. Then the digestion is deranged, and that is why some of the hogs get sick. It is not cholera, and as Phil. Thrifton says, "There is no sense in squealing about bad luck and providence. It is simply lack of care, and a bad case of destructive feeding." The chances are, some of the hogs will die, and the most of them are so impaired that the corn will be fed at a loss. By changing feed, and by care and good handling, they can be got back to a fair appetite. But there will only be a gain of a few pounds to the bushel fed, compared to what there would have been if they had been commenced with sooner, and fed more moderately until brought up to full feed; and it is best to continue to feed on grass, in the place of a lot, until the hogs are about fed out, for a certain amount of grass as rough food is essential to their health.

FOR WINTER FEEDING.

Late in the fall or for winter feeding, they should be put up in closer quarters and fed on a dry earth or board floor, and given bran or mill feed slops twice a day, with occasionally a feed of vegetables of some kind, or else cut up clover hay and mix corn-meal or mill feed with it, then wet it with hot water and let it stand a while before feeding. This makes good roughness, and something they will appreciate. They should always have a dry, clean, warm place to sleep. All pen fed hogs, or hogs fed in dry lots, should receive this attention if you wish them to do well. Do not compel them or any other stock to drink bad or ice water, or go without any; eat one kind of food all the time; stand around and shiver with cold, and sleep in the mud, if you expect to get well paid for your feed and labor.

NEGLECT OF FARMERS OR FEEDERS.

"A very large proportion of farmers do not provide comfortable shelter for their hogs. They have tried the experiment and know that they will not freeze to death in fence corners. Well, if they do not freeze to death, it is simply because they burn up in their systems enough of the farmer's corn (which would otherwise make pork) to keep themselves warm. It would certainly be much cheaper to provide them with suitable protection against the inclemency of the weather, than to expect them to keep themselves warm by burning corn. An open shed, under which about one-half the hogs can stand is not sufficient, and forces part of the hogs to pile upon top of the others, where some are liable to be seriously injured. Of course, in a cold night, hogs will do this to a greater or less extent, but by suitable quarters it will rarely be done to their injury. Sheds, of course, may be made too warm, and subject the animals to colds, but because this is true, no careful farmer should dispense with them.

Many people also realize less from their feeding operations than they otherwise would, by attempting to prepare for sale, at the same time, an irregular lot of hogs of different ages and conditions. In consequence of their diversity part are ripe for market a long way in advance of others, and consume considerable corn while waiting for the others to be got into the desired condition. A better way would be to select lots as nearly uniform as possible, that they may all be ready for market at about the same time. After they are worked off, another lot may be finished off, and so on.

Many people have an ambition to make their hogs as heavy as possible, and seem unwilling to sell a hog until they know it has reached such a weight as to render it almost impossible to put on another pound. These extra-heavy hogs are very fine, but it is too often the case that the last hundred pounds has been put on at such an expense as to eat up all the profit of feeding.

An animal, having gained fifty pounds in weight, will not put on another fifty pounds on the same food that was required for the first fifty, and the third fifty will require more food than the second fifty, and so on until a point is reached where no amount of food will increase the weight. So a certain weight hog, (varying with individuals, and perhaps with breeds,) can be fed at a large profit, and beyond this they will make but very small returns."

HOW MUCH PORK WILL A BUSHEL OF CORN MAKE?

"The great question of the value of corn for swine has never been, and cannot be actually demonstrated. How many pounds of pork a bushel of corn will make is what no man has yet found out. All experiments in feeding have only proven what certain hogs, under certain conditions, have made to the bushel of corn. Now, whether this gain was ten pounds, more or less, to the bushel fed, established this, and no more, that in certain conditions, so many pounds of pork have been made from a bushel of corn. There are so many things to be taken into account, as age, breeding, the season of the year, mortality, etc., that anything like a general average is almost, or entirely, out of the question. If anything is well established in feeding, it is, that the young of swine, as well as other animals, will make a very much better gain from the food consumed than older animals."—Dr. Stetson.

Following the Doctor's suggestions, I will add that the gain is always much greater in warm weather than in cold; and old corn either soaked or cooked before being fed is much better, and will produce more pounds of flesh than if fed dry, for it is much easier masticated and digested. The way to feed corn in any form to get the greatest returns from it is on grass. Three bushels fed then to young hogs will produce more pork than five bushels will, fed later in the season to older hogs. The best profits in raising and feeding hogs can be obtained until they will weigh about two hundred and fifty pounds; after that the profits are less. This, again, shows us how important it is to take care of the young hogs, and not keep them any longer than we can help.

WILL IT PAY TO GRIND AND COOK CORN FOR OUR HOGS?

"I have experimented a little on this subject, and all are welcome to my deductions; but I neither ask nor expect that the world will be turned upside down at my say so. I think it will pay to make swill, gruel, or soup for sows giving milk, just as well as it will for the dairyman to feed his cows on soft or green food to encourage the flow of milk. To make such food for sows, I know of no better way than to grind or cook, either with steam or over an open fire. I think it will also pay to prepare drink for pigs in the same manner, especially where large numbers are raised, and better drink cannot be obtained. All know that nature's element, milk, cannot be equaled, even in the laboratory of the chemist; and when milk cannot be obtained in sufficient quantity, make their drink palatable, as near blood heat as possible; anyway to get large quantities of milk into their stomachs. I have used two parts of corn and one of oats, ground together, and added to this an equal bulk of wheat middlings. This has proven satisfactory to the taste of the pig, and

I never saw anything but good effects from its use. It is a well established law in the physiology of digestion, that it is not the quantity of food eaten that nourishes the body, but the quantity digested, or assimilated. If it is the last feather that breaks the camel's back, so it is the extra grain of corn digested that pays. It takes a certain amount of food to supply the natural waste of the system, and all above this quantity is stored up in the form of fat and muscle. Corn, soaked in cold water, for from twenty-four to forty-eight hours, is rendered very much more digestible in the stomach of the pig than when not so treated. Always keep in mind that the greatest quantity eaten and digested is the true secret of success in fattening animals.

A few words as to the importance of fluids in the system to aid assimilation. All animals, from man down, that, in a state of health, consume a large quantity of fluids, take on flesh in the same proportion. It is not the nourishment contained in the lager beer of our Teutonic friends that gives them their barrel-shaped abdomen. The same quantity of water, pure, and uncombined, with the same amount of nutriment consumed, would produce the same result. Show me a fat man, woman, or child, or any other animal, and, if not proven great drinkers, they are the exception, and not the rule. The chemist will tell us, that it takes so many pounds of green grass to be equal in nourishment to a given quantity of dry hay. But everybody knows that grass is more "hankered after," and more readily assimilated and taken up by the digestive apparatus, more especially in animals that do not chew the cud.

There are just three things that give the hog its commercial importance: First, their flesh can be preserved for use, and kept for an indefinite time, as the flesh of no other domestic animal can be. Secondly, their extraordinary fecundity, six, twelve, eighteen and twenty-four, or even more pigs, at a single litter. A sow would hardly die of old age, before she might become the common ancestor of more hogs than are now to be counted in these United States. The third, and most important characteristic of the hog is, that he is a hog, ever ready and anxious to assimilate any article of food that comes in his reach. In plain English, the hog has a stomach made for digestion. All that any hog wants is plenty to eat, and his neighbors must look out for themselves. Yea, verily, any hog with a full stomach is at peace with himself and the world."—Dr. Stetson.

Like Doctor Stetson, I have had some experience in grinding and cooking food for animals, not only hogs, but for dairy cows; and, as I am so frequently asked this question, "does it pay to cook food for hogs, or other stock?" I will here give my opinion upon this subject. There is no doubt but that greater gains can be derived from cooked food than from uncooked food, but if enough to pay for cooking it, is the question. My experience is this: When the price of grain and other feed is high and where labor and fuel are cheap, as is often the case, it will pay to cook food for stock, or at least for some kinds of stock, such as milchcows or sows suckling pigs, in order to increase the flow of milk; or, for young pigs, to aid in digestion. But where grain is cheap as it is in most parts of the country, and there is much expense attached to preparing the food, by grinding, cutting and cooking it, I doubt very much if enough gain can be made in the operation to pay for doing so. Any young animal with good teeth will grind and digest its own food, when not over fed and crowded; when a crowding process is used, and the animal is being forced to produce either milk or fat, it is best to cook, or, at least, soak the feed, so as to be more easily digested. Where the cost of machinery, the labor of running it, in cutting or grinding the feed, the cost of fuel and labor in cooking it, are all taken into consideration, it is a question if there is enough profit derived thereby to pay the general farmer for doing so, or, at least, I have seen it well tested by practical men, and abandoned entirely. There are times though, when it can be done at a profit, but they are only when feed is high, and the cost of preparing it is low. There is some grain that should never be fed unless it is cooked, or soaked. For instance, wheat; if it is fed dry, to stock, they do not properly masticate it, and when taken into the stomach, it swells so as to cause bad results; and old corn is better cooked, or soaked, twenty-four hours before feeding, as it is more easily digested.

FEEDING HOGS FOR A SPECIAL PURPOSE.

Farm, Field and Stockman says: "When hogs are put up for final finish on corn they are expected to return a fair profit for the expense incurred in the shape of a fat carcass. It has been a time-honored custom in this country to fatten with corn, and but very little other food is used after the hogs are penned. Although a fat hog is desirable, yet the majority of farmers prefer to have the meat interspersed with a proportion of lean. That the carcass may be improved in quality without loss of weight, by judicious feeding, has been plainly demonstrated at the Missouri Agricultural College, where several lots of hogs were fed on different kinds of food. In addition to corn the food consisted of shipstuff, used alone, and also on some lots in connection with corn. The hogs fed on whole corn consumed less than did hogs fed on corn meal, but the gain was greater from the ground corn in proportion to quantity.

In comparing the value of corn and shipstuff, two lots of pigs were used for experiment, the period being from March to November, the one lot on whole corn, and the other on shipstuff.

One corn-fed pig dressed 82 pounds to the 100 pounds, and a shipstuff-fed pig 80.6 pounds. On severing the heads of the corn-fed pigs, scarcely a trace of lean meat could be seen, while in the shipstuff-fed pigs it was decidedly more abundant. Lean meat was also selected from the thighs, loins and shoulders of each lot, and examined under a microscope. The shipstuff-fed pigs carried less fat, even in the fibres of lean meat, than the corn-fed lot. The results were sufficient to show that the exclusive use of corn meal for a feeding ration is detrimental to a vigorous and healthy muscular development, producing a pig easily subject to disease, distasteful and more costly than necessary. The relation of the shipstuff to the meal in the trials deserves attention. It was found that 93 pounds of shipstuff gave the same gain that 100 of corn meal gave. Shipstuff, however, has been considered of but little value heretofore by farmers, which has seriously interfered with its genersl use. Repeated trials with it showed that 100 pounds gave 28.1 pounds gain, and 100 pounds corn meal gave 26.4 pounds gain. We have repeatedly advocated the importance of keeping pigs in a growing condition during their early stages, and the use of different kinds of food, as it promotes a better quality of carcass, and we are qualified to know that the experiments of the Director of the Missouri Agricultural College is the same.

In feeding hogs on corn alone, the animals are deprived of many essential elements demanded for purposes of growth. Laying on an excess of fat renders the meet unpalatable. A comparison of the weights above shows that there is but little difference in the gain between corn and shipstuff, while the quality of the meat from the hogs fed on shipstuff is superior. Nor is it necessary to use shipstuff alone. Hogs may be increased in weight by using ground oats as well as shipstuff, and while being made fat in one respect, will also have a large proportion of lean meat. The opinion, however, is that corn is absolutely necessary for hardening the fat, and must not be omitted, but it is really not superior to other grains."

When corn is ground into meal, it should never be fed alone, as it packs too close in the stomach, or intestines. It should have whole oats, barley, rye, or course bran mixed with it. If crushed fine, cob and grain, together, and then cooked, it is better than the meal, and can be fed alone. The cob has not only a large amount of nutriment in it, but prevents the packing of the meal.

"Corn is a staple crop, and farmers find it more convenient for feeding to hogs than anything else, and we do not advise them to discard its use; but the farmer who desires to produce pork of the best quality should feed ground oats and shipstuff in connection with it. Nor should roots and a variety of food be omitted, as such food conduces to the health of the animals, and this is very important, owing to the fact that a healthy hog will grow and increase rapidly. It should be considered also that good, warm, dry quarters will save food, and greatly conduce to greater attainment of weight."

PROFESSOR SANBORN'S EXPERIMENTS.

Professor Sanborn, of the Missouri Agricultural Colledge, according to some of the agricultural papers, reports interesting experiments of six years experience in feeding pigs upon whole corn, corn meal and ship stuff, and in all his experiments the ship stuff proved the superior feed. He calls attention to the fact that 93 lbs. of ship stuff gave the same gain in live weight as 100 lbs. of corn, and says: "This has been the continous result for six years," which he regards as a demonstration of its correctness, as the first three years experience was with 30 head of pigs. These experiments are valuable, and should prove beneficial to all swine breeders, and especially those that regard all other feed for swine second to corn.

CHAPTER VI.

Pure Bred Swine.

PEDIGREED SWINE.—WHERE THE PROBLEM COMES IN.—PRIVATE REGISTRY.—A GOOD TIME TO BUY PURE BRED SWINE.—THE SHOW PEN.—THAT FINE PIG AND ITS CARE.—DO NOT GO TOO MUCH ON THE COLOR.—WHERE TO KEEP THE YOUNG BOAR.—BREEDING SWINE FOR BREEDING PURPOSES.—THIS BUSINESS DEMANDS A GOOD PROFIT.—WHEN TO BREED THE SOWS.—TAKE CARE OF THE BROOD SOWS AND PIGS.—FITTING SWINE FOR EXHIBITION OR SALE.

PEDIGREED SWINE.

A great deal has been written, and is still being written about pedigreed swine; in fact, here of late, more so than ever, as all pure breeds are being registered in their respective herd books, and of course it brings out hot discussions pro. and con. as to the fallacy of it. The breeders of pure bred swine, supported by the agricultural press, claim that they should be registered, because the general public demands to know the history of an animal when it is offered for sale. Registered stock is worth the most money because, and only because, the herd book tells precisely what the purchaser is getting when he buys. No one claims that the fact of registry multiplies or strengthens the merit of the animal. It simply tells where the animal came from. A thorough-bred animal is just as good in itself without registry as it is with it. But how are we to know that? Simply this: If the animal is entitled to registry it must be purely bred, and if it is not entitled to registry it is considered a grade. Here is an animal declared by its breeder to be perfect and pure bred, but he declines to register his stock, and, of course, can not give any registered pedigree. He may declare the herd book a fraud, and of no value, but can give a pedigree without going to a register. The answer to this is, if the pedigree is worth anything it will run back to registered stock, and, if the breeding has been pure, the animal is entitled to registry.

"It is to be taken for granted that every man recognizes the established principles of breeding; that he acknowledges that there is such a thing as prepotency, and acknowledging that, that he knows unpedigreed stock may produce its like or may not. If this well-known truth is not recognized, the only advice to be given is, to keep out of stock breeding. But it is recognized, for it cannot help being. And that recognition settles the matter concerning the value of registering."

But do these swine herd books tell the purchaser precisely what he is getting when he buys? is another question. It is naturally to be presumed with them as with other herd books, that they do. But on account of swine being so prolific is where the problem, if there is any, comes in. The swine breeders claim now to have these registers so formed that fraudulent pedigrees cannot be entered. That is, in order to register, the pig must trace to registered stock. This was done to prevent fraudulent breeders from selling bogus pigs, and to prevent the records from becoming too cumbersome.

Now, if the swine breeders have these books so formed that they can control the records, and trace the pedigree of a hog as the pedigrees of cattle and horses can be traced, so as to expose and keep out fraudulent breeders, they have accomplished something that will go a long way toward improving American swine. This will evidently be the case now, more so than in former years, as the different improved breeds are more numerous, and more on an equality, and all striving to gain first honor. Therefore it will put the breeders of all the respective breeds more upon their guard, as they must depend upon pure blood and merit, more than pedigree and color, to gain or hold first honors; but the breed that will win, is the breed that has the quality. Whether the public records can control that quality, it stands in the future to show.

PRIVATE REGISTERS.

There is one thing that every breeder of swine that breeds for breeding purposes should do: That is, keep a correct private record of all the stock he sells or keeps for breeding purposes. This is not only necessary in order to keep from selling his customers pigs too near of kin at the present time, but also in the future. Then if he records his stock in the public records, in case his herd is diminished by sickness he can trace back, by referring to his registry, all that is left, and in this way make less mistakes than where he trusted too much to his memory. Even if they are only breeding a few hogs, this is absolutely necessary.

In breeding for home use, that is, when a breeder gets his customers from his own, or adjoining counties, it does not make so much difference as to whether his stock is recorded in the public records or not, unless so desired; for his own private register is all that is generally needed to satisfy any customer, providing the hogs have the quality. Where a breeder advertises largely, and expects to ship stock abroad to all parts of the country, he will almost be compelled to adhere to the custom, as in these days it does not do to be a mite behind in any business, and it is easier to float with the current than against it.

A GOOD TIME TO BUY PURE BRED SWINE.

Every few years there seems to be a lull in the excitement that prevails throughout the great corn producing states upon improved breeds of swine, and many gentlemen who have invested large sums of money in founding herds for breeding purposes, abandon the business as an unprofitable one, owing to the great falling off in the demand for pure bred pigs.

It is true that the quality of the swine throughout the country at large has been greatly improved by the efforts of the leading breeders during the past years, and that first-class specimens of all the leading breeds may now be found in almost every neighborhood; but it must be borne in mind that there are none of our domestic animals that deteriorate so rapidly as swine; and it will require but a few generations of neglect to lose all the excellence that years of care and attention have attained. Careful selection of the very best for breeding purposes, good judgment in coupling, generous feeding, and the utmost care to avoid the bad effects of too much in-breeding, are all essential to prevent the deterioration, which is inevitable when these are neglected.

Then is an unusually favorable time for men of judgment

and skill to embark in the business. The neglect of the past year or two is beginning to be seen and felt. Prices are low, good breeding stock can be bought for almost a song, and the prudent man should take time by the forelock and prepare for the great demand for good, pure-bred swine, which is certain to speedily follow the present season of neglect and indifference.

Those who wish to commence breeding pure bred swine will find this a much better time to buy good breeding stock than when the demand is greater, for three reasons; First, being no demand, the breeders are more negligent as to the care of their stock, and therefore it is not so fat, and one can see better what they are buying. Second, as they are heavier stocked, and want to sell out, there is a much greater advantage in making a selection as to what they would be, if they were scarcer of stock or did not want to sell. Third, they are not so apt to be so high in their prices, which very often is quite an item to the new beginner.

SHOW PENS.

New beginners who are contemplating the breeding of fine stock, should not visit fairs or show pens for the purpose of buying their breeding stock, or, if they do, should use good judgment and discretion as to what they buy. Not because exhibitors do not show their best stock, for as a rule they do, but because they are likely to be over-fat, and have been so tampered with, fed all kinds of feed, and received such attention, as the new purchaser could not give them in their new home; or, would most likely fail to do so. Therefore, they are not so likely to do as well, and be as profitable as those that have never been on exhibition. The animal that is to develop into a strong, vigorous one, with the greatest amount of vitality and force, must be fed so as to produce force and fiber, and not fat only. This, the exhibitor may not have had in view. He may have fed only for plumpness and fine appearance. His interest is to please the eye in order to sell the animal, or win the premium. Fat covers up defects and rounds out perfection. This is the reason a fat animal with fine appearance always wins the premuim, and out-sells one that is in only good breeding condition. And then, when an animal has taken a premium, it always attaches a fictitious value to it as a breeder, that is of no value to the buyer. In most all cases it will be money saved and money made, to visit some of the breeders, and look over some of their stock at home, and buy out of the field in preference to the show pen. This precaution is just as essential in buying any other stock as it is in hogs, especially cattle or sheep. Hogs, cattle and sheep are more likely to be over-fat than horses, and more likely to be barren. A great many fine show yard animals are barren and will not breed, and are only traveled about from one show to another for the purpose of showing them for the premium, and wait for an inexperienced buyer, so they can put them off. In buying these fine and high-priced animals, it is always best to secure with them a written certificate or guarantee, that they are breeders.

THAT FINE PIG AND ITS CARE.

There is so much disappointment among buyers of fine pigs that it may be well to give the subject a little attention. As a breeder remarked, "The breeder or farmer who sends off for a choice pig, and pays from twenty to one hundred dollars and express charges for it, naturaly expects upon its arrival something very fine, and would be expected to think enough of his purchase to give it good care and to have a place for it when it arrives at the farm. But truth on both sides of this question compels the statement that the majority of the buyers are disappointed upon the arrival of the pig, or if not, often do not know how, or neglect to handle it, in such a way as to secure the greatest benefit from it, and to keep it up to the standard it had attained before its purchase," providing it was a good one. Now as I have been engaged in the breeding of fine hogs for about ten years, and I think all honest breeders of fine hogs will agree with me, I will give to the readers of this work the benefit of my experience in the business. First, when the purchase of a fine pig is contemplated, the purchasers should visit some responsible breeder and select it themselves, or at least assist in doing so. They know what kind of hogs they have, and what they wish to mate the hog with, better than the breeder does, and by having quite a number of hogs to select from, they can no doubt suit themselves better than most any breeder could by writing to him, and then both will be better satisfied, and the trip is most always worth the expence in one way or another. If the distance is not so great but that the journey can be made in a day, with a team, there can most always be enough money saved by doing so, to well pay for making it. Second, remember that the best pedigree is the pig first, then its ancestors. If they are all of such quality as to suit the purchaser, some confidence can be put in the paper, providing the party is honorable. "There are to-day more swine sold by recommendation than any thing else in this universe—far too much—but it is the buyer's falt if he gets left. Every man should buy on his own judgment, and then have no one to blame." In buying by correspondence, the purchaser should try and make his order as plain to the breeder as possible.

If it is a male pig that is wanted, describe not only the kind of pig that is wanted, but the kind of sows that he is expected to be used with. This not only gives the breeder the knowledge of the kind of a hog that is expected, and what is expected of him, but gives him a chance to use his judgment in what should be expected, and in this way he can very often select a pig that will give much better satisfaction.

DON'T GO TOO MUCH ON THE COLOR.

Unless for some good reason a pig of a certain color is wanted, I would say, don't "hanker" too much on the color—better discard the color than any other good point. Any of our pure breeds are true enough to their color. One thing more: too much must not be expected in a pig two or three months old. One may order the kind of pig he wants, and the breeder may think he has got a pig that, judging from its ancestors, will make the kind of hog wanted.

Give it time, and then if it proves a snare, the next time a pig is wanted, see it first before buying it, and do not blame the pig or the breeder because its pedigree was furnished, for that was only on paper; nor the editor of the paper that contained his advertisement, for he probably knew no more of the man than you did, and like yourself, was imposed upon. Once the pig arrives at its new home, care should be taken not to feed it too much for a few days.

The kind of food it should have at first is very important. It may have been boxed several days, its feed has been dry, and of drink it has had none; hence, laxative feed is the kind it needs now. Turn it out and give it a drink of cold water first, after that some good house slops or milk, with mill feed or oats in it for a few days, and it will soon recover from the effects of its trip, and come back to its usual appetite and condition, when its feed can be gradually increased. A great many buyers of fine pigs want to give them too much care in the way of feed when they first get them home. They will feed plenty and often; first one of the family will feed them, and then another one, and before they are aware of it, the hogs are foundered, and they wonder what ails them. Too much feed, and usually too much corn. These ideas will do for one or more pigs, either sex.

WHERE TO KEEP THE YOUNG BOAR.

"There is no place better for the young boar than a grass lot, large enough to furnish him fresh grass and room for exercise, out of sight and hearing of other hogs. Here he will excerise enough to keep strong and in prime condition, if fed regularly and judiciously. He is half the herd, and he must be kept quiet and in strong condition, if he is to impress his qualities with surety on the coming pig crop. A pig thus cared for, if well bred, will not likely prove a delusion and snare. A pig of equally good breeding and qualities, penned into a dry lot, with corn and mud, and brimming sows always in sight, will soon be out of condition, and is likely to be a restless, thriftless shoot by breeding time, without the strength and force that should belong to the successful sire. His owner gets disgusted with his late purchase, and denounces the breeder of the pig; whereas, the fault is not in the pig or breeder, but in the ignorance and carelessness of the owner."—Breeders' Gazette.

BREEDING SWINE FOR BREEDING PURPOSES.

There is no material difference in breeding swine for

breeding purposes and feeding purposes. The successful breeder of feeders can easily become the successful breeder of breeders; for the same law and rule governs both, the system is the same, and to be successful with either one, the person must have a natural love for the business. This desire for the business is the first and most essential element, for then there is nothing that is too much trouble for the breeder of breeders to do. He will always have his hogs fat and looking well, no difference how the weather is, or how much work it may take. If the weather is cold, he will get up all hours of the night to look after some favorite sow that he is expecting to farrow, and never forsake her, until he sees her and her new born family safe. Then he will carefully house, feed and care for her and the pigs, never neglecting them for a single day, or even a feed—until they are disposed of. There is no feed too good for them to eat, no difference how much trouble it may be to prepare it—it must be done. They are carefully watched and kept out of the mud, and if they do get in it, it is washed or cleaned off. The house or pen is kept warm, but well ventilated and clean of filth or vermin. Good feeding troughs are provided for both sow and pigs, and kept clean. The pigs and sometimes the sows are turned out every day for a ramble or exercise, the time being governed by the weather. But as to feeding, that is done as regularly almost as the clock strikes, and at least three times, and often five times a day; the age of the swine, or when preparing them for some special purpose, governing that to some extent. The feed is always of the best, and carefully given in quanity as the size or condition of the swine may require it. Every precaution is taken not to make them wild, always preferring to call instead of drive them, for, by this means they can keep them quiet so they can be carefully handled at all times, which is a very important thing with all hogs, and especially breeders. By complying with these rules and some more I will speak of farther on, coupled with good judgment, plenty of money, and a good place to carry on business, anyone can become a successful breeder of swine for breeding purposes.

THIS BUSINESS DEMANDS A GOOD PROFIT.

The business of breeding and handling pure bred swine, as well as other pure bred stock, ought to, judging from the nature of the case, be a profitable one. The cost of conducting the business, not only in procuring the stock and caring for it, but the risks that are combined with it, and the cost of suitable buildings and fixtures, demand for the operator a good margin on which to work. The breeder who begins by working too close in this direction, or neglects his business, must fail outright and quit the business in disgust. There are many instances known of in this country where the breeding of pure bred swine resulted in the accumulation of considerable wealth. A great many wealthy men, though, have gone into the business of breeding pure bred swine, as a pastime, or a source of expected profit, but finding it no easy matter to accumulate a fortune at it, quit the business; for the reverses are sometimes heavy, and even under the most favorable circumstances it is not always profitable.

The breeding of pure bred stock of any kind, in order to be made profitable, requires money, good judgment and management, not only in buying the stock, but in the management and selling of it, in the latter case especially.

In order to make it both profitable and pleasant, as I said before, the breeder should have a natural love and desire for the business. A good situation is also necessary, although most any place can be made suitable with labor and money. A dry, rolling piece of land, with plenty of good water and shade, is the best, for it is much healthier and far more pleasant than a wet, level place. In purchasing the breeding stock to begin with, nothing but first-class individual stock should be purchased at any price. It should be purely bred of whatever breed the breeder desires, and of good, thrifty, growing stock. Good judgement should be used in procuring this stock, for it is not always the highest priced animal, or those that are purchased the farthest away from home that are the best.

"Breeding stock of any kind is often held above its worth. It is not infrequently the case that a breeder asks much more than the value of the animal, or the cost of its production will warrant. The purchaser must be on his guard on this point. This, however, is rather exceptional, for, as a rule, breeding stock is worth all it commands in the market."

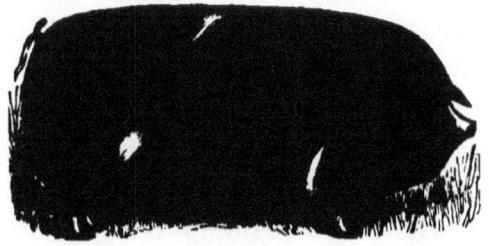

WHEN TO BREED THE SOWS.

Once the stock is brought together again, good judgment must be used in the breeding of it, so as to have the pigs come at the proper time. If the herd, or any part of it is to be exhibited the coming season, the pigs must come so as to be of the proper age to suit the premium list; or if only intended to be sold during the season without being exhibited, it is best to have them come as early in the spring as possible, so as to have the advantage of as much age as the former case will omit, and to be as early in the market as possible, in the latter case; as pigs with the advantage of a few weeks in age have quite an advantage over the younger ones, either in the show pen or in the market. Of course, in order to have these early pigs, and to save and care for them, good quarters of some kind are certainly necessary. It is not necessary that these buildings should be so costly, but they should be so constructed as to be warm, easily ventilated and kept clean. For information on this subject see plan of pens. Now the next thing on the programme is the care of these hogs. This is something that breeders cannot afford to slight in the least, if they expect to compete with others. They must have these hogs fat, sleek and clean, looking well at all times, and ready for a purchaser, for in this business, like any other, no man knoweth when a buyer cometh. Therefore, be ready, at all times and for all kinds of customers, for the least thing will sometimes drive a buyer away; such as a coughing pig, or the hogs not fat and looking well, dirty, filthy pens, and perhaps some of the pigs or hogs lying around in the manure pile or a dusty shed. The buyer will soon begin to talk about disease and leave. Remember that nice, fat, clean, sleek hogs, with everything around clean, pleases the eye; and that is what is wanted if the sale of the hogs is expected, and the breeder expects to prosper.

TAKE CARE OF THE BROOD SOWS AND PIGS.

As the sows are bred, each one should be carefully registered so as to know when they will farrow. There is but little variation from sixteen weeks as the time sows carry their pigs; the older ones not infrequently going beyond a few days, and the younger ones farrowing a few days earlier than this. If proper care be taken in the management of the boar, allowing but one service to each sow, the dates at which the pigs should come can be made a matter of record, and the necessary attention given the sows as the time for their farrowing approaches, when they should be put up separately, and in time, in order to prevent any accident that may cause the sow to lose all or part of her pigs. If their quarters are warm and dry, it is about all that is necessary, except in extreme cold weather, when the pigs may need looking after. Here is one place where it pays to have the sows quiet, for, at the critical hour, assistance can be given the pigs to get around to their mother's breast, and after they are all snug and safe, if she and the pigs are covered up with an old horse blanket or a piece of carpet, she will remain quiet long enough for the pigs to get dry and warm, and nurse. After that there is but little danger of them perishing with the cold; and in this way, sometimes, a fine litter of pigs can be raised, that would otherwise perish. The old saying, "take care of the pennies, and the dollars will take care of themselves," will hold good in swine breeding; take care of the pigs and the hogs will take care of themselves. In one case, without pennies you have no dollars, and in the other, without pigs you have no hogs.

As to the feeding of the sows and pigs, I suppose

enough has been said on this subject in former writings of this work to instruct the readers.

FITTING SWINE FOR EXHIBITION OR SALE.

From four to six weeks before the exhibition or sale of the swine, they should be put up, and become accustomed to being handled, washed and brushed, which should be given them every day or two. After they are brushed dry they should be oiled; this will make the skin soft and pliable, and the hair glossy. For this purpose there is nothing better than lard and sperm oil, equal parts mixed. Dampen a sponge or wollen cloth with it and oil them, but do not use too much oil, as it will show, look bad, and cause remarks.

If in the summer time, when the weather is hot, they should be kept out of the sun during the hottest part of the day, and should not be allowed to wallow in the mud. In case they do, it should be washed off in the evening, and not allowed to remain on over night, as it will cause the hair and skin to become rough. Never maim, or disfigure the nose, tail or ears in any way, if it can possibly be avoided. If they have been rung, cut the rings in two, and take them out before exhibiting them.

If one wishes to use ear marks, I know of no better plan than the patent ear tag. These should be put in the ears at, or before weaning time, so as to guard against mistakes as to what sows certain pigs belong. Then tags are numbered, and the numbers should be carefully registered. In putting them in, care should be taken in the operation, for they may cause the pig to carry a bad ear, especially if the ear becomes sore.

Some breeders object to these ear tags, as they claim they gather mud, and sometimes are the cause of the ear being frozen, or becoming sore, and use in their place an ear punch, an instrument similar to a leather punch. With this they punch holes in the ears, and thus mark the pigs. Where this is done, the pigs should be carefully registered, giving the number of holes in the ear, and the position also as to what sow such pigs belong.

In order to take them to fairs or exhibitions of any kind, and in order to ship them if sold, each hog should be boxed in a good, strong, but light box, with a small trough or tin vessel in it, to water and feed out of. If the breeder is well supplied with cards, showing whose hogs they are, what kind they are, how old they are, how much they weigh, and if for sale, he will save answering a great many questions. Now, one thing more to the new beginners. Once they have thrown out their card to the public, they must not expect to sell all the hogs that are needed the first year they are in the business; for if they do, they are liable to be disappointed. It takes time, energy and a great deal of experience to establish a reputation as a first-class stock breeder that commands respect and patronage.

CHAPTER VII.

SELECTIONS OF SUBJECTS.

IMPROVE YOUR STOCK.—SCRUB HOGS.—FIXING THE CHARACTERISTIC OF A BREED OF HOGS.—AN ILLUSTRATION OF HOW TO FORM A BREED.—MERIT AND PEDIGREE. —ROOTS, VEGETABLES, PASTURE, ETC., FOR HOGS.—RINGING HOGS.—HOW TO HOLD THEM.—OUR HOGS.—TRICHINAE IN HOGS.—HOW A PIG SUDDENLY BECAME PORK.—SLAUGHTER WITH THE BULLET.

IMPROVE YOUR STOCK.

The advantage of good stock over scrub stock is daily becoming more evident, an incontrovertible argument in favor of the former. This is a pleasant fact to contemplate by those breeding up their herds, and should serve as an incentive to future effort by others who have hitherto refrained from so doing. The improvement in stock throughout the country is marked, but the large increase of pure bred stock, the frequent public sales and the reasonable price at which they sell, enable men to make still more rapid improvements in the grading up of vast herds in the West, that cut the chief figure in our meat supply.

In passing through the country now, one cannot fail to note the changes that have taken place in most sections, as regards the improvements in all kinds of stock, and especially swine. People have begun to know the difference existing between a good hog and a scrub one. One may occasionally find a person who has made no improvement in his swine, but he is only an exception. He will soon fall in the ranks, for it is evident to anyone that it is as easy to raise a good hog as a poor one, and far more profitable. Pure bred swine of most all kinds have become so plentiful that it is no longer a difficult or costly matter to procure them, and once procured, they re-produce themselves so rapidly that it is very evident that in the near future the pure bred, or high grades of swine, will take the place of the native, or scrub hog, even in the most remote rural districts.

Other improved stock has made very rapid progress in the last ten years, and no doubt will continue to do so in the future, for the more plentiful it becomes, the easier it is obtained, and the more enlightened the people become, the more it will be sought after; but on account of it being more costly, or slower to reproduce itself, it can never make the progress that swine can or will. Every effort should be made to grade up all kinds of stock as fast as possible. As the use of good males of most all kinds of stock is now obtainable at a reasonable price in most all parts of this country, the people should not be slow to patronize them. By this means it takes but a few years to make quite an improvement in any kind of stock, and the idea that the market will become overstocked with any kind of good stock is all wrong. The demand will always exceed the supply.

"It does not pay to breed or to feed poor hogs. The hog is a voracious animal, and unless his voracity can be turned to profitable account it is better to have nothing to do with him. The great majority of farmers who breed pigs do so without definite aim toward producing a profitable animal. Some of them have got a nondescript sort of stock of no particular breed, and remarkable only for combining as many of the bad qualities and as few of the good points as it is possible a hog can have. Having come to them as it were as a common legacy, they look upon it as being a bounden duty to perpetuate the race. Yet bad as these hogs are, they have two redeeming points. In the first place, they are hardy, and have good constitutions; and in the second place they are capable of being rapidly improved at small cost, by crossing them with the modern improved breeds of pure-blooded sorts. Use what breed you will to begin the improvement, if it is only persevered in by those who understand the business, it must result profitably. A good thoroughbred boar costs money. We will say twenty-five to fifty dollars for a really first-class young one, three to six months old. But one is enough for a whole neighborhood, and if several will club together to purchase and keep one among them, or agree to pay a moderate sum for each sow they may get served, the cost will be small to each."

As to what breed is best to originate the improvement from, much will depend upon circumstances. If medium sized hogs are desired, use the Berkshire, Yorkshire, or Essex; for those who want larger hogs, giving from three to six hundred pounds when fattened, will find nothing better than the Poland China, or any of our other improved large breeds. Once they have made a choice of any one breed, it should not be changed unless they are thoroughly convinced that they have made a mistake; but everything should be done to improve it, always selecting and retaining the best sows for breeders, and every time boars are changed, try to get a better one.

FIXING THE CHARACTERISTIC OF A BREED OF HOGS.

"The time required in which to establish a breed, and the difficulty of the undertaking, depends largely on two things—the number of the characteristics desired to be fixed, and the rapidity with which the class of animals selected reproduce themselves. It is obviously a very much less difficult task to secure the reproduction of one characteristic than it is to secure half a dozen. It would be much easier to produce a breed of hogs which should be uniform in color, without regard to size and time of coming to maturity than it would to secure uniformity in all these points. The rapidity of breeding is an equally important element. Compare the horse and hog in this regard. A long life time would not enable one to do more with the horse than could be done in ten years with the hog; in each case the breeder being confined to his own animals. Before the effects of a second cross could be seen in the case of the horse, the hog breeder, starting with a single pair, could have a herd of hundreds, with a good degree of uniformity. Producing young once or twice a year, and several at each birth, the hog, of all our domestic animals, gives much the best opportunity for selection. Swine reproduce at so early an age, so many at a birth and so often, that in no other field can the student of the science of breeding and the art of selection and crossing so readily note results and acquire information by actual experience. Indeed, with a single sow and her descendants, for a period of five years, an observant, intelligent man may learn more concerning the laws of reproduction and the effects of inbreeding and crossing, than with any other variety of farm stock in a lifetime.

Estimating the produce of a single sow at a very moderate rate—one litter a year from the time she is one year old, and that from each of these litters there should be saved three sow pigs, which in time should be equally productive—we shall have, by the time the first sow is five years old, a herd of 1,024 females. These will have been produced at 341 different litters, and the most remote will be five generations from the first dam. But when we consider that it is quite within the limits of possibility that each sow will produce two litters a year instead of one, the number of descendants and the opportunity for observation are materially increased, as this would give us nine litters from the old sow alone, instead of five, as in the preceding calculation, and the total number of female descendants possible in five years, where two litters a year are produced, counting only three females to the litter, would be 2,683.

If, as is claimed by many, five generations serve to fix any given type with reasonable certainty in any of our domestic animals, it is quite within the range of possibilities for each farmer to create a breed of hogs for himself, in the course of five years. This case of fixing its characteristics, which the hog possesses in so marked a degree, enables any farmer to secure a stock which possesses in a very large degree the qualities he desires. If he will use well bred boars of the breed he prefers for four or five years, selecting the sows with care, his entire stock will very closely resemble the pure bred animals of this breed.

If he wishes, he may produce a new breed, or modify an old one, but in the large majority of cases this will not be a wise attempt, as those now common at large equal anything he would probably produce."—National Live Stock Journal.

AN ILLUSTRATION OF HOW TO FORM A BREED.

Following this I will give an illustration obtained from a farmer, who was a very successful breeder of swine, showing how he improved and modified his common breed of hogs and successfully formed a much more profitable one. This illustration may be of benefit to a great many who are contemplating improving their swine by giving them ideas as to how the work is done. By following these rules any breeder can improve in a few years the most mongrel breed of hogs we have, and transform them into a fine and profitable breed, by using good judgment and some patience. In talking with this farmer he gave his experience as follows: "Some thirty years ago I had what we called the Chester-White breed of hogs. I took great care in breeding them, and was also a generous feeder; by this means I had formed what was considered the best hogs in my part of the country. But they were too large and slow to mature to suit me, as I have always stuck to one system of breeding and feeding. I have always bred my sows so they would have pigs from the middle of February to the middle of March; then I would breed such sows as I wished to keep over again, and get another set of pigs soon after harvest. This first set of pigs I never let go hungry. I would feed them all the corn they wanted on good clover pasture, and by June, or some later, I had them ready to go to market, and generally struck a good one. The other pigs I aimed to carry until the following June, or later, as the market suited me. As to whether I have been successful or not, all I have to say on that subject is,

I commenced with limited means and am now worth over sixty thousand dollars. But, as to the hogs, as I said before, mine were too large and too slow to mature to suit me. So I began to look around for some way to get a hog that would put on more fat at a younger age. I had heard so much about the Berkshire hogs that I bought a good pair of them, and tried them a year or so, but I was soon convinced they did not suit me, for they would not keep still long enough to eat, and then, when turned out in the woods to range, though they would live where any other hog would starve, they would get wilder than deer. Experience in stock breeding generally brings about some good results. So here is where I struck it: I picked out some of my best, large white sows, and bred them to the Berkshire boar. The pigs from these sows were very uneven in size, but out-fed the pure Berkshire pigs, or my old stock of hogs so much, that I was convinced I had made one step toward improving my hogs. I saved some sows from these half-bred pigs that were nearest my idea of a hog, and also retained one of the best boar pigs. These sow pigs I bred to one of my best Chester-White boars, saved the best sow pigs from that cross, and bred them back to the boar pig I had saved. That cross proved to be just the hog I wanted. This breeding I have kept up for over twenty years, guarding against inbreeding too close; such as son to mother, father to daughter, or brothers to sisters. My hogs are always uniform in size and color, being white, with occasionally a black spot on the skin, and are of good size and quick to mature." Then the old gentleman tapped me on the shoulder and said: "But let me tell you, my friend, that it took patience and care to get them just right, and it takes the same care to keep them that way. Any one starting in expecting to form a breed of hogs or any other stock, in a cross or two, had just as well not start, for it takes time, patience and care." In talking with this gentleman I was soon convinced that he was very partial to the white hog, but could give no particular reason, except that they stood upon their feet better than the Poland-China, and stood traveling better than any other breed he had ever tried or seen, except the Berkshire, and they were too small and wild.

IN AND IN-BREEDING.

The aforesaid illustration only shows how all our improved breeds of stock are formed by in and in-breeding, and may serve as an example for those who have never made it a study; for it is only by in and in-breeding, guarding against too close a cross, or too violent an out cross, always retaining those animals of both sexes for breeders that show the characteristics most desired, that any established breed can be formed. Where no violent out cross is made, and the families are kept together, and the progeny is not uniform in its characteristics, just that long the breed is not thoroughly established.

MERIT, PEDIGREE AND COLOR.

The time was when the pedigree of an animal alone was sufficient to stamp it as first-class and of superior excellence. Although pedigrees are still adhered to, breeders have discovered the fact that they have been entirely too exclusive in this respect, and that many good animals possessing superior merit have been overlooked, because of supposed ignorable ancestry. As if determined to push their own claims, the discarded colts when given the privilege on the turf, forged their way to the front, the neglected heifers filled the pails to overflowing, and the chance pigs attained weight not believed to be within their reach. Acting upon the suggestion that an improvement in stock might be effected by breeding only from animals of merit, though of good blood, I will say from my own experience and from that of others who have come under my observation, never discard a good breeding animal, one that has proven itself such, (unless compelled to) for one of a more fashionable pedigree, about which nothing is known. When a change has to be made, try and find another good one that has proven itself equal to, or superior to the one you had, even if it is somewhat aged, as it very often will pay much better than to risk a young one, unless it is an exceptionally good one, and from good ancestors of which something is known.

The greatest evil of some of the fine stock breeders for the past years is, that they have adhered strictly to pedigree and color, and neglected quality or merit. This is especially the case with short-horn cattle, Berkshire and Poland-China hogs. I will venture the remark that they are not as good to-day as they were a few years ago. The color craze—red with short-horn cattle, and black with Poland-China hogs, then the fashionable pedigree of this stock, as well as with the Berkshire hog, has detrimented the breeds. This is being acknowledged all over the country, and is the cause of farmers seeking other breeds. This color craze, gray or fawn color, was started by the Jersey breeders, when the Jersey boom was first started, but some timely suggestions from some of the breeders that merit was more essential than color, soon put a stop to that, and the butter test took its place.

Now, some critic will say right here that the public demands the pedigree and color. While the pedigree is all right, providing it is backed up with merit, I will again venture to remark that the public will not know anything about the color if the breeders do not start it. Any of our pure bred stock is true enough to its color, if nature is left to place it as she sees fit, but it is the quality and merit that want looking after. Nothing will prove this more than the horse. Do people demand a bay, black or any other color, and of a certain pedigree in preference to quality, especially when left to judge for themselves? No, indeed; whereas, they may admire a horse of dark color, where he has all the other desired qualities, more than one of a bad color, yet the horse they will choose is the horse with the largest and best form, or that can pull the largest load, or go a mile the quickest. And the same with cattle or hogs; it is the quality that is wanted, and if the general stock grower can not find it in one breed, he will seek it in another.

ROOTS, VEGETBLES, ETC.

I will here give the experience of different ones as to roots, vegetables, pasture, etc., as food for hogs.

ARTICHOKES FOR SWINE.

"Use the Brazilian artichoke. I have not heard of a sick hog where it is used. It destroys all stomach and intestinal worms, constipation, indigestion and fever caused by corn-feeding in the winter, and we find our hogs so healthy and vigorous that they will not take disease, although they have their noses together through the fence often with diseased hogs. I would advise all farmers to plant a small patch of the Brazilian artichoke, as the seed can now be had cheap; and from my experience I am certain they will save your hogs and save hundreds of bushels of corn. I have three acres of them, and shall plant three more in the spring."

Another one says: "The value of the artichoke is so little known that I desire to give the farmers the benefit of my experience. I have had three years experience with artichokes for hogs. Three years ago I had about seventy-five head of hogs, big and little. Adjoining my hog lot I planted about an acre of Brazilian and a few hills of the White French, the two best varieties of artichokes known. After frost had killed the tops, I put my hog fence out around a part of the artichokes, giving my hogs full privilege to 'root, hog, or die,' and you would have been surprised to see how they used the instrument God has given them to unearth the kind of food their nature requires. Forty years ago, when hogs ran out in the wood and prairies, hog cholera was unknown. Thus be wise, and study the wants of this animal, so valuable to the farmer of the West, and supply these wants. This can be done by every farmer, by planting a patch of artichokes in one of his feed lots not used in summer, or near by his lots, and let his hogs have access to them in all the open weather from October first to May first. This has been my plan for three years. I have had each year from seventy-five to one hundred hogs, and have kept them healthy; while my neighbors, who fed only corn, suffered severely from cholera. For winter use, some should be dug and put in the cellar. I dug some last fall, and cooked and mixed them with meal or bran. They make excellent swill, and for this the White French is better, as it is the sweeter, has a larger tuber, grows nearer the surface, and is easier dug. They are also excellent for milchcows in winter. I can raise one thousand bushels of artichokes as easily, and on less ground, than one hundred bushels of corn. They should be planted on good, dry land, and the ground should be plowed deep and harrowed, then marked both ways with a three runner potato marker or some other way. The rows should be three feet apart each way. I then cut the tubers into small pieces, about two eyes to each, then plant the way I mark first, and cover with a cultivator. As soon as weeds start, harrow well, and when large enough cultivate as you would corn. In this way I raise from six hundred to eight hundred bushels to the acre. I would not have you understand that artichokes take the place of corn to a very great extent, but they loosen the bowels and keep the hogs in such a condition that a bushel of corn will put on more flesh than when fed on corn alone."

The author has so frequently herd the Brazilian artichoke favorably spoken of as being good for hogs, and knowing they possess rare properties, as an appetizer, etc., copies these experiments written to agricultural papers, for the benefit of those who may be unacquainted with the artichoke, or those who may wish to grow them.

NOTE.—I suppose the seed of the Brazilian artichoke can be had of any good seed firm.

ROOTS FOR HOGS.

"Two years ago I planted one acre of roots, mostly sugur beets, and raised seven hundred bushels. The beets were at the rate of one thousand bushels to the acre, and carrots six hundred bushels. I think sugar beets the best feed to grow shoats. In the winter I put four hundred bushels into the barn, and covered them with hay and straw. But the severe cold weather in January froze them solid, so I could not feed them to my cows, as I intended to when I put them up. So I put them into a kettle, and cooked and fed them to my shoats, half a bushel of meal to three bushels of beets, and I never fed anything to hogs that made them grow so fast as they did while I was feeding these frozen beets.

On rich soil one thousand bushels can be easily raised to the acre. I shall try it again this year on a piece of old hog pasture. It wants three pounds of seed to the acre, put in drills with Comstock's drill, rows eighteen inches apart. If on new ground it requires but little tending to keep the weeds down. I tend mine mostly with the drill cultivator."

The author would be willing to vouch for what this man says, if he would have said that corn and sugar beets would make shoats fatten faster than any other feed; for I do not think there is any food that would surpass it. We know that corn contains a larger amount of fattening element than other grain, and sugar beets have the same properties over other roots, and the two conbined could not help but form a great fattening food; in fact, so much so, that if fed largely, they would produce enough fat to be injurious to the hog, especially where intended for breeding purposes.

GROWING PUMPKINS WITH CORN.

"Pumpkins are valuable for stock in autumn and early winter, or as long as they can be conveniently kept, though the amount of nutriment, in proportion to bulk to be taken care of, and their liability to decay, have led most farmers to discard them, and adopt roots and squashes for succulent food. As a rule, every crop needs all the ground it occupies, and all the air and sunlight available. Corn is a 'sun-plant,' and to shade the soil and lower stalks with the dense foliage of pumpkin vines, must be more or less injurious, even if the latter do not rob the former of any needed nutriment. On very fertile, new soils, with short-stalked varieties of corn, in localities where frost is not to be feared, it may be allowable to plant pumpkin seed in every third or fourth hill, in each second or third row. With favorable weather, the corn will produce about the usual yield, and after the early gathering of the corn, the growing pumpkins thus exposed to full light, will ripen up those pretty well developed. As a rule, let the pumpkins have the whole ground; but still better are the harder fleshed squashes, which will probably supply more nutriment than field pumpkins, whether for man or beast.

SQUASHES.

"I have found that an acre of the Hubbard squash will fatten more hogs than any corn which could be raised on the same ground, and the squashes will keep through the winter. I plant twenty feet apart each way, which is thick enough, and little cultivation is required. The crop is easily gathered, no digging or husking being required. The plants are rampant growers, and are out of the way of the bugs in a week, early in the season. From six to eight tons have been obtained from an acre, estimated by the wagon load."

RAISE SOME PUMPKINS AND SQUASHES.

It seems that of late years the raising of pumpkins and squashes has been greatly neglected by the farmers, and it is now only occasionally that we see a corn field spotted over with the golden pumpkins, as in former days. Why is it? Has mother earth so depreciated in quality that she will not raise them any more? Or has our improved corn plows made it impossible to raise them? If these are not the reasons, it must be because the farmer thinks them not worth raising and gathering. I think a great many farmers under-rate the true value of them as food for hogs, and fail to appreciate them as they should. Any thing a hog will eat with as much relish as they will pumpkins and squashes, is certainly good for them, and they should occasionally have a mess of them. It is very seldom but that corn-fed hogs will leave corn, upon pumpkins being thrown to them, and devour them greedily. This goes to show that they want a change of food, and relish vegetables. When mankind is deprived of vegetables for a long time, they crave and want them, and often sicken and die for the use of them. The hog, "like his two-legged brother," is the same way. Many a lot of hogs have died, that a wagon load of pumpkins would have saved, if given in time.

RAISING RYE.

Rye is the earliest grass crop that can be grown. If seeded down in the fall it not only gets a good start if the season is favorable, therefore affording a slight opportunity for grazing in the fall to those who are not favored with pastures, but it comes out luxuriantly in early spring, and affords green material when other grasses are dormant. It grows on the sandy soils as well as on those that are heavy, but thrives best on a fertile, light loam. Rye is an excellent feed for young pigs early in the spring, and every farmer who has no early pasture for them should sow a patch for that purpose. After it becomes too hard for use, it can be plowed under, as it makes a good fertilizer for most any other crop.

"Swine may be raised very cheaply and to be healthy, if only the proper attention is given to the matter of their food and pasture. Every swine breeder should have a piece of clover pasture; yet green rye, oats, millet, Hungarian grass and green peas all make excellent and cheap hog feed. Where a pasture cannot be had, no other crop will make better feed, nor more of it, than green sweet corn fodder, or a crop of oats and peas mixed. Have these crops planted in a lot next to the hog lot, and cut and feed to the hogs as needed, but not until they have come nearly to maturity. By planting a second time on the ground which was first relieved of its crop a constant supply of these provenders can be maintained from the first of July until frost comes."

PASTURE FOR HOGS.

"The subject of good pastures for hogs in summer is becoming one of special interest to farmers. So also, the providing of a supply of roots for them during the winter, is beginning to receive deserved attention from the nore progressive and successful farmers. The continuous and excessive use of corn has long been deemed wrong both in theory and in practice, although comparatively few feeders ever seemed to have considered how it might be avoided. The light, however, is breaking, and a radical change in the management of hogs as regards their feeding seems fast going on. This change, we doubt not, will result in a very marked decrease of disease among swine. Of the grasses most suitable for hog pasture may be mentioned: timothy, red clover, blue-grass and orchard grass. In timber pasture, where red clover would not do so well on account of the shade, white clover will be found valuable. The best pasture is one containing several kinds; but it is no easy matter to keep a variety of grasses on the same ground. The more hardy will sooner or latter crowd the others out."

The best pasture is blue grass, as it keeps green most all the year round, and affords grass both early and late. Red clover alone is about the poorest pasture there is for hogs. Early in the season it is of too luxuriant growth, and then it soon becomes hard and woody, and has a tendency to cause constipation. When the first crop is taken off, and the second crop comes up, especially where it is of a luxuriant growth and hogs are turned in on it, it has the same tendency to cause sickness as an over-feed of new corn has. When sowing clover for pasture for hogs, it is always best to mix timothy, or some other grass seed with it.

RINGING HOGS.

My experience in ringing hogs leads me to think it an advisable measure, when rightly done and at the right time. The assertion sometimes made that hogs, if habitually allowed to run at large, will not injure meadows or pastures by rooting when turned upon them, cannot be relied on. They may for a while behave themselves very well. I have known them to roam a pasture for weeks and scarcely turn a sod. Then I would make up my mind that rings could be dispensed with; when, soon after I had quit watching them, the rascals would, from some unaccountable reason, get to rooting, and in a short time do more damage times over again than it would have cost to ring them. So I have at last concluded that the safest way is to use the rings whenever hogs are allowed to range where their rooting would be an injury.

I do not advocate the continuous use of rings the year round, nor their use on swine of all ages and sizes. In the spring of the year they are generally the most needed.

If hogs that are treated to rings in the spring are still on hand in the fall, it is usually best to remove them, particularly if the hogs are turned on mast, or allowed to follow cattle in feed lots or stalk fields.

It sometimes happens that a valuable brood sow acquires such bad habits as lifting gates or breaking fences. A couple of rings in the nose of such an animal will put her on good behavor the most effectually of any thing I ever tried. So also a sow that is vicious and cross to other hogs; a good ring in her nose will prove to be a wonderful tamer. A stock boar, if inclined to be unruly, should be treated the same way.

If a sow is cross and unruly to her pigs, take a piece of small wire, a size larger than broom wire, and four inches long. By the use of an awl, insert this wire in the center of the rim of the noise, and then twist it together: this forms a long probe and will strike the pig before her nose will, which will cause the pig to get out of her way and save itself from a blow. It will also cause the sow to behave herself better than a ring will. I have nothing to say as to which are the best patent rings; they are all good enough, some, perhaps, being more easily applied, or adjusted, to all purposes, and lasting longer than others. I have always used the round or triangle rings. I insert the rings through the partition of the nose (the same as putting a ring in a bull's nose) instead of through the rim of the nose. Never use but one ring in a hog's nose, if it can possibly be avoided, and insert that in the center of the nose, or, as spoken of before. When it is necessary to put in two rings, which is sometimes the case with sows or large hogs, insert them close together, less than an inch apart, one on each side of the center of the nose. By this means one avoids hitting the chords that are on each side of the nose, and which, if the rings are put through, causes the nose to become very sore and painful. The rings should not be set too deep, and see that they close up smooth where they come together, as the cause very often of hogs being injured by ringing is due to its being improperly done, and by the use of such inhuman rings as horse shoe nails or too heavy wire. Here is another plan to keep hogs from rooting, which I have practiced some, and have seen others adopt with good results: Cut the cords on each side of the nose; they can be observed by pressing the nose down. Use a small, sharp-pointed knife; insert under and cut up. This will take all the power out of the nose, and it will not get sore.

HOW TO HOLD LARGE HOGS TO RING THEM.

For the purpose of holding large hogs to ring them, there is no better or simpler plan that the use of one of Shook's Stock Machines. This machine is so valuable, cheap and simple to use for handling all kinds of stock, that every farmer can afford to have one.

SHOOK'S HANDY STOCK CATCHER AND HOLDER

Is the farmers' choice for the purpose for which it is intended, for the following reasons:

1. It is the only invention of the kind that can be converted into several different forms for the handling of different kinds of stock. It can be changed into a bridle, halter, twitch, slip-noose, or lasso for the purpose of hand-

ling all kinds of stock, large or small, with perfect security, and without injury. It is also one of the best bull staffs in use.

2. It is longer and lighter than any other instrument of the kind, being six feet long and weighing less than four pounds, which is quite an advantage on account of the ease and security with which it can be handled. Yet it is cheaper than any other; and is made of the best of material, so that it will last for years without repair. In case it is broken, any one can repair it at a trifling cost, owing to its simple construction.

No farmer should be without this machine, as it is a great labor-saving invention, often doing the work, in the hands of a boy or man, that would otherwise require the efforts of two or three strong men. It can be had of dealers, or will be sent free to any address, upon receipt of price, $3.00. State, county, or shop rights for sale. J. B. Shook, proprietor, Circleville, Ohio.

DIRECTIONS FOR THE USE OF THIS MACHINE.

Take hold of the staff back well at the small end with the left hand, and hold the rope and staff back of the ring with the right hand. In order to catch and hold a hog drop the lasso over the nose of the animal, or else in the mouth and around the upper jaw; then pull quick and hard upon the rope, and it will close up tight around the nose or jaw, and the ring in the center of the staff will hold the rope secure. A hog thus secured can easily be held while a ring is put in its nose, or its tusks taken out, or for any other purpose. The lasso can be made any size desired for catching calves, sheep or any other stock. In order to form a rope halter or bridle, for the purpose of handling a bad horse, run the lasso out long enough to go over the head of the animal, then reach through the lasso with the left hand, and catch the rope back of the eye of the machine, and pull it through far enough to go over the nose or through the mouth of the animal. To fit it up snug, pull on the end of the rope to take up all slack, and the ring will hold it secure. With this machine thus fit to a horse, it is no trouble to handle it; no matter how vicious it is. The bull staff is formed by using the hook, or snap at the small end of the staff. Around the shank of this hook is a spiral spring which holds a clasp in place; press the spring back, and the clasp will turn to one side and remain there. Now hook the snap in the ring in the bull's nose, then press on the clasp, and it turns in place, and forms a solid hook or snap, perfectly secure, and strong enough to hold any bull.

OUR HOGS.

A Chicago paper says:

"The government has set a professional gentleman to trap trichinæ at the Union Stock Yards in this city. That portion of the world which will insist upon eating uncooked pork have a decided aversion to the active wrigglers which sometimes sport in the muscles of our hogs and have no objection to capering in the muscles of pork consumers. But those who think that cooked food is better than raw, do not worry much over trichinæ in pork.

If a hog is permitted to eat anything and everything, it will likely be infected with trichinæ, and if it is much infected it will show it by its general appearance.

As a sanitary matter the pork question, according to the secretary of the State Board of Health, is of no importance. Far more are choked to death accidentally on beef each year than die from eating trichinous pork. Our pork is better and freer from trichinæ than the European article and far more nutritious. Government experts have shown that about two per cent. of all swine flesh is infected. It has been proven that trichinous pork exposed to a heat of 150 to 160 degrees Farenheit—heat equal to scalding water—renders infected flesh absolutely innocuous.

The United States consumes five times the pork she exports. Deaths from trichinæ have been known in Germany and France since 1830, long before importation of American pork. Two million German born and five million American-German eat our pork in the United States. In five years, in Philadelphia, there were 92,764 deaths, from trichinæ 3. In New York, in ten years, 170,838 deaths, with five from infected pork. In Boston, 43,680 deaths, from trichinæ none. Baltimore, fifty-four years, 264,324 deaths, from trichinæ none."

TRICHINÆ IN HOGS.

Hogs are not naturally infested with trichinæ, unless they swallow or otherwise imbibe the germs of the insect to be found only in feculent matter in a state of fermentation or decomposition, either moist or in the dried, impalpable condition of a fine dust inhaled into the lungs— in which latter case they affect first the liver and then the colons and bowels, and the disease acquires the cognomen of "cholera," by the changed symptoms and malignant nature of the disorder.

Unfortunately for the swine race under domestication, they are not as fastidious in their taste as their fellow-beings of the bovine family, hence the consequence is that nutritious food is seized upon, though mixed up with fecula in a state of fermentation, which if it were separate the hog would no more touch than the horse or ox, who by more fastidious tastes shun it even in the grass growing near to it and smelling of it. Yet the cow can be found to eat fecula in a state of fermentation, and thereby become liable to the infection we call trichinæ in pork, just as easy as the hog can be saved from such liability by reason of offering it no temptation to get it, or forcing the animal to breathe it in dust; only in the cow the disease would be called "pleuro-pneumonia," or perhaps farriery might call it "murrain," or some other symptomatic name quite as unintelligible.

The whole subject we desire the reader to understand is, that neither hog, cow nor man or other animal is subject by nature to any infectious disease, except the germ of the infecting parasite be imbibed either by the stomach or some other imbibing organism of the animal body, or in the case of external infection, and that all parasite life originates in matter in a state of fermentation, somewhere in or between the vinous and the putrefective stage of it; and that the matter imbibed is in the state of fineness of particles composing a gas, or in the more infinitesimal, primary state of spontaneous or electric combination. And lastly, from experience that hogs fed on grass and grain and slop or milk, before entering into the putrefective state of fermentation, unconfined in filthy stys and confined atmospheres and noxious gases, are not subject to any disease, much less trichinæ; while any animal is subject to the diseases known to man only as indicated above."

The National Stockman says: "The swine need to be treated radically, different from the usual methods employed in their feeding and care. Too much hog cholera pervades the hog growing districts; and it is caused almost wholly by not observing proper sanitary conditions in their feed and care. A hog is not necessarly a filthy animal, and even if he is, to make meat suitable for human food, he should be reared in strict cleanliness, and fed on only such food as will be most conducive to healthy growth. The parasites, such as trichinæ, which seem to make the system of the hog their home, are no doubt the offspring of the system of feeding and methods of their rearing. Filth and unwholesome food will beget these parasitical diseases in the human body, and other diseases also, and could we reasonably expect a disregard of these sanitary conditions which the human family has to observe so closely, to be carried on for years with the hog without producing at length just the results which have been observed in the cured pork which has made so much trouble with our export trade? A change must be made, and on many of our most advanced farms it has already been made; and the filthy pen and muddy yard have been dispensed with for the clean pastures. But yet corn, the great progenitor of so-called hog cholera is still used too much in feeding young and growing swine; and the food of fattening hogs is confined entirely too exclusively to this heating and fever-producing grain. The eyes of many of our swine breeders are becoming opened to these facts, and they are making radical changes in their system of feeding. Corn, of course, is still their main food; but an exclusive corn diet, from berth until made into pork, has been changed for clover pasture, roots, etc., and a variety of grains."

Cleanliness with raising and feeding hogs is just as essential as it is with other stock. The idea that anything is good enough for a hog, is an idea of the past, and is one that should not be practiced in this progressive age. The meat of a clean and well kept hog that has been fed on a variety of good food is far sweeter and better and more healthy than one raised in the filth. The practice of feeding hogs in the mud and filth, and the constant use of bad water, over-feeding of corn, clover, or any other food, is very wrong, and will bring on disease. A change should be made. That is, feed two or more kinds of food at a time. If they are being fed on old corn or running on clover that has become old, they should have once a day some wet food or swill, made of mill feed and ground grain, oats, barley or corn, or what is still better, crushed corn, as it is more bulky and affords roughness. This will aid digestion and prevent constipation, and prove very beneficial in this way as well as to cause the hogs to fatten much faster. These sloppy foods are something that hogs at times necessarily need, or else roots or vegetables of some kind to take their place; also salt or a better substitute to take its place, once or twice a week. But treat hogs as you will, they are as liable to disease as any other stock, and when sick should be cared for. "Humanity and sound policy demand this."

Never under any consideration whatever, use the meat of hogs that show any indications of disease, for it is in the flesh of these hogs that the parasites are found that cause trichinæ, and it is by the use of diseased pork that this terrible disease is caused. There is no more danger in eating good healthy pork, either raw or cooked, than there is in eating some other meat the same way. If the lungs, liver, melts and kidneys are sound (void of ulceration), you can eat the meat with safety, as you please. If not, it should be well cooked at all times before using. This may sound strange to some who read it, as they may think all persons cook their pork before eating it; they do, as a rule, but a great many farmers and others too, of every nationality, eat raw ham the same as dried beef.

The investigation of trichinæ in pork, by Dr. Detmers, as given here, and taken from the Farm Field and Stockman, Feb. 24, 1885, substantiates the above suggestions, and serves more upon this subject, of which I will speak further on.

TRICHINÆ IN PORK.

A careful investigator, Dr. Detmers, says: "That I am correct in ascribing the principal sources to trichinæ in hogs to the bad habits most of our farmers have of leaving hogs that die of swine plague, and of other diseases, too, unburied, will appear from the following: We had very little swine plague and very few losses from that disease in the West in 1883. The winter of 1882–3 was a severe one, the spring of 1883 was wet, pouring rains were frequent, and the summer following rather backward and cool, all conditions unfavorable to the preservation and development of the swine plague germs (diplococeus suis). In August, when I announced my trichinæ investigation, I examined mostly last year's hogs over a year old, and found 3½ per cent trichinous; in September some younger hogs, or hogs less than a year old, commenced to come in, and I found only 2.43 per cent affected; in October, when most of the hogs examined were less than a year old, the percentage came down to 1.62 per cent., and in November, when nearly all the hogs examined were young animals, the very low percentage of .73 was reached. Besides that in some of the hogs found to be trichinous the trichinæ were already calcified, or in a state of calcification, which shows that the same cannot have recently invaded the animal organism and were probably over a year old. Further, as said above, hogs from countries never seriously invaded by swine plague were almost invariably found free from trichinæ. In one car-load of hogs from Dakota, one animal was found to be trichinous, but the trichinæ were old, showed incipient calcification, and it is tolerably safe to say that hog, very likely, was not a native of Dakota, but born and invaded by trichinæ in Illinois, Iowa, or some other State, from which many people recently emigrated to Dakota. Another proof that the prevalence of swine plague, or numerous deaths caused by that disease, and that consumption of the dead hogs by the living, constitutes the principal source of trichiniasis in swine, is furnished by the following facts: A few years ago, when swine plague was extensively prevailing in the West, and when the losses caused by that disease were far greater than they are at present or have been during the last two years, the percentage of trichinous hogs reported by other investigators was much higher than that found by me in the fall 1883, from August till date, notwithstanding that my examinations have been made in a most thorough and conscientious manner, and with a microscope that has as large a mechanical stage, which permits a systematic examination of every portion of the slide. If numerous deaths of hogs by swine plague or from other causes, and a subsequent consumption of dead hogs by the living, does not constitute the most fruitful source of trichiniasis, the decrease in percentage of trichinous hogs coincident with the gradual disappearance or decreased prevalence of swine plague cannot find a rational explanation."

HOW A PIG SUDDENLY BECAME PORK.

In a new book just published, Mr. Phil. Robinson gives the following graphic description of how a pig suddenly became pork at a pig-killing establishment in Chicago. We should be sorry to vouch for the precise accuracy of the statements: "A lively piebald porker was one of a number grunting and quarreling in a pen, and I was asked to keep my eye on him. What happened to that porker was this: He was suddenly seized by a hind leg and jerked up to a small crane. This swung him to the fatal door through which no pig ever returns. On the other side stood a man. The two-handed engine at the door stands ready to smite once, and smite no more, and the dead pig shot across a trough and through another doorway, and then there was a splash. He had fallen into a vat of boiling water. Some unseen machinery passed him along swiftly to the other end of the terrific bath, and their a water-wheel picked him up and flung him on to a sloping counter. Here another machine seized him, and with one revolution scraped him as bald as a nut. And down the counter he went, losing his head as he slid past a man with a hatchet, and then, presto! he was up again by the heels. In one dreadful handful a man emptied him, and while another squirted him with fresh water, the pig, registering his own weight as he passed the teller's box, shot down the steel bar from which he hung, and whisked around the corner into the ice-house. One long cut with a knife made two 'sides of pork' out of that piebald pig. Two hacks of the hatchet brought away his back bone. And there in thirty-five seconds from his last grunt—dirty, hot-headed, noisy—the pig was hanging up in two pieces, clean, tranquil, iced! The very rapidity of the whole process robbed it of its horrors. Here one minute was an opinionative piebald pig, making a prodigious fuss about having his hind leg taken hold of, and lo! before he had made up his mind to squeal or only squeak, he was hanging up in an ice house, split in two. He had resented the first trifling liberty that was taken with him, and in thirty-five seconds he was ready for the cook."—National Stockman.

SLAUGHTER WITH THE BULLET.

"Ordinarily, when butchering day arrives, the fatted swine are driven from their pen into the yard. Here one is caught at the first attempt (possibly), and after much tussling is turned upon his back and killed. After this the herd becomes wild; much chasing, tumbling, and tugging (I trust no swearing) is indulged in, and finally, after human strength has been expended that might have gone far toward sawing a cord of wood, the doomed animal, half dead with fright, with heated blood coursing in his veins, has his throat torn open with a bungling implement, and thrust here and there, often in vain search for the vital current. My dear sir, I plead with you, in the name of humanity, in the spirit of civilization, to avoid this torture of helpless, unoffending creatures by shooting them. A small ball from a rifle or revolver will cause instantaneous insensibility, after which the bleeding may be accomplished without lessening your self-respect. The shooting will cause no emotion in the herd—it does not realize that any killing has been done. In slaughtering cattle I have seen inexperienced men strike the head of the victim with an ax three or four times, breaking the horn before striking the correct spot. This is outright murder, and would disgrace a savage. I have seen the heaviest beeves killed without pain by a bullet no larger than a pea. In shooting with a pistol the weapon should be placed within a foot of the spot to be struck (the forehead, just above the eye) unless the shooter is an expert."

The author has frequently seen hogs killed as described above, and knows it is not only bad for the hogs, but also for the one that does the work. Therefore, I think it would be much better to use a rifle, to quietly and mercifully shoot them.

CHAPTER VIII.

BUTCHERING AND CURING THE MEAT.

PREPARING TO BUTCHER.—RACK TO HANG HOGS ON.—A REGULAR SYSTEM.—KILLING and CLEANING THE HOGS.—HOW TO CLEAN THE INTESTINES.—CUTTING UP THE HOGS.—PREPARING THE LARD, SAUSAGE AND PUDDING—PREPARING OR CURING THE MEATS.

BUTCHERING TIME.

When the time arrives to butcher, before commencing, everything pertaining to that day's work should be got in good order. Every farmer knows butchering takes all day, and some times part of the night, as it comes in that part of the year when the days are short and the weather liable to be cold and bad. Therefore, one should have everything in good order, and leave as little other outside work to do as possible. If there is much stock to feed, the feed should be so prepared that it can be given to the stock quickly that day. A good supply of dry wood should be hauled up, prepared and put in the dry, so in case of snow or rain, it will not get wet. Then look after the butchering tools, so that they are all together and in good order. The knives, cleaver, ax and sausage machine should be well sharpened.

If the meat tubs and lard firkins need cleaning and hooping, see to it in time. Get the kettles, scalding tub, hog hook and gambrels together, so there will be no need hunting them when wanted. The hogs should be inclosed in a small lot or pen, as near as possible to where they are to be killed, for it saves hauling them so far. If there is no place already fixed to hang the hogs, one had better be prepared beforehand than to wait until the hogs are ready to be hung up, and then fix a temporary one that is liable to fall down and cause trouble. I will here give a description and cut showing how to make the best hog hanging rack I have ever seen for farm use. It is not only strong and safe if well put up, but is the easiest to hang hogs on. Three men can hang on this rack with ease a hog that will weigh six or eight hundred pounds. The cut itself will almost describe the rack.

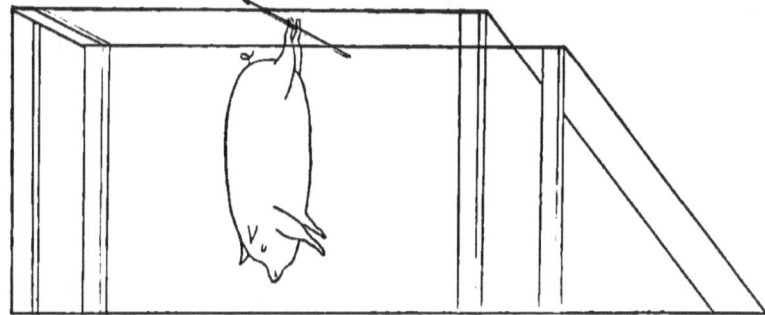

It is made by setting four posts, 4x6, nine feet long, in the ground, 2½ feet apart one way, and 12 feet the other, outside measure. When finished it ought to be 7 feet high. For the stretchers from one post to the other on which to hang the hogs, use 2x8 joists. On the inside of the posts at the top, cut a notch large enough for the stretchers to rest on. Then spike or bolt them securely to the posts. The back end of the rack can be fastened together by a good inch board being nailed to the posts, having it project above the posts an inch, to keep the hogs from being shoved off the end. The front end has two stretchers, 2x6 and 10 feet long, running from the ground to the top of the rack, and fastened to the top stretchers on the inside, to be used to slide the hogs on. The gambrel sticks to be employed on this rack must be 2½ feet long, in order to reach from one stretcher to the other, as the hogs hang between them. Where a rack of this kind is desired, from 16 to 24 feet long, there must be two center posts to strengthen the stretchers. The advantages of this rack over any others are: First, if the platform that the hogs are scraped on is put against the ground stretchers, it requires but little labor to slide the hog off of it, upon the rack; second, one half of a hog can be taken down at a time when cutting them up, or they can be cut in halves, in order to let them cool quickly. As for a place to clean the hogs on, a sled, or a wagon box turned upside down, with some good strong boards on it, will answer the purpose. For a scalding tub, a large barrel is better than a hogshead, as it does not require so much water, and does not get cold so quick.

A REGULAR SYSTEM.

At all packing establishments, hogs are cleaned and cut up under a regular system. But it is only occasionally that a farmer has any regular system of doing this work, and it is seldom that two persons do it alike. There are some who will kill the same number of hogs, and work them up in about half the time, and do the work just as well as others. Why is this? Because one works under a regular system, and the other has no system at all. Butchering hogs is hard work at best, but if properly managed, a large amount of work and time can be saved, and the work is just as well or better done.

KILLING AND CLEANING THE HOGS.

When several hogs are to be killed, after the water is

BUTCHERING AND CURING THE MEAT.

hot and everything ready to commence, two should be killed at once, as two can be scalded with the same water as one, and this saves heating water so often. There are some farmers who are experts in bleeding a hog, while others make a very bungled job of it and damage the shoulder. This is a simple operation. When once the hog is down, turn it on its back, use a short, sharp-pointed knife, and place the point in the center of the throat with the edge back. One thrust down and back will reach the vital part; and in drawing the knife out cut the incision some three inches long. This will cause the hog to bleed freely. If much blood, mud or snow adheres to the hog, it should be cleaned off before being put into the scalding tub, as it will chill the water and cause a bad scald. In order to have the water the right temperature to get a good scald, fill the barrel one-third full of boiling water, then add to this one or two gallons of cold water. This will be hot enough if the barrel is not too cold, but when it is, it may not require any cold water. If a half gallon of wood ashes or a half pint of lye is put in the water, it will cause the hair to slip better. When the water is too hot it will set the hair so it will not come off. In scalding the hog, always scald the fore part first, for that is the hardest to scald. Keep moving it, turning it over and then draw it out to air it and axamine to see if it is scalded enough. This is the case when the hair slips off easily. Then turn the hog around, and the hind part will soon scald. Now, while the second hog is being scalded, the first one should be cleaned, for while it is hot it can be cleaned much quicker than when it gets cold. Clean the fore part first, commencing with the feet and head and then work back. Here is where the lively work begins, and where a corn knife or hoe can be used with good effect to help remove the hair. When the first hog is cleaned hang it up, and then wash and scrape it, and soon follow with the other one. When the intestines are removed, wash the blood out and rinse with cold water. In order to let the hogs cool quickly, split them down on each side of the back bone, leaving them together at both ends. Then by the use of a stick spread them apart in front. Now, the first two hogs are taken care of, and the others follow suit in pairs.

HOW TO CLEAN THE INTESTINES.

As soon as the intestines are removed, it is best to clean them at once, while warm. This is done by first separating the paunch from the other parts, and then remove the lard. Then divide the large intestines from the small ones; separate the large ones and remove the lard by the use of a knife. The lard can be removed from the small ones by taking it in one hand and the intestine in the other and pulling them apart. To prepare the small intestines for sausage casings, empty them and keep them in hot water while cleaning them, which is done by scraping with a case knife upon a smooth board. If the water gets too cool, pore off a part, and put in some more hot. There is no need of turning the small intestines when cleaning them in this way. For casings for puddings, take those parts of the large intestines that are smooth and straight, turn them inside out, and clean them the same as the others.

CUTTING UP THE HOGS.

When the hogs are cool and fit to be cut up, commence by taking off the head and cutting it up for such purpose as is desired. When the heads have not been well cleaned, put them in scalding water, and clean them. Cut the head in two on a line with the mouth, take out the tongue and clean it, by putting it in boiling water, which will cause the rough skin to peal off. The under part of the head, or jowl, if not intended to be smoked, can be made into lard, sausage and pudding by cutting off the jaws for pudding, the lean of the other part for sausage and the rest for lard. The upper part of the head except the brains, is not of much use except for pudding. Cut out the ears and eyes, then split the head in halves, take out the brains, and clean the balance by cutting out the nose bones. Where the nose is not wanted, cut it off half way back to the eyes. The hearts and tongues if not wanted for other use can go in the puddings, one half of a liver to every three hogs. If the lard is not to be pealed and the rinds put in the puddings, the meat, now prepared, can be put over to cook and be out of the way. Enough water should be put on the meat to cover it. Now cut up the balance of the hog as follows:

Take out the back bone, remove the lard, and break the back bone at every other joint. Cut off the legs above the hocks and knees. Take out the leaf lard, ribs and tender loins, remove the piece in front of the shoulders for sausage, then the ham and shoulders, cutting the ham round and the shoulder square. Cut off a good strip of the belly and back for lard. Square up the remainder and cut it into pieces of such size as are wanted. Then put the meat away to thoroughly cool out before being cured. To clean the feet, put them in boiling hot water until the toes can be removed easily. Scrape and wash them thoroughly, and they are ready for use.

PREPARING THE LARD AND SAUSAGE.

While some are employed in cutting up the hogs, others may be preparing the lard to render and the sausage meat for use. With a reasonable amount of help and proper management, this work can all be going on at the same time. To prepare the lard for rendering, cut it into squares of an inch or more in size, and as soon as enough is ready to fill a kettle, it can be put on to cook, and a half gallon of water should be put in the kettle to keep the lard from burning before it commences to cook. No more lard should be added to this while cooking, but as soon as done, when the cracklings turn a light brown, take it off, run it through the lard press, and place it in another kettle to cool a little before it is put in the cans or ferkins. Another kettle full, or even two at the same time can now be treated in the same way. If the sausage meat is to be ground, it ought to be cut into squares, as by this means it does not become so stringy. Have the meat warm, but use as little water as possible while grinding it, as it keeps better if ground dry.

PREPARING OR CURING MEATS.

To season the sausage so as to be palatable to all, is very hard to do. But nearly everybody will find one of the following recipes to suit: To forty pounds of ground meat, use one heaping pint of salt, one fourth pint of pepper, five table-spoons of coriander and three table-spoons of sweet-marjoram. Mix thoroughly, prepare for the table, and it is good enough for a king.

Another: For the same amount of meat, use the same amount of salt and pepper, and one-half pint of sage. To this can be added two table-spoons of Summer Savory, if liked. When the sausage is not put in casings, it can be made into cakes and cooked ready for use, then packed in jars, always pouring over each layer the fryings until the jar is filled. Then heat and pour over them enough lard to cover them. In this way they can be kept until quite warm weather. When they are put in casings, they can be prepared in the same way, or hung up and let dry and then smoked a little, which will improve them, but too much smoke makes them bitter. To season the puddings while grinding the meat, to ten pounds of meat add three good sized onions; then mix with this four table-spoons of salt and two table-spoons of pepper; stuff them, and then put them in the same water or juice that the meat was cooked in. Bring to a boil, take out and dip in cold water. Put them in a vessel to cool, and when they are cool, they are fit for use.

The back bones and spare ribs can be salted light, packed in a jar and put where they will keep cool, or else a weak brine put over them. The side meat can be cut in strips of three to the side, packed edgewise, with the skin side out in a large stone jar and pickled pork made. Brine for pickled pork, should be as strong as possible; it ought to be strong enough to bear up a good sized potato. Make by stirring into warm water as much salt as it will dissolve, and when cool, pour it on the meat. In packing the meat put some salt in the bottom of the jar when commencing, and also add an ounce of saltpetre to twenty pounds of meat, distributed through the meat as packed. If it begins to sour, take it out of the brine, rinse well in cold water, cleanse the vessel well with hot water, re-pack in brine. When the brine seems thick and ropey, the meat is not doing well and must be looked after. When the sides are wanted for bacon, they can be cured with the hams and shoulders. For a dry salt cure, as soon as the meat is cooled out one should begin immediately to salt it. A clean oak or molasses barrel is the best to use. Cover the bottom with salt, and, commencing with the hams, the shoulders and the sides last; put each piece in a tub and salt and rub both sides thoroughly with it. Pack in the barrel as closely as possible. Put plenty of salt between the pieces and layers of meat. When packed, leave three weeks and then take it out and re-pack it. Leave three weeks more, take it out, rub well with black pepper, hang up and smoke. Use corn cobs, green hickory or sassafras wood, taking care to have smoke, but not fire enough to make heat. When smoked enough, which will take from five to ten days, take down, wrap in paper and put in a muslin sack, tie tight and hang up in a cool, dry, dark place.

A quick sugar cure: For one hundred pounds of meat take one quart salt, one pint brown sugar, three table-spoons of black pepper and two tablespoons of saltpetre; dissolve the saltpetre in hot water, and pour over the other ingredients; mix well and rub thoroughly, and leave it lie thirty days. Look after it occasionally, and rub the preparation over it, then hang up and smoke.

The worms in meat are caused by a small black bug, and not by a fly, as some suppose. Meat should always be sacked as soon as smoked, for these bugs appear very early in the spring.

A brine for pork: To one hundred pounds of meat, take ten pints of salt, five pints of brown sugar or New Orleans molasses, two ounces of soda and one ounce of saltpetre, with enough water to cover the meat. Mix the salt and sugar, rub the flesh side of each piece with it, and pack in the barrel, having first covered the bottom of the barrel with salt. When the meat is all in, make a pickle of the remainder as follows: Put the salt and sugar in water, dissolve the soda and saltpetre in hot water, add it to the brine, and pour over the meat. Put on a sufficient weight to keep it down, and leave in for six weeks. Then take out, sprinkle with black pepper, and hang up to smoke. Brine for beef is made the same way, except to use two pints less salt. If the brine gets thick or ropey, boil and skim it, let cool and put it back. The pieces that are intended for dried beef must be taken out in three weeks, and cured by drying or smoking. The others must be kept in the brine.

To heep hams: For one hundred pounds of meat, take eight pints of salt, two tablespoons of saltpetre and four gallons water; put hams in this pickle, keeping them well under the brine; in April, take out, drain for a few days, slice as for cooking, fry nearly as much as for table, pack in stone jars. When full, put on a weight and leave stand until cool, then pour over the fat fried out. Prepared in this way, they retain the ham flavor without being smoked. The last three recipes were taken from the Buckeye Cook Book, a book dedicated to the plucky housewives who master their work instead of allowing it to master them.

"Bad dinners go hand in hand with total depravity, while a properly fed man is already half saved."

CHAPTER IX.

HOUSES AND TROUGHS FOR SWINE.

REMARKS.—HOW TO BUILD HOG HOUSES OR PENS.—FIRST DESIGN OR PLAN.—SECOND DESIGN.—THIRD DESIGN.—FOURTH DESIGN, A PORTABLE HOUSE.—TROUGHS FOR SWINE.

HOG HOUSES ARE NECESSARY.

Houses or pens for swine are, as a rule, indispensible with the successful swine raiser. Their use is so often needed at all times of the year and for so many different purposes, that after a person once builds a well arranged hog house or set of pens, he will wonder how he has ever done so long without them. There are many farmers who think it so costly an operation to build a hog house or some pens, that they never commence them. That is very often a mistake, for most farmers could build themselves a very comfortable hog house or set of pens at a very small expense, except for the labor, and that can very often be done at such times as they have no other urgent work to do, and therefore the cost would be very light, especially when compared to their value. In order to show how this may be done, the author will give several different designs or plans of building hog houses or pens, from which any one could choose a plan to suit his surroundings.

In building a structure of any kind, it is always best to have a definite plan, and aim to adopt it exactly to your wants, as far as practicable. A little forethought in choosing site, determining dimensions and arranging details before the building is commenced, will accomplish much for future convenience. Changes from original plans are very expensive, cause delay, and are often unsatisfactory. These rules will hold good in building pens for swine, as well as for any other use. The comfort and requirement of the stock and the storing of food and supplies must all be taken into consideration. The first thing to decide on is always the location. Sometimes this is hard to do, as there are several things to be taken into consideration. The other farm buildings may be built in such a way that it is difficult to choose a site which will make the house or pens convenient to use, and yet far enough away from the dwelling. If a proper place is chosen, the lots joining the building can very often be formed without the use of very much fencing. For these reasons, before one attempts to build, the work ought to be the subject of careful study. Any farmer who intends erecting buildings of a costly nature, would do well to spend some time in examining good buildings belonging to other farmers, or in studying plans which are accessible in books or papers. A house or set of pens for swine should be on the highest ground attainable within the desired place. The point to be preferred is toward the south. The next best is toward the south-east. It should be so built that it can be well ventilated and cleaned, and also admit the light and warmth of the sun. It should have lots so attached that the hogs can have access to them for exercise and air. Whatever the plan, in the first place such houses must be dry. As the hog in winter spends a good part of his time in his bed, it should therefore be a comfortable one, as comfort is essential to contentment and thrift of all animals.

The bed should be dry, warm, and well ventilated. I prefer a dirt floor for this department, as it should be separate from the feeding room. A dirt floor is warmer than one of boards, and becoming rounded out fits the shape of the animal, and he rests much more comfortably. Hogs that sleep on a board, brick or stone floor often have lumps raised on their limbs, and they frequently become sore and painful. In order to have a dirt floor dry, it should be raised considerably above the surrounding level.

The sleeping room should be tight and warm as possible in cold weather, and have means of cleaning out and ventilation when moderate, and should at all times be supplied with clean, dry bedding. Leaves, prairie hay or corn stalks, make good beds. Straw will do, but must be changed often, as it wears out fast and is very liable to become damp. For a feeding department, a pen on the south or east side of a building, with a tight floor sloping a little from the building, will answer every purpose.

Adjoining this feeding floor and the sleeping department, also, if possible, there should be the manure pit or lot, so that the cleanings of both places can be thrown out. When feeding time arrives, the hogs should be compelled to pass through this lot and held there a short time to make their discharges before passing upon the feeding floor. Finally a supply of good water troughs and water, and a crib of corn, all arranged for convenience, are essentials not to be overlooked.

FIRST BUILDING DESIGN OR PLAN.

I will give first a simple and cheap design or plan for

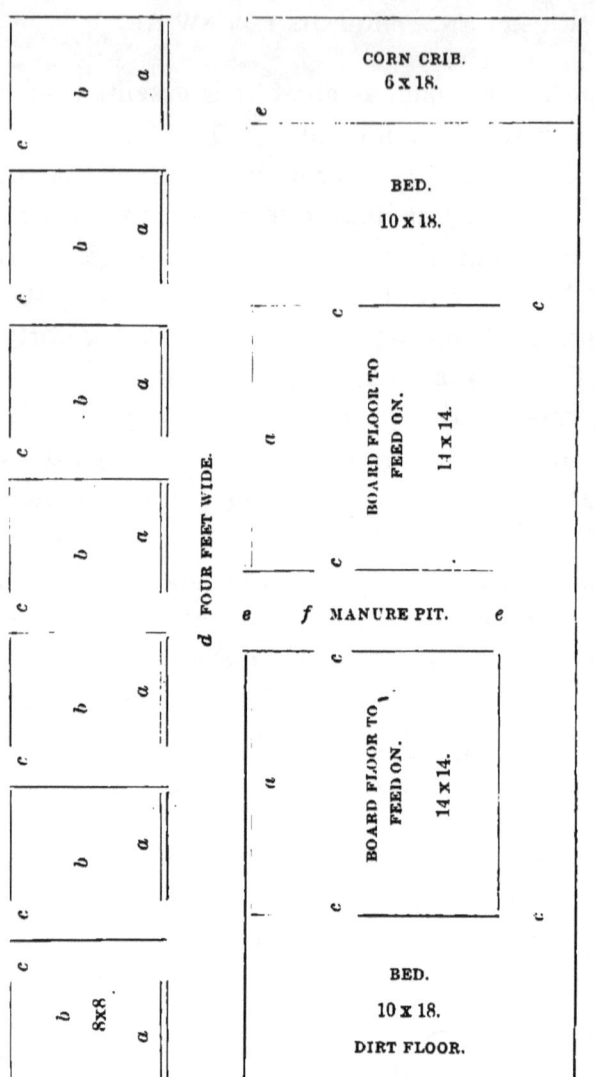

breeding and feeding pens. The draft is only designed to give a general idea of the arrangements, which are simple, and may be varied to suit the convenience of almost any farmer. The cost, except the labor, could be made light. The building can be made twelve feet wide and of any length desired. The pens should be 8x8, which will leave an alley or passway under cover four feet wide. There should be a door to each pen, 2x3½ feet in size, to accomodate large sows. Unless the building is unnecessarily high at the back part, this door should be hung. Where the building is high enough, a drop door can be used. If possible, each pen should have a lot attached to it for the use of the sow. At the front end of each pen, cut a door large enough to allow the pigs to pass in and out. This can be closed by a sliding door, and so arranged to suit the size of the pigs by raising it and holding it by a pin. By this means the pigs can be fed in front of the pen by themselves. The partitions between the pens should be so arranged that they can be swung up out of the way, or taken out, thereby throwing two or more pens into one, forming a sleeping or feeding place for several hogs. This building should by all means face the south or east. If four feet high behind, and eight feet high in front, it will do. or it may be higher if wanted. The front part of the pens for 3½ feet high should be boarded up tight, also the ends of the building and the back part, all but the doors. Boards 16 feet long are the right length. They will close up two pens in front, or cut in two will form the partitions, and will cut to a good advantage in boarding up the back part, or to form the doors. They are also of the right length for the roof, where boards are to be used which make as good a roof as is necessary.

After boarding up 3½ feet of the front part of the pens, the upper part can be closed by falling doors, one for each pen, hung above by hinges or by a 2x4 piece set in the uprights, by rounding the ends and boring holes in the posts. When these doors are down they ought to close up the open space tight, or when swung up they will be out of the way so as to admit the sun and air. This should be done at all times except in cold stormy weather. The pens should be provided with a smooth, tight board floor, so as to keep out the cold and save the feed; and a good plan is, at the back part of the pen between the door and partition, to place eight inches from the floor a shelf six inches wide, for the pigs to get under so the sow cannot lie on them. At the ends of this pen can be built corn cribs of any length desired, with a ten foot passway between the pens and cribs. This can have a dirt floor and be used for hogs to sleep in. In front of this building and running in the same direction lengthwise with it, can be formed a feed lot for other hogs, with a feeding floor, manure pit and a sleeping apartment at one end, or a corn crib, sleeping place, feeding floor and manure pit.

In forming this second lot, if the corn crib and feeding floor, etc., are at one end, the other end of the lot should be open, or vice versa.

In forming the first set of pens, where lumber is high, they can be covered with prairie hay or straw; the back part can be made do for a fence and banked up in the winter with straw or corn-fodder, and the doors and lots formed in front of the pens. When there is no board floor put in the pens, they should be filled in with good

HOUSES AND TROUGHS FOR SWINE.

clay six or eight inches deep, then looked after often and kept dry and clean.

At the end of the alley there can be an elevated walk constructed, sloping from the alley out, and of the right height at the back end to suit a wagon when backed up, for the purpose of loading hogs. The hogs can be turned in this alley-way and driven into the wagon. A light board shield that can be carried easily, should always be carried behind the hogs when loading, to keep them from running back.

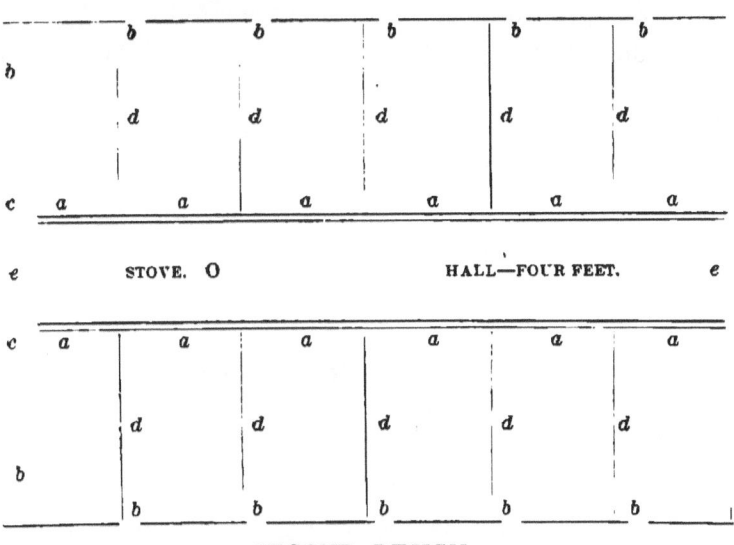

SECOND DESIGN.

Pens, 8x8, or 8x10. *a a a* Trough. *b b b* Doors for Entrance and Exit of Hogs *c c* Doors opening from Pens into the Hall, which, when both opened at once, fasten together, and close the Passage into the Hall. *d d d* Movable Partitions. *e e* Doors for Entrance to Hall.

This draft is similar to the first, except that it has a double set of pens constructed alike with an alley-way between them. This makes a building twenty feet wide, or wider if liked, and any length desired, and has to be roofed both ways. If well built, it can be made very comfortable in cold weather by the use of a stove, which is an important feature, should a cold snap occur when pigs are expected. The doors at the ends of the alleyway can be made in two halves, in order to have the upper half open for ventilation when wanted, and there can also be a window over the door to admit light.

The pens on each side at one end of the building should have doors 2 feet wide, which should open into the alley. These hooked together form a passage way from one side to the other. When partitions are out, both sides can be used for feeding, or one side for feeding and one for lodging. Partitions can be stowed away overhead, and replaced when wanted for sows. This building can be built on a cheap plan, or made more costly if so desired. According to the design in the Breeders' Gazette the pens should be set on stone piers, about 1½ feet high. Sills, 8x8 inches; joists, 2x8; plates, 4x4; rafters, 2x4, 2 feet apart; roof, ⅛ pitch, with two good ventilators in peak, right distance apart for appearance. Seven feet from top of sill to top of plate. Stock board 14 feet in length, cut in the middle, can be used for the sides; battened all around; sealed up inside with common lumber to bottom of windows; tar paper used on sides and roof; two-inch plank for floor; shingled roof. This comprises about all needed for the structure.

At one end of this building if desired can be formed grain bins and a feeding room, with a steamer or stove of any kind to cook food and heat water. Or it can be built one and one-half stories high, with a granary overhead through the center of the building at one end, and a place for bedding material at the other end. In this

HOUSES AND TROUGHS FOR SWINE. 139

case it would be harder to keep warm unless floored overhead.

THIRD DESIGN.

This draft or plan is very much like the last one, except that it has a main floor at one end to prepare the feed and is intended to be either one or two stories high. The diagram will explain the building.

These diagrams, rude as they may seem, will no doubt be plain enough to give any one an idea how these pens are constructed, and enable them to build a house or set of pens to suit their wants. The doors at the back part of the pens, if so arranged to raise and fall in opening and closing, can be opened and shut by the use of a small pulley over the top of the door and a rope reaching from the top of the door over the pulley to the alley way.

NOTE.—When a hog house is built up off of the ground, which is the best way to build them if possible, it should be well banked up in the winter to keep it warm, and the dirt or other material should be removed again in the spring so as to admit the air. By this means it can be made more comfortable and healthy.

A BATH BOX.

The box marked j in this diagram is 4x8 feet and a foot or more deep. It should be made of two-inch plank and water tight. The end next the alley way must be made slanting, and have some slats fastened on it on the inside some three inches apart to keep the pigs from slipping when going in or out of the box. One side should be set against the partition, and the other side can have some movable boards on top of it, held in position with slats at the end, and high enough so that the pigs cannot

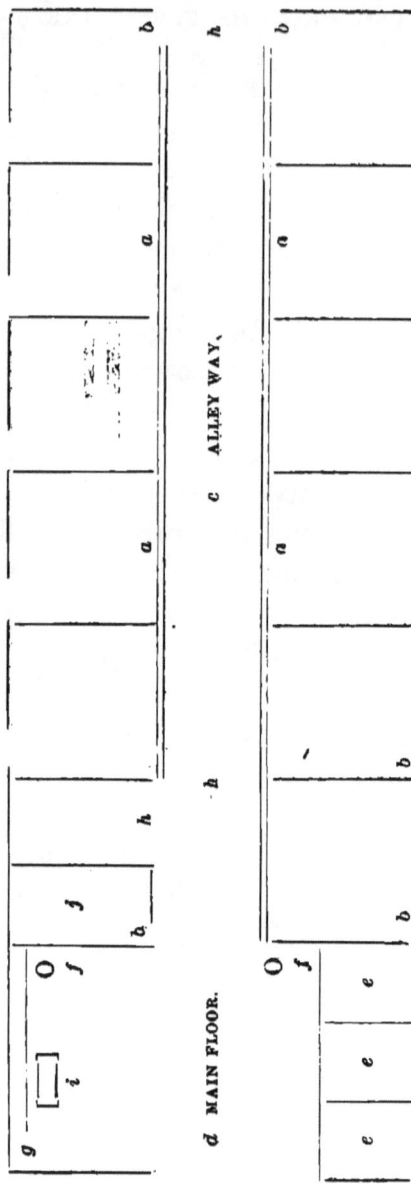

SECOND DESIGN FOR BUILDING.

a a, Troughs. *b b*, Doors for Entrance and Exit of Hogs. *c*, Alley way. *d*, Main Floor. *e e*, Feed Bins. *f*, Swill Barrels. *g*, Stairway. *h*, Doors. *i*, Stove, or Steamer. *j*, Box, to be used for washing hogs in summer.

get over. The box is the same length as the pen. The end next the alley way must have a door or gate to open into the alley. After the pigs are once in the box, this can be closed to keep them in. A light, movable walk, for this end of the box, for the pigs to go upon, is also necessary. By turning the pigs into the alley way and going behind them with a slat frame about as wide as the alley, they can be made to walk into this box without any trouble for the purpose of washing them. In this way a half dozen or more pigs can be washed at a time and then turned out and another lot put in. As soon as through the water ought to be drawn off, which can be done by having a hole in the bottom of the box. In the winter, or any other time, this box can be used to mix feed in, and in that way made to answer two purposes.

The old saying, "What ever is worth doing, is worth doing well," will hold good at times in washing pigs as well as feeding them.

Swine seek their wallow of water or mud only, to allay their most uncomfortable heat of body. Therefore they need, in hot weather, a shallow bath in which to cool themselves and cleanse their skin. This plan of bath is so simple, that, in any convenient hog house, it can be adapted for a large or small lot of pigs at little expense or labor. A bath box similar to this can be made at a convenient place outside and supplied with water, and the pigs will not require any teaching to avail themselves of it.

A box for this purpose should not be over eight or nine inches high. It can be of any width or length desired and should be put in the ground, bedded in puddled clay to make it water tight. Plank or gravel put around it, to prevent mud, is all that is needed.

A MOVABLE PIG HOUSE.

A light portable pig house, large enough to accommodate a brood sow, is often very convenient. It can be taken into a field, grove or grass lot, at any time to accommodate a favorite sow and pigs, or some nervous sow that does not do well when housed close to other sows and pigs, or where she is disturbed. It also comes handy to set in a lot to shelter a boar, ram, some choice pigs or poultry for a time. I will describe how to make a house of this kind, as given by L. N. Bohman to the Breeders' Gazette. Also a cut, showing a house as described, except that it has a sky-light to admit the sunshine in cold weather, which is very beneficial to young stock. Any farmer can at a very small expense build a few houses as thus described, which he will find very useful at almost all times of the year.

HOW TO MAKE THE HOUSE.

"Provide four scantlings, 2x2, 12 feet long, two scantlings 2x4, 12 feet long; fifty feet of flooring for roof, and 75 feet of flooring for sides and ends. Let the flooring for the roof be the best, free from knots and windshakes. Cut four rails or nail ties, 2x4, 6 feet long, for the back and front. Now cut siding enough for the back, 3 feet long, and then two boards one foot wide, 4½ feet long, for the front. Nail two of these boards to the flat side of two of the rails above named, letting the outer edge of each board project one inch past the ends of the rails, and have the rails flush with the ends of the boards; taking care always to put the siding square with the rails. The bottom rail, on edge, keeps in the bedding, and is not too high for sow or pigs to get over easily. For the back, nail the three-foot boards to the two-inch face of the rails, letting top rail be at the ends of the boards and project one inch at the ends of the rails, and the bottom rail be eight inches from the other ends of siding, which when set up allows the bottom rail to prevent the sow from crushing pigs aginst the side.

After the siding is nailed as above, make mortises 1x2 inches just under the rails of the back, and two inches from the edges of the boards. In the front make the mortises 1x2 above the bottom rail, and the top mortises opposite those in the back. The front and back are now complete.

Cut four rails, 2x2, 5½ feet long, and make a tenon, 1x2, 3 inches long, by cutting into the rail one inch and ripping back to the shoulder, which makes the tenon on one side of the rail. Draw-bore these tenons with a five-eighth bit, and put them into the mortises of the back and front, so the outside of the rail is flush with the siding at the front and back; put in the drawpins and the frame is complete.

Now cut the siding for the two ends and nail it to the rails as they stand, and you will have no trouble in taking apart and putting up again. Draw a line from top of the front to the top of the back, and saw to it for slope of the roof. This done, cut three slots, 2x2, for rafters to rest in, one notch six inches from the front, one three inches from the back, and the other notch half way between these two. Take the three rails, 2x2, 6½ feet long, that were left after cutting the four side rails, and lay in their notches so they project three inches at each end. Saw the roofing to project eight inches at the rear and three inches in front. Lay this flooring from the roof carefully and paint each joint as laid. When done, paint the roof well. It will pay also to paint the house with oil and Prince's Brown, which is cheap and lasting. The front of this house is now open, 4 feet high, less 8 inches, the width of the rails. The closed sides should set north and west, to exclude cold winds, and the open front face the east and south, to admit sunshine.

We have a movable front and swinging door to close all up if a sow is to farrow there in early spring. The movable front is made by having the battons project one inch at one side, so as to catch within the siding. On the other end of the battons we have a button on each to catch the upper and lower rails. By swinging a door in the remaining space the house is closed, and there is complete protection against storms. We use these movable fronts in early spring until the pigs are old enough to endure the cold, when the front is taken off and laid away. If the house is set up on a dry spot where the water will not run under, or if a trench is cut behind for the drip of the roof to run off, the inmates will be more comfortable than in any of our big houses.

Each spring and fall we take these houses down and whitewash inside, and never have a new litter begin life in the old filth of their predecessors. With a clean house, on a clean, fresh sod, the young things start life without being handicapped by disease. The sow should become accustomed to the house two weeks before farrowing, and the swinging door should be kept open. The night she is to farrow it may be closed, and then the pigs are safe from any storm we ever have in this latitude.

A handy man can make two of these houses in a day, and the cost of material does not exceed $2.50.

The above description is for a house without the skylight. The sash and lights cost about $2. In bright, cold, or windy days, in March or April, the glass lets the sunshine pour into the bed, which the pigs enjoy. We cannot get too much sunshine for the pig in the spring of the year.

These movable pig houses will be found most convenient on small farms where permanent hog houses are not provided. To the tenant who wishes to give his pigs better care than the quarters of the rented farm afford, they will be found of especial value, as he can move them as he does his implements and stock. To move one from one lot to the other, a sled may be slipped under, or the house can be taken down by removal of the pins, and placed in a wagon, or carried piece by piece by one person. On flat land, where drainage is poor, it will be well to make a floor of inch boards, cut so that the pens set down over it. This keeps the floor perfectly dry. The floor should fit the house, so that there will be no danger of a pig's foot or leg being caught between the floor and house. In order to prevent killing the grass and destroying the sod, we do not allow the house to stand long in one spot. Move often to keep the soil and grass fresh. With clean beds, in clean houses, on clean sod, we may hope to raise healthy pigs, if fed judiciously and bred for constitution rather than color and fat.

TROUGHS FOR SWINE.

Every farmer in this wide land of ours, from Ocean to Ocean, is interested in hogs. No well regulated farm should be without them. They fill a niche in mixed farming that no other animal can supply. They largely subsist on stuff that would otherwise be wasted. They are economizers. If you are opposed to raising hogs for sale, at least try and keep a few pigs to consume the waste. It will pay to do so.

The trough is as essential as the breed, and should be well filled. The breed is the machinery and the trough supplies the raw material for manufacture.

Since information on making troughs for swine may be of value to some of the readers of this book, I will endeavor to explain how to make a few troughs that will be found practicable to use. First, the old log trough, made by squaring up a stick of timber, 9x12 and of any length, and hollowing it out by the use of an ax or foot adze, is a good stationary trough, for the hogs cannot upset it, and if made of good timber, will last for years. A trough similar to it can be made by spiking and bolting together three two-inch boards, with end pieces well set in. To keep hogs from crowding one another, upright pieces can be fastened on the sides about a foot apart; if set against a fence or in a pen, only one side should have the pieces. Light troughs for pigs, or for general use where they are to be lifted about, can be made in the same way out of six inch fencing boards. The eves-trough, made by nailing together two boards edge-wise, of any length, width, or thickness, and then nailing on or setting in end pieces, is a common and handy trough. Large troughs made this way, can have a wide board or two narrow ones, runing lengthwise in the center of the trough and braced by pieces from the edge of the trough to them, to keep the hogs from crowding or getting over the top. Troughs for small pigs are made low and nearly square, as more pigs can get to them, and they cannot be upset; they are also easily cleaned. Oak lumber is the best to use to make troughs out of, as it will last longer and hold the nails better. The hogs can be kept out of the trough until the feed is put in by means of a wide board, or two put together with strips. It should be wide enough so one edge can rest on the edge of the trough or on slats put across the trough, and the other edge fastened to the pen or fence by straps or hinges; this board must be in a sloping position, the board or shute that carries the swill into the trough, being under it. When the hogs are wanted in the trough, raise the board by the use of a rope or strap fastened to the outer edge of it and fasten it up. As soon as the hogs are done eating, it can be lowered again; in this way the hogs can be kept out of the trough and it can be kept cleaner than when they have free access to it all the time.

CHAPTER X.

Prevailing Causes of Swine Disease.

WHAT CAUSES CHOLERA.—SWINE FEVER.—ITS PREVAILING LOCAL CAUSES.—CERTAIN BREEDS CHOLERA PROOF.—COMMON ERRORS IN FEEDING.—WHEAT STUBBLE PASTURE.—CONFINEMENT, BAD FOOD AND WATER.—STRAWSTACKS, MANURE HEAPS AND BARNS.—ITS INFECTIOUS CHARACTER.—DANGER ARISING FROM RUNNING STREAMS OR POOLS.—DANGER IN EXPOSURE OF DEAD HOGS.—THE PERIOD BETWEEN EXPOSURE TO CONTAGION AND ITS ATTACKS.

HOG CHOLERA AND SWINE FEVER.

What causes hog cholera or swine fever? is a question which has been often asked, and for which many answers have been proposed, but among the hog growing people of this country, it is as far from solution as ever. While certain theorists and their advocates talk "filth" all the time as its cause, others unmercifully condemn the improved breeding of swine. The farmer knows there is something in this when carried to the extreme, but he is often puzzled to know why his hogs get sick, when kept in clean quarters and not pure bred, while his neighbor's pure bred hogs are in good condition; and on the other hand, it not infrequently occurs that the farmer who keeps pure bred hogs, loses his, while his neighbor owning native bred hogs has his herd in a thrifty condition. In studying the cause of this epidemic, too much attention cannot be given to the local causes, as well as the artificial condition of the patient. "It is true, when a rapid growth is attained by artificial means, we lose in vitality, hardiness, and constitution." This is especially the case in the improved breeds of hogs, which now weigh as much at nine months as the old hardy breeds did at eighteen. Instead of roaming at large, unlimited by field or pen, as the old native breed did, and maturing more slowly, they have been subjected to confinement, fed with corn, cooked food, distilled or other slops, etc., which were entirely unknown to them in their native state, thus, opening up the way for hog cholera and other fatal diseases. This cause has also been increased by inbreeding too close, or breeding from too young or runty and inferior animals. To obviate this, too much attention cannot be given to the selections of thrifty and well matured animals as breeders, and treating them as near like nature as possible.

CERTAIN BREEDS CHOLERA PROOF.

No breed, however, is exempt from this disease. Even the "Hazel Splitter" with all his vigor of constitution could not resist taking this disease when exposed to it in its epidemic or coutagious form. The representation that any improved breed of hogs are cholera proof is a fallacy. It is true, the better constitution a hog has, the better fortified he is against such epidemics. Hence a hog, forced in growth all the time, is more liable to disease, than one grown more slowly—because its digestive and other organs become impaired and its ability to resist the attacks of disease is thereby lessened.

The present practice of raising swine artificially by the use of such stimulating foods as will secure a rapid growth and quick development, is the most fruitful cause of disease among swine otherwise well cared for.

COMMON ERRORS IN FEEDING.

Unquestionably many healthy hogs are made sick and die, by the thoughtlessness of their owners in suddenly changing from dry feed to green corn. The vast amount of saccharine matter taken into the stomach of the animal, impairs its digestion, and on failure of assimilation the food ferments and sets up an inflammation in the stomach and bowels which either produces an active diarrhea or severe constipation. Both these conditions are often noticed in a herd of hogs at the same time, and apparently arising from the same cause.

The same effect is produced on hogs when taken from short dry pasture fields, where they have been kept for some time, and turned into a stubble field where there is a rank growth of clover, or into a clover field, where the second crop is growing rank. The disastrous effects of these changes are more easily noticeable if the change be made during a warm, wet time, as under such circumstances fermentation takes place in the stomach of the animal more quickly than at any other time. Another fruitful cause of sickness from which farmers suffer greatly is allowing hogs to run in matured clover fields and feeding old corn, or not feeding at all. The effect noticeable in this class of cases is almost universally a constipated condition of the animal. The same fevered and constipated condition is noticeable when hogs are shut up in pens, or lots, and fed old dry corn in large quantities, for the purpose of fattening.

WHEAT STUBBLE PASTURE.

Another dangerous practice which causes the same

trouble, is that of turning hogs into a wheat field, in a dry time, particularly so, when the herd is small or the field very large, and the amount of wheat left on the ground in harvesting is considerable. The hogs begin eating the dry wheat at once, and continue just as long as they can find it, unless they get sick before it is all eaten, which not infrequently occurs. The dry wheat, when taken into the stomach without proper mastication, is almost certain to clog the stomach, and remain undigested, producing a bilious condition of the animal, resulting in fever and constipation.

Practical demonstrations have proven that wheat should never be fed to hogs unless ground, soaked or cooked. The farmer who is fearful of having his fields rooted or torn up by his hogs, is careful to put rings in the nose of each pig as soon as weaned, thus depriving it of a taste or smell of fresh earth, and the use of an instinct which teaches it in bilious attacks to search for bugs, worms, and other insects as well as roots or vegetables, the natural excitants of the stomach, liver and bowels. He never once thinks of the necessity of furnishing the animal an artificial substitute for these. Dr. Koch, an eminent German scientist and a standard authority on cholera in the human species, says: "Cholera will have but little effect among those who keep the digestive organs, and the kidney and liver in a healthful condition." Following this suggestion of Dr. Koch's, the author has, by repeated experiments, practically demonstrated that swine are subject to the same physical laws as the human race respecting the administration of medicine for the prevention of diseases. And by giving attention to the local condition of the animal and furnishing it with proper remedies, if administered in time, not only will the diseases arising from local causes be removed or prevented, but exposure of the herd to swine fever, cholera, however contagious, will not result disastrously.

CONFINEMENT, BAD FOOD AND WATER.

Confining hogs in a small lot or pen and compelling them to drink stagnant and filthy water, and in the winter season, ice or snow water, or scanty feeding, or dry corn, or musty, moldy and unwholesome food, causes worms in the intestines of the animal, which most generally produces unthriftiness, constipation and disease; such treatment will sometimes produce diarrheæ or other ailments of the digestive organs. The foregoing illustrates the common errors in feeding hogs, which have resulted in the disease, called cholera or swine fever. Aside from the errors in feeding which I have briefly enumerated, there are other causes of disease which frequently occur which I will mention: First, allowing hogs to run in fields along streams, or in bottom or low lands during wet seasons, when decaying vegetable substances are throwing out their poisonous miasma. Many thus contract disease similar to malaria fever, which, if neglected, may and frequently does become fatal. A timely application of proper remedies which will act upon the liver and kidneys without irritating the digestive organs will almost invariably relieve this difficulty, and it does not require close attention on the part of the feeder to discover this condition of the animals. Second, the habit of turning hogs into a wood lot in seasons when there is a large quantity of oak mast, is very dangerous, and not infrequently results in the death of a portion, if not all the herd. It may be inquired why did not the hogs of "ancient days" die, when they had nothing else? The reason is plain to a practical observer, and is the same as before assigned. "The "ancient hog" was by nature calculated to root for such things as his system required, such as roots, insects, toads, snakes and young animals which tended directly to overcome the powerful effect of the astringent properties of the seed or jackoak acorn. This variety of mast is far the most dangerous, as its astringent properties are proportionally greater. Continued feeding upon these nuts injuriously affects the urinary and other organs.

The cultivation of the land and removal of timber, have left the fields free from roots and herbs, mice, insects, and other varieties of such food as formerly was found and eaten, rendering the hog entirely incapable of obtaining the needful remedies for such condition as above described. Any prudent farmer will see at once how necessary it is to supply this necessary want, and do so, instead of allowing the hogs to die.

STRAW STACKS, MANURE HEAPS AND BARNS.

Another and potent cause of disease is, the manner in which hogs are kept, and particularly so where the farmer entrusts the entire care of the animals to the employes about the farm, who naturally take little or no interest in the condition in which they are kept, in order to avoid extra labor, and attention in caring for them. The owner having neglected to provide suitable quarters, the hogs are expected and allowed to shift for themselves as best they can. And in cases of this kind they very often seek an old straw stack, fermenting manure heap, dusty shed or barn in which to sleep. This cannot be too severely condemned. Here they crowd together in large or small numbers, according to the size of the drove, and sometimes even burrow beneath the straw or litter, and are thus compelled to breath the "impure and noxious gases engendered thereby." These taken into the system poison and weaken it, and generate disease, which, sooner or later, takes a malignant form, in the way of typhoid or lung fever, and becomes epidemic and contagious and spreads over a large scope of country. In my practice I have often traced the first disease that was known in a neighberhood, to some farm where I was satisfied it started in this way. In other instances it was traced to farms where the swine were allowed to sleep in dusty sheds or under barns. Here they are compelled to breathe or inhale the impure air and dust found in such places, which is very dangerous, especially where the buildings are occupied by other animals. The "solid and liquid excretions" of the other stock, mixed with that of the swine, or the excretions of the swine, mixed with the dry litter of sheds or barns, present the means for the germination of disease. In warm or wet weather, the evils that arise from swine sleeping in the above named places are more noticeable and more dangerous than at any other time; as the hogs which are crowded or piled up in such places become very warm and wet with sweat, and upon coming out into the cool air, undoubtedly take cold and thereby contract a more fatal malady. By observation, I have very frequently known this to be the cause of a very malignent type of disease, especially with fat, young hogs or pigs. This being the case, the farmer or owner of hogs should see at once how important it is to remove the cause, and give the hogs such treatment as would release the local trouble, before it had taken a fatal form.

ITS INFECTIOUS OR CONTAGIOUS CHARACTER.

When the disease has assumed a malignant form, it is the same as the Asiatic cholera, or typhus or typhoid fever with the human family, and similar to epizootic and pneumonia with other stock, being infectious or contagious. It has been practically demonstrated, by good authority, that hog cholera or swine fever, is a "germ desease" capable of being germinated, propagated and transported in various ways. And perhaps some of the ordinary methods of spreading this disease, cannot be better described than to quote from the American Stock Book as follows: "It has been a great mystery to the farmer how the disease spreads from place to place without apparent actual contact. It was like fighting in the dark to attempt to prevent it, and many gave up in despair and stoically awaited its coming, or after a few cases had occurred, ceased all remedies or precautionary measures, saying: "what will die, will die anyway." There is no doubt but what it is under favorable conditions infectious and conveyed by germs or spores in the air. It is most difficult to draw the dividing line between the epizootic nature of the disease, and the contagious form. There is no doubt but what the infectious nature of the disease may, under a predisposing condition of local causes, etc., take the contagious form, which is far more malignant, sweeping and fatal in character. That a few spasmodic cases may occur in a drove, which if neglected, may so increase in number and violence as to become highly contagious. This contagious matter is of a fixed character, and is present in the blood, the discharges, and of course in the place inhabited. It possesses great vitality.

DANGER ARISING FROM STREAMS OR POOLS.

It is not infrequently the case that swine afflicted with this contagious disease will go to a running stream to drink, and standing or lying in the water, die. The stream carries the virus from such dead animals for miles along both its banks. And hogs drinking the water below are almost certain to contract the disease. The same class of exposure is met when buzzards which have gorged themselves on the carcasses of diseased hogs, seek a pool of water, and after drinking, vomit the contents of the craw, either into the water or on the banks. Hogs drinking the water or eating such material are certain to at once become diseased.

DANGER IN EXPOSURE OF THE DEAD HOGS.

Where dead hogs are buried shallow, or piled up and left to decay, the grease from them will penetrate the ground for quite a distance, carrying with it the poisons, virus or germs, which away from the air retain their poisonous qualities. Hogs coming in contact with those places will in many instances root up and eat the earth where such dead animals have decayed, and in such cases, they invariably become diseased. There is also a practice of feeding the dead hogs to the herd, many farmers claiming by so doing the living animals are benefited. But in all his many years of experience the author has never found this to be the case—unless the dead bodies were first well charred, when there may be some benefit derived in so doing.

The methods of exposure to this disease, the author has found to be very dangerous; and when hogs become diseased from either of these causes, such attacks almost invariably are attended with fatal results. The germs of the disease in such case having been brought directly in contact with the mucus membrane of the mouth or stomach, and the warmth of the animal furnishing the germs with the needful elements of growth and formation, the hog speedily becomes diseased, past all hope of recovery, unless such treatment be resorted to at once, as will enable the animal to throw off or overcome the effects of the poisonous matter. This alone should prove to the farmers how important it is to burn diseased hogs as soon as dead. For by so doing all this danger is obviated, and the germs are entirely destroyed. If left lying where they happen to die, or if they are hauled out and piled up, or buried shallow, the carcass or a part is likely to be found and devoured by hogs, or else the bones and flesh will be carried about, and sometimes for miles by dogs or other animals and deposited in such places as hogs will find and devour them soon afterwards, and become diseased,

Dr. Detmers, a celebrated scientist and careful investigator of the swine disease, says: "The dead hogs should be buried at least four feet deep or cremated." The author knowing that the farmers will not go to the trouble of burying them four feet deep, still repeats the advice in his writings of former years, to burn them, as that obviates any further trouble.

THE PERIOD BETWEEN CONTAGION AND ITS ATTACKS.

"The intensity of this contagious matter seems also to vary according to the form and malignancy of the disease. The period which elapses between exposure and the attacks is not always the same, varying with the form the disease assumes, from a few hours to a few weeks. As we have stated before, an infectious disease may become malignant and contagious, and one form of the disease does not necessarily impart the same type to another, but depends more upon the primary seat of the malady in the patient. It may take the enteric form or the external carbuncular character. It may localize its attacks on certain organs with well defined symptoms, which are more prolonged in their results, or, it may affect the whole organization, and destroy life in a few hours." The experiments of Drs. Law, Detmers, Salmen, Sutton, Budd, Osler and others, in inoculating sound hogs with the virus or poisoned blood of sick ones, have shown the period of incubation to vary greatly, sometimes proving fatal the first day, and in other instances, not until the fifteenth day. Dr. Detmers gives the period, "from five to fifteen days, or an average of seven days." The author's experience and observation in having well hogs with sick ones, have placed the period of infection from three to thirteen days, but the majority of cases occuring in from seven to nine days.

CHAPTER XI.

INVESTIGATION OF SWINE DISEASE BY THE GOVERNMENT.

INVESTIGATIONS BY THE GOVERNMENT.—DISCOVERIES OF DR. H. J. DETMERS, JAMES LAW AND OTHERS.—EFFECTS OF THE SWINE DISEASE UPON OTHER ANIMALS AND UPON THE HUMAN FAMILY.—GERM THEORY.—OPPONENTS OF THE GERM THEORY.—PROOF THEREOF.—WHY SUMMER IS THE MOST DANGEROUS SEASON.

INVESTIGATIONS BY THE GOVERMENT.

In support of the practical experience of the author set forth in the preceeding pages, I cannot do better perhaps than to give some extracts from Drs. James Law and H. J. Detmers, in their excellent report to the Commissioner of Agriculture of the United States, in 1880, upon the cause and effects of hog cholera, swine fever, or what they called, hog fever or swine plague. In experimenting in this direction and others, Dr. H. J. Detmers and Dr. James Law, while investigating this disease in the fall and winter of 1878 and 1879, and in 1880, being a part of the commission as appointed by the government, made some discoveries which I consider of value, and I will give such extracts from their report as I think may be useful to the general farmer, in order to show more plainly the cause and effect of hog cholera or swine fever and its treatment. Dr. Detmers says: "When I first commenced my investigation, in the fall of 1878 and in the winter of 1878 and 1879, I had clear sailing, because an abundance of material was always available. The disease presented itself almost everywhere in its malignant form. I endeavored first to ascertain the nature and the cause or causes of the disease, the means and manner of its spreading, and the working of its morbid process; secondly, to discover the means necessary to check its spreading and to prevent its outbreak, and to learn the most practical means of prevention, that is, such as would most likely be the least objectionable to the farmers, and prove both effective and easy of application; thirdly, to ascertain whether and to what extent an attack of swine-plague terminating in recovery is able to destroy further predisposition or to produce immunity from the effects of a subsequent infection." "Hence, as it was my intention to find reliable means of prevention, and to subject the preventives to a severe test, it was not advisable to inoculate from any case of swine-plague that presented itself or was convenient. But I made my selections, and only used material from malignant and typical cases of swine-plague, also refusing to use any material from cases showing putrefaction; therefore, I am sure I have made no mistakes." The learned doctor's investigations show that hog cholera, swine fever, or what he named "swine plague," though a disease peculiar to swine, can, under favorable circumstances, be communicated to other animals, and under very favorable circumstances probably to human beings, but not likely to the barnyard fowls.

The author has satisfied himself that the disease cannot be communicated by working with diseased hogs in any manner, he having been frequently bitten when handling them, and he has many times held post mortem examinations of hogs that have died of cholera when his hands were sore and often raw in places without ever experiencing any unpleasant results from so doing. Dr. Detmers says: It can and may attack one and the same animal twice, and even three times, but if it does, the second and third attacks are always mild ones and not apt to prove fatal, unless complicated with other diseases. As a rule, however, the first attack, provided the animal recovers, produces immunity from the effects of a subsequent infection, at any rate for some time, and it may be for life. The same seems to destroy fully or partially the condition necessary to the development of the swine plague germ. Even an interrupted attack, or in other words an infection that has been prevented from causing serious morbid changes, either by medical treatment or otherwise, as a rule, seems to produce immunity from the effect of a subsequent infection, the same as a fully developed attack.

HOW IT AFFECTS THE LUNGS.

"The morbid process of swine plague can have its seat in almost any organ or part of the body. Yet it must be considered as characteristic of the disease, that the lungs invariably are more or less affected, and constitute in a large number of cases the principal seat of the morbid process. At any rate, in over two hundred post mortem examinations, I found this to be more or less the case. This stage of the disease, severe affection of the lungs and heart, is more frequent in severe cold weather, and more acute, and fully as fatal as in warm weather, a fact easily explained in the habits of swine crowding together and lying on top of each other when the temperature is very low. Whenever investigations have been made, the examiners have found the symptoms and post-mortem appearances of the disease the same, and hence agree as to the propriety of designating the affliction under the head of a general disorder. But during cold weather it does not seem to spread so readily from one farm to another as in warm weather, but as to its spreading trom one animal to another in the same herd in which it previously existed, no difference can be obseved.

"Further, whenever the morbid process of swine plague has become sufficiently developed to produce morbid changes, serious enough to manifest their existence by a rapid emaciation, the growth and thrift will be impaired, but the growth and thrift, it seems, remain more or less unimpaired only in such cases. Some years the disease is of a much milder type and less complicated than others, and the symptoms less varied, but otherwise exactly the same.

WHEN THE DEATH RATES INCREASE.

The death rate in a herd of affected swine is increased or decreased respectively by the malignancy of the disease, which, it seems, depends largely on the one hand, upon the rapidity with which the swine plague germs develop and propagate, and on the other hand, upon the size of the herd, the condition of the premises on which they are kept, the number of diseased animals in the herd, and the mode and manner in which the animals are attended to.

"Everything else being equal, the mortality, as a rule, will be the greater, the more rapidly the disease is spreading from one animal to another, and the more abundant the infectious principle. This is easily explained. The larger the herd and the greater the number of animals diseased at the same time, the greater is also the quantity of the excretions containing the swine plague germ; consequently the more abundant the means of infection, and the more rapid the spreading of the disease within the herd. Again, a rapid spreading causes many animals to become affected at the same time and thus increases, not only the sum total of the number of germs discharged with the excretions of the diseased animals, but also the quantity of the infectious principle taken up by each individual pig. As a consequence the single attacks become the more malignant, and the more malignant the single cases, the more rapid will be the dissemination of the infectious principle and the spreading of the disease."

INTESTINE AND LUNG WORMS.

"In my post-mortem examinations I frequently found worms in the stomach and intestines, also in the bronchial tubes and lungs. But these worms do not constitute the cause of swine plague, and their presence is merely an accidental complication, well calculated, though, to increase the malignancy of the morbid process, because their presence necessarily weakens the constitution of the animal, and thus facilitates the operations of the germs. On the other hand, worms always thrive better in a diseased or declining organism than in a healthy animal. The same of course cannot be said of worms found in the bronchial tubes, because in every case of swine plague the lungs are more or less diseased, and it is difficult to determine how much or how little the presence of those worms may have contributed in bringing about the morbid changes. In parts of the lungs but little affected by the morbid process of swine-plague, but affected with lung worms, the mucus membrane of the bronchial tubes presented a little swelling, or what may be called a catarrhal condition."

OPPONENTS OF THE GERM THEORY.

The Doctor, in support of his theory, says:

"The opponents of the so called germ theory of disease, well knowing that a complete separation of the germs from the animal tissues and fluids is impossible, demand absolute proof, without offering any evidence whatever in support of their own 'theories' or even demonstrating the existence of anything akin to what they claim constitutes the cause and infectious principle of infectious diseases."

As further proof that the swine plague germ and nothing else constitutes the infectious principle of swine plague, he offers the following: First, if one inoculates a well hog with the virus of a hog that has the swine plague, it will contract the disease, and this virus can be retained for quite a while, and favorably cultivated in urine or other liquids and if healthy hogs are inoculated with it, it proves fatal. Other animals, especially the rabbit, and rats or mice, can be successfully inoculated and die of swine plague. Once affected they may carry the disease long distances. Second, if portions of a hog which has died of swine plague are fed to a healthy hog, it proves fatal, and healthy hogs will contract the disease if put in a pen with sick ones, or where sick hogs have been kept. This proves that it is infectious and contagious. Open sores, wounds or scratches attract and absorb the infectious principle, if floating in the air; hence a hog in this condition is more liable to contract the disease than one that has no eruption of the skin. Third, in warm weather, and especially if wet, the disease spreads from farm to farm much faster than in cold weather. Fourth, hogs kept separate and in the open air, will not contract disease as quick as hogs will that are kept in large droves and allowed to sleep about old straw stacks, etc., because nothing is more apt to absorb the contagious or infectious principle, and to preserve it longer or more effectively than old straw, hay, or manure heaps, composed mostly of hay or straw; for the contagion that is absorbed by or clings to such material will remain effective and be a source of spreading the disease for a long time.

Following this, the author will give some extracts from Prof. James Law's report, as to how the swine plague germ may be stored up and transported from one place to another. This will be followed by an account of such treatment as recommended by Drs. Law and Detmers, as preventive of the disease, and some remarks will then be given as to theoretical and practical ideas, and then the author's practical treatment.

Danger of storing up the virus and increasing its potency:—The learned Doctor says: "It is evident that we must guard more sedulously than ever against the possible storing up of the virus of swine plague in confined spaces where it has little access to air, and above all when there is superadded organic matter and moisture which may serve to maintain the vitality and assist in the propagation of the poison.

We cannot too severely condemn the current practice of allowing pigs to crowd together by scores and hundreds in the debris of rotten straw stacks and dung heaps, where they lie like sardines in a box, and even piled one above the other, closely enveloped in the masses of decomposing dung or litter, which not only shuts out the pure and wholesome air, but generates an abundance of noxious gases to take its place and weaken the system.

This doubtless contributes much toward laying the system open to the attack of whatever germ is imported into the herd. It probably does not generate the germ, otherwise the plague would be even more prevalent than it is. Yet the resulting condition of the blood of the pig, the lack of oxygen, and the growth of the virus in this state of the fluid, in harmony with the principle we have been considering, must enhance its virulence and increase the mortality. But it is the intensifying of the poison which has passed out of the body which is especially to be feared. In deposits from the breath, skin exhalations, urine, or dung of the pigs, the germ must find in the damp and more firmly packed lower layers of such refuse, and in the damp, close soil beneath, saturated with decomposing organic matter, the best field for its preservation and for the conservation or increase of its virulence. If the pressure of liquid charged with organic matter could be done away with, the virus would lack for food and would be more readily destroyed. If the air could be freely admitted to all parts of the mass and soil, the virus would soon perish or be transformed into a harmless material. But as it is, this warm bed of the herd supplies the conditions which we have found to be essential to the preservation of the plague germs and to the increase of its potency. In connection with this question it should be considered that among our domestic quadrupeds, the pig requires the very largest amount of oxygen in proportion to its body-weight.

CROWDING IN CONFINED SPACES UNDER BARNS.

It is very dangerous when hogs crowd together in large numbers, in a confined place under barns occupied by other animals. Here the solid and liquid excretions of the stock above pass, to a certain extent, through the floor, and thus mixing with the excretions and exhalations of the pigs, accumulate in the confined area, saturate the ground, and produce constant emanations that deteriorate the air and undermine the health of the animals that crowd together in the close and stagnated atmosphere. Such sleeping places may, therefore, be set down with manure heaps and rotten straw stacks as propagators, though they may not be germinators of the plague. In the present state of the swine industry in the western states, the swine plague is so wide-spread that the chances are always favorable to the extension of the contagion, and no herd, however well cared for, can be looked upon as safe; yet the danger may be greatly enhanced by such management as to surely contribute to the multiplication and potency of the germ.

DRAINS AND LIQUID MANURE PITS.

So called improvements are often fraught with unseen danger. Sewers serve to spread typhoid fever, diphtheria and cholera; warm, air-tight barns propagate consumption and glanders; and closed, covered drains, cesspools, liquid manure tanks, or unventilated spaces beneath the floor of a pig pen, are liable to spread hog cholera. If these are indulged in, they should be properly ventilated by inlets for fresh air, and the latter should on no account be opened into a close pig-pen to befoul its atmosphere. Emanations from such close, confined drains and pits are always unsanitary and injurious to animals requiring such abundance of pure air as do swine, but they must become pre-eminently plague-pits and passages when once the hog cholera germ has been introduced in them. Mr. Law continues in quite lengthy details as to where and how the hog cholera germ may be propagated, and sooner or later escape to assume its malignant form. His suggestions are good and cannot be too carefully read and studied by any one, and especially those who have heretofore had no knowledge of the hog Cholera germ, or the opponents of the so called "germ theory" of diseases.

Danger from railroad cars and vessels.—"It must be apparent that many of the objections to wooden piggeries apply no less to railroad cars. The joints and crevices, the accumulation of filth, and the absence of all systematic disinfections, the constant use of the cars for successive loads of swine, and the impossibility of obtaining perfect drying and airing in the intervals between trips, all combine to make these vehicles the bearers and disseminators of contagion. The absence of air in the masses of accumulated manure, and in the interstices of the wooden floor or wall will even go far towards adding a new force and malignancy to the poison that may be introduced. In boats there is the additional danger of the close atmosphere between decks and the bilge-water in the hold, attaining increased virulence and malignity and spreading a more inveterate type of the malady than that from which it was derived."

Why summer is the most dangerous season.—"Various considerations will show the especial danger of summer. In winter the germs cannot multiply, being laid up in litter or congenial soil, not dead, but inactive, like the dried and stored seed, ready to start a new growth and increase when subjected to the warmth and moisture of spring and summer. Thus it is that the disease often disappears during the winter months, but breaks out anew on the return of genial weather. In summer the germ in the soil, building, or other places, is free to grow and multiply, and buried more or less deeply, it is constantly liable to be set free by the rooting of the hog. The germs thus rooted up from a depth in the soil are likely to be far more dangerous than those that may have been left on the surface, having met with little air to produce a salutary modification. In summer, too, the hog exposed to the scorching rays of the sun is rendered feverish and more susceptible to the action of disease poisons. The air that he breathes is much more rarefied, contains far less oxygen in a given volume, and thus the purification of the blood is likely to be less perfect than in colder weather, and cause the blood to be more conducive to the production of a malignant germ. If the hogs are fed, as is too often the case, even in the extreme heat of summer, almost exclusively on Indian corn of the proceeding year's crop, this adds its quota of costiveness, intestinal irritation and fever, to favor the disease in its worst type. Finally, it need not be overlooked that summer is the season of the greatest number of hogs, and especially of young hogs that have never had the plague, and are therefore especially susceptible to its ravages."

VALUE OF LOOSE, DRY EARTH AS A DISINFECTANT.

"This appears to depend largely on its antiseptic and deodorizing properties. Finely powdered dry loam or clay are direct antiseptics, and have the power of absorbing the noxious gases produced by organic decomposition and the growth of facteria. There are besides porous in an eminent degree, and transmit through their substance a large amount of atmospheric air which produces the less obnoxious fermentation. Hence in earth closets the disagreeable odor may be entirely suppressed. In the case of anthrax carcasses the virulence may in time disappear, and in hog cholera the same good results be attained. But it must be observed that it is the dry, pulverulent, porous earth alone that will act in this way. Moisten it and pack it firmly, and its good qualities may be at once exchanged for evil ones, and it may become a dangerous propagator in the place of a destroyer of infection. Dry earth is not a potent and speedy disinfectant, like chloride of zinc, or lime, but will act slowly in this way if dry, open and porous. It may be used in certain cases as an auxiliary to other disinfectants, and its action is mainly valuable as showing how the porous dry soils are slowly but permanently destructive to such poisons as those of anthrax, chicken cholera, and swine plague."

Preventives that will prove beneficial: In treating diseased swine that are ailing with the genuine hog cholera, swine plague, Drs. Law and Detmers say: "First, remove the hogs from all infected places and the sick from the well ones; then use as disinfectants in the operating yards or pens, chloride of lime, chloride of zinc, sulphate of iron or carbolic acid, the latter being considered the best and safest, and guard the well hogs with every conceivable precaution against the introduction of the diseased germs through accidental channels, as by other animals or fowls carrying the diseased flesh of those that have died, or otherwise, as spoken in this work. Second, the system can be habituated to the poison and fortified against it, by a succession of small doses of medicines, for if a germ is once introduced, though of mitigated fever, it may increase so as to develop to an altogether unexpected degree. Third, pains should be taken to supply pure air, and surroundings to avoid extremes of heat and cold, to give gently-laxative and easily-digested food, and to correct any unhealthy condition of the functions, above all of the digestion. Finally, when all have recovered, disinfections of the premises should be conducted in a very thorough manner."

In reading the extensive writings of the learned doctors, the author has learned that they do not claim that once the swine plague has assumed a malignant form, that, by the use of carbolic acid, as a disinfectant, the disease can be checked or cured, but if used in time and with good sanitary measures it is very beneficial, either as a cure or preventive.

THEORETICAL AND PRACTICAL IDEAS.

The Western Rural says:

"People deal largely in theory. We have tons of theory upon almost everything. This is the result partly of the necessity upon the part of some to say something, whether there is any sense in it or not. Men are often paid for talking and writing, and the machine must run. If they are inspired with a specially warm desire to appear to earn their money, they will often incubate and hatch a theory which nobody else ever thought of, and which, perhaps, it would have been well if nobody ever had thought of. They may keep on harping upon such a theory until practical men adopt it, only to find that it is good for nothing and wholly false. These theorists have nothing to lose by such failures. They make their profits from theories, but the practical operator must make his from successful work. It is, therefore, highly desirable to move cautiously in the adoption of the theories of the professional teachers. We often waste time in reading a smoothly worded address by some professional theorist, who would command much more attention from an ordinary audience than many a practical man would, who knows more in ten minutes than the professional ever knew in his whole life. It is plain facts that the world stands in need of—facts that are demonstrated to be such beyond the possibility of doubt; demonstrated by every day experience, and by the experience of years.

In agricultural and stock papers, and others, too, and even in some veterinary books, there are always to be observed two classes of writers, the theoretical and practical. Both write, however, as if they were telling just what they knew to be true. But it is not difficult to determine which is the theoretical and which is the practical. The practical writer comes right to the point. It is to be observed that in every line he is telling his experience. Sometimes what he says is not in the smoothest language, but it is worth its weight in gold. Frequently the writer expresses fear that he will not be understood, and expresses regret that he has ever attempted to write at all. Such a man can never fully realize how his effort is appreciated by the public. There is never any trouble in discerning what such a writer means. It is the theoretical writer who bothers the reader, for there is nothing to go by frequently, except what the writer says, and if that happens to be ambiguous, the dilemma is a serious one."

The public delights to have solid experience, and that is what the author of this work has kept in mind all the time, and shall throughout the entire work. He will insert nothing but what he knows by actual experience or observations, to have been thoroughly tested and practically demonstrated to be of value.

C. B. Burleigh, in the "Home," says.

"Whoever adds to the general fund of human knowledge, or explodes an incorrect theory, is a public benefactor. Science numbers its martyrs by thousands, and the world is better and wiser for the lives of men who, with heroic devotion, have sacrificed themselves in establishing eternal truths. Experiment, though unsuccessful, is never worthless. The discipline and example of earnest effort are always beneficial; and it has often happened in human history that, in following out some steadfast purpose, incidental discoveries have been made of infinitely more value than those originally sought. In fact a large proportion of scientific discoveries are accidental, rather than the result of direct experiment."

And this again is what the author has kept in view through his work—to exclude all theories, or avoid giving such as will be of no value to the readers of this work, and endeavored to give only such as would prove beneficial to its many readers, and educate the masses instead of the few.

CHAPTER XII.

Treatise on Diseased Hogs.

INTRODUCTION.—HOG CHOLERA, SWINE FEVER, TYPHOID PNEUMONIA AND THEIR SYMPTOMS.—DIRECTIONS FOR GENERAL TREATMENT.—WHEN MEDICINES FAIL.—HOW TO MIX THE MEDICINE FOR SWINE, POULTRY, AND OTHER USES.—INCURABLE CASES.

The following treatise on diseased hogs and poultry is based upon practical knowledge and scientific principles, from work, careful study, experience and practice in the field by the author from 1878 to 1885. The marked progress made by me during the past four years in the practise of treating diseased swine, and the demand for more imformation upon this subject from my numerous patrons renders a new volume upon these subjects indispensably necessary. Not that the principles of my medical practice have been materially changed, but greatly improved upon and simplified. Having made some new and valuable discoveries, both in medical compounds and modes of treating the different diseases of swine, I will in this edition give the added experience of those years of constant labor and observation in my only and chosen profession; and in presenting my works to the public, I feel confident that if the rules herein given are carefully carried out, that any diseased lot of hogs can be saved, and the disease entirely eradicated or prevented on any farm or in any neighborhood, and hundreds of farmers and feeders that have tried it testify to the same.

This treatise is the work of years of practice in the field, and is the only work of the kind ever published that tells you what and how much to use, when and how to use it, so that you can use it, and that will do the work. The location of the internal organs are nearly the same in a hog as in a man, and as far as practicable the treatment is about the same.

I do not cure every disease known to swine with one mixture of drugs, but explain in a plain way and in plain English and German, the symptoms of the different diseases. The name of the drugs and the amount of each is given in the same way, so any person of common capacity can understand and use it. Although I do not use the common drugs which are used in most proprietary medicines, or by farmers who have recipes of their own; such as copperas, sulpher, red pepper, venetian red, resin, saltpetre, calomel, or arsenic, and these, or a part of them mixed in oil meal, shorts or coal oil; yet the drugs which I do use are common, cheap, and as easily handled as those named. My mode of administering medicine to swine—in fact, the only successful way, is to mix it in their drink or wet feed. Being less manageable than any other stock they obstinately resist all attempts at coercion, and drenching is rarely practicable, and caution and great care should be observed by the inexperienced in administering medicine in that way. If hogs are too far gone to eat or drink, the chances of recovery are against them, but by careful treatment even in this stage of the disease, very often they can be saved. In my treatment, as to the management and the administering of the medicine, I shall endeavor to make it so plain and practical that any person can read and readily understand it, and by its practice make the treating of diseased swine a success.

This treatise has been thoroughly tested by many of the best breeders and feeders of Ohio and other States, not only as a cure and preventive for the many local diseases, but as a cure and preventive for the swine plague in its most malignant and contagious form. It bears these unqualified endorsements. The testimonials used by me in any way are all bona fide, and from persons of good standing in their respective communites or professions.

And now, during my extensive practice in treating diseased swine, which has brought me in pleasant intercourse with many of the most prominent breeders and extensive feeders, and in sincere appreciation of their many courtesies and favors, especially in tendering their names and influence in commendation and endorsement of my system of treatment, or in testimony of services in treating their sick hogs, I would, to them, courteously inscribe this volume.

HOG CHOLERA—SWINE FEVER.

I will first mention the three most fatal diseases known to swine, and their symptoms, and known all over the country as hog cholera—swine fever. With cholera, the symptoms are vomiting and purging, and often attacked by severe cramps, as with colic. Those thus attacked generally refuse to eat, but frequently the appetite remains good until death, which occurs within a shorter period of time than with any other disease. With typhoid fever the symptoms are lameness, sluggishness or unthriftiness, with disposition to keep the nest, being cold and chilly, or with a high fever and excessive thirst and loss of appetite, scanty, high colored urine, constipation, and frequently diarrhea, swollen ears, and a rapid emaciation. With typhoid pneumonia these symptoms are accompanied by coughing. When hogs are afflicted with any of the above named diseases their treatment is about the same, which I will now describe:

First, I will give the directions for handling and treating hogs in large droves, which can be adapted to any number; either where the trouble is only local, or where they have contracted a malignant type of disease, the directions should be carefully read and followed as closely as possible, to be successful.

Directions for general treatment: As soon as it is observed that hogs are not doing well, they must be attended to at once; to delay a day or so with them, the same as with other sick stock, may prove too late. First, observe closely the condition of the hogs, whether the symptoms show constipation or diarrhea, in a bad form or not; also, if they are troubled with a cough, and if you can attribute their sickness to any particular local cause. Thus by close observations, very often the cause can be removed with but little expense or labor. As so much has been said before this about what may produce sickness with swine, I will only name here a few things that may be the cause, which may assist the owner or handler of the hogs in discovering the cause and removing it. First, a violent change or an excessive amount of food of any kind; Second, the use of old dry corn albumen alone, or dry grasses; Third, dry grasses alone, especially clover; Fourth, scanty feeding, or the use of stagnant, ice or snow water; Fifth, turning in wheat fields and allowing them to eat too much dry wheat; Sixth, the use of stone coal; Seventh, turning hogs on a luxuriant field of second growth clover, especially in a warm, wet time; Eighth, allowing them to sleep in old rotten or chaffy, loose straw, or manure heaps, where they are liable to get too warm, or compelling them to sleep out in cold weather, thus chilling the blood by getting too cold. Any of these causes will produce sickness, either in a mild or malignant type. Very often when the trouble is discovered while yet in its mild form, it is easily removed by prompt treatment and change of food. When the hogs are in a constipated and fevered condition, it can be removed by the use of laxative food and the medicine as described in this treatment for general use. This given in sloppy or wet bran, ground oats or barley, will soon remove all constipated or fevered condition of the animal. This treatment can be assisted to act quicker by feeding some green corn, pumkins, roots, or turning them on fresh grass. In case the disease has taken the other form, and diarrhea is the trouble, it can be checked by the use of the same medicine, but it acts better by using shorts or rich midlings, with which to make the swill or feeding dry, and confining the hogs in a dry lot or field for a day or so. This same treatment, also, never fails to remove all trouble arising from worms or any ordinary cough.

WHEN MEDICINES FAIL.

When sanitary means are neglected, any medical treatment will fail. When hogs are allowed to pile up in straw or bed in manure, either in or out of the stable, it is not worth while to give them any medicine; and disenfectants are of no avail. That cause must be removed. And the same is the case where the hogs have no shelter in the winter time, and their beds have become foul, damp and packed; they must either be renovated or the hogs removed. In the first place—when hogs are observed to be sick, it is best to remove them to another place immediately, so as to get them away from their old beds, etc. When this cannot be done, remove the old bedding by pulling it away or spreading it out, and give them new bedding if necessary, and do not allow them to pile up in loose straw or manure. They get too warm or contract cold, thus increasing the disease. This, of course, is all the more necessary when the hogs are afflicted with a malignant form of the disease.

Select the sick and ailing from the well ones: This is something that must be strictly observed. Separate all the sick or ailing hogs from the well ones, and put them where they can be cared for. Better take out some that show no signs of disease than to leave in one that does, for it will surely inoculate others. Put the sick in a dry and comfortable lot where they cannot get water. By this means they will become thirsty and can be induced to drink what is given. See that they have sufficient shelter to protect them from the cold storms of winter. A change from warm weather to cold is very bad on them, especially if wet, and in the summer they should have shade, so that they can get out of the hot sun; if not they will lie in it so long as to perish. In a very hot and dry time they will have to be looked after often on this account. A lot where they can exercise is better than a close pen. An orchard, wood or grass lot is often the most convenient and best place to lot them, except in cold or bad weather, when it may be necessary to put them in pens, so as to give them the necessary attention. This is something to which I wish to call the atteniion of all who use my treatment. Never undertake to treat sick hogs in a close pen, especially in warm weather.

GIVE THEM EXERCISE AND AIR.

In order to have hogs do well they must have exercise and air, and if the lots are too small, they will lie down too much, and should be turned out in a field so they can run around or be driven about some every day, for the following reasons: First, it not only has a tendency to cause the contents of the bowels and the urine to move off more freely, which is very essential with those in a constipated or fevered condition, but better distributes their passages so they do not come in contact with them. It is the poison that passes off through the bowels and the urin, that is to be most feared and avoided; not only with swine, but with the human family, when afflicted with a malignant type of disease; such as cholera, typhoid or yellow fever, etc. These poisonous discharges distributed in small quantities over the ground and exposed to the air soon lose their poisonous qualities, but if allowed to accumulate in any way, and especially when they are mixed with the bedding or dry litter, such as old straw or straw manure, they will retain their vigor for some time. Second, the excercise gives them a chance to graze, or increase their appetite, and they are more liable to eat and drink what is given them. Third, they have a chance to root and bed in the fresh earth, and that and the fresh air has a tendency to help remove the fever. But if confined in a close pen, especially in warm weather, where the fresh air cannot have free circulation, and they are compelled to breathe the hot, poisonous air, and come in constant contact with their poisonous discharges, the chances are that they will die.

It should be mentioned that all diseased hogs which have rings in their noses should have them cut out at once, as the nose is liable to become very sore, and the rings interfere with their eating or rooting. But in taking out these rings, care should be taken not to injure them much, as it may kill them. In taking them out use a pair of sharp pincers. When the hogs are confined in pens, the pens should be thoroughly cleaned every day and sprinkled with water mixed with carbolic acid as a disinfectant, using two tablespoon fulls to one gallon of water; or use lime, or lime and charcoal together, for the same purpose.

GRADE THE SICK.

Sick hogs should be graded into two or more lots; that is, put the smaller or weaker ones by themselves, so they can drink. When this is not done the larger or stronger ones will push them away from the feed. This should be attended to at the start, for if they miss a feed or two, it often happens that they cannot be induced to drink after that. Success depends a great deal on how carefully they are sorted or fed. They must have attention, and especially when there are many hogs the disease assumes a malignant form. Those which show no signs of sickness, or still eat and drink well, can be put in lots or fields to themselves and treated as directed. Yet, all must be treated, for when once the disease has started in a herd of hogs, it will continue to spread unless something is done to check it. When there are other hogs on the same farm or one adjoining, and they are not looked after and properly cared for, they are liable to contract the disease. But, if good sanitary means are used, in connection with the Tonic Powder that I herein prescribe, the disease can be controlled and confined to a few hogs, or a small scope of country. In caring for sick and well hogs, the well ones should be cared for first, and never go direct from the sick ones to the well ones, especially in warm, wet weather, as some of the excretions of the sick may in that way be carried to the well, and thus cause them to become diseased.

THE NEXT THING TO BE DONE.

After the hogs are properly sorted and put in their respective lots or pens, it is best to let them go twenty-four hours or more without food or drink, unless the weather is very warm. They may then be given some water with soda, copperas, lime or carbolic acid in it as hereafter directed. By confining the hogs thus they become hungry and thirsty, and can be compelled to take the medicine more readily, and it will act quicker and better on an empty stomach than a full one. Meantime see that there are plenty of troughs in which to give them feed or drink. These should not be too large, so as to interfere with their drinking. Have plenty of them and keep them clean. For this reason there is nothing better to use than six inch fencing boards, edged together with end pieces. These can be of any length desired, and will be light to lift about from one pen to another, or can be taken back and forth from any part of the farm by a team, in order to treat two or more lots of hogs.

THE BEST WAY TO PREPARE THE FEED.

When there are very many hogs to be fed, it is best to prepare a barrel of swill at a time, as it will take a barrel or more to feed them, when they are in large droves, and if it is not all used at once it will not spoil until the next feed, or for a day or two, even in warm weather. When it is prepared in this way, it can be made of one strength better than if mixed in small quantities, and by different persons each feed, as often occurs. A barrel of swill will feed from seventy to one hundred and twenty hogs, depending upon their size, and the fatality of disease, etc. Hogs which are very costive will require more swill than those which are not, and large hogs more than small ones. This will have to be governed by the feeder. After the medicine has begun to take effect, no more should be given than enough to keep the bowels in a normal state.

TO MAKE A BARREL OF SWILL.

For forty or forty-five gallons of swill take two bushels of bran, mill feed, ground oats or barley; put it in the barrel, then add the drugs, as given in the first four numbers of the recipe. (See recipe.)

Take five pints of No. 1, two or more pints of No. 2, from one-third to half pint of No. 3, four tablespoons of No. 4, then fill the barrel with milk, slops, or water, and add no more liquid until the whole is used up. Stir the swill well while feeding, and feed only what the hogs will drink up clean, twice a day; in most cases, especially in warm weather, they should be fed three times a day. Do not keep it by them. Give them only what they will drink up clean. Three gallons is enough for five or more hogs, according to size. In order to get the hogs to drink the swill, it is sometimes necessary to sprinkle bran, oats, or meat cracklings in the troughs, all of which are good and beneficial. Be sure that the hogs are all up around the troughs when fed, so that they all drink. Success depends a great deal on this; when they will not drink they must be drenched. (See directions.)

Diseased hogs should be kept under treatment from five days to two weeks, according to fatality of disease. Sometimes they recover very quick if properly cared for, and then again slow, the same as with any sick animal; and for this reason it is best not to despair and quit because they do not get well in a day or two. As they begin to improve, any kind of light food is good to feed them. It is very easy to tell when they begin to improve, as the urine will come more abundant and clear, and their discharges soft and regular. In using this medicine for sick hogs, allow no water or corn for four or five days, and but little corn for a few days after a cure is effected. This, again, is something that must be strictly observed; do not feed sick hogs corn while under treatment, especially old corn. It seems natural for all feeders to want to feed corn if the hogs will eat it, and with this one thing I have more to contend than anything else. New corn is not so bad, because it is not so heating or hard to digest. Sometimes I put shelled corn in the swill barrel and let it soak. This is good after the hogs have begun to show some improvement, and is very good to entice them to eat.

TREATISE ON DISEASED HOGS. 185

AS A PREVENTIVE, TO BE FED AFTER THE SICK ONES HAVE BEEN TAKEN OUT.

In feeding large herds, where it is not convenient to feed the swill, use this same medicine, Nos. 1, 2, 3 and 4, (and the amount of each as given in the recipe;) mix, use one pint of this mixture in one half bushel of wet bran, which is enough for twenty or thirty head, and feed twice a day for three days. This will act upon the entire system and check the disease. It will be found the most reliable and cheapest remedy that can be used as a preventive, where they have been exposed to the disease, and the swill cannot be given. But it is better to give the swill as directed, to all the hogs, than to do any other way, as they get the medicine better. In the use of corn (at all times when feeding the medicine) feed light for a few days where the hogs have been exposed to disease.

TREATMENT FOR GENERAL USE.

This treatment is intended for all the ordinary diseases known to hogs, either as a preventive or cure, and can be relied upon, as it is a powerful blood purifier, and also acts as a diarrhetic. It prevents inflammation or ulceration of the intestines, breaks the fever, regulates the bowels and destroys all intestine worms, thus relieving or curing the patient.

Special Notice: The first four ingredients of the recipe as it is filled out are just right for a barrel of swill of forty gallons, for ordinary diseased hogs for general use, or as a preventive, when hogs have been exposed to disease. But it is necessary sometimes to make a change in it to suit more mild or more severe cases, as follows: If for pigs, use one pint less of No. 1. But for large hogs which are very costive or badly diseased, add one pint extra of No. 1 and also add No. 5, as given in the recipe. This will increase the strength and it will act quicker and better. But in two or three days it can be reduced again as above. That is, use only five pints of No. 1. If they are coughing, keep on using No. 5. If not, omit its use.

For a Cough: If hogs are coughing and the first four numbers as given fail to break it up, then add a heaping table spoon of No. 5 to a barrel, or a level teaspoon to three gallons of swill. A gallon of swill is enough for three or more hogs, according to size.

FOR PIGS OR VERY SICK HOGS.

Sometimes very sick hogs or pigs refuse to drink the swill made as described. If they do put them and those which have the diarrhea by themselves, and use Nos. 2, 4, 7 and 8, as given in the recipe, to forty gallons of swill. (See recipe).

Take two or more pints of No. 2, four tablespoons of No. 4, five pints of No. 7, and four tablespoons of No. 8. To this can be added two pounds of powdered charcoal with good results. Especially in all cases of diarrhea, as it is an absorbent, and in cases of dysentery it is soothing and improves the consistence of the stools; it is good in the case of gasses on the stomach, as it abates the pain and sickness. It also is a disinfectant, appetizer, and aids digestion.

With sick hogs, use plenty of No. 2. I often use one gallon to forty gallons of swill.

In using the above avoid the use of corn meal in the swill; use bran, shorts or midlings, two bushels to a barrel, and after the hogs begin to improve, use the first four or five numbers as given. This I prefer to the other, if the hogs will drink it, as it is a powerful blood purifier, and controls the bowels and urinary organs better.

Hogs or pigs which have the diarrhea can be treated very successfully in this way: Take sweet milk, let it come to boiling heat; in two gallons of this milk put one half pint of soda; to this add three gallons of swill, made of the four or five numbers of the recipe. This is the best treatment for typhoid pneumonia or fever, or ailing pigs with scours (cholera infantum,) that can be given. If they are still sucking the sow, give the swill to her also. But the prepared milk is not necessary for her, unless the pigs are very young; otherwise the swill can be given full strength. If the sow is not showing any signs of disease one feed a day for two or three days will do for her. But the pigs or very sick hogs that this milk preparation is made for, should have it twice or three times a day for a few days as the case may require.

If swine which are being fed on warm feed, get sick, the swill that is given them should be fed cold, and the same way in the summer. In winter, the swill is best made blood warm.

How to drench a hog: In extreme cases it may be necessary to drench, but it should be avoided if possible, and should be done with great care, as an over-exertion will very often kill the hogs. They should be put in a close place where they can be handled with care, and should not be run or dogged, as it is liable to kill them. Then take a piece of small rope, stand beside or across the hog, put the rope in its mouth, and hold its head well up; give it only what it can swallow with ease, and be careful not to give anything while it is squealing, for the medicine will go into its wind-pipe and kill it.

In drenching, the use of an old soft shoe is very good. Cut a hole in the toe of the shoe, then put the toe in the hog's mouth and pour the mixture in the mouth of the shoe; in this way the hog can keep its mouth shut, so it can swallow, and it is not so liable to squeal.

Drench: For a hog that will weigh one hundred pounds that is constipated, in one half pint of sweet milk put one tablespoonfull of No. 1, one-fouth of a pint of No. 2, one teaspoon of No. 3, and one-half of a teaspoonfull of No. 5, or ten drops of No. 8. Increase Nos. 3 and 8 according to size of hog; give once, and if it still refuses to drink the swill, give the second time, which is as often as I ever found it necessary, until they would drink the swill, as described for sick hogs, or general use, which should be given for a week or more, in order to cleanse their blood and system. In case the hog has diarrhea, omit No. 1, and use a tablespoon of powdered charcoal.

HOW TO GIVE INJECTIONS.

It is necessary at times, in cases of extreme costiveness to use injections in order to save an animal. This is the case with hogs as well as other animals. Very often a hog's life can be saved in this way, and it may not take but a few minutes to complete the operation. It can often be done by one person, but in most cases it requires an assistant. Put the hog in a close place where it can be handled quietly. Then the assistant, by the use of a wide board, can confine the hog to one side of the inclosure. The injection can now be easily given by the use of a syringe. Use soap suds and a small amount of turpentine, (a teaspoonful to one gallon of suds.) Avoid all violence, as any worry may kill the animal. In this way several hogs may be given injections in a very short time, and be the means of saving them, when otherwise they would die.

EXTERNAL APPLICATIONS.

The use of external applications properly applied, are just as necessary in the treatment of swine as they are in the treatment of other domestic animals or the human family, to produce counter-irritations, or by their cooling effects, help to remove pain and fever, and relieve the suffering patient. Those I herein describe are cheap, easy to make and use, and their effects are beneficial. For sick hogs that are feverish, mangy or lousy, take one gallon of coal oil, one gallon of lard, two tablespoonfuls of carbolic acid, mix, make warm and grease the hogs well with it. When there are several hogs, they can be closely confined in a scale-pen or any small inclosure, and the mixture put in a sprinkling can and applied in that way. This will remove all mange, scurf or lice, cleanse and heal sores and assist greatly in removing fever. This preparation should be applied to every lot of diseased hogs when put under treatment, and if necessary repeated. It is good to use on swine when castrating them. I consider it better than tar; it will also remove any scurf or itch, with horses, cattle or sheep, lice on any domestic stock, or scurf on fowls, and is valuable to grease the heads and the throats of fowls with when they are sick, especially with roup. In using this preparation on anything but hogs, it must not be used too heavy—just enough to dampen the affected parts.

In order to remove lice on hogs, fowls or cattle, leave out the carbolic acid; the coal oil and lard will do just as well. With fowls, grease them under the wings and about the head and throat. With cattle, grease them clear around the neck, and along the back to the tail, also in the flanks; this will soon remove all the lice. But in order to keep them off, good attention should be given to their surroundings. Their stables, houses or pens should be thoroughly cleaned and whitewashed. If some carbolic acid is put in the whitewash, it is good as a disinfectant.

Rheumatism liniment: Made by taking turpentine, three ounces; ammonia, three ounces; gum campher, two ounces; chloroform, one ounce; opium, one ounce, arnica oil, one ounce, tincture of cayenne pepper, six ounces; coal oil, one half gallon. Mix and always shake well when using.

When this liniment is wanted, it is best to copy it off and have some druggist put it up, so as to avoid any mistakes, or at least the first seven articles; the coal oil can be added at home. This is an excellent remedy to remove any trouble arising from kidney disease, paralysis, lung or throat trouble, rheumatic or neuralgic pains, either with swine or the human family. Its penetrating powers are wonderful.

Carbolic acid, copperas or soda: These dissolved in water and used to wash or sprinkle hogs with in the summer time, when very warm, are beneficial remedies. One pound of copperas or soda, dissolved in four gallons of water, or two tablespoons of carbolic acid in the same amount of water, is the right strength for a wash. These, when well applied, have a great tendency to remove fever; also the same is true when they are administered internally; when given as a drink, it should not be more than one-third as strong, as when used as a wash.

As a fattening agency, or a tonic powder, as a preventive against disease, to be used at all times to keep the hogs in good health, and make them thrive fast, take No. 1, eight pounds or pints; No. 7, eight pounds or pints; No. 4, one pound; powdered charcoal, one pound. Mix; use one pint of this mixture in one half bushel of wet bran or ground grain of any kind, except corn meal. This is enough for twenty or thirty hogs at a time, and should be given once or twice a week, or as their condition may require it. It is better than salt and hickory ashes, copperas and sulphur, or any other preparation I have ever seen or heard of.

It should always be used when commencing to feed corn at any time, or on a new herd of hogs which are brought on the farm, so as to guard against disease. A small expense at the first indication of disease, or as a preventive, will save hundreds of dollars in the end. This mixture, or the one given for general use, will be found invaluable to use with hogs at all times, especially when they are running on a dry or stubble pasture, or black, mucky ground, and also when on a heavy growth of matured clover, or when being fed on dry corn, either of which is liable to cause constipation or sickness. They should receive it regularly once or twice a week. In feeding large herds the mixture can be made in a box and then put in barrels and taken out in the field with a team, the hogs all called up and then fed on the ground. In feeding it in this way it should be put out quickly, so they all get it. I have fed some three hundred hogs at a time in this way with good success.

This tonic powder will keep them in a high state of health and make them thrive very fast, especially where they are being highly fed, or running on mast the latter part of winter or in the spring; mast is then very dangerous, especially jack oak (red oak) acorns. But where hogs have been exposed to disease, or are diseased, mix the first four numbers as directed, adding the fifth if coughing, and use in swill at all times if possible.

TREATMENT OF SOWS WITH PIG.

For diseased sows that are with pig use the first four numbers of the recipe as given; mix, use one half-pint of this mixture and No. 6 as given in the recipe, to four gallons of sweet milk or any good slops. This will prevent abortion, and is good to give to sows a few days before and after farrowing; it will keep them from eating their pigs. This mixture is a powerful anti-spasmodic, and will prevent convulsions of various kinds, spasms of the stomach, bowels, etc. It is also cooling and waylays fever and prevents constipation, which causes sows to eat their young; and when a habit is once learned it is hard to break them off. In fact the only sure cure for an old habitual pig or chicken eater is the butchers' block.

Diseased sows which are with pig will have to receive good attention, and in time to prevent them from losing their pigs, for when once they are badly diseased, they are almost sure to lose them, and often do so when under treatment. This has lead some to believe that it was caused by the medicine, but such is not the case. The medicine mixed as directed will not do any harm, unless an overdose is given, when it may make them quite sick for a few hours, but they will soon recover. Sows that are half gone or more with pig should be kept away from other hogs. They are very often injured by being overlayed, or otherwise, and in that way lose their pigs.

HOG HABITS OF SLEEPING, OR OBJECTIONS TO PENS.

Where hogs are confined in close, small quarters, it is important that some absorbent be provided. Straw and leaves are both objectionable. Hogs are apt to become overheated at night on account of their crowding propensities. They like to sleep three double. When litter of any kind is provided the danger is greatly increased. Straw is one of the poorest conductors of animal heat that is known of, and as a consequence its use for littering is highly objectionable. Leaves or corn fodder are either one better than straw when litter of any kind is used, as it does not become so foul and warm. Dr. Law says: "Dry earth is a better absorbent than anything else, and conveys away animal heat, although not so rapidly as to chill the animal." This is one reason why I recommend out door treatment for sick hogs at all times, when the weather will permit it. The dry or fresh earth has a great tendency to reduce the fever. Then again, they can be kept cleaner and separate, and do not come in contact so much with one another or with their poisonous discharges; and they also have the benefit of the fresh air, or in cool weather, the warm sun.

A prominent writer says: "Especial care should be taken to secure for swine a good supply of fresh air, especially in the fall, when the atmosphere is unusually liable to foulness. Swine sleep just as close together as they can get, and will breath second-hand, and for all I know, forty-second-hand air, without reference to decayed teeth or foul stomach. It is needless for me to tell you that this is liable to produce disease unless fresh air be supplied liberally, and just as useless for any one to try to convince the swine that it is highly improper for them to do so. The only remedy is to supply plenty of fresh air.

Directions as to medicines repeated: 'The directions for treating hogs when in large numbers, and for mixing the medicine, have been extended by the author probably more than necessary; in order to make it more plain and to give the reasons why such treatment is used, it is necessary to again give the directions for mixing the drugs which constitute the different medicines, used in the various treatments of swine, and also poultry, before taking up the description of local diseases.

In order to make the medicine for any use as herein directed, taking the amount of each drug as given in the recipe and putting them together as given in the treatment Nos. 1, 2, 3 and 4, make the mixture for general use. If necessary, add the fifth, in order to increase the strength. If to this mixture is added one pound of powdered charcoal, it makes the medicine I can and sell. For all severe cases of sickness with swine or poultry, this is the most valuable to use. For pigs or for hogs which have the diarrhea, take Nos. 2, 4, 7 and 8; to this add two pounds of charcoal. Either one of these mixtures will make 40 or 45 gallons of swill. For sows that are heavy with pig, use the mixture made of the first four numbers, as for general use; to one-half pint of this mixture add No. 6, as given in the recipe. This will make four gallons of swill strong enough for use. For the tonic powder, use Nos. 1 and 7, equal parts, No. 4 and charcoal equal weight; mix and use one pint of this mixture in one-half bushel of wet bran or groud grain of any kind (except corn meal), to twenty or thirty hogs once or twice a week, as their condition may require.

MEDICINE FOR POULTRY.

For poultry, as a cure for cholera, roup or gapes, in one gallon of soft food of any kind, bread, meat scraps, bran and milk, etc., (never use corn meal,) use as follows: No. 1, two tablespoonfulls; No. 2, one-half pint; No. 4, one tablespoonfull; No. 8, one tablespoonfull. Mix thoroughly, and feed once a day for two or three days. As a preventive, once every two or three weeks, owing to condition of fowls. For small chicks use less one-half, or omit No. 1.

No. 4, carbolic acid, which is about the right strength for any use as given in this treatment, is made by taking one-fourth crystal carbolic acid, and three-fourths rain water. Always buy pure drugs, and use strictly according to directions.

Never give this medicine to horses, cattle or sheep. It is very strong and more or less poisonous. In keeping some of these drugs around the house, they should be kept secluded from children or other persons not knowing what they are, especially Nos. 5 and 8.

INCURABLE CASES.

In treating swine, as well as any other domestic stock, especially when in large droves, and when the disease has assumed a malignant form and they have been allowed to run for some time without treatment, there are almost always some incurable cases. And anyone claiming a specific "a cure all," for hog cholera or swine fever, cannot be too severely condemned. Such a claim should prove to any one, who stops to think, even for a moment, that such treatment is a humbug. As long as we have no specifics for the cure of the diseases of the human family which we have every means of treating promptly, why should we expect it for so fatal a disease as hog cholera or swine fever. These fatal diseases with swine can be told by the following symptoms, which, even under good sanitary or medical treatment, unless promptly attended to, seldom recover. First, severe constipation, accompanied by high fever, rapid emaciation, lameness, and often bursting and sloughing off of the ears. These are symptoms of typhoid fever. With typhoid pneumonia, these are accompanied by a severe cough, and when once either disease has assumed such a form that chronic diarrhea sets in, and the ears and body become cold to the touch, then the case will prove fatal. This is also the case when blue, purple, or red spots appear under the throat, chest and belly. This shows that inflammation of the lungs or bowls, or both have set in, and the case is most always hopeless. The same may be said of those patients which bleed at the nose and ears, or have bloody passages. This is caused by hemorrhage, by the bursting of the tissue linings of some of the vital organs, bowels or intestines. Frequently the disease assumes a gangrenous form and settles in the limbs, and often one or more slough off, especially the feet. They will live in this way sometimes a long while and frequently recover, but never do any good. They are a loss to their owner and had better be killed. With what may be termed cholera, vomiting, purging and severe cramps, as if attacked with colic, will soon prove fatal if not well treated. When the patients survive a few days, they may be, and frequently are, affected as before described. Any of these fatal diseases are known under the name of hog cholera, swine fever, or swine plague, and in treating them not only must the best of medical means be used, but the best of sanitary means. When this is done, and in time, before the disease has assumed a malignant form, almost if not all the hogs can be saved. In treating any herd, when even afflicted in the most violent form, if well cared for, the largest part of them can be saved, and the disease kept from spreading. Therefore, it is much better to treat them than to let them all die, or to ship them to market to be eaten by our fellowmen.

WHY MY TREATMENT IS A SUCCESS.

Very frequently in talking with farmers and professional men, they will say, "If the 'germ theory' is correct, anything that would be given the hog that would kill the germ, would kill the hog." This is no doubt true to a certain extent. But I do not claim that the medicine I use destroys the life of the germs direct, but what I do claim is that swine afflicted with swine fever, known as hog cholera, or swine plague, can be given medicine that will so affect the system, as to check and prevent the propagation, or multiplication of the germs, and have such an effect upon the bowels and urinary organs as to cause the poisonous effects of the germs to be passed off through these channels; and these poisonious discharges exposed to the air, soon loose their poisonous effects.

Therefore, when treating in the open air, and especially when the hogs are allowed some range so they do not come in such close and constant contact with their passages, the disease can be checked and cured. This is the main secret of my treatment, either as a cure or as a preventive, and why it is a success while so many others are failures.

. The main points in treating any diseased animals are first to know what ails them; then be sure that the medicine that is given them will have the desired effect to assist nature to cast off the disease.

David Crocket said, "Be sure you're right, then go ahead."

The author does not claim that this is the only treatment that will cure diseased hogs of hog cholera, but it is the best that has ever come under his observation, and is the most practical treatment ever published; and if it is the means of saving the swine of a few farmers among the many, it is a work well done.

CHAPTER XIII.

LOCAL DISEASES, AND THEIR TREATMENT. REMARKS.

THE LOCAL DISEASES.—PNEUMONIA.—DIPHTHERIA.—KIDNEY DISEASE.—INFLAMMATION OF THE BRAIN.—CATARRH.—PILES.—WORMS.—SWEATING PIGS.—SCOURS.—FROSTED HOGS.—REMARKS.—MY PROPOSITIONS.—FOR SALE.

THE LOCAL DISEASES.

In describing the local diseases and their treatment, I shall endeavor to make it as short and plain as possible, so that the general farmer can understand and treat them successfully. I hope the readers of this work will not say, "Oh, I have seen that tried before, and it won't work." Give my treatment a fair and impartial trial, and I am satisfied you will be successful. In describing the different forms of diseases, I will name them as known by the farmer or feeder of swine, as well as by the more scientific names.

THUMPS—PALPITATION OF THE HEART.

This is the last stage of lung disease, and is only observed in very sick hogs or pigs, and if cured must be given good attention, and in time. It is often caused by an over-accumulation of fat around the heart and lungs in over-fat pigs, or with weak and deficient bred pigs, caused by breeding too close, or breeding from weak and inferior stock.

Symptoms: Breathing rapidly and laboriously, like an

over-exerted animal. Treatment: Use medicine as for general use; one tablespoonfull twice a day in sweet milk, or any good slops, and give on tongue one-half teaspoonfull of No. 5, once a day; also bathe the chest and sides over heart and lungs with the rheumatism liniment, or coal-oil and turpentine, equal parts; this is very good. Continue treatment until relief is given.

LUNG FEVER—PNEUMONIA.

This is an acute lung disease and is a dangerous and common disorder. It commences with a severe chill and fever, accompanied by a deep, hoarse cough, and locomotion difficulty, seeming to be weak in the back.

It seems to be an affection of the lungs, commonly called lung fever, but it is really caused by the blood being impoverished by the non-removal of the natural acids by the liver and kidneys. Pneumonia is always proof of diseased kidneys and liver. Indeed, this is true of many other lung disorders, also. Pneumonia is a very common and fatal disease, and if cured must be treated with care and in time. Treatment: The same as with thumps; or, for a large lot of hogs use the medicine made of the first five numbers of the recipe, and sprinkle them well with coal-oil, lard and turpentine. Give them soft, laxative food, and good, dry quarters.

STRANGLES, SORE THROAT, QUINSEY, DIPHTHERIA.

This disease can be first observed by the difficult breathing and swallowing. The throat becomes sore and swollen, and in the more advanced stages in a diphtheria form, the animal often sits upon its haunches like a dog in order to breathe, and frequently strangles and dies in that position. Very often this disease becomes epidemic, similar to distemper or epizootic with young horses, and proves fatal. It is in a certain degree contagious; that is, by contact with the shreds coughed up by the diseased ones, well hogs will take the disease as readily as it is communicated by the human family, and owing to this, in its fatal type, is frequently mistaken for cholera—swine fever. It is caused by sudden changes of atmosphere. Allowing hogs to pile up in strawstacks, manure heaps, and other warm places during cold weather, is one of the most fruitful causes of this disease. When they are allowed to pile up in such places, upon coming out, especially on a cold morning, the cold air strikes them, and any one must know that such sudden changes will produce this or some other more fatal disease, and especially with pigs or young hogs.

Treatment: Separate the sick from the well ones, divide them up into small lots, and give them good, dry quarters. With those that are very sick give them twice or three times one-fourth pint of No. 2, one teaspoonful of No. 3; for a pig, one-half this amount, and bathe throat and chest well with rheumatism liniment or turpentine. With those that will still drink, the medicine can be given in sweet milk or any good slop. Those that show no indication of the disease, can be given as a preventive, the medicine for general use, and should not be allowed to run with the diseased ones.

Kidney disease—paralysis of hind quarters: With this disease hogs become weak in the back, the hind parts will wriggle about, and finally the pigs will sit down on their haunches; after some effort they will get up again and run rapidly straight ahead for some distance, then swing to one side awhile and then go to the other side, and finally get down and are unable to rise again, and drag their hind parts about until death occurs, which is almost sure to come unless something is done for them. Treatment: Use the medicine as for drench; it can be given in slops. Repeat the dose two or three times once a day or oftener if necessary, and bathe the back across the kidneys with the rheumatism liniment once a day for three or four days.

Blind staggers—inflammation of the brain. This is very frequent with hogs. Symptoms: At first the animal becomes dull and stupid, the eye red and inflamed, and the bowels constipated. In a short time, if not relieved, the animal runs wildly about, usually in a circle, seems blind and the breathing becomes rapid and laborious. Treatment: Give twice a day in some sweet milk or rich slops, a tablespoon of the first five numbers mixed as given in recipe, and bathe the head between the eyes and ears with rheumatism liniment, turpentine or any strong liniment that will produce a counter irritation.

Founder. Caused by over-feeding and lack of exercise. Symptoms: Loss of appetite, and so lame and stiff they can hardly get around. Treatment: Use swill as for general use for a week or more, and give on tongue a tablespoon of powdered alum. In very severe cases repeat this dose in a day or two, and avoid the use of corn. Feed light and soft food of any kind and turn them out for exercise.

Rheumatism. This is something that swine are as subject to as any other stock. It is often caused by close confinement, and especially on board or stone floors, or when being compelled to sleep in a damp and cold place. Symptoms simaril to founder, being sluggish, with indisposition to move, accompanied by fever, pain and swelling of afflicted part. Frequently the swelling is of a wandering character and changes about from one location to another. Treatment: Use the swill as for general use and bathe afflicted parts with the rheumatism liniment.

Snuffles with pigs. This is caused by catarrh in a chronic form. Caused by repeatedly contracting cold and being neglected, and frequently by improper breeding, the same as pigs with thumps. This is thought by some breeders to be hereditary, and no doubt is, when those badly afflicted are used as breeders. But this can be said of any other badly diseased hog; unless they are perfectly cured they should not be used as breeders. The treatment for this disease is light and soft food at all times while under treatment. Use the medicine as for general use. To this add No. 8, as given in recipe, to a barrel of swill, or a teaspoonful to two gallons, or ten drops to a dose.

Piles with hogs. Piles are a disease which frequently occur with hogs, but are not dangerous, as they seldom, if ever, cause death, but are very painful, and the animal so afflicted will not do well unless cured. Piles are seldom discovered until the knots are visible, but occasionally may be, after the disorder has so advanced that blood passes off with the excrements, or the hair around the anus is blood stained. They are caused by the use of rich and heating food, or sour slops. They occur more with still fed or pen fed hogs than any other kind, and often with hogs that follow cattle. Treatment: Use the swill as for general use; avoid the use of corn, feed light with soft food of any kind, or turn them on grass. An injection of warm salt water or salt and vinegar is very good, but when the gut is much protruded it should be replaced first, before giving the injection. This can be done by oiling it with any kind of oil.

Intestine Worms. These sometimes accumulate to such an extent in hogs as to be injurious to them, and often cause death by strangulation, as well as constipation and unthriftiness. Symptoms: More or less coughing, hair looks rough, appetite good, but hogs do not thrive. Treatment: The same as for general use, which will soon remove all trouble. Cause: Close confinement or dry and musty food, stagnant, snow or ice water, and neglect to give them the needful care, in the way of a change of the proper kind of food or remedy, to overcome the evil effects of the above named causes.

Sweating pigs. This is caused by a lack of vitality, the same cause that produces night sweats in human beings. Divide the pigs up into small lots, and keep them out of their bed during the day. Compel them to exercise and use the medicine as for general use for a few days, which will remove all this trouble.

Scours—Cholera Infantum. Many of our swine breeders sustain considerable loss annually by their pigs dying from this disease, which is caused by the bad quality of the sows' milk. The disease is more apt to make its appearance when the sow has been fed upon dry corn or musty food. It generally attacks them within two or three days after their birth, but sometimes after they are much older. I have never failed to check and cure this disease when I used the following treatments: Use the medicine as for general use; to this add No. 8. Ten drops to a tablespoonful of the above mixture, given to the sow in some sweet milk or good slops, twice a day for two or three days, will give relief. Or the treatment for pigs given on page 194, will be certain to effect a speedy cure.

Blood poison, scrofula or cankerous sore mouth. This is a common occurrence with unthrifty and badly kept pigs, often caused by the use of musty and unwholesome food, or the bad quality of the sows' milk, and very often dirty pens and dirty udders will make young suckling pigs sore about the mouth and head; also, frequently the tusks of young pigs are so prominent as to cause them to bite and lacerate their lips, which become sore, and in either case the inflammation will spread. Treatment: When pigs are not doing well, use the medicine as for general use. When the pigs are still sucking give the medicine to the sows also, and apply externally upon all the parts where any sores appear the following mixture: Coal oil and lard, equal parts; to one-half pint of this add one tablespoon of carbolic acid; this will heal the sores. This is good to use on hogs when being castrated, or on very mangy ones. When either the pigs or pens are dirty, both should be thoroughly cleaned and kept that way. Sometimes pigs have what is called "measles"—pimples all over the body. They usually appear first about the head or flanks, and are caused by the blood being impoverished or poisoned. This, if neglected, will very often turn to scrofula or cankerous sores. But if treated as directed, and when the hogs areconfined, turned out on the fresh ground, they will soon recover.

Mange. This, like most all other diseases of the hog, is infectious or contagious, and is similar to the itch in the human family, or scab in sheep. It is quickly and easily cured by using the swill as for general use for a few days to cleanse the blood, and applying thoroughly this treatment: Take coal oil or black oil, such as is used for machinery, and lard, equal parts; make warm, put it in a sprinkling can, get your hogs in a close place and give them a good sprinkling once every month or six weeks. This is the best treatment that can be given them. It rids them of all mange or dandruff, opens up the pores, and helps to promote health generally. The same mixture is good to use for lice, in fact is the best thing that can be used, and should be applied once a month or every six weeks; this will rid them entirely of the pests. I have used this for the past fifteen years with good results, and have never had any cause to change it. This is one of the first things that should be done with a lot of diseased hogs after you put them under treatment, is of great benefit to them, and should not be neglected. In extreme cases of mange it may be well to give the animal a thorough washing with soap and warm water, then apply the treatment as given. Never use the coal oil alone, especially in hot weather, as it will scald the hog, and cause the hair to come off.

LICE.

Lice are a great pest to hogs as well as other animals, and one they should be kept rid of. There is no doubt they will do better off than on, and the time they are employed in rubbing them off, as some let them do, could be more profitably employed putting on flesh by keeping quiet. Treatment the same as for mange. Some make use of sulphur and wood ashes, coal oil or black oil alone. All are bad and will scald the hair off, and often do harm. The cleaner you keep the hog house or their nests, the cleaner you can keep your hogs of the vermin and the better will be their health and condition.

FROSTED HOGS.

This is something that occurs more or less every winter with all kinds of hogs, and often proves very injurious, especially to fine pigs, which are intended for the breeding or show pen, by disfiguring the ears or tail, and causing the hair to come off in spots, which makes them look very bad. Treatment: To one ounce of saltpetre, dissolved in as little water as possible, add one tablespoonful of spirits of camphor, one of oil of sassafras and one-half pint of coal oil. Bathe frosted parts once a day for a week. (Hogs which are intended for show use should be clipped in April, then the new coat of hair will come on more even.)

The above mixture is invaluable for frosted flesh, either with stock or the human family, and will also remove the soreness from corns or chilblains.

HOW TO PREVENT THIS.

It should be borne in mind that there are but few of our domestic animals that are more keenly sensitive to cold than the hog, and no farmer should endeavor to keep more of them through the winter than he can provide comfortable quarters for. During the winter months they should receive especial attention. If they are permitted to do so, they will seek the fermenting manure heap, on account of the heat which is therein engendered; but this in no case should be allowed, as it is a prolific source of disease. Provide them with a warm place, well ventilated, protected from the winds, and with plenty of dry bedding. It is only in extreme cold weather that hogs freeze or suffer if kept dry. Don't permit a very large number to pile up together in the same bed. Feed bountifully, allow them free access to the sunshine on pleasant days, and they will repay you for your care by a constant increase in flesh. But, on the contrary, if they are allowed to lie in the manure heap, or to shiver with cold on the bare floor, with the thermometer below zero, all the food that is given them is simply wasted. It will pay better to kill them at once, and save feed, than to waste it upon hogs so kept. The main secret of success with hogs in the winter is comprised in three words—food, warmth and ventilation.

BLACK TEETH WITH HOGS.

Very often I am asked the question, do black teeth kill hogs? Or some one will say that a certain person was going through the country pulling out the black teeth of hogs, saying that "they were what caused hog cholera." Now it is all a mistake to suppose that black teeth cause death to hogs. Black teeth never kill hogs any more than botts kill horses, and it has been proven by practical men long ago that such a thing is impossible. Of course hogs may occasionally have a bad tooth that would be better out than in, but not often, especially if it is an upper jaw tooth, for then corn or other food will pass through the cavity caused by pulling the tooth into the nose, and cause more trouble than if it had been let alone. Therefore, I will say that if anyone wants to pull out your hogs' teeth, tell him you will leave them alone to crack corn with.

The same is true of smut poison. If a hog never died until it died of smut poison or black teeth, there would be no use for hog medicine. What are called black teeth is a symptom of disease, and shows a necessity for a treatment of the general system. All pigs have the little black teeth in the middle of their jaws, which worry people so much. These are the teeth in the males which make the tusks, and in the females which keep the rope from slipping off of the jaw when they are caught to be rung. When the pigs are young these teeth are very small, but sometimes so sharp that they lacerate their tongues or cheeks so that they cannot nurse or eat well, and then they "do miserably." When a pig shows these symtoms, these teeth should be broken off smoothly with a pair of pincers. Taking the pig between the knees and putting a small cord with a slipping noose around the upper jaw will cause it to open its mouth, and at the same time it can be held firmly.

A PREVENTIVE IS BETTER THAN A CURE.

The old saying, "An ounce of preventive is better than a pound of cure," is a true one in swine raising. And therefore, by observing and remembering some things which I will now brifly speak of, it may be worth a great deal of money to the many readers of this work:

First, I will again mention how the disease may be carried from one place to another. Second, as to buying or handling diseased hogs. Third, as to their food and care. When the hog cholera—swine fever is in a neighborhood, it can be conveyed from one lot of hogs to another, by having hogs along a stream of water where there has been diseased ones above. This is very dangerous, especially in dry seasons when the water is scarce and stagnant. There is also a good deal of risk in having them in fields adjoining those in which diseased hogs are, or by allowing strange hogs brought on the place for any purpose, as weighing, breeding, etc. But the greatest evils, and those that spread the disease over the greatest scope of country the quickest, are by driving diseased hogs along the public road, or having them exposed where they have died. I have known whole neighborhoods for miles around to be inoculated in this way. Hogs that die of cholera or any other sickness should be burned immediately. This is an easy and the best way to get rid of them, for then you are certain that your own farm or that of your neighbor will not be inoculated by this diseased flesh being carried around by dogs or other animals, or by fowls, or by the stench being carried in the air, which is thought by most farmers contagious. That all diseases known to the hog are infectious or contagious, is certainly an undisputed fact, therefore we cannot be too careful. In buying hogs for feeding or breeding purposes, great care should be taken not to buy those that show any indication of disease, and if they are to be shipped home in cars, see that the cars are clean and have been sprinkled with air slacked lime or a strong solution of carbolic acid, as a disinfectant before loading them.

A few hints as to feeding hogs might be beneficial to a few, but no rule can be given that would be or can be adopted by all feeders; but hogs, like any other stock, should be fed regularly twice or three times a day, and only be given what they will eat up clean, a change of food, the use of pure water, and salt regularly twice a week, and a grass or wood lot for range.

Now I am aware that some persons claim that hogs do not need any salt, but that does not prove it to be so. I have also heard people claim that sheep did not need any water, and one claim has about as much foundation as the other. Salt, and hickory ashes, when they can be procured, is one of the best things that can be given hogs, and is something that they should' have once or twice a week. But the tonic powder made according to the instructions in this book, is much better, as it contains the properties so much needed, being a stronger and better preparation than the former.

Cleanliness with raising and feeding hogs is just as essential as it is with other stock. The idea that anything is good enough for a hog is an idea of the past, and is one that should not be practiced in this progressive age. The meat of a clean and well kept hog that has been fed on a variety of good food is far sweeter and better and more healthy than one raised in the filth. The practice of feeding hogs in the mud and filth, and the constant use of bad water, over-feeding of corn or any other heat-creating food, is very wrong, and will bring on disease. A change should be made. By being careful and observing these rules, a great deal of trouble and money can be saved. An artificial food or compound should also be used as given in this treatment, for a blood purifier and appetizer, which acts beneficially on the stomach and kidneys alike, it being valuable in sickness and health. In ages of time past as well as at the present time, compounds have been popular with the people for the improvement of the health of animals, and follow economy and civilization.

For this purpose use the treatment as given for general use on page 185, or as for the tonic powder, on page 191.

SPECIAL NOTICE.

Do not take the recipe for the treatment of hogs and poultry to a drug store to have it prepared. Make out a memorandum of what you want, and mix the medicine at home. Do not loan the book or recipe to any one for the purpose of treating their hogs, or make the medicine for anyone, without my consent. Remember you have signed a contract to that effect. The treatment as given in this book and my recipe, for the cure and the prevention of the diseases of hogs and poultry, is protected by letters patent and copyrights, according to the Laws of the United States, and anyone infringing upon my rights will be prosecuted to the full extent of the law and my purse.

REMARKS.

It can readily be seen by examination that this book contains a plain, practical and improved modern treatment of all the various diseases of swine, never before published. It is just such a book as has long been needed, and fills a vacuum long felt, and should be in the hands of every breeder and feeder. It is written in plain English, and is free from technicalities which so frequently blind the average reader. Common terms are used in describing symptoms, treatment and remedies, thereby enabling anyone to readily understand the nature of all the diseases and how to treat them, something never before given in the cheap works of this kind that have been sold through the country or published through the newspapers—through charity. My long experience and extensive practice in the field for years, in the treating of diseased hogs and poultry, has enabled me to properly compound a medicine to be sold to the public for this purpose only, that I consider is superior to any other remedy known, and is free from much of the cheap rubbish that goes to fill up the majority of the remedies made and sold at an extortionate price by druggists and others, who know nothing whatever of the diseases of swine or their treatment—especially with the so-called condition powder, which is made and recommended for all kinds of stock. The powder never was made which is fit for horses, cattle or sheep, that will cure diseased hogs; and it is by the use of these powders and worthless hog powders, causing so many failures, that has caused so many people to think that diseased hogs cannot be cured. But that idea, like many others, is becoming a thing of the past, and thousands of farmers and feeders who make constant use of my medicine testify to the same. Besides the numerous recommendations I furnish at all times with my medicine or works, I have hundreds of others from the best farmers and breeders at home and all parts of the United States who have tried my treatment. Three years ago I sold four hundred copies of my " Treatise " to good farmers, under a contract that they could be tried for six months, and if they did not give good satisfaction, upon the return of them I would refund their money. Ninety-eight per cent. of them were kept and highly endorsed.

And now that my treatment is greatly improved and simplified, it will bear the most critical examination. What I claim is first, that there is no other work of this kind published upon which there has been so much time, or practical experience spent in its completion as on this.

Second, that none has ever been sold and tried under as severe tests as this one, and is as highly endorsed and recommended by such an array of men of high authority and practical experience.

Third, that there is no other person known that has ever had the experience in this business that I have had. In all my travels, which have been quite extensive in the past four years, I have never met anyone that would undertake to compete with me, and I have frequently treated herds with the best of success that had baffled all other treatment, and have never failed to give entire satisfaction to all persons for whom I have worked.

Fourth, that all attacks or criticisms are caused by ignorance, jealousy or envy of my great success on the part of persons not competent to judge, and who do not compare with the high character of the men who recommend me and my treatment.

For my own benefit, as well as for others, I will answer a question here that has been very often asked me. "Why do you not sell your treatment to the government; they offer a hundred thousand dollars for a cure?"

Others will say, "Certain States offer ten or fifteen thousand dollars for a cure." Now I have heard this so often, and often, too, from good authority, that I supposed there was something in it; but upon investigation I found it all false. There never was, and probably never will be such an offer. It would not make any difference how good a cure any person had, to cause such an offer would take the united efforts of the entire agricultural press and people. The only way this terrible scourge can be controlled is for every swine breeder or feeder to take an interest in it, and make use of the best method of treatment that is known. And believing that I have that treatment, I take the following plans to place it within reach of every one:

First, by placing my medicine upon the market, so that any one can get it. Second, by selling my Practical Treatment to all who may wish to buy it for their own use, which is the best way, especially for those who handle very many hogs. Third, by selling to veterinarians or others who may wish to use and sell my treatment, the right to do so.

This book, with my recipe, will show my full treatment for swine and poultry, and can be had at any time by addressing me, and remitting ten dollars ($10), or it can be had of anyone selling my medicine.

MY PROPOSITION TO THE PUBLIC.

I will visit any part of the United States, Canada or England at any time requested for the purpose of treating diseased hogs, and guarantee to do all I claim, or make no charge beyond traveling expenses. If in visiting diseased herds of hogs any place and treating them, I warrant a cure of at least three-fourths of any herd of fifty head or more, and will check the disease in three or four days from spreading any further, no difference how bad it is. My terms, either by day or head, are very reasonable, or my treatment as given in this book, if used as directed, will cure or prevent the diseases of hogs or poultry better than any other methods ever published. If it is given a fair and impartial trial and is not what I claim it to be, I will cheerfully refund the money paid for it, by complying with the terms of the contract under which I sell it. I also believe that the medicines I make and sell to the public for the cure and prevention of all the diseases of hogs and poultry, will excel any other medicine known to the profession. It can be had of druggists, or send direct to me and I will send by return express, prepaid, six pounds for $2.50, or 13 pounds for $5. For larger orders a liberal reduction will be made.

BEWARE OF COUNTERFEITS.

My medicine as a cure for diseased hogs or poultry, can also be used as a preventive, is put in tin cans of four sizes and sells at the following prices: Thirteen pounds, $5.00; six pounds, $2.50; two and one-fourth pounds, $1.00; and one pound, 50 cents. They are wrapped with green wrappers, and all bear my name and address, J. B. Shook, Circleville, O.

I also prepare a dry preparation, or powder, as a preventive or tonic powder, to be given hogs once or twice a week, as their condition may require, which will keep them in the best of health and cause them to fatten very fast, which I sell at twenty-five cents per pound, delivered to any address in orders of not less than ten pounds. For orders of twenty-five pounds or more a liberal reduction will be made, or it can be had of dealers at the same price. Now this is only half the price which is asked for other swine powders, and my goods are warranted to do all I claim for them, or the money refunded. They will go as far in use as any other dry powder, for they are made of pure drugs and free from oil meal or shorts, the bulk of most all dry swine powder, or condition powder.

In sending for any amount of medicine of any kind, or for my treatment or book, remit the money by post office order, draft or check, and your order will receive prompt attention, and goods will be sent by return express.

FOR SALE.

In order to more rapidly and effectually introduce my treatment and medicine for swine and poultry, I offer for sale State and County Rights at common sense prices, with full instructions how to compound the medicine I sell to druggists. I also furnish the directions, wrappers, circulars, letters, cards, posters, etc., to work it with, if wanted at publishers' price, and usually a large amount free with the sale, also the farm right recipes, contracts and small book of instructions, and when wanted I will furnish this book at a very reasonable price. This is something that will pay any one to buy and work, as it will not only pay well in any neighborhood, but be very beneficial. And besides it is well protected by letters patent, copy-rights, etc., necessary to protect an invention of this kind. No great additional expense need be added to first purchase, as all the advertising matter can be got of me at cost, which is low, and then you have the benefit of all my newspaper advertising, which is extensive and still increasing. There are but few if any investments of the same amount, that could be made, that would pay as well as to buy a State or County right on this invention. I have frequently known inexperienced men to make $100 a week selling this medicine and the treatise. It always sells readily, and the better it is known the better it sells. The profit on the medicine is as much as any one could wish, and the farm rights the same. From $500 to $1,000 can be made out of a county in one season, if worked. Prices low, terms reasonable. Correspondence cordially invited and cheerfully answered.

THE AMERICAN POULTRY.

A TREATISE ON THE

PROFITABLENESS OF POULTRY,

WITH INFORMATION AS TO THE BEST METHODS OF REARING AND HAND-
LING THEM, WITH A REVIEW OF THE VARIOUS DISEASES TO
WHICH THEY ARE SUBJECT, AND THE MOST PRACTI-
CAL TREATMENT THEREFOR.

CHAPTER XIV.

Profitable Poultry Raising.

POULTRY RAISING.—SELECTED POULTRY SUGGESTIONS.—DIFFERENT BREEDS.—PRACTICAL SUGGESTIONS AS TO HATCHING, REARING AND CARE.—THEIR DISEASES AND HOW TO TREAT THEM.

POULTRY RAISING.

The raising of poultry, like the raising of other domestic stock, if conducted on scientific principles, can be made much more profitable than if conducted on a haphazard plan. But this business, probably more so than the raising of any kind of stock, in order to be profitable, depends largely upon the situation. When one is within easy access to a large city, where the market is good at almost all times of the year, and both the fowls and eggs can be sold direct to the consumer or dealer, the profits are much better than when the products have to be sold in a village or small town, where the supply always exceeds the demand, or else to be shipped some distance to market, and then most likely pass through a commissioner's hands. When poultry raising is conducted on a small scale, it is much more profitable correspondingly, and especially when connected with some other business, than when conducted alone on a large scale. Therefore, when experiencing with a few fowls, to ascertain what can be done, one must not suppose that the same returns correspondingly could be made from a large number; for with poultry, as with swine, as the number increases, the chances of success diminish; not only do the advantages in caring for them diminish, but the danger arising from fatal diseases greatly increases. The question as to whether poultry raising pays, is a question settled long ago by the farmers' wives. As a farmer remarked: "Any housewife can make from her dairy and fowls more than any two men can make raising cotton and corn, and with one-tenth the capital and at one-hundredth part of labor. Many a man is working like a slave, groaning at his debts and troubles when freedom is just within his reach. It lies in the scrubs that he despises; it roosts with the chickens on the fence, if he only knew it." This statement may be a little strong, but still for the same amount of capital and labor invested, there is but few things about the farm, when properly managed, that make as good a return as the poultry yard, and there are but few things with most farmers that are as badly neglected, and for farmers' wives and daughters who desire to do some extra work that will pay in cash, I know of nothing that will pay as well in proportion to the time and capital invested as a small flock of fowls well cared for. It is a certainty that raising poultry for egg production pays the farmer. As a general thing the fowls that the farmer keeps in his barnyard and on which he expends but little, pay best of all his live stock, but when attention is especially paid to fowls, properly fed, housed and attended, after deducting the cost of keeping, care, interest per cent. from the amount for which their eggs sell, there is in nine cases out of ten a larger balance on the credit side of the ledger than is found in connection with any single department of farm industry.

PATIENCE AND CARE.

A little watchful care is needed, and a little patience to go with it helps to make the raising of poultry pleasant and profitable. In early spring, when there is much to do in watching the breeders, making new nests for the layers, gathering and assorting the eggs for hatching and anxious waiting for signs of broodiness among some of the early layers, a little patience and care are good things.

These little jobs, the odds and ends of the poultry business, seem trifling to those who do not keep poultry, but still they must be attended to in time if we desire to make the pursuit satisfactory and remunerative. We may say there is no real labor about it, think it is more of a duty than a task, and we feel better satisfied at the end of the season when we see something for our patience and care.

To be successful in poultry keeping one must have a liking for the pursuit. Few ever make much progress or attain distinction if they feel that it is a forced task to keep fowls for what they bring to the pocket. Of course remuneration should be one of the primary objects, but at the same time one should like them and care for them willingly, though it is a matter of dollars and cents. If we give the object of poultry keeping a sensible thought, we will find that it gives recreation, amusement and daily pastime to the attendant; and when we see what we have accomplished during the hours of relaxation from other cares it will remind us of the benefits of patience and care.

Selected poultry suggestions: By carefully reading and observing the following notes, and adopting their advice as far as practicable, poultry raising can be made profitable in any locality. A specially important matter in the keeping of fowls on a large scale is to secure a near market for them. Hotel-keepers, restaurant proprietors, boarding-house-keepers, etc., will often buy in large quantities and at good rates, when the "goods" suit and the seller is deemed reliable; but if the dealer on a large scale has only the general market to rely upon, he may soon conclude that poultry-keeping does not pay. It is a business dangerous to enter upon when not well considered. The man who wishes to understand as much as possible about poultry-keeping, should buy and study the leading books and papers on the subject. Avoid those published in the interest of some particular breed or breeder. The farmer who objects to books giving instruction on this or any other subjects, is as much at fault as a doctor or lawyer who should claim that he has no need of books. His profession would vote him a fool at once. The pleasure and interest that are awakened by the first step in the right direction go far towards gaining the experience necessary to success. Profit and loss do not depend upon accident or chance, but are necessary consequences of wise or unwise methods of procedure. I have very frequently heard ladies say: "I cannot raise poultry; I have no luck with them; they all die for me, or something kills the little ones, or the hens will not lay." Let me inform you, kind friends, that there is no such thing as luck. If your neighbors are more successful than you, it is because they have better methods, or are more diligent and attentive to their fowls.

Very often when ladies complain of having no luck with poultry, and when the case is investigated the cause found is that their fowls were allowed to roost in trees during the winter, with no feed except what they got from around the corn crib. Poultry, like other animals, require housing in winter and a variety of feed, and if otherwise cared for prove unprofitable.

There is nothing connected with poultry raising, whether for exhibition or market, that a woman cannot do better in a general way than most men.

Poultry keeping is a healthy and engrossing pursuit. It is pleasurable as well as profitable; it affords amusement, and well repays for the time and labor spent while engaged in it; but it should never be undertaken by any but those who take an interest in it, and find pleasure in the work.

A flock of hens will pay for themselves before they are one year old, if they are rightly cared for. You can then sell them, if you choose to, for a good price, and raise another lot, but it is not advisable to do so, as the second year is the most profitable; but do not keep them after they are two years old, for after that age they do not pay so well.

Those having the same kind of stock that have been on the place for years and years without crossing and improving should look to fanciers and breeders for better stock than they have, or they ever had. They will be surprised to see what a difference it will make to introduce into their flock one or more pure bred cocks.

While you are thinking of ornamenting your homes, stop and consider what an ornament a beautiful pair or trio of Wyandotts, Dark or Light Brahmas, Hamburgs, Cochins, or some of the pretty strains of improved fowls would be. Five dollars invested in inanimate ornamentation would not attract nearly so much attention, nor receive the admiration of visitors as the same amount expended in high class fowls. Did you ever pass a farm-yard where there was a flock of improved poultry that you did not have to stop and admire their beautiful and uniform bodies, plumage, and appearance? It always creates a sensation to get a valuable pair or trio of fowls from a distance. The neighbors will speak for a pair of the offspring, or setting of eggs, and were you willing to let them go you could get several times the price of the original fowls the first season for their produce. This is not merely supposition, but it is true. Five dollars per trio seems like a large price, when common fowls sell at three dollars per dozen, but with good care a person can raise enough to pay for the parent stock the first season, and sell the produce at three dollars per dozen—the price of common fowls. So there is no money to be lost, even at the worst calculations. Nothing reproduce so fast as poultry. A pair of fowls reproduce themselves from twelve to forty times the first year, and at the end of the year the produce is in full development, and the fac-simile of the parents ready to be sold at the same (considered by some fancy) prices.

It costs no more to raise the best breeds of poultry than the common barn-yard fowl, while the returns are more than double. Get a setting of eggs from some reliable breeder, and convince yourself of this fact.

Most every people under the broad vault of heaven, excepting the nomadic tribes of Asia and Indians of America, raise poultry for pleasure and profit.

IMPROVE YOUR FOWLS.

In order to increase the size of common fowls, the cock selected should be a Cochin or Brahma, which will give a heavy feathering, compact size and small comb. Such a cross will lay earlier than the pure Brahma or Cochin, and make better nurses for chicks. This cross is well suited for cold climates. For warm climate, or where quality of flesh is desired, or the production of eggs, or as an out-cross for any of the large breeds, the Leghorns will prove profitable. It is only a greenhorn who is caught with the idea that a new and much-puffed variety of fowls, just discovered or imported, is better than anything yet known. Only give the old sorts good care and they will do well enough, and often a great deal better than new sorts at fancy prices.

LIGHT BRAHMAS.

The light Brahma fowls are handsome birds when in full feather, and doubtless have as many merits, all things considered, as ony other breed, if not more. A new beginner with poultry can hardly do better than to try this old reliable and valuable breed. But in saying this I am not advertising anybody's flock, and have none for sale. A cross of the light Brahma and white Leghorn, makes a very valuable fowl. Some persons prefer a cross of the Leghorns in order to gain early maturity and increased egg production, but object to the cross, as the infusion of Leghorn blood is so potent as to greatly reduce the size, which is not desirable in market fowls. Such reduction, however, will only occur for a single season, as the larger breeds of cockerels may afterwards be used. The Leghorn cross will always be found a very valuable one.

THE OLD BLUE HEN.

The "old blue hen" is a term applied to the extra good common hen. She is found on every farm and enjoys a reputation second to none. She has performed her duty faithfully and well, has always been a favorite, and is never forgotten. Long after she has passed away her qualities are extolled and her merits compared as a standard of judgment with hens of every other breed. She is the model by which the usefulness of all other hens are measured, and often she is pensioned and spared from the knife as a reward for her extraordinary capacity of egg production.

But, somehow or other, no farmer ever succeeds in raising a whole flock like the old blue hen. He never has more than one of that kind. Carefully he selects her eggs for sitting, and cautiously he watches the nest where she lays in order to secure them. He places the eggs under a good hen, or allows the old hen to hatch them herself. The chicks come out sprightly, grow fast, and arrive at maturity, but the pullets do not prove old blue hens. They usually turn out to be the most worthless scrubs on his farm, no two being alike in shape, color or size, and finally the farmer comes to the conclusion that there is nothing stable in feeding fowls for a special purpose.

But the trouble with farmers in such cases is, that while they are particular about the old blue hen, they have not noticed that they have no old blue rooster. They forget that the rooster is everything, and that he impresses his qualities upon all his offspring. If the old blue hen is expected to produce something excellent when mated with a worthless barnyard mongrel, she is expected to do what would not be looked for in cattle, sheep or other stock. Farmers, the moral of this is that you should use thoroughbred males only, for in no other manner can a common flock be improved.

PLYMOUTH ROCK.

The Plymouth Rock is a very valuable breed in most respects, being an average layer, quick maturer and of good size, and void of the leg feathers so much disliked by most farmers. They are a quiet but industrious breed, and cross well with the common breeds. They are the old Dominique improved, and if you remember the old saying, "Never mind the old speckled hen; you had better let her be, for she lays two eggs every day, and on Sunday she lays three." The improvement though, has not been in the laying quality, as much as in the form and shade.

AMERICAN DOMINIQUES.

The Dominique is thoroughly an American bird, and it combines many of the good qualities of the pure-bred varieties. Its hardiness, symetry and general utility are only more appreciated by the addition of harmony of colors—being so blended as to be always pleasing to the eye. Like memories of by-gone days, always growing in remembrance, the American Dominique, so justly entitled to the appellation, comes to the front amidst the furor for something new, claiming our attention for long-established virtues and for its present improved appearance.

POULTRY INVESTMENTS.

"Nothing risked, nothing gained," is an old adage that is nowhere more applicable than in the poultry business; and there is no business in which it is so frequently ignored. So many are under the impression that the chicken business is too "small a fry" to invest anything in it, and that any one investing only a small amount in that way was simply throwing money away. The business cannot certainly be started on nothing, and run itself; that those who do make money in that business have more than the usual amount of skill and business tact.

We must admit that an ordinary amount of common sense and judgment is required to carry on any branch of business successfully, and the poultry business is no exception to this rule. But a corresponding amount of capital is needed to meet the requirements of the trade, and to insure comfort at least. What would we think of a man starting out to make a fortune (or even a reasonable amount of money) on stock of any kind, who would start by procuring, or having already on hand, a poor, degraded lot of scrubs, and then turn them out to gather their living as best they can, leaving them to take shelter from driving storms under trees or behind fences, and should they come to the barn to seek shelter, to be driven away to seek their own shelter? You would soon pass judgment on him and mark him down as doomed to the misfortune of failure, which would seem inevitable, for it would be unjust and contrary to the laws of cause and effect for such a system to succeed.

I need not make the application; you can see at a glance that the shoe fits, and I suppose you will have to wear it until you can make a change for the better. I wonder how many of our readers have ever seen fowls roosting in the trees, on fences or under a few loose boards in mid-winter, simply because "anything is good enough for the chickens."

I imagine many have seen such a sight, and perhaps in their own yards; we hope many have repented ere this, and are on the high road to success. Persons keeping fowls in such a manner have no need for the huxter until nearly June; perhaps not then, for men do not gather figs from thistles, nor eggs from hens that are so nearly frozen to death that the food they receive is scarcely sufficient to keep "soul and body together." It would seem that many of us do not deserve eggs, or even fowls, for such inhuman treatment. There is no branch of farm economy that will pay such a handsome dividend on the capital invested as the poultry business, where it is carried on in a systematic manner. Comfort must always be the ruling watchword which necessitates a moderate investment.

MAKE CAREFUL SELECTIONS.

In order to keep the character of a flock to full vigor and stamina it is important to be careful in selecting only those that are the best. If you intend to discard anything, let it be from the bottom. Always reserve the best to breed from. The transmittal of good qualities can be done only by those that are perfect, and he who is careful in selecting only those best fitted for the purpose of improvement, not only elevates the poultry in his own yards, but confers a favor and benefit on everyone who patronizes him. It is by sound judgment, careful observation and unceasing watchfulness that the present breeds are becoming better and better as time passes along. By all means, if poultry is an object, do not trust to any haphazard risks, or unfounded hopes, but rely solely on the best attention that can be personally given.

The fall is the time in which to make selections of the pullets that are intended as winter layers. It must be considered that fowls are adapted for particular seasons, according to the breeds. The Leghorns commence laying very early, but unless given warm quarters and the best of feed, rarely make good winter layers. In fact, all fowls should be made comfortable during the winter season; but there are breeds endowed with heavier and closer feathering than others, which are thereby enabled to retain the animal heat longer. An examination of the Leghorn hen will demonstrate that the body under the wings is sometimes nearly naked, being covered only by wings, while the body of the Brahma is covered not only by the wings, but also by a heavy fluff feathering, soft and downy, which is serviceable during the long season. There may be exceptions, but such is usually the case.

Leg feathering, however, is of no advantage, as the feathers keep the legs continually damp, where the fowls are confined on heavy clay soil. The comb is another obstacle to the Leghorns, Black Spanish and Plymouth Rocks, such fowls having tall, single combs, which are easily frosted when exposed to severe cold winds, or when they become wet, as the danger of freezing is thereby increased. The combs may be cut off close to the head, as also the wattles, if necessary, which operation is not necessarily dangerous, but sometimes beneficial, when the combs are very heavy.

In selecting the winter layers it is best to reserve those that were hatched early. If the small breeds are kept, the pullets hatched as late as the beginning of June sometimes begin to lay about Christmas, but those a month older will give more satisfactory results. The large breeds —Brahma, Cochins and Plymouth Rocks—require more time during which to grow and mature, and pullets of such breeds, when intended as winter layers, should be hatched as early as possible, March being the month preferred, but later hatched pullets of the large breeds often begin to lay early, and produce quite a number of eggs before spring begins. Langshan pullets begin to lay nearly as early as Leghorns, which is a good quality for a breed of large fowls, and the crosses of the Langshan with mixed or common fowls also produce good early layers.

CULL THE FLOCK.

Each year select out and get rid of all the old fowls. January is a good month to do this, as they will bring about as much then as at any other time, and further expense in the way of care and feed is saved, also the risk of death or disease by having too many together. Always retain the early hatched pullets and last year's hens, as they will be the most profitable ones. Early pullets are the birds for early winter layers. The man misses it who sells them for broilers at a low price, and the early, molting hens are the ones that will be your winter layers next to the early pullets. If the hens begin to molt early they will get through the process before winter sets in, but if they begin to molt after cold weather comes they will not lay until spring, whether they finish before spring or not. A hen usually requires three months during which to molt. Little or no profit can be expected from old fowls, those in excess of two years. Very valuable hen-mothers may sometimes be retained several years longer for chicken-raising, but the rest should be gotten rid of. The most profitable fowls are pullets.

GAME FOWLS.

In January, or the fore part of February, get some pure bred cocks to mate with the hens retained, using good judgment as to the breed, if a cross is desired. Too many cocks in a flock are worse than too few. The right proportion is a matter for some study, and depends, in a measure, on the capacity of the cocks. Very clumsy ones should be avoided.

INCUBATORS.

Incubators can doubtless be made useful on many farms, by giving them close study and attention. No success need be expected without that. But when the purchase of one is being contemplated, I would advise the purchase of a small or cheap one to start with, and by experimenting with that, it can be ascertained as to whether it is profitable or not. There are but few things that can beat nature producing life. They may be one, but I doubt for the general farmer, if they are as cheap and reliable as hens. Of late years poultry keeping has become a pursuit of care and system to make it a success, and it is in the order of business with poultrymen to be preparing for the spring trade. We have our monthly work before us, and every month has its allotted share, whether it is preparing for the shows, selecting and mating the breeders, putting things in shape for hatching and caring for the broods, and so on through the whole annual routine.

Spring has many drawbacks, and at the same time we are most sanguine about doing great things, our plans and prospects may fall through and burst like a bubble. Our hens which we have anxiously watched for the past few weeks, to see signs of broodiness, are deceiving us by their merry cackle. Sometimes this is provoking when we have made up our minds to have some early chicks. But there is another feature about it; every baker's dozen brings in a few dollars, and we are quieted for the time being. Some breeders will get mad and resolve to have an incubator which will, they say, "do away with this eternal watching and waiting for hens to sit. It can be set up at all seasons; it will regulate itself; it needs no coaxing to incubate, nor no food during the time of work but some hot water, and the chicks will roll out by the dozens." Now that is all very well to talk about, but you must prepare for disappointments.

HOW TO FEED FOWLS.

Feed regularly and in variety. Hide the grains in chaff or leaves, and let the fowls hunt and scratch them out. Never throw huge masses of food before them if you wish them to do well.

Fowls in confinement must have grass provided for them, or they will not thrive. Careless observers will be surprised to know how much grass a hen eats in a year. A small flock will keep down all vegetation in a yard of considerable size.

Instead of giving all the skimmed milk and buttermilk to the pigs, allow the hens to have a share, all by themselves, in nice clean pans, and see if they don't pay you as well for it. A little bran or meal stirred into it helps powerfully. Charcoal in feed will produce a greater amount of flesh and fat in poultry than the same quantity of feed without.

Indian corn should be fed sparingly in the summer season to fowls, as it has a tendency to fatten to excess; but if fed whole once a day, and in the evening, it is beneficial. Charred corn is an excellent food for laying hens, and serves to keep them healthy and vigorous. Do not feed entirely, but give once a day, and be careful in preparing it, or it will burn to ashes. Ground or cracked corn is better fed in the morning, and if mixed with other food is better than if fed alone. For chicks, feed meal or soft food wet with milk during the day, and in the evening cracked corn, wheat, or some other whole grain.'

The last thing that the little chick does before leaving the shell is to draw into his body the yolk of the egg, from the white of which the body of the chick has been developed. So the first food given it should not be materially different. Boiled eggs, crumbled into little bits, form the most natural food that the little chick can have. But don't be in a hurry to feed it. Full and plump as it is when it comes from the shell, it will not need food for at least twelve hours. In that time it has learned the use of its legs, and is much more active than at first, and will readily pick up food that its wise old mother invites it to partake of.

Soft food, with now and then seeds and small grain, is much better for young chicks than an exclusive diet of whole grain. Young birds, like suckling animals, cannot masticate solid food, for the organs of mastication and digestion are unable to perform the work in a healthy manner.

The great objection to soft food, such as corn meal dough, is the way in which it is usually mixed up for chicks. When it is porridgy it is not fit for them, as it sours in their crops, and causes diarrhea. Stale bread crumbs sopped in milk, "Johnny-cake," brown bread, boiled rice, cracked wheat, millet, and a little cooked food occasionally, will make them grow nicely.

When the chicks run around and pick bugs, seeds, cracked corn and wheat, it is good for them, for then they are able to partake of more solid food. They should have no more food at a time than what they will pick up clean, for if left to be soiled or trampled upon it is unfit for use; and once rejected, they seldom touch it afterwards.

It is noticeable with fowls, particularly young birds, that they will pick up fresh food as often as it is dropped to them. Variety of food, or change in the manner of cooking and preparing it, makes it more relished. It costs no more, or at least not much more, to provide a variety of food than one or two kinds. Still many breeders use but one or two kinds of grain during the year, and believe there is economy in it.

In the winter season, fowls can get but little to eat except what is given to them by hand. They may be able to pick up something in the barn-yard, where grain-fed cattle and hogs are turned every day, but a great many poultry keepers have no stalls or barn-yards for poultry to forage in, hence they are entirely dependent on their keepers for support.

The food and the manner in which it is fed has a great deal to do with the health and well being of fowls in the winter season. They like a variety of food at all seasons, but especially in cold weather. When fed a variety of good food and housed well, you may expect a good supply of eggs in winter.

Feeding requires judgment; for fowls, in order to lay and give good results, must be given a variety, green food being allowed as a regular addition to the supply of grain. Meat in some shape is also essential, and good quarters and pure water are very important. As eggs bring better prices in the fall and during the winter than at any other time, the breeder will be well rewarded for the care he may bestow if the fowls are properly attended to and their wants amply supplied.

Exercise is very important with all fowls, whether old

or young, and especially to laying hens, where eggs are to be used for breeding purposes.

It is desirable in winter to have the floor of the hen house covered with chaff for the fowls to scratch in, for this keeps them active, and gives them the exercise they so much need.

Every hen in high health has a bright red, or crimson-colored comb. All laying hens show that color. It is always absent from a hen which has "sat" three or four weeks. She is not in a laying condition.

Egg shells should be crushed before feeding them to the fowls, for when fed whole it is apt to teach them the habit of eating their eggs. I think to burn the egg shells, and feed bone dust or ground oyster shells would be better, and would prevent this habit. Iron nails thrown into the drinking water will make a good tonic for the fowls, or else use an iron vessel in which to give them their drink. In absence of this a tablespoonful of tincture of iron in half a gallon of water is good. The want of pure and fresh water accounts in many instances for the lack of eggs during the winter season. Fowls require a constant supply of water, and without it will not lay.

Good care for poultry is especially necessary during the molting season. Feed generously, and provide shelter from inclement weather, for at this period their system is thoroughly drained, and they are liable to disease.

NESTS FOR SETTING HENS.

A writer says: "We have found by many years' experience in the setting of hens and rearing of poultry, that the best nest for setting purposes is the sod box. It is made as follows: Take a square box, or make one 12 or 16 inches square and about 14 inches deep, cut out a blue-grass or timothy sod just large enough to fit the bottom of the box, and about four inches thick ; place the grass side down, as it is good to hold moisture; place about two inches of straw or grass on this—the finer the grass the better—dampen the nest with milk-warm water before setting the hen; then dampen every five days until the eggs are hatched. If the hen is a good sitter, you will get a hundred per cent. from the fertile eggs. Turkeys, geese, and all fowls in the wild state, build nests on the ground. The sod box makes up for the deficiency in dampness."

This advise is very good, for no doubt the proper way to make a nest for a hen for any purpose is to follow nature as close as possible, or else let her make her own nest. Another good way to form a nest is to saw a barrel in two in the center, then cut off two or three of the staves, so as to form a place for the hen to get in; turn the barrel upside down, and form the nest on the ground. This makes a dark and damp nest, such as nature requires. Have a watchful eye on the sitting hens. A hen should not be entrusted with the eggs until she has left her nest once or twice, and returned to it without too long an absence. Arrangements should be made whereby she will not be interrupted by other fowls. Food should be within her easy reach, so that she need not be long in quest of it. Corn is the best food for her, and green or soft food should not be given her during this period, as they induce a laxative condition. A dust box should be provided, so she can take her baths; for the hen is a cleanly creature if she has an opportunity to be so.

Fanny Field says: "A beginner wants to know how poultry raisers manage to make one hen own two broods of chicks; says she has tried it more than once, but the hen would fight all the chicks except her own. Didn't go to work right, my dear; you must mix the two families before the hen finds out how many children she has of her own, and what they look like. Slip the extra chicks under the hen before she leaves the nest, and in ninety-nine cases out of a hundred she will think that she hatched them all. Or if you take the hen from the nest before she gets ready to leave, give her all the chicks when you put her in the coop. Sometimes a dark hen will object strongly to a single white chick, but if she has half a dozen of that color she will own them all.

POULTRY IN THE GARDEN AND ORCHARD.

It is a very excellent practice to place newly hatched broods in an enclosed garden that the older fowls do not have access to. Confine the mother hen in a coop, which may be placed in the shade of any small fruit tree or bush. As chicks require soft and delicate food at first, it is difficult to feed them if their coops are placed where the rest of the flock can pillage freely, but if allowed access in the garden, they will run about, doing no harm. Their little bodies and feet have no impression on the soil; they do not scratch, seem never dissatisfied, but find pleasure only in the pursuit of food, or in basking in a warm corner in the sun's rays. While in this stage of infantile innocence the little creature can in the garden perform a vast amount of good. Their little eyes spy out and little bills gather myriads of insects that are not easily visible to the human eye. Perhaps owing to the very minute nature of the food they gather, arising from their characteristic voracity, they are always roaming about and doing useful work. This is a matter that should be practiced when possible. I believe that if farmers and fruit raisers knew the benefit arising from such management, they would at once adopt it, for in almost all instances whenver a fruit tree is in the poultry yard, it seldom fails to bear. Knowing this to be the case, it could be made very profitable, as far as practical, to confine the poultry in the orchard. The good results are more noticeable with plums or peaches than with apples, as they destroy the worms that are destructive to that fruit.

SUNFLOWER SEED.

I do not suppose that the sunflower will very soon command itself to the general run of farmers, as a crop, however valuable it may be. But there is no doubt that as a valuable food for poultry, the seed of the sunflower is worthy of consideration. As it is so easily grown and gathered, every farmer should try and raise a large amount and store it away in order to feed to poultry in the winter, as it is a very valuable food, and especially as a change of feed.

POULTRY HOUSES.

Poultry cannot be kept to advantage unless they have a properly arranged house for their accommodation. This is just as necessary to their well being as it is that the cattle or horses should have a good barn. Poultry houses need not be expensive, but should be built snug and warm. The three principal errors most common in the management of poultry are: First, allowing too many fowls to mass together. Second, neglecting to keep the house and yard as clean and as disinfected as they should be. Third, allowing them to roost in the peach or apple trees around the house, or in a rail pen with a leaky roof. If you have not built a comfortable poultry house, it is time to be at it, if you want to get any good of it, or rather if you want your fowls to. In the fall is the time to look well to your poultry houses, and see what is needed in the way of repairs. To begin with, the houses must not only be air-tight, but be heated by the sun or artificial heat, and can be of any design you desire. The building may be a lean-to, fronting the south or south-east, with windows in front; or, made with a roof having a long slope on the south side, with an ordinary greenhouse sash to admit light. Proper means should be taken to ventilate the house, but the ventilation so constructed that the draught will not strike the fowls, as it is liable to cause disease and freeze their combs. Do not complain because your hens lay no eggs, if you have allowed them to have their combs frozen. It will take them some time to repair the damage which your neglect has caused. You are guilty, and suffer financially. They are innocent, but must suffer physically.

There is a good demand for eggs in winter, and the farmer should endeavor to have his hens in such condition that they will produce eggs at this time, when they are worth twice as much as they are in summer.

The best and most natural flooring for hen houses, all things considered, is clean, dry earth upon an earth floor. In cleaning the house, always take out part or all of the loose earth with the manure and replace it with fresh earth.

One of the principle advantages of having a separate house for poultry is in being able to save their droppings. These should not be allowed to accumulate all winter, but should be removed at least once a week, as they are a fruitful source of disease if not so removed. You will be surprised how many barrels of the best of fertilizer you will have next spring, if you thus save the droppings from twenty well fed fowls.

In the winter, when you think the hens eat their eggs, first be sure they have any to eat. Second, remove the cause, and it will soon stop the habit. It is usually acquired by several hens crowding into one nest, thus breaking the eggs. The hens soon find they are good to eat, and that the shells supply their peculiar appetite for bone, and so are apt to continue it. It is a bad plan to throw the empty shells into the poultry-yard without first crushing them fine, or mixing them with other food. Crushed oyster shells and broken bones will supply the hens with what they want. These should always be where the hens can get them, and it is wonderful what an amount of them they will devour. It is folly to suppose, as some, that the few egg shells they give them ought to supply them with shell-making material for all the eggs they expect them to lay. I have seen the lime picked off of white-washed buildings as high as the hens could jump, and have heard the owners complain because the "vile hens" wouldn't refrain from this practice. Give them fresh shells, or at least bone material of some sort, every day or two, and it will not only increase the production of eggs, but prevent the hens from eating them.

Also charcoal and lime should be allowed fowls always. Let them have all they will eat. Even if the fowls are not confined, but especially so if they are. Charcoal pounded up into bits of pieces about the size of a grain of corn, or a little finer, should be put where the fowls can have easy access to it, and they will soon make use of it.

GOOD AND POOR EGGS.

The difference between an egg laid by a plump, healthy hen, fed with good, fresh food daily, and an egg laid by a thin, poorly fed hen, is as great as the difference between good and poor beef. A fowl fed on garbage and weak slops, with very little grain of any kind, may lay eggs, to be sure, but when these eggs are broken to be used for cakes, pies, etc., they will spread in a weak, watery way over your dish, or look a milky white, instead of having a rich, slightly yellow tinge. A "rich egg" retains its shape, as far as possible, and yields to the beating of a knife or spoon with more resistance, and gives you the conviction that you are really beating something thicker than water or diluted milk.

A fresh egg has a clear, yellow color when held to the eye so that the sun or a bright light can fall upon it. The fingers should enclose it so that the light is excluded from passing between the fingers and the shell. Eggs which admit no light are bad. Some dealers who handle large quantities of eggs "candle" them—that is, examine them in a dark room by holding them near a candle or lamp, to see if light will pass through.

HOW TO PRESERVE EGGS.

The different methods for packing and keeping eggs for future use are as numerous as the different cures for fowls. But a method that we have always found to be successful, and one that can be relied upon, providing the eggs are fresh and the packing properly done, is to cover the bottom of a keg, cask, jar, or whatever you choose to pack in, with a layer of fine salt two inches deep; upon this place the eggs, small end down, and far enough apart so that they will not touch each other or the sides of the receptacle; then put on another two-inch layer of salt, then another layer of eggs, and so on till the package is full. This is, on the whole, the best method for house-keepers, and for those who have only a small number to pack for market. The salt can be used over and over again.

Pickled eggs won't boil. Whenever they come in contact with hot water, the shell dissolves partnership in the middle.

WEIGHT OF EGGS.

Shall eggs be sold by number or by pound, is a momentous question that is said to be agitating several Parisian scientists. It has been learned that the average weight of twenty eggs laid by fowls of different breeds is two and one-eighth pounds. The breeds that lay the largest eggs, averaging seven to the pound, are Black Spanish, Houdans, La Fleches and Creve-Coeurs. Eggs of medium size and weight, averaging eight or nine to the pound, are laid by Leghorns, Cochins, Brahmas, Polands, Dorkings, Games and Sultans. Hamburgs lay about ten eggs to the pound. Thus there is a difference of three eggs in one pound weight. Hence it is claimed that in justice to the consumer, eggs should be sold by weight.

It would be found better, both for the producer and consumer of eggs, to sell by weight rather than number, for as the market is to-day, small eggs sell for the same as nice, large ones.

VERMIN—LICE.

We all know what a dust bath is, for we have seen the fowls, hundreds of times, at work dusting themselves. A heap of ashes, pile of dirt, or a scooped out place in the ground, any convenient spot that affords a good opportunity for fowls to throw the dust over themselves, is suitable as a place for a dust bath.

They dust themselves in order to rid themselves of vermin. They can very easily get rid of lice if you give them a chance, but unless they are protected against their return, the fowls cannot keep themselves rid of them. The dust bath drives away the lice, but only for the time being. If the quarters are filthy, they will soon swarm with lice; and as soon as evening comes, and the birds return to roost, the lice attack them again. There are two kinds of lice that trouble them most. One kind remains on the body until driven off by the dust bath, but the other kind " loves darkness rather than light, because its deeds are evil," and so it attacks them when on the roost, like the chinch or bed-bug, and sneakingly hides away on the approach of day. They inflict terrible suffering on the fowls, and there can be no thrift or enjoyment of health in the presence of these detestable parasites. To be rid of them is to put the quarters in a clean condition, and there is nothing equal to a thick daubing of whitewash with some carbolic acid added. It will not do to give the quarters one cleaning and then stop.

A careful use of kerosene oil will keep off lice. Coal tar is also frequently used to good advantage for the same purpose. Apply it with a brush into every crack and crevice where there is any chance for vermin, and it will keep them off.

There is no use in cleaning your poultry houses unless you burn the old nests. They will be sure to harbor more of the various kinds of poultry parasites than you can ever exterminate with a whitewash brush.

Lice are a great pest to poultry, as well as to any other stock, and it is impossible for them to do well with this annoying pest sucking the life-blood away from them all the time.

If you notice a fowl drooping, or standing off by itself "all drawn up in a bunch," watch it closely. If you can see no indications of cholera, if it eats when food is thrown toward it, but quickly resumes its uncouth position, examine it carefully to see if it is not infested with vermin. Several kinds of lice give trouble in the poultry house, but those very small ones, scarcely discernible to the naked eye, are the worst. Examine carefully under the wings, and in the fluff of the bird. If you find them you may not be able to get rid of them without "doctoring" the whole flock, and the premises they occupy.

Treatment: Apply light on the head and around under the wings, coal oil and lard equal parts, mixed. This will soon rid the fowls of them, but will be of little use unless the roosts and nests are thoroughly cleaned. All poultry houses should be looked after three or four times a year, or oftener, if necessary; the nests cleaned out and replenished with new straw, and sprinkled light with flour or sulphur; the roosts and floor well cleaned of droppings, and the floor well sprinkled with air-slacked lime, the roofs and sidings kept well whitewashed, and all openings that permit a draught of air direct upon the fowls kept closed. It is in this way so many catch cold, which soon brings on a more fatal disease. They should have clean water to drink at all times, and once a week give them one tablespoon of tincture of iron to a half gallon of water, or else use an iron vessel, or a trough with some old iron in it for them to drink out of. Avoid the use of musty food at all times and change their food often. By so doing it will go a long ways towards insuring health and prosperity among your fowls.

DUCKS.

We are occasionally led into wondering why more ducks are not bred and marketed among our poultry breeders in America. We have now in this country three or four varieties of imported ducks, at the head of which the Pekins stand to-day, without question, for size, early maturity, hardiness and thrift. The Aylesbury (pure white, like the Pekin), the Rouen (brown or parti-colored, and the Cayuga (black), are notable and of good quality. Each of these varieties, within my knowledge, have been successfully bred upon a country place where there was neither pond or rivulet for their amusement.

The ducklings were hatched under hens, and the ducks were raised with the other poultry and fowls on the estate, with similar feed and care, the owner claiming that for marketing purposes ducks can be reared, like other fowls, upon dry land, without any perceptible difference in their thrift during the season. The Cayuga duck has not been extensively propagated until of late years, although it is well worthy of cultivation, and the best of dark ducks. Ducks should be allowed as much liberty as possible, as they are not partial to confinement, like chickens. When they are kept in the poultry yard with hens they become quarrelsome, and do more damage than they are worth, and for that reason should be kept separate, or allowed to run free.

DUCKS AND DUCK HOUSES.

As a poultry breeder remarked: "There is money in

ducks, and a goodly quantity of it, too, provided you know how to get it out and have the facilities for breeding them successfully. The one thing essential is plenty of running water; a small stream or pond near by is most excellent, and far better than a river or large stream, in which latter the young ducks are apt to fall an easy prey to snakes, turtles, etc. Artificial ponds can be constructed, though these are often objectionable, on account of their liability to become stagnant. If this can be avoided, by some way insuring its being kept fresh and pure, it is as good, to all intents and purposes, as a stream.

In breeding ducks, keep them in the yards in the morning until about ten o'clock, by which time they will have laid their eggs; after that they can be given their liberty. Keep the ducks laying all through the breeding season, and set all the duck eggs under hens. As soon as the young ducklings appear, transfer them to a commodious coop with their foster-mother, and make a small pen for them. Keep a shallow pan or small trough in the pen, and keep constantly supplied with clean, fresh water, until they get well grown and fully feathered; do not let them frequent the pond or stream, but give them plenty of room to run around on the grass, when the dew is off. When they get fully feathered, let them out into swimming water, and they will be happy.

It is surprising what a large flock of young ducks can, in this way, be reared from a single trio of ducks in a good season, as ducks get most of their living off the grass. Breeding ducks cannot be kept up in pens, for they copulate in the water, and unless they have swimming water their eggs will generally be unfertile ones.

Any little, low, shed-like houses will do for ducks, and

the only thing necessary to keep them properly is to keep the place clean and well supplied with fine hay as a bedding."

RAISING GEESE.

The old gray goose and his mates of the white or mottled variety, so commonly seen about the barn yards in certain localities, are bred in considerable number by farmers and poulterers who have the conveniences and facilities for rearing this fine water-fowl, but the Embden or Toulouse geese are better.

Three or four geese only should be mated to one gander, and generally two are sufficient. Laying begins in April, or early in May. After the goose has laid her litter, from ten to fifteen, she will arrange her nest in sitting order and line it with feathers. If the eggs have been taken from her they should now be returned, and she allowed to cover them. As the process of incubation is of considerable length—from twenty-eight to thirty-two days—she must be encouraged to leave the nest often for food and exercise. A supply of clean water and vegetable food, raw and cooked, and also corn should be given to keep her in a healthy state. An occasional visit to a pond of water can do no harm, provided it is not prolonged until the eggs become chilled.

OUR NATIONAL TURKEY.

"Our National bird is not so much the eagle—which few of us ever see, except at the Zoo, remarks a writer in the Philadelphia Star, or rarer still, on the gold pieces but the more savory, the more festive turkey. The turkey may not soar so high in a patriotic sense, but he touches the National heart more tenderly, especially about Thanksgiving or Christmas time, when men are so susceptible to the tenderest influences of life.

Some writers assert that turkeys were known to the ancients, but a writer in the New York Era tells us this is an error. It is a nice question, too, who first introduced the turkey into France, and when. In many parts of France jesuite is a familiar name for turkey. The very name in the French language would seem to attest its American origin, for this country was formerly designated Indes Occidentals—hence dindon. Besides this is the only country where the turkey is found wild.

TURKEY COCK AND HEN.

A turkey in prime condition, properly cooked, is a dish of which few persons refuse to partake. The young hen turkey, plump and fat, is usually preferred; though a young "Tom," being larger, and weighing from fifteen to twenty pounds, can hardly be surpassed when well roasted. The old turkey is best for boning, and is excellent when boiled. Wild turkeys are always to be found in some markets during the winter season. Their flesh is darker than the tame, and has a gamey taste. A Capon turkey, however, is the most delicious of all, being more tender, succulent and finer flavored." Well fattened and well-dressed turkeys will bring two or three cents a pound more than the lean bird. It will not only be better for the purse, but for your manhood, to send nothing but finished products to the market.

Those who have turkeys should feed liberally from early fall to Thanksgiving or Christmas. The demand for good turkey dinners is increasing.

FATTENING TURKEYS.

The Bronze is the king of turkeys. In short, they are noted for their great size and rich, changeable bronze colors. They are always beautiful; are pretty good foragers, and it costs little to raise them where grasshoppers and insects are plenty. They are No. 1 layers, hardy, and easy to raise; they make a very rapid growth, and if the winter is not too hard, and does not set in too early, young gobblers will weigh twenty-five pounds at about six months of age, and hens about thirteen or fourteen pounds. Turkeys, unlike chickens, grow all winter, and make weight for the seed they consume. The bronze do not fully get their weight until they are about three years old. At maturity, hens weigh from fifteen to twenty pounds, and gobblers from thirty to forty pounds each.

"In most sections turkeys are very profitable, and no

doubt the weight can be made from about the same feed and trouble that is given to the rearing of small, common turkeys. It pays to keep the best blooded stock, if we get much larger returns from our outlay.. We give it as a fact, which many persons do not understand, that turkeys shrink from three to nine pounds in shipping, as being nervous they eat little, and the journey worries them. They soon recover, however. Customers are apt to weigh them upon receipt, and many a seller gets a cursing for sending lighter weights than he represented, when it was owing to the shrinkage of the birds. They should not be weighed under three or four weeks of good keeping after their arrival on a new place. Shrinking happens the same with other fowls, too."

DISEASED POULTRY—THEIR SYMPTOMS AND TREATMENT.
CHOLERA AND ROUP.

All kinds of poultry, especially chickens and turkeys, are subject to diseases similar to those of the hog, (known as cholera and roup,) and is as infectious or contagious with them as with hogs. This view of the matter suggests the propriety of adopting such measures with the first cases in a locality as shall prevent the spreading of the disease in any way. The diseased, in any case, should be kept apart from the healthy ones until they have well recovered, and upon the appearance of the disease should be cared for immediately. Fowls show signs of sickness immediately after they are attacked. Perfect health with poultry is best shown by the bright scarlet color of the comb, their cheerfulness and elasticity of step. As soon as the fowl feels unwell the comb changes color, at first pale and then purple, and they refuse to eat or leave the roost, often remaining there until death.

HOW TO TELL A SICK FOWL.

The comb and wattles are the parts of a fowl to examine first in case of sickness, as they should always be of a bright scarlet color. When the comb looks white, or pale, or black, something is wrong; even lice will cause the comb to change color to a certain extent, when there is refusal of food, for no healthy fowl will refuse to eat if fed on a variety of food, unless already full. Thirst, to a great degree, is another sign; and a nervous, uneasy look is a warning. A sick fowl often drinks to excess, especially when attacked by cholera; but again at other times, it refuses both food and drink. Sometimes a hen will go moping about with drooping wings, with no other signs of sickness. Whenever the comb, however, does not show a bright scarlet, and the fowl is not lively, it should be examined and treated immediately. Delay is dangerous with fowls, and sickness among them is hard to eradicate if not driven off early. A fowl may suffer from a want of certain food which it cannot get in confinement, and unless gratified will show signs of sickness. For this reason, often a change of food will effect a cure.

CHOLERA.

This name is given to a disorder of obscure origin and character, which has proved itself to be one of the most rapidly destructive known to poultry keepers. It is by far the most common in the South and West, where also it is most fatal, but it has often appeared in the eastern states, and is now becoming very common. The causes of the disease do not need to be detailed here at any great length. Anything that tends to lower the constitutional vigor of the fowl will render it liable to an accession of this disease. Unwholesome food, impure and stagnant water as a drink, exposure to the weather or to the depressing heat of the sun without shade, all of these causes increase the liability of the fowl to this disease, as well as to many others. The more active and restless birds are first attacked, although no age is exempt. On damp and clay soil the disease is more prevalent than on sandy or gravel soil. Very large and high fed fowls soon fall victims.

Among the causes most prominent in fostering the disease is, an over-crowded condition of the coops, and allowing them to become very filthy. In the first place, such a condition of things is directly depressing to the fowls. In the second place, the bad air makes good soil for the development of poisonous "germs." Cholera has been known, however, to attack flocks that are not kept in houses at all. Such cases can be explained by the fact that fowls thus kept are generally badly protected from the weather. Cholera seems to be most prevalent in very hot and in very dry seasons. It is infectious, but the infection does not seem to travel far. Fowls roosting near fowls sick with cholera catch it, but whether from them or their droppings does not appear. Dr. Solmon says, it is only infectious or contagious through the discharges, or by eating portions of those that have died with the disease, or by eating flies, worms or other insects that contain the blood of the diseased ones.

Observers of eminence are of the opinion that it depends on a special poison, which comes into the fowl from without; that this special poison first affects the blood, and that the deteriorated blood produces the changes in the liver, and so forth, which constitute the disease. It is called cholera, because, as in the Asiatic cholera of the human race, it is accompanied by much diarrhea, is very fatal, and attacks many individuals at a time, but yet it is altogether a different disease. The name cholera, to which we have become well accustomed, is probably as good as any that can be devised. The organ most changed is the liver. This is found enlarged, dark green, full of dark blood, congested and usually very tender; it can be very easily crushed in the hand. The gizzard is soft, and sometimes much smaller than natural, and contains half digested food. The crop and intestines are often full of sour, fermenting food, and ulcerated. The coudition of the liver is the main thing to be noted. Of course, you will find the brain, nerves and lungs more or less congested, full or darker blood than usual, and the heart, perhaps, enlarged. The liver is not only the organ the most changed, but seems to be the first attacked. It comes suddenly; in some cases a fowl well to-day may be dead to-morrow, and a whole flock may be thus rapidly carried off.

The discharges at first are yellowish green, or "like sulphur and water," becoming thinner, greener and more frothy as the disease goes on. The breathing becomes heavy and fast, the crop fills with mucus and wind, the food is not digested, the eyes close, and in a few hours the fowl dies. There is weakness, sometimes extreme; the fowl may be unable to stand well, and have a general sleepy, moping appearance. There is much fever, great thirst, and a rapid, weak pulse.

Treatment: Use the medicine as directed on page 195 in English, or — in German. Separate the sick from the well ones, and thoroughly renovate, as far as practicable, the roosting places, by removing all the manure and hauling it away, and whitewashing the roosts and houses, and sprinkle the floor with copperas water and carbolic acid, or lime. I will not say this treatment will save all those that are attacked, which it often does, but I will say it will do more than nineteenth-twentyeths of all the treatments ever published or sold, and is easily used.

ROUP.

During damp weather the roup sometimes makes its appearance, even when the fowls have received the best care that can be bestowed. There are many forms of roup, and it becomes contagious in flocks when allowed its way unchecked; but the mild form is usually a cold, the symptoms being a stoppage of the nostrils, which gives the well known hoarse breathing, with the mouth opened. It sometimes appears also as a disease of the throat, and other times the eyes and head are affected, in all cases attended by general debility, loss of appetite and depressed spirits. The most essential object should be to separate the sick fowls from the others and remove them to a dry, warm location, feeding on soft, nutritious food.

THE AMERICAN SHEEP.

A TREATISE ON

Sheep Husbandry.

ITS PROFITABLENESS, WITH PRACTICAL INFORMATION AS TO BREEDING, REARING AND HANDLING, ALSO THE ORIGIN AND CHARACTERISTICS OF THE VARIOUS BREEDS, WITH SUGGESTIONS AS TO FEED AND CARE.

CHAPTER XV.

Treatise on Sheep Husbandry.

SHEEP HUSBANDRY.—WHY WOOL GROWERS DO NOT FAIL.—INFORMATION AS TO BREEDING.—REARING AND HANDLING.—ORIGIN AND CHARACTERISTICS OF THE DIFFERENT BREEDS.—SUGGESTIONS AS TO FEEDING AND CARE.

SHEEP HUSBANDRY.

Sheep husbandry in the United States is becoming one of the great pursuits of this country. In former years the entire interest in raising sheep was for the wool clip, but of late years the production of mutton has been given some attention. The Americans still give more attention to the production of wool than mutton, while in England the reverse is the case. This is only a natural result of the different conditions of the markets and surroundings. England is the best mutton market in the world, while wool commands the best prices in the United States. That these conditions will change is not a matter of very much doubt, especially in the east, and near large cities, where there is a demand for mutton, and especially lambs, but still the time has not come yet, when mutton sheep are as profitable in this country as in England. The American demand now seems to be for a sheep which grows the finest fleece on a medium carcass, producing both wool and mutton. Wool must be, for some time to come, of at least equal importance with mutton; and in many portions of the country, from necessity, in the far west, away from the meat raising markets, the wool must be the main object.

With this business, as with any other, the question is often asked, Does sheep raising pay? Judging from the reports as given from all parts of the country one year with another, it is very doubtful if the breeding and raising of any other stock pays as well for the capital invested, as that of raising sheep. Mutton, it is claimed, by the aid of a good fleece, should be raised cheaper on the high-priced lands of the Eastern States than beef on the cheap lands of the far West. While in the far West, where sheep are raised on a larger scale upon the cheap lands, it is claimed they pay one hundred per cent. upon the capital invested.

If these claims are true, and no doubt they are, sheep husbandry is without question profitable.

WHY WOOL GROWERS DO NOT FAIL.

Another question which is often asked, is why wool growers do not fail, as other business men do; and is answered by a wool grower: "Simply because the growth of wool and increase is as perpetual as the times in which they live. It matters not how dark the night is, the wool continues to grow; and it matters not how the wind blows, or how it may storm, gestation is never longer than one hundred and fifty days. The lambs will average one-half females, and often twins, and they breed the next year, making "double-compound," a perpetual growth, and no loss. Everything that does not go into market goes to enrich pastures. Though the landlord may be sick, it does not stop the growth of the wool and lambs. Not so with other business. The merchant, mechanic, or the man who works for a salary, has nothing to grow while he sleeps. When his labor ceases his income stops, and his expenses are perpetual. It is true there are perpetual expenses attending the sheep business, but under the most unfavorable circumstances, where they can live on the cheap grass lands without feeding, the meat of the wethers will pay all expenses, without drawing on the wool or increase of the ewes. Hence it is like a perpetual stream, flowing into a basin. It is only a question of time about filling it to overflowing. The great drawback seems to be that men do not relish living away from thickly populated settlements and towns, depriving themselves of society, for the sake of making money. This objection can be obviated in all new countries. There are villages constantly springing up, near which good sheep farms can be had, where the owner can visit his flock daily, and also give his family the benefit of schools and society. There are many such now on the plains, and one is reminded of the patriarchal days, for there is no lack of society in the shepherds and in the family, and the long summer day and evenings are pleasant. In short, the way to success and happiness is to build up an independent civilization. To a man of energy and some means, such a life is pleasant and attractive. It is hard to answer the common inquiry as to what the profits of the business are. As much depends upon the individual care and management as in any other business, but I am safe in saying one hundred per cent. per annum, net profit, is realized by wool-growers that make a permanent business of it. Many intelligent wool-growers are of the opinion that should wool yield only twenty cents per pound they would have a more pleasant, certain and remunerative business than any other branch of agriculture in these United States."

Taking the judgment of those who follow the business, there is no doubt but that sheep husbandry, judiciously and scientifically followed, is one of the best paying pursuits of the American people, and especially with the general farmer who is engaged in mixed husbandry.

Sheep are especially suited to the small farmer, and to the farmer of limited means, on account of the small amount of capital and limited range necessary to provide for a small flock.

And it is a well known fact that, with the keeping of sheep, the land does not deteriorate, but its fertility is constantly increased. So that on lands which have been used as sheep walks, when a crop of any kind of grain is desired, a marked increase is invariably noticed, as sheep distribute their droppings more evenly than cattle, and on the highest ground—where they are most needed.

Again sheep are closer feeders than any other farm stock and great foragers, consuming a greater variety of food than any other stock; thus often proving beneficial as well as profitable in reclaiming an old farm, or one which is covered over with briers, and it will pay well to purchase a flock of sheep to aid in subduing them.

A comparison was made by Linnæus, the naturalist, as to what kind of stock ate the greatest variety of forage. He found; The horse ate 274 species of ordinary forage plants, and rejected 212; cattle ate 276, and rejected 218; while sheep ate 387 species, and refused but 141. The value of the different foods for sheep is a matter of no small amount, and one on which the success of the flocks depends more than on any other in the far West or elsewhere, when kept in large numbers. In the present state of the flock industry every experiment looking towards the cheapness of foods should be eagerly welcomed, and no doubt the fodder, sorghum, root, and millet crops will play an important part in furnishing this cheap food. Two sheep can be raised where one is raised now, if judiciously cared for, and shepherds would do well to try, on a small scale at least, the crops mentioned, and alfalfa besides. But in attempting to cheapen the cost of rearing the flock, the wool and the carcass should not be forgotten, but let them be steadily improved each year.

Sheep breeding and wool growing are arts which allow of no half way measures; but the whole attention of the breeder must be given to the management and care of his flock, if he expects the highest success.

INFORMATION AS TO BREEDING.

In breeding sheep, as with other stock, every one should be governed somewhat as to their situation. The eastern farmer, or those living near large cities, where they have the advantage of a good meat market, can no doubt make the production of mutton more profitable than that of wool, or the farmer who keeps a few sheep can give them better attention than where large flocks are kept; and perhaps those farmers who cannot well keep large numbers could handle the mutton breeds to better advantage. They require just such treatment as these farmers are best prepared to give them.

The papers from different sections state that the consumption of mutton has increased greatly of late. Is not this due, to a great extent, to the improved quality of the mutton? If so, cannot the demand be much further stimulated by feeding the people on better mutton still?

The English sheep breeders pay more attention to mutton than wool. If we, in this country, would follow their example, we would hear no more clamoring about the tariff on wool. It is bad enough to fear Australia, with thousands of miles between her shores and ours, but the difficulty lies in our failure to realize all that is possible from the sheep industry, and our failure of breeding a better mutton sheep, and striving in which to select and grade up the quality. The Oxfords, Shropshires, Hampshires and Southdowns are becoming numerous, and are as far superior to the scrubs as an electric light is to a tallow candle. Not only do they possess size, but certain characteristics that improve the quality of the carcass and enable the breeder to secure a higher price for excellence, as well as for greater profit for weight.

It is not altogether the weight that breeders must consider, though weight is a very desirable matter. We wish, in our markets, better mutton, of a juicy, marbled, attractive quality, that commands a sale as soon as it arrives, and which will always be in demand. Such mutton is as easily produced as that which is inferior, and we are safe in guaranteeing a heavier fleece also. The lambs from the improved breeds, or grades, are also more saleable than those from natives, to say nothing of their rapid growth and heavy weights at an early age. We have alluded to this subject for the purpose of advising the farmers to endeavor to raise better mutton, for by so doing they can laugh to scorn the tariff, and derive a larger revenue in a single season from mutton than they can from wool in twice that length of time.

THE COUPLING SEASON.

"Where the highest type of perfection of offspring is desired, the condition surrounding their begettal needs to be looked after as carefully as those necessary to their proper and rapid development after birth. As a rule, it is not good policy to allow rams to run with the flock during the coupling season. When so allowed, all control over the crosses is surrendered. The heavier and more pugnacious rams soon become masters of the situation, though not without much injury to themselves, as well as their weaker antagonists. Rams that have quietly lived together all the previous season, will be found no exception to his rule, when turned with a flock of ewes during the rutting time. Add to this the further act that much vigor is expended by repeated service of the same ewe, and but little experience is required to predict an offspring lacking in some of the characteristics of lambs begotten under more favorable conditions. When but one ram is to be used, and the service required of him quite limited —say not more than twenty-five ewes—the lazy man's policy of "turning in" may find some excuse; but then only with the understanding that he is separated from the flock during the night, that both ewes and ram may have the rest requisite to a proper discharge of their reproductive functions. We are aware that a different course is generally pursued—the exception being found among those breeding high-priced animals—but are satisfied that it is so pursued at a loss to flock-masters in delaying the building up of a thrifty and profitable flock."

SELECTING A RAM.

A sheep grower gives the following points in selecting a ram: "Every discreet shepherd who is about to purchase a ram, seeks these three desiderata: First, the maximum wool with the minimum of yolk. Second, the greatest amount of muscle done up in the least wrapping of skin. Third, an animal that will reproduce himself the greatest amount of times, i. e., constitution, wool, mutton. In a humid climate one dare not concede a single point in constitution. Unless the flock master has personal knowledge of the animal's exceptional vigor, he should demand a good barrel, ribs well sprung out, eyes large and prominent, and square rump, body coupled up rather short, ears thick and soft, and they and the face covered with fine, white, silky hair. But in the skin resides the surest test. I have known a ram to have nearly all the above points and yet be delicate; but I never knew one having a bright, rosy skin to be lacking in robustness."

THE EWES.

The ewes should be bred so as to have the lambs come as early in the season as possible, so they can be saved; better lose two in the spring than one in the fall. As the ewes near parturition they should be well fed, with an occasional feed of laxative food, roots, or oil meal and bran. They should be provided with shelter during lambing time; and so arranged that they can be kept warm at cold times. In case they have any difficulty in lambing, they should not be assisted for at least a few hours, but let nature alone. When any assistance is given, let it be with caution and gentleness. In case of any trouble or sicknes, see veterinary department.

After lambing a ewe should not move about much. If she is weak, give her some good whisky or whisky gruel. If her teats are closed against the efforts of the lamb, try and squeeze them out with the wetted fingers; or in case they have grown shut, open them with a knitting needle, being careful not to insert the needle too far. If they are inflamed, bathe with some cooling lotion, and hold her while the lamb nurses. If she disowns the lamb, or is wanted to adopt another, shut her up with the lamb away from the other sheep, and hold her while it nurses. Bathe her nose and the lamb's with whisky, which will sometimes bring her to terms.

THE LAMBS.

New born lambs that can help themselves should not be interfered with. If so weak they cannot stand, they should be held up to nurse, and in case the ewe has no milk, use a nursing bottle with a gum nipple; these are now sold by dealers, and should be kept in readiness for use. The milk of the cow, fresh and warm, is just right for the lamb. It should be given often, but too much should not be given at a time. If the lamb be chilled by the cold, it should be taken in the house to the fire and cared for, by warming and feeding it. When quite weak give it milk and a little whisky, which will soon restore it.

In castrating lambs, there are two methods used. I have seen both performed with good success. Neither one is difficult, and can be done by any farmer. The first is, to cut off the lower end of the scrotum, press the testicles upward and make an incision in the inner skin and thus remove them, the same as is done with a pig. The other plan is, after removing the end of the scrotum as usual, seize the testicles with a pair of pincers, and remove them by a quick jerk, without cutting the inner skin. This is thought by some to be the best method that can be used.

WEANING LAMBS.

They should be weaned at four months of age, and put on a good piece of fresh grass. In absence of this, or when a rapid growth is desired, they should be fed on green fodder, roots or grain, so as to keep them growing fast until matured. This is the great secret of raising sheep or other stock—early maturity. As cold weather approaches, they should be sheltered and well cared for.

THE MUTTON BREEDS.

The improved mutton breeds which have found most favor in the United States, are of the long or middle wool. Of the former, the Leicesters, Cotswolds, and New Oxfordshires; of the latter, the Southdowns, Hampshires and Shropshires. The Leicester sheep are unexcelled in earliness of maturity, and none make better returns for the amount of food consumed than they do, but they require better shelter and care than any other variety. The ewes are neither so prolific, nor so good nurses, as those of other mutton families, and the lambs are delicate and hard to raise. The mutton is only medium in quality, owing to the great amount of fat. The fleeces are composed of a long combing wool, and average with select flocks, about ten pounds each.

THE COTSWOLDS.

The Cotswolds are a larger, hardier and more prolific sheep than the Leicester, and the ewes are better mothers; their wool is valuable for combing use, but the fleece is no heavier than that of the Leicester, but their mutton is far superior, as it is not so fat, and the fat is better intermixed with the lean meat. They are much used in crossing other breeds and varieties, and are decidedly the favorite long wool sheep of America. The Lincolns are as large as the Cotswold, though in other respects, as now bred, very strongly resemble the Leicester; but the fleece is longer and heavier, and unsurpassed in luster, commanding, therefore, the best prices in the market.

THE SOUTHDOWNS.

The Southdowns are the oldest established short-wooled, improved mutton variety. In size they rank with the Cotswold, but have a lighter fleece. Their mutton is very choice, and commands a better price than that of any other breed. They are hardy, good feeders, and excellent nurses.

THE HAMPSHIRE-DOWNS.

This family is the result of a cross between the Southdowns and a long-wooled English variety of greater size, and better constitution. They are coarser than the Southdowns, but possess nearly all the good qualities of that breed and are hardier, and the mutton commands a good price. The Shropshire was also produced by a cross of the Southdowns with a hardy short-wooled stock; and some have a dip of the Leicester and Cotswold blood. They are large, and unite to an uncommon degree the good qualities of the short and long wools. This mutton is of good quality, and the ewes prolific and good mothers. The Oxford-downs are a comparatively new family, and are a cross between the Hampshires, Southdowns or Shropshires, and their characteristics are about the same as the Shropshires, though they vary some in their appearance and quality.

THE MERINO.

The American Merino is a descendent of the old Spanish or French Merinos, judiciously crossed and bred almost exclusively for the production of wool. They are a small, compact, hardy breed, with a very dense fleece, shearing some eight pounds per head, of a short, oily wool. The Merino is well adapted to be kept in large numbers upon the plains, or rough, poor land. They are great walkers, traveling a long ways for food, and are freer of disease than the larger mutton breeds. Almost all sheep demand for their health dry land, but with the Merino, dry land is indispensable. There may be wet land in their range, but they must not be confined to it. They will thrive on less feed than other breeds, and can travel further to obtain it. Hence they are well suited for all countries where sheep raising is done on a large scale. The ewes are very prolific, good sucklers, and the lambs hardy. The Merino, on account of its density of fleece, with which it is well protected, and its hardiness in constitution can stand more exposure than other breeds. The

Merino cannot be matured under three years; this makes it necessary that this breed must always remain a large producer of wool, and any course of breeding tending to lessen the fleece is a move in the downward direction. A noted breeder says he believes that the continual use of smooth, long-wool rams was contrary to the correct principles of breeding, and always resulted disastrously, and what sheep-breeders had yet to learn was that they needed density of fleece, more than length of staple. Mutton sheep, to do well, require richer soils than the Merino, and those yielding regular and good food, but they most all do better on a rich upland than on low land.

What constitutes a good sheep? This is a very important question, yet perhaps no one could give an answer which would be satisfactory to all sheep breeders. One breeder admires size and symmetry, another desires to breed a medium sheep—good for mutton, with medium fleece—while another cares nothing for the carcass, as long as he can grow a fine fleece of the greatest weight. A sheep adapted to every section and to every breeder's surroundings cannot be grown in the same animal, so that a description of a breed which would be one man's ideal, perhaps, would be entirely unsuitable to any other man or his surroundings.

A good cross is obtained, when early maturing lambs or size is wanted, by using a cotswold buck, or a buck of either of the down breeds, with Merino, or common ewes. The fecundity and excellent nursing qualities of these ewes give them the first place in breeding for early lambs; or a common flock of sheep can be bred up to a great improvement, by the use of a pure buck of the characteristics desired, and the best ewes of that cross retained and bred to another good buck of the same breed.

A COTSWOLD RAM.

The realization of profit does not always depend upon immediate results. The breeding of a common flock to a profitable basis requires some time and means; but the end should be more carefully kept in view than immediate profit. The flock should be carefully sorted each year, and nothing but the best retained for breeding purposes. Sometimes large prices can be obtained by letting a dealer take the pick of the flock, but this would be worse than folly, and would ruin the prospects for years to come. The flock should be graded up to a high standard, even at considerable cost; and it should be remembered that the choice of the flock which has been bred so carefully for years, is worth more to the owner than anyone else.

In breeding, it is always best to give both the subject and the flock some study, and learn exactly what class of wool your flock now clips, and what kind would pay you best to raise—then breed for this type alone. This is very important in securing an even clip of wool of average quality. This, of course, cannot be done in one season. But by carefully selecting the breeding flock and using a ram of the same type of wool, in a short time the flock can be bred up to such a point of excellence that their fleeces will be uniform in quality and difficult to tell one from another. Until such is the case, as long as in sorting each fleece has to be thrown into a separate pile, or as long as a mongrel clip is raised, just so long will the wool have to be sold at a disadvantage.

SUGGESTIONS AS TO FEEDING AND CARE.

Good shelter, as well as food and water, is indispensable for sheep in the winter time. Their feed should be composed of a variety of foods. Hay, corn-fodder, corn, oats, mill-feed and roots, intermixed and given regularly.

In growing sheep, the first requisite is an intelligent shepherd, the second good sheep, and third good care, including good feeding. This states in few words all there is in sheep-growing; but those unversed in the matter would be surprised to find out just how much intelligence and skill, how much care and feed, and how much capital is invested, in rearing a fine flock to produce profitable results. The spring is the time when sheep require the most careful attention, and is also the season in which, as a rule, there is the greatest mortality among them. At this season the sheep are weakened in vitality by the long winter's cold and storms, and their system is not able to withstand the climatical changes which occur at this time; and unless very carefully tended they must succomb in their weak and debilitated state, to the inevitable. The sheep now should have an increase of grain food, and their feed be changed, and some kind given them which will tempt the appetite. The weak ones should be put by themselves and receive extra care.

In turning sheep out to grass in the spring, it should be done only an hour or two during the day at first. In this way they are not so liable to scour, as the change from dry to green food is less sudden. If they do scour when turned upon grass, feed some corn and bran dry, which will check it.

The sheep should be prepared for the summer by being tagged in early spring, before being turned on grass, their feet trimmed, and the animals carefully watched, that maggots do not get on them and destroy them. One principal argument for early shearing is that it obviates all danger of trouble with these dangerous pests of the flock. Nothing is more conducive to the welfare of the flocks than just such management as will always keep the sheep comfortable, thrifty and in good health. If this is done nothing more is needed to insure the highest condition and profitableness of that flock according to its grade. It is important that the flocks be carefully sorted, and the weak sheep not allowed to run with the stronger ones. Sheep of different ages and conditions should be sorted into separate flocks, and the weaker ones have a little extra feed. Old sheep ought to be in a lot by themselves, so as to take time to eat their feed, like old men and women take more time to eat. Feed a half bushel of grain morning and evening, to fifty head; this is enough in one lot to feed right and do well.

In culling out the flocks in the spring, about as good disposal as can be made of the culls is to fatten them on grass. The sheep can be fattened very rapidly, as well as cheaply, on good grass, with the aid of some grain twice a day, and the local butchers will, as a rule, pay a fair price for such muttons. Dispose of all the yearling underlings. The reason for parting with yearling underlings is this: They are liable to breed disease among the flock, and nothing should be retained unsightly to the eye of the flock-master. The more evenly sheep are graded, the more evenly will they thrive.

The day has gone by when a man's flocks will be estimated and valued by their numbers. Henceforth it will be the income that each sheep will yield that will determine the value of the flocks, whether it be in wool or mutton. Therefore keep none but the best.

Good sheep require good care to maintain their excellence, or they will soon deteriorate.

Do not undertake to keep sheep on low, undrained lands. They will surely contract disease, and a sick sheep is about as mean a thing as I know of, a sick hog not excepted.

There is nothing more injurious to a sheep than to lie on a fermenting manure pile. Therefore keep them well bedded. They, of all stock, must have dry and comfortable quarters.

The sheep is exceedingly neat and even fastidious about its food and drink, and hence should have clean grass and clear running water. Though they use less water than other animals, often passing whole days without it, it is none the less necessary for their comfort and health that it should be accessible.

Salt regularly twice a week, or keep rock salt where they will have free access to it. It is essential to their health. It has been proven by actual experiment that beets or turnips can be raised, lifted and stored for six cents per bushel. At this cost they certainly are a profitable food for sheep, and any one who has not tried raising and feeding turnips to sheep cannot have a full appreciation of the benefit derived from this cheap food, and in the increased thrift of their stock. There can be no doubt of the advantage of the English method of feeding compared with ours, if we compare their immense fat muttons with ours; and in all the feeding districts of the English provinces turnips are fed in immense quantities.

Good corn fodder is an excellent sheep feed. It is loosening, cooling, and relieves constipation. Also early made, properly cured and stored hay, either clover, timothy, or millet, is far superior to matured hay for sheep.

Frequently the agricultural papers advise farmers to pasture their orchards with sheep. Any one having the least practical knowledge of the nature of sheep knows that they would rather peel a nice, thrifty young apple tree any day than eat the most tender grass, and that they will even peel quite large trees. Therefore, they should never have access to the orchard. A change of pasture is good for sheep, but medium short grass, on high or dry land, suits them best. In the fall, if the pasture fails, do not put off feeding them hay or grain too late, unless a good crop of pelts is wanted in the spring.

CARE OF SHEEP—THINGS TO BE REMEMBERED.

First, keep sheep dry under foot with litter. This is more necessary than roofing them. Never let them stand or lie in mud or water. Second, take up lamb bucks early in the summer, and keep until December following, when they may be turned out. Third, count every day, and if any are missing hunt them up and see what ails them. If any sheep is hurt, catch it at once and wash the wound; and if it is fly-time, apply spirits of turpentine daily, or wash with a solution of carbolic acid. If a limb is broken, bind it with splinters tightly, loosening as the limb swells and bath with arnica. Fourth, keep a number of good bells on the sheep, as they are a protection against dogs.

Fifth, begin graining with the greatest care, and use small quantities at first. Feed grain, if you have to sell half the sheep to pay for grain for the other half. Sixth, separate all weak, thin or sick from the strong in the fall, and give them special care. Have some rye for weak ones in cold weather, if possible, and be sure to get it. Seventh, never let the sheep spoil wool with chaff or burs. Remember that burs in the wool are removed only by machinery, and therefore reduce its value. Cut away the weeds that produce burs. Eighth, if a ewe loses her lamb, milk her daily for a few days, mixing a little alum with her salt. Ninth, have the lambs come as early as possible, so they can be saved. The early lambs require more attention than late ones; but when fine fat lambs are finished in time to meet the early market, it is doubtful whether any other kind of stock pays better. Tenth, give the lambs a little mill-feed in time of weaning. In preparing them for market, keep in mind that the more fleshy and fat they can be made, the better prices they will command. This is, in reality, much more important than extreme size. Eleventh, let no hogs eat with the sheep in the spring, by any means. Twelfth, never frighten sheep, if possible to avoid it, and kill all the dogs that bother them, your own not excepted. Thirteenth, cut tag-locks in early spring, which will prevent foulness or maggots. Fourteenth, for scours, give ginger and powdered charcoal in wheat bran; prevent by taking great care in changing dry for green food. Fifteenth, if one is lame, examine the foot; clean out between the hoofs, if unsound, and apply tobacco with blue vitriol boiled in a little water, and never buy lame sheep and bring them on the farm, as by this means foot-rot is spread. Sixteenth, shear at once any sheep beginning to shed its wool unless the weather is too severe, and save carefully the pelt of any that die. Seventeenth, the wool business is not likely to be overdone in this country, as we do not now supply our demands, and the market will increase as rapidly as the supply. Eighteenth, the crossing of the long wools and Merinos cannot be done without sacrificing the fineness and combing qualities of the fleece. Wool is a commodity—a manufactured article, which requires the highest intelligence and skill in the production of a fine article. Nineteenth, have at least one good work on sheep, to which you can refer, as in this progressive age, no one can make the raising of stock a success without some study.

THE AMERICAN CATTLE.

A TREATISE ON

THE CATTLE INDUSTRY

OF AMERICA,

CONSISTING OF A DESCRIPTION OF THE VARIOUS BREEDS, AND INFORMATION AS TO BREEDING, GROWING AND FEEDING; ALSO THE MOST APPROVED MODERN METHODS OF DAIRYING.

CHAPTER XVI.

The American Cattle Industry.

THE CATTLE INDUSTRY.—VARIOUS BREEDS.—FAMOUS COWS AND STEERS.—HOW TO SELECT BREEDERS.—VALUABLE BREEDING, GROWING AND FEEDING SUGGESTIONS.—MANAGEMENT OF BULL, COWS AND CALVES.

THE CATTLE INDUSTRY.

The growing of cattle in North America has become one of the great live stock industries of the world. The congeniality of the climate, as well as the soil in most all parts of North America, are such as to produce abundance of grass and feed, and thereby render the growing of cattle profitable; and the last few years has shown a great increase in this industry. Not only has the natural increase of population, and the advance of civilization greatly increased the production of cattle, but men of immense fortunes, both in America and foreign countries, have embarked in the business of raising cattle in large numbers upon the vast plains of the West, for the production of beef; and now herds of one, or even ten thousand head, are of no uncommon occurence. Following this great increase of the production of cattle, naturally has come the introduction of the strains of good blood, and now America is well represented with large and numerous herds of pure bred cattle of all the improved breeds, namely, the Short-Horns, Herefords, Polled Angus, Galloways, Red Polled, and Devons, which represent the beef breeds; while the Holsteins, Jerseys, Gurnseys and Ayrshires, represent the dairy breeds. The characteristics of all these cattle are such as to well adapt them to the wants of the American people, when pure bred, or crossed upon our native stock. The most of these cattle are too well known to demand any special description or comment, but I will give a brief description of each breed, as to their origin and characteristics, for the benefit of those who may not be well acquainted with them, and who may be contemplating the purchase of some of the new breeds.

THE SHORT-HORNS.

The Short-Horns are one of the oldest and best established improved breeds of cattle known. They first originated in England, and were known as the Teeswater, or Durham cattle. Charles and Robert Colling were the first and most successful breeders of these most famous cattle, commencing about one hundred years ago. The bull Hubback, the founder of the breed, was purchased in 1785, by Charles Colling, at a low price, and was raised by a poor man upon the highway. He was of medium size, compact form, admiral touch, and of a yellowish red color. He was so easily fatted that he soon became useless as a bull. This bull was bred to the cows owned by the Collings, and later an infusion of the Galloway blood was introduced in their herd. This progeny was inter-bred until 1810, when they had succeeded in forming a very fine breed of cattle. "Messrs. Bates, Booth, and other breeders of England, have done a great deal to improve this fashionable breed of cattle, and in 1850 Mr. Bates sold the Dutches family, part of which were calves, for an average price of $581, and in 1853,

THE SHORT-HORN.

Lord Ducies' herd averaged $760, for sixty-two head. Since, individuals of superior excellence, have been sold at fabulous prices." As now bred, the improved Short-Horn is less in height, broader, more compact, and heavier than of former days. In color, they vary from snow white to cherry red, though the red and white, or roans, predominating. They are easily kept, fatten readily at any age, and obtain as great a weight, at any age, as any other breed. They are heavier milkers than any other beef breeds, and very valuable to cross into the native cattle. The public sales of Short-Horns that occur nowadays bring forcibly to one's mind the fact that the day of fancy-priced Short-Horns is at an end. "It was only a few years ago when, at the New York Mills sale, one cow realized $40,000. Another of the same herd was taken to England for Lord Bective at about $30,000. This was in 1873, but $20,000 and $35,000 respectively were paid for two heifers at Windermere six years ago. At the Dunmore sale, in 1875, $22,500 was paid for a bull, and the same year in Toronto a Duchess heifer less than six months old brought $18,000. In 1876, a pair of Duchesses realized $21,000 and $23,000 respectively. In 1879, at Dunmore, two Duchesses were bought at about $15,000 apiece by Sir Henry Allsopp, and their progeny came into the ring in good form at one of the recent sales, but failed to realize any of the above named fancy prices."

The price of finely-bred Short-Horns, however, are very far from what they used to be, but this does not prove any real practical decadence in the Short-Horn breeding interests. Short-Horns are as good as they ever were, and the fact that the Duchesses no longer bring such fabulous prices only indicates that the excellence of the race has become more generally distributed, and that as a whole Short-Horns are now of more real practical value than they were in the olden times, and the prices that they command at public and even private sales now-days, put them within the reach of all enterprising farmers.

THE HEREFORDS.

The Hereford cattle are also an English breed, and in their characteristics resemble the Short-Horns very much. They are uniform in color, being a light red, with white or mottled face and breast, belly and feet. Their horns are longer than any other improved breed of cattle except the Devons; hair soft, silky and curly, showing them to be a breed of great vitality. They are fully as compact and heavy as the Short-Horns, and less in height. They are noted for being quick maturers and great rustlers, and have become quite fashionable of late years in America, to improve our native cattle.

ABERDEEN—POLLED ANGUS.

This is another breed of cattle that has become very fashionable of late years, and has been heavily introduced into America. They are of Scotch descent; have no horns; very compactly made; about the size of the Herefords, and covered with a heavy coat of curly, black hair. As quick maturers and rustlers, they have no superiors, and should prove very valuable upon the plains, as well as with the general farmer.

THE GALLOWAYS

Are of the same origin as the Angus, and resemble them very much, except that they are some rougher in form, more slow to mature, and have a more curly coat of hair. Hon. Wm. M'Combie, of Tillyfour, Scotland, was the chief founder of the black polled cattle. His name was no more inseparably linked with the fame of the polled cattle of Scotland than is that of the Collings with Shorthorns, or of Tompkins with the white faces of Herefordshire.

The red polled cattle are also of foreign descent, and resemble the Angus very much. They are said to be good handlers, quick maturers, and good milkers. They are of good height and smooth, but not as compact as the Angus, and covered with a smooth, red coat of hair. Any of these polled breeds are said to be very hardy, and can endure a great amount of cold and exposure, and thrive upon a more scanty fare than the Short-Horns or the Herefords.

HOLSTEIN—HOLLAND, OR FRIESIAN CATTLE.

These cattle were originated in Germany, and are one of the oldest improved breeds known, but have not been introduced into America very much until of late years. They are now becoming very fashionable, and are considered the leading dairy cattle for milk and cheese. In color, they are black and white spotted; not as compact and smooth as the Short-Horn, Hereford, or Angus cattle, nor as well adapted for beef, although they are as large, but far superior to them for the dairy, and are thus very valuable.

The Devons are an old English breed, and are very valuable for a rough, rugged country. They are a dark red, compactly made, active breed of cattle, hardy and quick to mature; good milkers, and the steers make the best of oxen. In size, they are smaller than the above named breeds.

ALDERNEYS—JERSEYS—GURNSEYS.

These cattle were originated on the British Channel Islands of the same names. While they vary somewhat in color from a light fawn, or squirrel, to a pale red, and also in size, yet their charateristics are about the same, as they are emphatically butter breeds. They are more noted for the quality of their milk than for the quantity, it being very rich; and the butter for its rich, golden color, hardness of texture and nutty flavor. The laws under which they are bred in their native homes are very strict, and well enforced, in order to preserve the breeds in their pure state.

The Jerseys have had quite a boom in America in the last two years, and many have been sold at long prices, their chief value being in the large amount of butter they are capable of producing. As a cow for the wealthy class in a city, or for those making butter for that class of people, they are valuable; but for the dairy, where milk is sold, or for the general farmer, they are of but little use.

The Ayrshire cattle originated in Scotland, and were bred exclusively for the dairy. They are a compact breed, in size and characteristics resembling the Devons, but are heavier milkers, and of a brown, or brown and white color. They, or the Gurnseys have more size, and are better adapted to the wants of the general farmer as a dairy cow than the Alderneys or Jerseys. But as a cross upon the native cow for the production of a cow for the general farmer's use, there is probably no breed equal to the Short-Horns, although some of the other breeds are highly recommended, especially the Holsteins, or Angus cattle.

NOTED COWS AND STEERS.

The famous Jersey cow, "Mary Anne of St. Lamberts" was dropped March 26th, 1879. Mary Anne of St. Lambert produced 36 pounds 12¼ ounces of mar-

THE HEREFORD.

ketable butter in seven days in the fall of 1884. The test was made in accordance with the rigid rules laid down by the American Jersey Cattle Club, and there can be no doubt as to its thorough accuracy and reliability. In the seven days covered by the test, this cow gave 245 pounds of milk, an average of 35 pounds per day; 36 pounds being the largest and 32½ the smallest yield in any one day.

The cow was fed by the manager at his discretion, and he informs us that at the beginning of the test she was eating thirty-five imperial quarts of feed per day, consisting of the following:—Twenty quarts ground oats, ten quarts pea-meal, three quarts ground oil-cake, two quarts wheat bran, and that this was increased up to about fifty quarts per day, the composition of the above food being varied. She was also fed a small quantity of roots and cabbages, and a few apples, and kept in a small pasture in company with another cow.

"Eurotus," a Jersey cow, was dropped in 1871. From the milk, given in one year from this cow, 778 pounds of butter were made.

The Holstein cow, "Mercedes," was dropped in 1878, and died in 1884. This celebrated cow ranked among the heavy milkers of the breed she represented, and from the milk she gave in thirty days, 99 pounds and 6½ ounces of butter were made, eclipsing all competitors in that length of time for the production of butter. The well known cow, "Aegis," with a milk record in one year of 16,824 pounds, was fourth in the list of milk records, the heaviest being 18,120 pounds, 18,005 pounds and 17,746 pounds. The cows with these records are all of one family.

It can be seen by this that great results can be produced by careful breeding, care and feeding.

At the fat stock show in Chicago, Illinois, in 1884, the Aberdeen Angus steers, "Waterside Jock" and "Black Prince," showed the merits of this breed as beef cattle by winning some of the principal prizes. "Water Side Jock" was nine hundred and ninety-nine days old, weighing 1,815 pounds, and won the first prize as a two year old on the block. "Black Prince" was three years old, weighing 2,300 pounds, and won first prize in his class on foot.

At the same time and place the cross-bred steer "Roan Boy," by a Hereford bull, and out of a Short-Horn cow, won some of the principal prizes, including the silver pitcher, given by the Breeders' Gazette for the best fat steer of any age or breed.

THE MONSTER STEER.

Probably the largest steer ever known or exhibited in America, was on exhibition in 1885, by J. R. McGregory, of Ripley, Ohio. He was a fair mountain of flesh, and could be compared to no other animal, except an elephant. He was dropped in Decatur county, Indiana, in 1879, being now six years old, and weighing 4,250 pounds. The author had the pleasure of examining this steer on the 22d of May, 1885, in Circleville, Ohio, where he was on exhibition. Mr. McGregory, at that time, was exhibiting him and a small Teeswater, or Currey cow, only thirty-four inches high, and weighing three hundred and fifty pounds, in the cities and towns of Ohio. The steer was a rich roan, and measured six feet and four inches in height, eleven feet and four inches around the girth, three feet and four inches between the hip joints, and eighteen feet

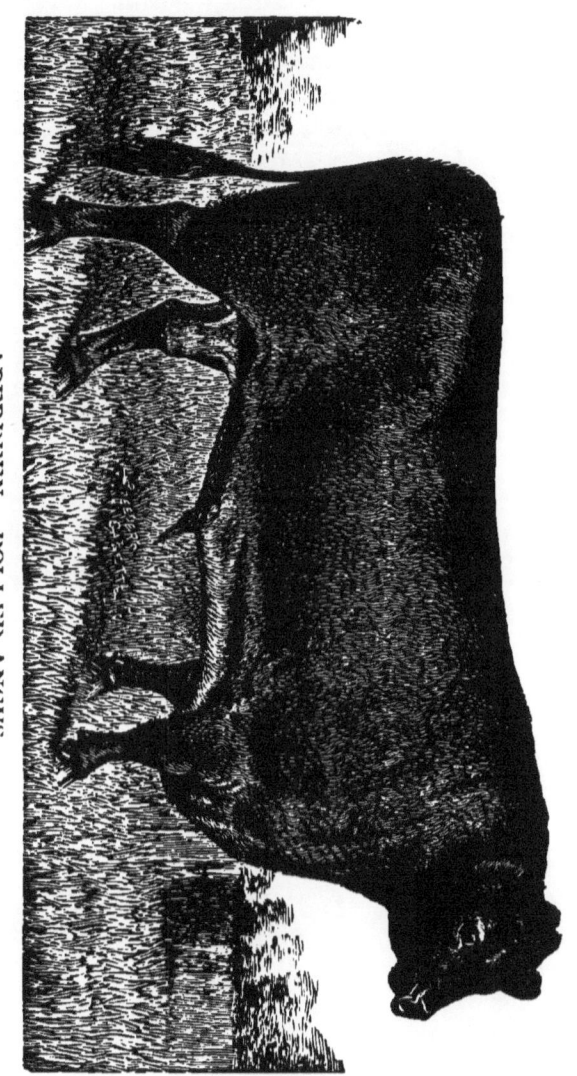
ABERDEEN—POLLED ANGUS.

from tip to tip. He was consuming one bushel of corn, sixty pounds of hay, and from eighteen to twenty gallons of water daily. He was said to be about three-fourths Short-Horn, with a good sprinkling of the blood known as the Seventeens, which he showed very much in the head and neck, also from the shoulder to flank. He was very fine in the brisket and rump, wide, straight back, well sprung ribs, and had good, strong, clean, bony legs, that would carry all the flesh, that could be put on him. He was only in moderate flesh, and was very active. The little cow was giving some two gallons of milk a day, and was very much admired. She was a dark red, and compactly made, which is characteristic of the breed.

As said before, this is supposed to be the heaviest steer on record, although there has been several heavy steers spoken of within the last twenty-five years weighing from 3,500 to 4,000 pounds, and all were composed of the Short-Horn blood, and generally a goodly sprinkling of the Seventeens.

HOW TO SELECT BREEDERS.

In the selections of cattle as breeders, as much care and judgment must be used as in selecting breeders of any other stock. The characteristics desired should be strongly marked with the animal, as would show beyond doubt that they should transmit those characteristics to their progeny, let that be beef or milk. Unless for some good reason, an animal of a certain color is wanted, I would say with them, as with swine, do not "hanker" too much on the color; better discard the color than any other good point. Any of our pure breeds are true enough to their color, but quality is the first and most essential point. Frequently at public sales of Short-Horns, a first-class roan animal is offered, and the knowing ones will whisper around that it has a cross of the Seventeens in it. That was an importation of Short-Horn cattle made in 1817, and known under that name. They were not thought to be strictly pure bred, and frequently will sell at a low price, as compared to a dark red one that may have been sold before it. But any farmer who wishes a good animal as a producer of stockers, had much better risk that one than a cherry red one, that may have a cross of Devon in it. One of the most essential points in any breeding animal is constitution. This, with cattle, is observed by a good coat of soft, silky hair, mellow hide, well sprung ribs, being good around the heart, with a strong, clean cut, neck and head, and a brilliant eye. Animals possessed of these qualifications, of either sex, and a clean, bony leg, are most always vigorous and good handlers. Other good points are a broad, straight back, prominent hind-quarters, well let down to the hock on a straight leg, full, deep barrel of medium length, with a full frisket and medium shoulder. The shoulder and the head with a bull should be more prominent than with a cow, and also the horns—if they have any, but either one should have a slim, bony tail.

THE CONTROLLING INFLUENCE.

The common accepted theory is, that the male parent has the greatest influence upon the offsprings in outward form, etc., while the female exercises a controlling influence on the vital functions. This cannot always be relied upon in practice, but is a very safe rule to be governed by. Therefore, in the selections of breeders, it is best to keep in the mind's eye the characteristics desired in the progeny, and select accordingly. If beef is the desired quality, select those of a large, compact form, that show by good handling that they are capable of making a rapid growth and maturing quick. If milk is the desired quality, select females that are prominent in the milk producing points, such as a prominent udder and milk veins, heavy hind quarters, a full deep barrel, wedge-shaped shoulders, slim neck and clean cut head. In selecting a bull he should be purely bred, of whatever breed be desired, and strongly possess, as said before, the characteristics desired in the progeny, and if his ancestors were possessed of the same characteristics, he is all the more valuable. Very often a good breeding old bull can be purchased for considerable less than a young bull, and the risks to obtain the desired results are much less. These points serve to emphasize the truth that nothing is so trustworthy an assurance that a given animal will be valuable as a breeder as the fact that it has produced good offspring in the past. In view of this, the high esteem in which young and untried animals are often held is not well founded.

HANDLING STOCK.

The term "handling stock" is a technical one, more particularly applied to cattle than other domestic animals, but a practical knowledge of it, even in sheep and swine, is considered important in this country, as well as in England, by all breeders, and is thus described: "In order for visitors to judge better of the quality of the animals submitted to their inspection, I think it is important that they should know what handling is; and although it is difficult to define in words, I will make the attempt, at the same time suggesting to every one who has not a practical knowledge of it to get some person who has, to give him lessons direct from the animals he is inspecting before him. It is this: When the fingers are moderately pressed upon the fleshy parts of an animal, and the hair, hide, and especially the flesh beneath have a fine, soft, elastic spring, it is called good handling; on the contrary, if they are coarse, thick, hard, and rigid to the feeling, with little or no spring under the pressure of the fingers, that is called bad handling. Of course there are as many degrees in handling, from very bad to very good, as there are grades of animals. The better an animal handles, the quicker it feeds—that is, the sooner it will mature and become fully grown for the purpose of breeding, or to fat for the butcher, and a good handler will do this at a much less consumption of food than a bad one."

BREEDING FROM SHOW HERDS DANGEROUS.

Inexperienced breeders cannot be too often warned against purchasing breeding stock at public sales and elsewhere that have been fed and pampered for the show-yard. In the height of the Short Horn speculation it did not make much difference; then barren show cows were carried from place to place, and appeared first in one breeder's catalogue and then another's, until they finally drifted out of the current and were stranded high and dry in the hands of some unsophisticated outsider, where they were never again heard from. Experienced persons steer clear of these show-yard animals, or at least will not buy them without a distinct and specific warranty that they are breeders; and it will be well for all who buy at public sales, made up mainly of old show herds, to follow their example. If these cattle fail to breed, they are worth simply what they will bring for beef, and no more; and the purchaser should have a distinct understanding to that effect before he makes a bid upon an animal old enough to breed, that does not show for itself. Breeders who offer stock that has been, in the main, bred and raised by themselves on their own farm, are not much troubled with barrenness in their cows, and when such cases occur they are usually sent to the shambles at once; but showyard animals, and those that have again and again been fitted up for the auction block, are so frequently made barren by the high feeding and forcing to which they have been subjected, as to put every experienced man on his guard when such animals are offered.

THE SCIENCE OF INBREEDING.

Although inbreeding is strongly condemned as ruinous to the vigor of stock, yet it is an admitted fact that animals produced by inbreeding transmit their qualities more prominently than do those that are the result of careful selection from different strains. Inbreeding as practiced on some farms is not done under the guidance or direction of the farmer, but in a careless and irregular manner. Inbreeding is a science, and demands the most careful judgment, as it permits of no middle ground whatever. Its tendency is either to improve or deteriorate the stock. Without inbreeding we would not be favored with many of our choicest and most popular breeds, as all of them have been established by a persistent inbreeding in order to fix the characteristics desired. Lord Western, in his effort to make a superior breed of hogs, resorted to but a single out-cross upon the Essex, which prompted him to use the Neapolitan as an admirable animal with which to blend the proper proportions of lean and fat, and even this out-cross may not be considered as such, the Neapolitan being really one of the original breeds upon which the experiments were begun. It was only by a judicious selection of the strongest and most vigorous of the herd that success was attained. Had the herd been left to breed in-and-in without a guide to assist in the selection of the best, the Essex hog would have passed out of existence long ago. Later on, however, even careful selection could not prevent the breed from gradually becoming enfeebled and weak, when the Berkshire, itself a closely inbred hog, was used to infuse new blood, and the process of inbreeding was again persisted in until at the present day we have a perfectly black hog without a white spot of any kind, which breeds true to color and stamps its features and merits on all its offspring.

The Jersey cattle are all closely inbred. But few pedigrees can be traced that do not run into one or two progenators of the whole, and our best butter strains are all descended from a single family. The rule of late years has been to select for breeding purposes only cows that have made records for butter production, they being closely inbred for that purpose. The surprise is that such animals maintain their constitutional vigor, but, happily for the breeders, the test of butter production is also the test of vigor, as the best cows are those that are vigorous and capable of digesting and assimilating sufficient material with which to accomplish the purposes desired; yet, with all the care that may be exercised in the matter of selection, the animals that prove superior are few as compared with the number that are not so fortunate. The results of inbreeding may be plainly noticed by even the most casual observer, in the delicate shape and structure of all Jersey cattle.

Nor can the horses be said to be exempt. Breeding

close into the Messenger blood, through Hambletonian, has certainly increased the speed of our trotters, and admitting that the instinct of trotting has been more firmly impressed, and yet there is a much larger proportion of failures compared with the success attained, if we consider the fact that the number of the whole is a hundred times greater than that of a quarter of a century ago. The form of the trotter, as well as that of the thoroughbred, shows plainly the work of inbreeding, for while the spirit and will force have been increased, it has required an occasional infusion of new blood (not, however, altogether foreign) to retain the stamina so essential to the roadsters.

One of the mistakes of inbreeding is the infusion of new blood through the male line. It should be through the female line only, as mistakes may be more easily corrected. The sire may improve or damage a whole herd or flock, while the dam is limited to the production of a single animal, and should she prove undesirable may be easily supplanted by a substitute, which is not so easily done in the male line. The breeder, however, is the one who really prevents injury, for a knowledge of his work permits him to study the characteristics of each animal from its birth to maturity, which affords him ample opportunity to lay out his plans with a definite purpose in view. Thus, in the hands of a skillful person, inbreeding is, at times, an advantage and a science, but if not done judiciously, it is hurtful and baneful."

STOCK RAISING THE MOST PROFITABLE.

There is no pursuit on the farm that affords greater pleasure or gives such sure profits as raising stock or operating a dairy. Not only is the produce of the farm more easily marketed when fed to the stock, but the fact of converting it into meat, milk or butter enhances its value and increases the profits in proportion to the labor expended. There is another feature in stock raising, and one of the most important, which is that the farm becomes richer every year. Therefore, when computing the actual profits obtained, we should calculate and enter into the account the value of the improvement made upon the farm.

The greater the number of animals that can be comfortably kept upon the farm the better. The more stock, the greater the fertility of the soil, and, hence, the larger the crops each succeeding year, which in turn permits of a still larger number of animals. And in raising stock the matter of improvement is a prime factor in the enterprise. Good feeding is important, but good feed gives the best results when good stock only receives it. The breed and the trough are twin essentials, and cannot be separated without loss. Fill the trough full, but let it be emptied by animals that are capable of converting the contents into the largest quantity of available product. There should be no waste of food nor loss of time. Use the most perfect animal to be found, if not too costly, for crossing on common stock, and thus grade up. Pure breeds, of course, are best, but if the foundation must be laid on common stock, make it a point never to use a mongrel sire. Aim to improve the stock, and the stock will improve the farm. The task is an easy one, but requires some little attention to succeed.

For profitableness we look to the animal as a machine We know that in almost every line of industry machines are constantly being replaced by others that can turn out from the raw material a larger percentage of manufactured product. In just the same way, if it is desired to produce meat, the old native animal should be replaced by Short-Horns, Herefords, or some of the other beef producing breeds, or their grades as greatly superior and more economical meat-making machines. If for the dairy, by the introduction of the Holsteins, Gurnseys, Ayshires or Jerseys, good results will be obtained. It is foolishness—it is financial stupidity—to keep and feed a scrawny, scrub steer or cow in these days of Short-Horns, Herefords, Gurnseys, Jerseys, Ayrshires, etc. Good grades can be had anyway, and at prices not above the reach of ordinary farmers. Farmers can at least secure a few good native cows, and from a good bull get good grade stock.

The two rules given are not based on theory alone. Their soundness has been demonstrated in practice, but they are not so widely adopted as they should be. There is an astounding number of scrub animals in existence to-day, racing along the road in summer, and shivering under straw stacks in the winter, which, the sooner they are abolished and replaced with good stock, the better it will be for the owner.

GROWING OR FEEDING CATTLE.

The growing of cattle, like the growing of any other stock, to be profitable, should be well conducted from birth during all seasons of the year, and the one successful principle of stock feeding kept in view; that is, to feed liberally from birth until the animal is disposed of. The proverb "well summered is half wintered," however true, is no more so than it is reversed—well wintered is half summered. Properly summed up, both propositions but amount to this: there is no time when the stock owner can permit his stock to deteriorate the thrift without inviting loss, and quite often, disaster. The beginner who expects to find any time during the year when his vigilance as an overseer, and liberality as a provider, can be relaxed without detriment to his stock, will have such delusion thumped out of him by the costly cudgel of experience, if he fails to heed in time the warnings of those who have come up through tribulations they would have him avoid, that he will wish that he had looked more closely after them during both summer and winter. It is poor economy to allow animals to run down during the fall, expecting to winter them well, or during the winter months, expecting that in the spring, when grass comes, they will recover and grow the same as if they had not been stinted.

Cattle may live and get through the winter on cornfodder and straw, but generally it will take much of the spring and summer to recover what is lost. Instead of being ready for market at two years, they must be kept longer, in order to make a slow growth.

We cannot reasonably expect stock to thrive in the best manner without grain during the winter. The amount, of course, depends upon the quality of the other feed. The best guide is their condition. They must not under any circumstances be allowed to run down. It costs too much to regain what is lost. I am aware that the old custom was to keep cattle until they were three or four, and even five years old. Hogs were not expected to have attained sufficient growth to fatten until they were from eighteen months to two years old. Of course improved stock has considerable to do with early maturity, but not all. Good stock, in order to grow, must be well fed. It is as easy a matter to stunt a full-blooded animal as a scrub, and good feed from the start will aid wonderfully in bringing out a scrub.

Experience has taught us that in order to receive the most profit, we must push stock right along. Give them a start to grow, and then keep it up by good feeding and good care. During the winter, as often as possible, give them a change, as they soon tire of one kind of feed, and a change is beneficial. Generally corn is the main reliance, and as a whole it is one of the best, if not the best stock feed we have. Yet with all this in its favor, a change to something else is better.

Good shelter will save feed, and if one must economize in feeding, do it by providing warm shelter. Not only will stock be in a better condition, but less feed will be required to keep them growing. The principal secret in profitable stock raising and feeding is to keep the animals growing, and yet to do it with the least possible expense.

Cleanliness should not be overlooked. To thrive well stock must have clean quarters, and when confined during the winter this requires work; but it will pay. See that they have plenty of litter, and that their quarters are kept as clean as possible. Where one has no barn room, very good shelter can be made by erecting rough sheds or wind breaks. Often this can be done with very little expense, and no difference how rough the structure is, so it breaks the wind off. The building of two high fences close together and filled in with straw or prairie hay, rough sheds erected and covered with the same material, or a hedge fence banked up with the same, will answer much better than nothing at all These structures should surround a high, dry piece of ground, and then the corn fodder fed on as small a scope of ground as possible, so as to form litter enough for dry bedding. Providing shelter for stock, simply as a question of economy in the consumption of food, cannot be considered in any sense an undue pampering calculated to render animals less hardy, or to detract, in the least, from their constitutional vigor. On the contrary, we believe suitable shelter, to which stock can resort in case of storms, will tend to promote these very qualities. An animal can, perhaps, endure the full force of a regular blizzard, but it is only at the expense of a certain amount of vital force, which must leave it in a worse condition than an animal which has not been called upon to endure this strain. There is much of the time when it makes but little difference whether an animal has shelter or not. In clear, cold, dry weather, healthy live stock appear to be in a large degree insensible to ordinary extremes of temperature; but the snows cccompanied or followed by winds which sift it into the hair, where it slowly melts from the effect of animal heat, tell very severely upon the condition of the stock. We have often observed that the storms coming late in the season or toward spring, when snows are damp and often mingled with rain, are more deleterious than those of midwinter. When the hair is damp or wet there is a constant evaporation of moisture which robs the animal of the natural heat and puts its powers of endurance to the severest test; and animals that have been subjected to all sorts of extremes and exposure during the whole winter, approach the close of the season, the most critical period of all, with depleted strength and vigor, and in the worst possible condition to withstand the severer trials which are then before them. As has been before suggested, it is not necessary that permanent or expensive structures be provided, but if nothing else can be afforded, poles and straw make a shelter very good while it lasts.

When possible, all fodders should be fed in racks and thus avoid wast. Some use a long manger, others a rack of some style. The way to form a very good rack is to set four fence post in a square twelve feet apart, board up all around three feet high, as for a fence, then place a center post and run boards diagonal from one corner to another each way, thus forming four three-cornered racks, in which to put the feed. This can be made and set down, and then moved when so desired. Again, cattle should be salted regular twice a week, or rock salt placed in a trough where they can have free access to it, which is much better, as then they will only take a small amount at a time, and more frequently.

WATER FOR STOCK DURING WINTER.

See also that the animals have a good supply of water, and not half ice. It is often the case that a large proportion of Western farmers make very poor provision for supplying their stock with water during the winter. Springs that afford a supply of water that is moderately warm are scarce, and few of these that exist are utilized to the extent they should be. Generally the water for the supply of farm stock is procured from a well in or near the farm yard, and is raised by means of a hand pump. The water is often nearly at the point of freezing when it is drawn, and is ordinarily conveyed into a trough that is lined with ice. Animals that drink the water suffer severely from cold. It is often the case that there is but one trough in the yard for the accommodation of a large number of horses, cattle and sheep of different ages. It is generally surrounded by ice on which the animals are likely to slip or receive injuries. The younger animals suffer most because they are hooked or pushed by those that are older and stronger. During very severe weather many farmers allow stock to have access to water only once a day, and as a consequence they drink so much that they suffer from cold produced by taking so large an amount of water into the system at once.

If practicable, stock should be supplied during the winter with water furnished from a spring, as it is generally several degrees warmer than that drawn from a well. The well should be covered, as should be the trough into which the water is conveyed. The practice of bringing water into barns and stables has given excellent satisfaction wherever it has been introduced. When it is not practicable to convey water into the buildings where stock is kept, a trough for holding it should be under sheds, and surrounded by a special platform that can be kept free from ice and snow. Young stock should be allowed an opportunity to drink while the animals that are liable to molest them are out of their way. In severely cold weather it is better to carry water in buckets to colts and calves than to allow them to suffer the exposure necessary to obtain it in an open yard. Unless during storms of long continuance, animals should have an opportunity to obtain water at least twice a day. If their only food is dry hay, straw, and corn fodder, they require considerable water in order to digest their food properly.

THE CARE OF THE BULL.

A bull should be confined in a well-fenced grass lot, away from the cows or other stock, and when wanted for service, the cows should be turned into the lot to him, as they are more easily got in and out of the lot, than he is to get back in the lot, when once out; and if not allowed out at all, he is not as liable to become breachy. Again, if he is allowed to run with the cows he is liable to become cross and troublesome to other stock, and will also exhaust himself by unnecessary service. In this lot should be a stable for his use at all times of the year, and his feed should consist of a mixture of corn, oats, millfeed, cut feed, hay and corn fodder, in the winter, and in the summer, if not used too heavy, plenty of good grass is sufficient, but where being used for a large number of cows, they should have some grain, and some method to provide him with plenty of fresh water at all times, should be arranged.

CARE OF COWS AND CALVES.

Cows, to be profitable, should not be neglected, and allowed to become poor at any time of the year; for no neglected, delapidated or run-down cow, can ever be profitable to her owner. No matter what they are kept for, beef, butter, milk or the raising of calves, the profits will depend upon their thrift, and when well fed and cared for, they pay cash down, and ask no trust. In the summer they should have an abundance of grass, and where their range is small, and the grass not sufficient to support them, fresh grass or provender of some kind should be mowed every day, and given them, or in absence of this, grain. In the winter, plenty of good food and shelter is necessary if any profits are to be derived from them, and the warmer and more comfortable they are kept, the less food they will require, and the better will be the profits obtained from them.

The philosophy of keeping animals warm and quiet is simply this: Part of the food animals consume is used just to keep the machine running. It is only the surplus above this that can be used for production of meat or milk. Now the percentage of food used in running the animal machine depends upon circumstances. The animal that is just warm enough and quiet enough to be comfortable and healthy uses much less food in maintaining the animal body than one that is exercised violently and is kept cold. It takes food to maintain muscular activity, and food must also be used as fuel to keep the animal warm. The colder the room, the more the fire is needed. It is possible, as now can be seen, for the warm, quiet animal to obtain a surplus for production from a ration that would just maintain the animal kept in the cold and in a less quiet condition. Does it pay to leave a window open in the room where we sit, and then burn twice as much coal as is necessary in order to keep warm? Does it pay to burn an unnecessary amount of hay and grain in order to keep animals warm?

It seems to me that it is much better to provide shelter for them, and save the feed. The man who does not study and seek to understand the requirements of his farm stock and their care, should never be a farmer. A farmer must have the well-being of his animals constantly in mind; and not only that, but their comfort ought to be of as much importance to him as his own. Not only ought this to be looked at from a dollars and cents standpoint, but from a humane one also. A man who has not enough humanity to make his stock comfortable, without any other consideration, is not a typical farmer.

Cows not well cared for cannot be expected to give much milk either for the dairy or their calves, or do well upon dropping their calves. A great many cows annually die thus, by neglect.

IMPROPER MILKING.

Again, many farmers milk their cows too near the time of calving, and a great many good milkers are injured by this hurtful practice. The physical welfare of both cow and calf, together with the quantity and quality of the milk, are materially affected by thus overtaxing her, and she should be allowed to reach the time of calving in the best condition possible. A cow should go dry at least six weeks, in order to gain flesh and strength before calving, and when not on grass, should be fed with a good milk producing food, as mill feed, oats, clover hay, malt and roots. Thus properly fed and cared for, the cow will be strong and able to nourish the calf and provide plenty of milk for it after birth. Cows that are heavy milkers should be looked after for some time after calving, and see if the calf takes all the milk; if not, she should be milked clean twice a day, until the calf is able to take all the milk, or it is taken from her. Some cows, when on good pasture, or well fed, require milking before calving, as well as afterwards, and should be closely looked after and cared for; for if neglected, they frequently are troubled with garget, or milk fever, which is very injurious to them, if not the cause of their death. The cows on the farm that are not pleasant and profitable to milk should be turned out with their calves, as soon as the calf is able to take all the milk and let run. This will pay better than to worry with such animals. When it is desired to make a cow own two calves and raise them, sprinkle the calves with salt. The cow will lick this off, and a repetition a time or two will often secure a permanent recognition of the calf.

WHEN CALVES ARE REMOVED.

When the cows are expected to be milked, the calves should be taken from them when three days old, or even younger, as at this age they are easier taught to drink, and then the cows do not fret after them so much. They should be put in a grass lot, or warm stable, according to the season, away from the cows, and fed for a few days, new milk, or new and sweet skimmed milk mixed, until a week or two old, when the skimmed milk will be sufficient. As they become older, mill feed and oil meal can be added to their feed with good results. One gallon of sweet skimmed, or even sour milk, made hot, and a quart of mill feed with a gill of oil cake stirred into it, then cooled to blood heat, and given a calf, will produce about as good results as fresh milk. Feed can be prepared in this way for a number of calves and put in a trough, and it will not require a very great amount of teaching to have them drink in that way. As they become older this feed can be increased, or else fed some dry mill feed and oats, crushed corn, fodder, pumpkins, etc., as the season may afford. Where pasture is plentiful, and calves are fed in this way, it is more profitable to keep the calves than to sell them to the butchers. Many a farmer has found himself a hundred dollars richer, without missing the cost, by keeping calves instead of sending them away, and as a general thing, if properly conducted, it is more profitable to feed the milk to the calves or pigs than to make fifteen cent butter. In weaning the calves, when fed in this way, or when they have been running with the cows, they should be fed some other good feed in the place of the milk, and kept growing right along, and not allowed to become poor and stunted; and as they increase in size and age, increase the strength and bulk of the feed, never forgetting that the road to success in stock raising is through early maturity. When calves are not intended for any other use than beef, they should be castrated at an early age—from one to four months.

THE FIRST YEAR OF A CALF.

There is not a farmer in the country who raises his own calves but who knows that the future value of them depends upon the first year's growth as a calf. If the calf is half starved, stunted and ill-used, there is not one chance in ten that when it reaches the proper age it will make a good animal, either beef, bull, or milch cow. The calf must have the very best of food and enough of it if the object is to make the matured animal a first-rate one, and indeed it is necessary, too, that with yearlings and two-year olds, attention should be given in such a manner as to insure the animal plenty of food.

A calf that is intended for a bull, in order to make a first-class animal, should run with the cow till he is six months old at least. If weaned earlier, feed on new milk just from the cow three times a day till he is six months old, then twice a day till eight months old, then once a day for a month or so longer. At an early day, say a month old, if not on grass, give him a little fine hay to pull at, and later let him have some oatmeal, a little oil-cake, vegetables, etc., increasing the rations gradually as he grows older. Weaning from milk should be gradual and in pasture time. Teach him to lead at as early an age as possible, and ring his nose at eight months, and handle him from that time on daily. After he is weaned feed as you would other cattle, to keep them in the best condition. Often a young bull treated in this way will show his superiority before maturity, and sell for a better price. In leading him, do not handle him too much by the ring. Put on a head halter, run the stub through the ring, then the pull will come more direct upon the head than the nose, and still have perfect control of him. Use him kindly; any abuse in any way only irritates him, and makes him afraid and cross, while kindness insures success. After he has become older and more self willed, use a bull staff, with which to handle him. When twelve or fourteen months old, he can be allowed to serve a few cows, but he should not go to more than two a week, and should be well cared for as spoken of in the care of the bull.

In growing heifer calves for the dairy, the important thing to accomplish is to grow the frame and muscular system, without laying on much fat. It is a rangy, well developed animal, with a vigorous digestion, that is wanted in the milch cow. The profitable milch cow must be a large eater, and make the best use of her food, in order to produce a large yield of milk. In rearing the heifer, then, she should be so fed as to give her a full development of all the vital organs, and this will necessarily bring her digestive organs into special activity.

Fat in the animal body seems only designated to serve as a cushion to the tendons and joints, to fill up and round out depressions, and, lastly, as a reserve of fuel to keep up animal heat in case of necessity. It is not the seat of any sensation, has little or nothing to do with the vital processes, and generally is merely inert ballast in the body. The food given, then, should not be designed to lay on fat—food containing an excessive amount of starch or oil should be avoided in feeding heifer calves designed for the dairy—but food rich in albuminoids and the mineral constituents of the body, is what should be sought. Therefore, if the heifer calves are taken from the cows at an early age and properly raised by hand, the results are as good as if allowed to run with the cows, and furthermore, they become accustomed to being handled, and are rather fond of the presence of the keeper, an important feature with a milch cow. Kindness helps to create a quiet disposition, and this education must begin when the calf is young—any habits acquired when young, are apt to cling to the cow when grown.

HOW EARLY SHOULD HEIFERS HAVE CALVES?

There is a great difference in the practice of farmers in respect to how early heifers should have calves. For beef purposes, three years old is probably soon enough; but for a milker, I would have the heifer come in at two and one-half years old, or sooner. She is then old enough to become a cow. I would not, as a rule, allow her to go to farrow too long, but milk her up to within eight weeks of calving. A cow thus trained will give more milk and be more likely to hold out longer in milk, if her after care is judicious and liberal, as it should be. Such treatment tends to form the habit of giving milk, and, as we know, habit is a sort of second nature. To couple the heifer with a bull one or two years older than she is, is preferable to a yearling, and better stock is likely to come from such. After the heifer has come in, her feed should be regular and liberal. In absence of good grass or hay, we must make up for what is lacking in some concentrated feed, such as oat-meal, shorts, oil meal or the like, but great care and judgment must be used not to over-feed or crowd, as the future cow may be ruined. Undue forcing shortens the useful life of a cow very rapidly.

It is often the case when a heifer has her first calf that the farmer thinks she will not give more milk than will keep her calf in good condition, and lets them run together, to teach her the mysteries of being milked when she has her next calf. In this decision there are two mistakes that go far to spoil the cow for usefulness. Cows are largely creatures of habit, and with their first calf everything is new and strange to them, and they readily submit to being milked, and think it is all right; but suffer them to run with the calf the first season, and a vicious habit is established that they will hardly forget in a lifetime. If they ever submit to be milked quietly, it is evidently under protest. But there is a greater objection than this—the calf running with the cow draws the milk every hour or two, so that the milk vessels are not distended with milk, though the quantity secreted in a given time may be large. But this is the natural time to distend the milk ducts and expand the udder to a good capacity for holding milk. When, with her next calf, you require the milk to be retained twelve hours, the udder becomes hard and painful, and the milk leaks from the teats, or more likely nature accommodates the quantity of milk secreted to the capacity to retain it, and the cow becomes permanently a small milker, and very frequently learns the habit of holding up her milk. Much of the future character of a cow, therefore, depends upon her treatment with her first calf. Everything that disturbs the quietness of a cow, impairs the milk, both in quantity and quality. To obtain the best results, therefore, there should be a regular time and place of milking, and as far as possible the milking should be done by the same person. Any cow can be milked dry in a few weeks by irregular milking, at intervals of twenty-four hours, and sometimes six. Separation from her usual company, a change to a new location, a strange milker, and, above all, a blustering manner and a scolding voice, are sources of irritation that, more or less, impair the milking qualities of a cow. No cow under the influence of fear will give her full quantity of milk.

UNRULY MILKERS.

The habits that a great many cows form of holding up their milk, kicking or jumping, and running when being milked, are very annoying, and the "theories" of how to break them of these habits are " as plentiful as woodchucks in cherry time."

My experience in handling from thirty to fifty cows daily, in the dairy, for several years, proved to me that the suggestions given in papers by different ones as to the means for subduing these cows were only "theories." To lay a wet cloth or sand bag across their loins, or buckle a strap around them in order to make them give down their milk, or putting a chain to their leg, or some patent contrivance to keep them from kicking, are all in the mind's eye, as far as a cure is concerned. By such treatment they may be subdued for a short time, but it is only a matter of time until the old habit is renewed. My experience with such cows was this: Unless very valuable as milkers, or for the blood that was in them for breeders, I would fatten and sell them to the butcher. When they were valuable as milkers, I would shut them up in close quarters where they would be compelled to stand.

This takes less time than to run after them. Then if they kick or hold up their milk, change milkers. It is possible, very often, that a cow will object to one milker, but will immediately submit to another. Never abuse or speak harsh to them. Kindness will go a great way towards conquering them. When thus treated, and they will insist upon kicking, take a small rope, fasten one end in a snap; back of that eight inches, fasten a ring, by passing the rope through the ring and tying a knot in it; put the rope around the cow's right hind pastern, and fasten the snap in the ring. Now tie the rope to a ring or post back of her, pulling the foot back far enough just so the toe can rest on the ground. Thus fastened, she is compelled to stand quiet, and this will do more toward conquering her than abuse. When they will insist on holding up their milk, and cannot be subdued, I would keep them to raise calves, or fatten them.

As a farmer said, "A cow is a curious animal. Like some other females, she has a nerve and a mind of her own, and when she gets nervous or makes up her mind, she will have her own way all the time and every time. In her tricks of kicking or holding up her milk, for instance; a cow can never be beat out of it, if she has once learned it. And just look at her quietly and sidewise while you are vainly trying to get a drop of milk out of her udderful, and notice her very peculiar expression. She is looking at you out of the side of her eye, as much as to say, 'I guess you won't.'"

CHAPTER XVII.

Modern Methods of Dairying.

DAIRYING WITH PROFIT.—THE BEST DAIRY CATTLE.—HOW TO JUDGE A COW—NECESSITY OF STABLING COWS.—LESS VENTILATION AND MORE BEDDING.—HOW TO FEED AND MILK.—THE MOST APPROVED METHODS OF MAKING BUTTER.

DAIRYING WIHT PROFIT.

The dairyman of course wants to make his profits as large as possible. This requires earnest effort and close attention to the details of the business. The making of good butter and cheese, and the selling of good milk, are the first requisites in this undertaking. There are many instances throughout the country of farmers making a grade of butter which sells at fifty cents per pound and upwards the year round, and in active demand even at that, while their neighbors, with equal advantages, make a grade of butter which is hard to dispose of at fifteen cents per pound. Here is where the dairy business is injured, to a great extent, by the manufacture of so much mean, trashy butter, that it seriously affects the market and demand for the better grades. Another thing that must be looked into in making the dairy profitable, is to get a herd of cows suited to what is wanted of them; that is, a herd that will give a large quantity of milk, or a large yield of butter or cheese. The cow that is good for either one of these is scarcely ever as good for either of the others, unless it is for giving a large quantity of milk which will make a large yield of cheese; and consequently it is important that if a large yield of milk is what is wanted that butter cows are not kept, etc. The feed supplied should be adapted to milk secretion and to the secretion of the butter oils. If these points are attended to carefully, it would be of some advantage to the dairy interests.

THE BEST DAIRY CATTLE.

It would be very hard to say what breed of cattle is the most valuable for the farmer engaged in the dairy business. This would have to depend somewhat upon the situation, and the purpose for which they are used. The ideal general purpose cow, that is pictured out by some of the correspondents of several agricultural papers, will probably never be found; and certainly not among any one breed of cattle; but the farmer's cow should be well-bred, of large size, a good breeder, and give a generous quantity of rich milk.

THE HOLSTEIN.

The Holstein breed of cattle, now so popular as dairy cattle, are of Dutch or Holland origin, and are one of the oldest established breeds known, though their introduction into this country has been somewhat recent. They have, as is claimed, four merits: first, as great milk producers; second, as good cheese-makers, third, good for butter; and last, for beef. While not as great in general for butter as the Jerseys, their general excellence in these respects places them in the front, as a general purpose breed without any rival, except perhaps the Short-Horns.

In yield of milk they seem to be confessedly at the head. One cow is quoted with a record of one hundred and twelve pounds in one day; another with 18,004 pounds in one year, or nearly fifty pounds per day, which is said to be the greatest yield on record, and the Holstein cow Mercedes, is credited with the largest yield of butter in thirty days, making ninety-nine pounds, six and one-half ounces in that time. While we may not judge any breed of cattle by the merits of a few specimens, yet the Holsteins are undoubtedly great milkers.

The Ayrshire cow, owing to her docility, being very easily managed, is valuable; for dairy purposes, she is equal to any other cow of her size, but she is inferior to the larger breeds for feeding purposes.

The Jerseys and Gurnseys, and especially the former, for quantity and quality of butter, have no superiors. They stand upon the same platform as the thoroughbred horse. They are each bred for one special purpose: the thoroughbred horse to run, and the Jersey cow for butter. No improvement can be made with either one, for their purpose, by the infusion of other blood. But as said before, in keeping cows for the dairy, or to give milk and make butter, keep only the kind that will give the greatest quantity of your speciality—butter cows, if it is butter; and if it is milk, then keep cows of one of the milk breeds.

But no matter what breed you have, something further is necessary in order to reach the best success.

THE JERSEY.

A good cow can generally be produced by good feed and care. A $5,000 Jersey cow will do poorly for butter on the care and feed that many farmers give their animals.

HOW TO JUDGE A COW.

In selecting cows for the dairy, by close observation very often their character can be told by their countenance, and their quality by their appearance.

"Man is not the only animal which shows his character by his countenance. Nearly all kinds of live stock, and especially cattle and horses, have something significant in their facial expressions. Gentleness and docility on the one hand, and wildness and ferocity on the other, crop out almost unerringly in the cast of the eye, or the pose of the head. An expert horseman can nearly always interpret the disposition of a horse from a square look into his eyes. Experienced dairymen also discriminate largely in the choice of milking stock by their knowledge of live stock phisiognomy. The same thing is carried into the fat stock markets. Butchers will nearly always scrutinize the countenance of a bullock before purchasing, and we have often seen them turn away from a handsome beef because it had a "wicked eye," which unerringly presaged trouble in getting it from the yards, through the streets, to the shambles. Stock drivers will, when wanted to take charge of an animal, ask to see it, and after a momentary front view will consent or refuse with a promptness which shows confidence in their ability to judge in this way. A bullock will sometimes be avoided by several drivers in turn, and without connivance, too, because he has a villainous "phiz." One who accustoms himself to reading the faces of cattle can soon become so expert that he can with difficulty be entrapped into an error of judgment."

Having had considerable experience in handling stock, I have found the following description, as given by Mr. C. Bordwell, of how to judge a good cow, of value. As the character has a great deal to do with the cow, and we must judge that by her countenance, we will commence at the head, and first notice the eyes. Thse should be large and of a bright color, showing a mild disposition. "The muzzle should be rather large, but the head small and rather bony, with the face dished and wide between the eyes; horns rather small and amber color; ears small, thin and yellow; neck thin and long, with clean throat; neck will drop a little in front of shoulders, making what I call a ewe neck; shoulders sloping, not heavy, but lean or bony; back level, with good width of hips. The back-bone should be rough or loose-jointed. I consider this one of the best points. As you move your hand along the back the joints seem to be farther apart and open. Barrel broad and deep at the flank, with the back ribs wide apart. Rump long and rather wide; thighs long, thin and wide apart, with legs short and bone fine; hoofs rather long but small; milk veins large, and where they enter the body you can stick your fingers in. Udder well forward and well up behind, with four good large teats set square and wide apart. Udder soft and pliable, and not fleshy, so that when the milk is drawn the udder is nearly gone. Tail long and slim, with a good switch. Skin should be soft and yellow, and covered with a good coat of soft, silky hair. The cow filling the above description, or nearly so, I have always found a good one."

In buying a cow, find out for yourself if she is what you want. Don't take anybody's word for it. A mean cow is such an intolerable nuisance that many men, and sometimes other members of the family, are strongly tempted to strain a point in order to get rid of her.

If possible, when she is in milking condition, milk her yourself, or see her milked, and judge her by the milk. To find out whether any individual cow is a profitable member of the dairy herd or not, a separate account should be kept of her milk and butter. If no such pains are taken it is not easy to tell just what the worth of a doubtful milker is. The true policy is to throw out every one which does not yield a profit, and replace her with a better one. It costs just as much to feed a mean cow as a good one. "Better pay more for a good cow than accept a poor one for a gift," is a true saying with dairymen. A good cow is one that will make from ten to twelve pounds of butter a week for ten months in the year, or one that will give from ten to 12,000 lbs. of milk in the same length of time. A poor cow, such as is kept by the average farmer in nameless sections of the country, to my knowledge, will make from two to four pounds—average three—eight months in the year, and probably give in that time four thousand pounds of milk. New milk weighs eight pounds and eight ounces per gallon. The poor cow will require the same amount of food if kept up, as the good one, and therefore must be kept at a loss.

No man can afford to keep a poor cow for making butter or giving milk. The best thing that can be done where one is saddled with cows that make only four or five pounds of butter a week each, or give but twelve or fourteen gallons of milk each in that time, is to raise stock and feed for the shambles.

MILCH COWS SHOULD BE STABLED.

Mr. J. A. Smith, a Western dairyman, writing of the importance of feed and proper treatment of dairy cows, gives some excellent suggestions on this topic. He says that "dairymen are often surprised at the light weight of their milk next morning after a cold rain-storm, through which their cows have suffered unstabled, and it is only a natural result of such treatment. The cow does not eat as much, for one thing; and another is, part of what she does eat goes to repair the waste of her system in withstanding the effects of the storm, and that keeps a per cent. out of the milk-pail, until she has recovered from the effects of such exposure. It is also true that a cow affected by short feed or painful exposure not only loses in the quantity of her yield of milk, but in the amount of fatty matter it contains. In a word, nature has so organized the cow that she revenges herself on her owner's pocket, for cruel neglect and short feed; and a farmer might just as well try to dodge taxes and death, as to escape the unwise treatment of a cow. In point of fact, when thus treated, she takes the cream first, and gives the owner what skim milk she cannot assimilate. The only way to get a profit out of her is to fill her so full that she runs over, and take the surplus for your gold mine."

These suggestions show the necessity of stabling the cows, so they can be better fed and milked.

Milking in the barnyard is an old custom that should be abandoned. It is inconvenient and unclean. It should go with the wooden pail and hairy butter, and never be heard of any more; gone and forgotten, too. It is a wonder that any farmer would permit it, and still more a wonder that farmers' wives and daughters would consent to it.

It is just as easy, and far more convenient, for the milkers to put the cows in the stable all times of the year, at milking time, as it is to leave them out in a lot; for in this way they are rid of the cold and mud, or heat and flies, and can remain quiet while being milked, instead of being chased around through the mud and snow. It is no wonder that farmers' daughters want to marry some city chap, who does not keep cows. If I were one—well, never mind; just try to build a cow-stable, so that the cows can be put up at all times to be milked, or at least when it is necessary, during a hot or cold time, and then see if the girls, as well as the cows, will not be in a better humor.

There is a prejudice among many farmers against keeping cows tied up in the barn the greater part of even the wettest and coldest days. It is claimed that the animals will not be healthy unless they are allowed the freedom of the yard all day. I have seen herds of animals belonging to well-to-do farmers standing backed up to cold winter blasts, or vainly trying to obtain shelter from a storm. I have also seen cows, under the irritation of the cold, chasing one another around the yard during the greater part of the day, and cows giving milk, too. Now this is not a rare occurence. There are a great many days in the winter when stock should not be out of doors longer than to give opportunity to drink. Milkmen know that the flow of milk rises and falls in quantity as the temperature rises and falls during the winter season, unless the cows are so well sheltered and cared for that they do not feel the severity of the cold. The object in having a cow stable is not only to make it more convenient to milk, but to protect the cattle from cold and wet weather, as well as to aid the keeper to feed in the way that will be of the most benefit to the stock with the least expense of food. It is the care in feeding and keeping that gives the profit, and these points must all be kept in view when arranging a stable. No one can build a permanent cow stable without expense, but such a building will soon pay for the cost it will incur. If built, the merits will soon become evident. The owner will soon say that he cannot get along without it, and his only regrets will be that it was not built sooner. In building stables for cows, as well as for horses, there are so many different plans, that I will not attempt to give any; all that is required is to have them convenient, dry and clean.

"There is possibly no more repulsive sight than a cow-stable, in which dirty cattle are housed. It has been demonstrated that cows neglected in this respect fail to yield a perfect flow of milk, and it is reasonable to suppose that such is the case. The richest of food may be given to them, but if condition in the stalls is neglected they will not thrive. The foul odor of a filthy stable must necessarily permeate not only the animal's hide, but it has been proven that the meat of stall-fed steers, fattened under these circumstances, is unwholesome; moreover, the milk, even during the period of milking, is liable to absorb the filthy emanations from such stables, and to become absolutely poisonous. It would seem, therefore, reasonable, that owners and dealers in cattle and milk should appreciate the importance of cleanliness and it's relation to health, even as a source of profit."

EXTRA VENTILATION RARELY NECESSARY.

It is a rare thing to have a stable so tight that any extra ventilation is necessary. Where this is the case, ventilators should be so placed that there will be no cold drafts upon the animals. In order to insure this, they should be placed as far away as possible from the stock. In no case should they be placed on the windward side of a stable, but should connect, if possible, with another building to prevent draught, and one in which the air is somewhat tempered. The ingress and egress of air should be at opposite ends to insure circulation, and at the same time prevent a draught, which would be more likely when placed near each other. The ventilators should be few and small, and should be latticed, overlapping each other, which would prevent strong currents. There is but little danger if stables are daily well cleaned out, of the air ever becoming foul enough or close enough to injure stock. The necessity of ventilation is usually more of whim than a necessity. When a stable is cold enough to freeze, ventilators are never required. To my mind, cattle sleeping on ice or frozen chunks of manure, is a barbarism that a humane or economical farmer would not tolerate. One would suppose that the dreams of the farmer, tucked up in a feather-bed, on a winter night, while his cattle were obliged to rest on an icy floor among frozen manure, could not be very pleasant.

GOOD BEDDING NECESSARY.

It is economy to give the horse, cow and other stock housed through the winter, a good bed. It has much to do towards saving food and keeping stock in a thriving condition, to say nothing of the obligations man is under to provide well for the dumb animals for him given to have "dominion over." Better to give stock comfortable beds through the usual seasons of necessary shelter and stabling, as they can be provided with very little difficulty and expense. There is usually refuse fodder, sraw or other matter, which can be utilized and made into manure by this process. A large amount of the excrements, by this practice, which would otherwise be lost, can be saved. Fine sand makes a good bedding material and a good dressing for any heavy soil. Sawdust is another article which can be used advantageously for the same purpose. There is no farmer who cannot provide plenty of litter, of some kind for his stock, and this by all means he should do and will do, if he understands his business and consults his own interests.

HOW TO FEED AND MILK THEM.

Cows, in order to be profitable, must not only be generously and regularly fed, but their milking should be done at as regular hours as possible, winter and summer.

The cows don't have watches, but they know when business hours come around, and are fretful if the business don't go on. Their feed, of course, will depend upon the time of year. During the best of the grass season, they may not need much if any feed, but if stabled at milking time, it is best to give them some dry mill-feed, as it not only prevents them from scouring, but entices them in the stable. When the grass is scarce or begins to get hard, the mill-feed can be increased in quantity and quality, or else some fresh grass cut and put in the stable for them. The main object in feeding summer or winter is to give a variety, at least enough of a change so that they will not get tired of any one kind. Corn is the great fat-producer, and should be mixed with the winter feed, but if crushed or ground, and mixed with cut hay and steamed, or fed wet, it is better than if fed whole. A rich fodder, as clover hay, needs less meal, while a poorer one, like straw or corn fodder, needs more. Cattle that are being fattened should also receive more meal than the heavy milkers. The feeder himself must regulate the amount given. He should be able to feed each individual one of the herd the quantity and quality necessary, and so keep them thriving by giving enough, but not too much.

To aid in mixing their feed, there should be a large trough close to the hay cutter. This trough should also have a sheet-iron bottom, and be fixed for heating or cooking, if wanted for that purpose. It takes but little additional expense to have the apparatus fixed for cooking. When so arranged small potatoes, turnips, pumpkins, and mangolds can be used to their best advantage. They are far more easily digested when cooked and do cattle more good. These and mill feed, barley or malt, mixed with cut clover hay or sheaf oats, form the best of milk producing food, and it is considered settled that the quality of milk is controlled by the quality of the food. How important it is then, to give to the cows none but the best and purest food. With no other stock is this so essential, for the reason that it has been fully demonstrated by competent authorities that the milk is a very prolific source of transmitting disease germs from impure food, and especially from impure water. Pure water—and no other kind should be tolerated under any circumstances—should be supplied to the cows, all they will drink, three times a day.

In feeding cows for milk it is a common practice to give each cow a pailful of water in which liberal quantity of bran has been stirred. This produces a large flow of milk, especially if the water is warm, but it is a big chore to feed a large number of cattle in this way. The importance of water requires that it should be handy, and a good plan is to have a tub or trough so arranged at the well as to protect it from frost in the winter; this filled with fresh well water and a liberal amount of bran and a little salt stirred in it, will help to promote a great flow of milk. A rapid, expert milker, who is at the same time kind and considerate to the cow, can also do much to increase the yield of milk. Slow milking of cows never secures the full product. The cow becomes tired of relaxing the udder muscles, and after a time resumes the more natural position of contracting them. This makes much stripping necessary, and a slow milker will never have patience to strip a long time. Partial milking soon dries the cow, and greatly reduces her value.

Always treat your cows kindly, have quiet attendants,

feed well, milk quickly and cleanly. Discharge all help that are noisy, or that would strike a cow.

In driving the cows, never hurry them; as when their udders are full of milk, or they are heavy with calf, it is very likely to do them permanent injury.

Besides the suggestions already given I will say that the way to make money in dairying is to keep the best cows, give them first-class treatment, use the best methods of cheese or butter making, and keep your eye on the market. Don't keep a poor milker, and seldom sell your best cows. The best cow for the dairy is not necessarily a thoroughbred; it is the one that yields the most milk or butter.

"While I do not wish to lay a straw in the way of progress of fine dairy cow breeders, and while I admit the excellence of the Jersey, Ayrshire and Holstein, yet I do protest against the constant revilement of our native cows. No animal on the farm is treated worse. Struggling among ragweeds in almost grassless pastures, furnishing blood for flies in the blazing heat of mid-summer, the effect of wrath, hail, snow, sleet, rain and polar winds, she still survives, ever patient and returning good for evil. If our abused native cow was treated half so well as her foreign cousin, perhaps she would be as famous as they."

MAKING BUTTER.

In making butter remember that it is all important to suit the tastes of your customer. Let your taste be subordinate to theirs.

In packing butter for the various markets, or furnishing it direct to customers, it should be salted and put up in packages to meet with favor.

"One of the first essentials to a good package of butter is the use of a pure dairy salt, free from any injurious ingredients, and one that will retain the flavor and good-keeping qualities of the butter. The use of poor salt, perhaps more than any other cause, has been the means of more loss to the dairymen of this country than can be readily estimated, especially when butter is held in storage for a higher market, the poorer grades of salt imparting a fishy or racid flavor, detracting in value from one to five cents per pound.

"In salting butter, one ounce to the pound is what is generally used. Butter should be exposed as little as possible to the air from the time it is churned until packed tightly in tubs, fit for market. Care should be taken never to overwork butter, as the grain and texture should be preserved. This point should never be lost sight of.

"Equally good results can be obtained by washing or working the milk from the butter, when skillfully done under favorable circumstances. In either case the only object is to free the butter from the milk, with as little injury to the flavor or grain of the butter as possible. In washing butter, the danger is mostly in injuring the flavor by introducing foreign matter in the water, while in the other case, their is more danger in overworking, and so injuring the grain. In localities where pure water cannot be obtained, washing should not be resorted to, for butter is always sure to take up the impurities contained, as it will taint of any decaying vegetable or animal matter that may be near. Many wells and springs which are thought to be pure and good have in them decaying substances which render them entirely unfit for any use, much less to wash butter with. Decaying organic matter so introduced into butter acts very much like yeast in dough; at least, it starts a fermentation, so to speak, which soon destroys the butter. Allow no surface water to get into the spring or well, or any filth to remain in them, and if they are not highly charged with lime, mineral or salts of any kind, there is no better or easier method than to wash the milk out quickly and thoroughly before salting.

"It is very difficult, if not impossible, to make good butter without having a good milk room. All the other conditions may be good, but if the milk be set in a room where the temperature is not right, or the air bad, the result may be poor butter. This fact is too often overlooked, but not as frequently as formerly. It is now very generally known that, to make good butter, milk must not be kept in the same room with boiled vegetables or other cooked food; or where there are vegetables, as in a cellar. But it is not so generally understood as it should be that the milk room should not be where there is any chance for disagreable odors to come from adjoining rooms. Too many settle down in the idea that if they have a room expressly for milk, it is all that is required; but this is a mistake. The milk room should be so far away from the cook room that it should be impossible for the odors which arise while cooking to enter it, though the door is opened.

If the farmer smokes tobacco he should be very careful never to smoke even in a room adjoining the milk room, or to go into the milk room after smoking, until the odor of the tobacco is out of his clothing, which, if he smokes very often, will not be until he gets a new suit. There are but few substances that absorb odors like milk or butter."

All buckets or cans that receive the milk should be kept clean and sweet. The milking should be done quickly and the milk put away immediately in the milk room. As soon as the cream separates from the milk, which is in forty-eight hours or less, according to the temperature of the room, it should be churned, and not allowed to stand and become rancid. Keep a thermometer with which to test the cream, and churn it at a temperature of about sixty-three degrees. Never try to secure the proper temperature by pouring water in the cream or testing it with the hand, but apply hot or cold water on the outside of the can, and get the temperature by the use of the thermometer. Wash the butter with pure cold water, add the proper amount of salt and coloring before commencing to work it. Avoid the use of the hand in working it. Use a ladle, or what is better, a lever. Don't spat it or draw the ladle over to smooth it, as that breaks the grain. As soon as the milk is all out it can be prepared for market by putting it in prints, or rolls, and wrapping each one separate in a clean muslin cloth, wet in strong brine.

Use good ash tubs or scalded stone jars for packing. Butter should be packed in solidly, so that when turned out it will not be full of holes and loose. Tubs should be soaked in good strong brine, or else thoroughly steamed, then weighed, and the tare marked plainly on each tub. "Fill to water measure." Soak the cloths well in brine, and have them large enough to cover the entire top. It is now ready to go to market, or to be put in a cool place free from all animal or vegetable odors.

PACKING BUTTER IN BRINE.

This method of packing butter for its more perfect

preservation, and one which is very effective, has long been in use in England. It is to pack the butter in cylindrical bags of muslin, which are put in a mold for the purpose. These bags hold about two pounds, and when filled are tied tightly and packed away in brine in tubs, pails, or casks, and are headed up just as pickled pork is. The butter will absorb no more salt, is perfectly free from atmospheric exposure, is enveloped in an antiseptic fluid, and is therefore entirely safe from change, excepting so far as this may occur internally from within by natural process called ripening. But this change goes on so slowly that the butter merely acquires a high and agreeable flavor, and no strong scent or taste is developed which would approach rancidity.

This manner of packing butter has long been in use in some districts of England, and the supplies furnished to the large universities of Oxford and Cambridge have been put up in a similar way for many years. The butter is made in long rolls about two inches in diameter, and these are wrapped in muslin and the edge secured by some stitches, the ends being tied.

Another method for packing butter, and one which is well adapted for the general farmer, is to work or wash the butter until it is free of milk, then pack well in a good sweet jar or ash vessel; cover the top over with a wet cloth; press down close all around, and cover with salt some two inches thick. When wanting to add more butter, remove the salt and cloth, pack as before, then replace the cloth and salt. Butter thus packed during the fall months will keep sweet and good until late in the spring.

THE AMERICAN HORSE.

A MODERN, PRACTICAL AND RELIABLE

TREATISE ON THE HORSE,

GIVING A BRIEF HISTORY OF THE DIFFERENT BREEDS, WITH VALUABLE INFORMATION ON VARIOUS SUBJECTS, AS TO BREEDING, REARING, HANDLING AND SHOEING, EITHER FOR THE FARM OR ROAD, FOLLOWED BY A PRACTICAL TREATMENT ON THE DISEASES OF HORSES, CATTLE AND SHEEP.

CHAPTER XVIII.

THE DIFFERENT BREEDS OF HORSES AND THEIR CHARACTERISTICS.

THE ANCIENT HORSE.—WESTERN PONIES.—CANADIAN KANUCK. — THOROUGHBRED. — AMERICAN TROTTING HORSE.—THE PACING ELEMENT.—THE DRAFT FAMILIES.—THE CLEVELAND BAY.

THE ANCIENT HORSE.

The horse is mentioned in Scripture at least fifteen hundred years before the Christian era. To what country he was indigenous is left in doubt; but from the information given in Scripture, it is reasonable to presume that Africa was the home of that noble animal.

Horses are not supposed to be indigenous to the Western continent; at least none of the first discoverers have left on record any evidence of their existence. History shows that Columbus, in his second voyage to this country in 1493, brought over horses, the first, no doubt, that ever saw the Western hemisphere. According to Herbert, in 1604 an enterprising French lawyer, M. S. Escorbot, brought horses and other domestic animals into Canada, from which descended the Canadian Kanuck, that for many years prevailed extensively in that country, and still exists, to some extent. In 1609, the English colonization ships, landing with immigrants at Jamestown, Virginia, brought over from England six mares and one horse, besides cattle, sheep and swine. In 1625, horses were imported from Holland to New Jersey by the Dutch West India Company. In 1629, Francis Higginson, an English emigrant, brought over horses and mares to Massachusetts, from which descended the first stock of New England. From these beginnings and subsequent importations, many millions of horses have spread over the United States. Some of the noblest steeds and greatest performers in the world are numbered among our running and trotting celebrities, of which I will speak hereafter. The horses found in the wild state on the prairies of North America, are undoubtedly descendents of the fine Spanish horses escaped or let loose in the exploring expeditions of De Soto and other adventurers, especially from the horses that escaped in the Spanish wars with Mexico and Peru.

The blood of the Barb and Turk, known as the Arabian horse, predominates in these ponies to a great extent, which, no doubt, accounts for their durability, for it is known that they are "tougher than a steak from a Texas thorough-bred steer." These ponies predominate all over the West, and are known under different names, according to the locality, as the Mexican, Texas, or Indian Pony, California Mustang, and in the territories as the Cayuse, or Spanish horse.

THE CANADIAN KANUCK.

This breed is supposed to be of Norman descent, and originated from the horses brought over from France by the first settlers of Canada. They possess the general characteristics of the Norman, without degeneration or any material change excepting that of size, which is attributed by some to the cold climate and scanty food on which they have been raised, and by others to a cross of the Norman and the Arabian. They were the first draft horses bred on the western continent, and spread over the United States. They are a valuable agricultural and general purpose horse, for a rough country, as they are active, easily kept, and grow fat at hard work. They stand from fourteen to fifteen and one-half hands high; possess an iron constitution, with strong muscled quarters; large bone in proportion to size; sound feet and legs, free from spavins, ringbones, or other hereditary defects. They perpetuate their strong points and leading characteristics to their issue, and when crossed with high-bred trotters or thoroughbreds, increase the bone. Many of our now noted trotting horses possess the blood of the Kanuck, as obtained through Old Pilot, a noted pacer brought from Canada to New Orleans, by Mr. Chas. Barker, in 1835, and from there taken to Louisville, Ky. He was a black horse, fourteen and one-half hands high, and could pace exceedingly fast. It is claimed that he paced two miles in 4.27; but was such a lugger on the bit that he had to be worked with a peculiar rigging attached to the saddle, in order to hold and control him. This rigging consisted of a stout crupper extending from the saddle to the tail. Attached to this was a regular harness breechen. Long, line-like reins extended from the bridle bit back through the rings in the brichen, then back again through the rings in the bridle bit, and then up to the saddle. Thus rigged, the little "black ram," as he was called, could fairly fly, and from his loins, through his grand daughters, have such trotters as Maud S., 2.9¾, and Jay-Eye-See, 2.10, been produced.

The breed of horses which now prevail, and are so established in the United States as to deserve particular description, are the thoroughbred race horse, American trotting horse, Norman, Clydesdale, English cart, and Shire horses.

THE THOROUGHBRED HORSE.

As ordinarily applied by breeders, the word "thoroughbred" simply means purely bred, or of unmixed lineage, and in this strict sense none of our domesticated animals can justly be called thoroughbreds, except the English race horse, because they all have more or less composite ancestry. When, however, that a certain strain or race has been bred within itself, without outcrosses to other or different strains, for many generations, until a marked and peculiar type is uniformly produced, that race, or strain, or breed is said to be thoroughbred, or purely bred.

The term thoroughbred was first applied only to horses in great Britain, bred especially for racing purposes, and was adopted as the name of the breed, and is still used for that distinctive purpose. Consequently, when one speaks of a thoroughbred horse, all intelligent horsemen understand that the race horse is ment. No horses are recognized as Thoroughbreds in this country that do not show an unbroken line of ancestry, on both sides, to animals recorded in the English Stud-book. No intelligent horseman will speak of a thoroughbred Morgan, a thoroughbred trotter, or a thoroughbred draft-horse, because, as before stated, the term, when applied to horses, belongs only to one particular breed, the running horse, called Thoroughbreds.

Mr. Youatt says: "There is much dispute as to the origin of the Thoroughbred horse. By some he is traced

through both sire and dam to Arabian origin. Others believe him to be the native English horse improved and perfected by judicious crossing with the Arabian horse, the Turk, Bard or Beduin, which, without doubt, is his true parentage."

England is entitled to the credit of originating and perfecting the thoroughbred in his present form. The Darley, Arabian, Godolphin, Barb, Byrley, and Turk, were among the most distinguished progenitors and founders of the breed. The Stud Book, which is an authority acknowledged by every English breeder, traces all the old racers to some Eastern origin, or Arabian horse. If the pedigree of an English racer of the present day be required, it is traced back to a certain extent, and ends with a well known racer, or in obscurity. For an American Thoroughbred, it traces to a well known race or an imported Thoroughbred. It must, on the whole, be allowed that the present English Thoroughbred horse is of foreign extraction, improved and perfected by the influence of the climate, and by diligent cultivation. The beautiful tales of Eastern countries of somewhat remoter days, may lead us to imagine that the Arabian horse possessed marvelous powers, but it cannot admit of a doubt, that the English Thoroughbred horse is more beautiful, far swifter and stouter than the famed courser of the desert, and those bred in America have proven themselves equal to, or superior to those bred in England. In former days the race horse was not brought upon the course until matured, generally at five years old. The consequences were that they remained sound, competent to train and run well at an advanced age. Now the system is changed. The majority of breeders start their colts at two years old, so as to give them a reputation for early maturity, and they train off or break down at three or five years of age, and the majority go off crippled into the stud.

Whether the introduction of two year olds upon the race course, so they may astonish the public by their fleetness, is best, is a question which more concerns the sporting man than the agriculturist, and yet it concerns the agriculturist, too, to some extent; for racing is principally valuable as connected with breeding, and as the test of breeding. But the breeding of the Thoroughbred horse is a business that belongs to men of ample time and means; for it takes plenty of both to make it a success. That the breeding of Thoroughbred horses is legitimate, in which any farmer may honorably be engaged, is too plain to admit of denial. It becomes simply a question of how far this almost universal passion may be carried. But whether it is wrong to run them at so early an age as two years, and cripple or ruin them for life, as is often the case, is a question that is easily answered in the affirmative, and is a practice that should not be tolerated by the breeders. The horse is as susceptible of pleasure and pain as ourselves. He was committed to us for our protection and for our use; he is a willing and devoted servant. Whence did we derive the right to abuse him? Self interest speaks the same language as reason in prompting us to take care of him.

THE AMERICAN TROTTER.

This celebrated and valuable breed of horses is of American origin, and is thoroughly composite. It is made up of different elements of blood of the Thoroughbred horse crossed with the native American mares, and their produce so inbred, that now the trotting horse is a distinguished breed, and more valuable than any other known. The horses which were most noted as the founders of the breed, and which became famous, are, Juston Morgan, Rysdyk's Hambletonian, Andrew Jackson, Mambrino Chief, Blue Bull and Pilot Junior. Further on, I will speak of these horses named, and give their breeding as given in history with a few brief remarks on their value as sires, but cannot give the history of the families in full; to do so, would require a large volume in itself.

THE FOUNDER OF TROTTERS.

The founder of the best trotting families was the imported horse Messenger, brought from England to Philadelphia, in 1778. The lineage of this noble sire traces back in the male line to the Darley Arabian, the sire of Flying Childers, but with the suspicion of an out-cross through his great grand sire Sampson. On the side of his dam the strain reaches Code, by Godolphin Arabian. From all accounts, Messenger was a horse of superior, though not handsome form, and possessed extraordinary power and spirit. His color was grey, which became lighter with age; was fifteen hands, three inches high, with a large bony head, and a rather short, straight neck. His windpipe and nostrils were nearly twice the usual size, while his withers were low, and shoulders upright, but deep and strong. His loins were strong and the quarters very muscular, while his hocks and knees were very large, yet the cannon bones were flat and clean. He carried his legs under him, and was always ready for action. This description shows but little of the form of the Thoroughbred, yet is typical of the form of his trotting descendents. This form, as well as the extraordinary vitality and endurance peculiar to him, he impressed upon his progeny, which being persistently driven and trained to trot, became more intensified and habituated regarding gait, until we have as the result of this skill of man, and this strain of blood, the final development of the trotting horse of America, the pride of the turf and road. Messenger died on Long Island, in 1808, at the age of twenty-eight, and stood for fifteen years in the vicinity of New York City. The roadsters and trotting horses throughout that section show the impress of his blood.

PROMINENT SONS OF MESSENGER.

The following were the prominent sons of Messenger, to whom we trace many pedigrees of the fastest trotters: Mambrino, Bishop's Hambletonian, Ogden's Messenger, Engineer, Commander, and Winthrop Messenger. Some of Messenger's daughters have contributed to the different families qualities which have given them prominence. The grandam of young Bashaw, the source of the Bashaws and Clays, was the daughter of Messenger.

PROMINENT GRAND SONS OF MESSENGER.

Among the grand sons of Messenger, Abdallah and Mambrino Paymaster stand pre-eminent. Of this king of stallions, Abdallah, "rough to look at," a son of Mambrino, and a grandson of Messenger, out of the mare Amazonia, too much cannot be said. In life he was not appreciated; in fact, was so neglected as to yield no profit in the stud, and was sold for $35 to a fisherman, who, not being able to work him on account of his temper, allowed him to starve to death. His greatest laurels were reaped years after in the honors bestowed on his sons. During late years his blood has been highly prized in the pedigrees of trotting horses, either through male or female line. Mr. Wm. F. Porter, in speaking of him, says, "Abdallah was foaled on Long Island, and was a rich mahogany bay, and measured about fifteen hands three inches, under the standard. He had a star and very possibly one white foot. He is presumed to be Thoroughbred, but the pedigree of his dam was lost.

Rysdyk's Hambletonian, a son of Abdallah, was the greatest progenitor of trotters the world ever saw, and by right of acknowledged pre-eminence, claims our consideration as the first on the list of great stallions. He was foaled in 1849, and died in 1876. His dam was by imported Bellfounder, his second dam was by Bishop's Hambletonian, son of Messenger, and third dam by Messenger. He is described by Mr. Holmes, who knew him well, as a strong, compactly made horse, close to sixteen hands high. His coat was ordinarily of the brightest bay, his legs black, the black extending above the knees and hocks, with white socks behind (in size precisely alike), and a small, white star in the centre of his forehead. His pictures are all utterly inadequate to convey any correct idea of the horse."

After the get of Rysdyk's Hambletonian began to show promise as trotters, and especially after Shark, one of his sons, came out and trotted several wonderful races under saddle, from 1862 to 1866, making a mile in 2.28½, and two miles in 5.00½, and Dexter, another son, who came out a year later, and swept everything before him, and in 1867 made a record of one mile in 2.17¼, which for so many years stood as the best performance on record, the "Old Horse," as he has long been called, became very popular in the stud, and was extensively patronized. Another of his sons, George Wilkes, came out nearly at the same time as Dexter, winning many races, and in 1868, made a record of 2.22, which stood for many years as the best stallion record. Then Gold Smith Maid and St. Julian, granddaughter and grandson, appeared upon the turf and electrified the world with their wonderful speed for many years. And they kept coming thicker and faster—first, the sons, and then the daughters, then the granddaughters and grandsons, then the great-grandsons and ... ... ntil his descendents became the most noted ... ... tting horses known, and the irresistible logic of trotting statistics to this day has clearly demonstrated the superiority of the Hambletonian blood over all others.

Hambletonian commenced service in the stud at two years of age, and continued successfully until two years before his death, when he proved no longer fertile. He served 1,833 mares, and got 1,325 colts. During the first three years he stood at $25, to insure; the next nine years at $35; the next year at $75; the next at $100; the next at $300; and since then at $500. His earnings in the stud amounted to $185,125.

Of his get, 37 have trotting records of 2.30 or better, or one 2.30 trotter out of every thirty-five colts. From this it can be seen that from the number of foals he produced, the percentage of 2.30 trotters were small. Some of his sons and grandsons in this respect, and also in the production of horses of great speed have surpassed him. Among those that may be mentioned that stand pre-eminent as great sires are Volunteer, George Wilkes and Harold. But it must be borne in mind that they have had the advantage of being coupled with better bred trotting mares, and the colts the advantage of the skill and knowledge of man as to how to educate the trotter. It has been practically demonstrated that neither Rysdyk's Hambletonian, nor many of his sons, have produced sensational trotters when crossed on Thoroughbred mares, although three-fourths of all the sensational trotters belong to the Hambletonian family, but have been produced by the cross of Hambletonian sires with well-bred trotting or pacing mares. This is not only true of the Hambletonian family, but with all other trotting families, that there are but few fast trotters that have been produced by breeding strictly Thoroughbred mares to trotting sires, or trotting mares to Thoroughbred sires. Less than twenty with records of 2:30 or better, would cover the entire list.

IMPORTED BELLFOUNDER.

Bellfounder was imported from England, in 1822. He was a remarkably fast trotter for a Thoroughbred horse, and has contributed a most valuable strain of blood to the trotters of this country. At three years old he trotted two miles in six minutes, and at four years old made ten miles in thirty minutes. The Bellfounder cross is highly prized, and is found in the pedigrees of the Hambletonians, Clays and other families. Rysdyk's Hambletonian's dam was by this great horse, and her speed, at four years old, was very great, seldom equaled, even in these fast times. She was a handsome dark bay mare, and queen of the road of New York City for many years."

Mambrino Paymaster was another noted son of Mambrino, and his dam was a large black mare, breeding unknown. Mambrino Paymaster was the sire of Mambrino Chief, the founder of the family which bears his name.

This strain of blood has become very fashionable and will be found in the pedigrees of some of the most noted sires or dams of sensational trotters.

MAMBRINO CHIEF.

"Mambrino Chief, br. h. 16 hands, was a very fast trotter for his day, having trotted a mile in 2:36, in the year 1854, after having made a season in the stud. But besides being himself a fast trotter, he possessed the most remarkable power of transmitting the ability to reproduce trotters to his descendents. He was foaled in 1844, and spent the earlier part of his life in New York, where his opportunities in the stud were limitted. He was afterward taken to Kentucky, and after making but seven seasons in the stud, died in 1862, at 18 years of age, and just at the beginning of the war, which hindered the development of his get for many years. In spite of this, and notwithstanding the fact that the development of the trotting horse was then but little understood, ten of his get trotted better than 2:30. Amongst these was the great Lady Thorne, who beat all the great trotters of her day with the utmost ease, including the renowned Goldsmith Maid, whom she beat every time she met. Her best record was 2:18¼, but those who knew her best, say that this was no measure of her speed, she being able to trot much faster." She was credited with trotting a mile in 2:08 in a trial, driven by the veteran driver Dan Mace, and this long before forty pound sulkeys or shin boots, etc., were known. After the trial, Dan said to the parties that timed her, "We will never live to see that mile trotted again."

The opportunities of Mambrino Chief as a sire, were vastly inferior to those of Hambletonian. His services in the stud were comparatively limited; he died before his fame was established, and his get had to contend with great disadvantages. But notwithstanding this he was to the West what Rysdyk's Hambletonian was to the East—the fountain head of a great trotting family. And history establishes the fact beyond question that no other stallions ever lived, of which we have any record, who possessed the power, to a greater degree, of transmitting to their descendents, running through successive generations, the ability to reproduce trotters, capable of the very best performances, with unerring certainty as the great stallions Mambrino Chief and Rysdyk's Hambletonian.

This cut, as taken from life, represents the standard bred trotting stallion, Mambrino Hambletonian, and his general appearance shows the characteristics of the two families which he represents. He is a dark bay horse, 15¾ hands high, and weighs 1,125 pounds. Sire of Stranger, record 2:22½; two miles 4:59. Coal Dealer trial, 2:24, dead; Red Jacket, stallion, trial, 2:26. He was sired by Ashland, by Mambrino Chief; 1st dam Blinker mare, by Rysdyk's Hambletonian; 2d dam by Young Patriot, sire of Volunteer's dam; third dam the Chas. Kent mare, the dam of Rysdyk's Hambletonian. Ashland's dam, Utilla, by imported Margrave; 2d dam, Too Soon, by Sir Leslie; 3d dam, Little Peggy, by Gallatin, he out of imported mare Mambrino, by Lord Governor's Mambrino, sire of imported messenger.

THE MORGAN FAMILY.

To this celebrated family of trotting horses, too little attention has been paid of late years. They in former days obtained much celebrity as a family of fast and fine road or track horses. But owing to but few of them being able to obtain records of 2:20, or better, and on account of their size, being rather small, they have lost considerable of the celebrity they once obtained. As a family of trotting horses with records of 2:30, or better, they no doubt are entitled to second place, the Hambletonian family holding first honor in this respect, as well as the honor of claiming all the kings and queens of the turf. As to the pedigree of the Morgan horse, there is some doubt, but the one as given by Mr. Justin Morgan is accepted as the one entitled to the most credit. The horse, Justin Morgan, the founder of the Morgan family of horses, was foaled in Massachusetts, in 1793, and brought from Springfield, Mass., to Randolph, Vt., in 1795, where he was kept for many years, and became celebrated as a sire of fine horses. Justin Morgan, ch. h. 14 hands, was sired by True Britain, by Traveller. Dam by Diamond, by Wildare, Thoroughbred. He was extensively patronized, and left a numerous and valuable progeny. There were but four of his sons left entire: Revenge, Sherman Morgan, Bullrush and Woodbury, or Burbank. The last three became distinguished sires. But as to the breeding of their dams, little or nothing is known. Sherman Morgan was probably the best son of Justin Morgan. He was the sire of Vermont Blackhawk, Sherman Blackhawk, and Vermont Hero, who perpetuated the blood of their sire through a long and illustrious line of trotters. Blackhawk was the sire of Ethan Allen, whose brilliant career on the turf gave him a record of one mile in 2:25, and with running mate of 2:15, but his fame in the stud far eclipsed his successful career of the turf. He was the sire of a great many fast trotters, and also the sire of Daniel Lambert, the sire of twenty-five 2:30 trotters, and the grand sire of H. B. Winship, with a record of 2:06, with running mate. Vermont Hero was the sire of Gen. Knox. Both their dams were of Hambletonian blood. Gen. Knox possessed more Messenger blood than Morgan, and his progeny show it by their records. Woodbury Morgan became famous as a sire of horses suited for martial display, on account of their beautiful form and graceful action. This is characteristic of the Morgan family, and very noticeable with horses possessing that blood.

THE BASHAWS, CLAYS AND PATCHENS.

The Bashaws descended from an imported Arabian stallion. Grand Bashaw was imported from Tripoli in 1820, and sired Young Bashaw. Young Bashaw was the sire of Andrew Jackson, who was the most famous trotting stallion of his day, and as a weight puller was unsurpassed in speed. His dam was of unknown blood. She was taken to Philadelphia in a drove of horses from the West. From the loins of this great horse, Andrew

Jackson, have descended the Bashaws, Clays and Patchens. He was foaled in 1828, and died in 1846. He sired Long Island Blackhawk, who was the first horse to trot a mile in 2:40, to a two hundred and fifty pound wagon, and from whom descended Green's Bashaw, the Mohawks, and many other trotters of note. Henry Clay, the origin of the Clay and Patchen branch, or family, was a son of Andrew Jackson, and was foaled in 1837. The dam of Henry Clay was a trotting mare of unknown blood, but was both fast and game. Henry Clay was possessed of great speed and endurance. Cassius M. Clay, son of Henry Clay, and sire of George M. Patchen, has done the most to establish the Clays and Patchens.

MESSENGER DUROC.

Duroc, son of the Thoroughbred Diomed, and the sire of Messenger Duroc, whose dam was a daughter of Messenger, is a noted strain of blood, and is found in the pedigrees of the American stars. Mares of this blood are very valuable to cross with Hambletonian sires.

THE PACING ELEMENT.

An important addition to the trotting element to produce trotters of great speed, is the pacing elements, which have been brought out within a few years, the chief elements being the descendents of Young Columbus, the sire of Phil Sheridan, and Old Pilot, the sire of Pilot Junior; also the Copper Bottoms, Red Bucks, Cadmuses, Hiategas, Tuckahoes and Blue Bulls. All have representatives among the fast pacers, and some of the families have assumed the trotting gait with great readiness, particularly the Pilots and Blue Bulls. Their tendency to that gait is shown in the fast horses that trace back to them. The trotting gait with the greatest speed has been produced

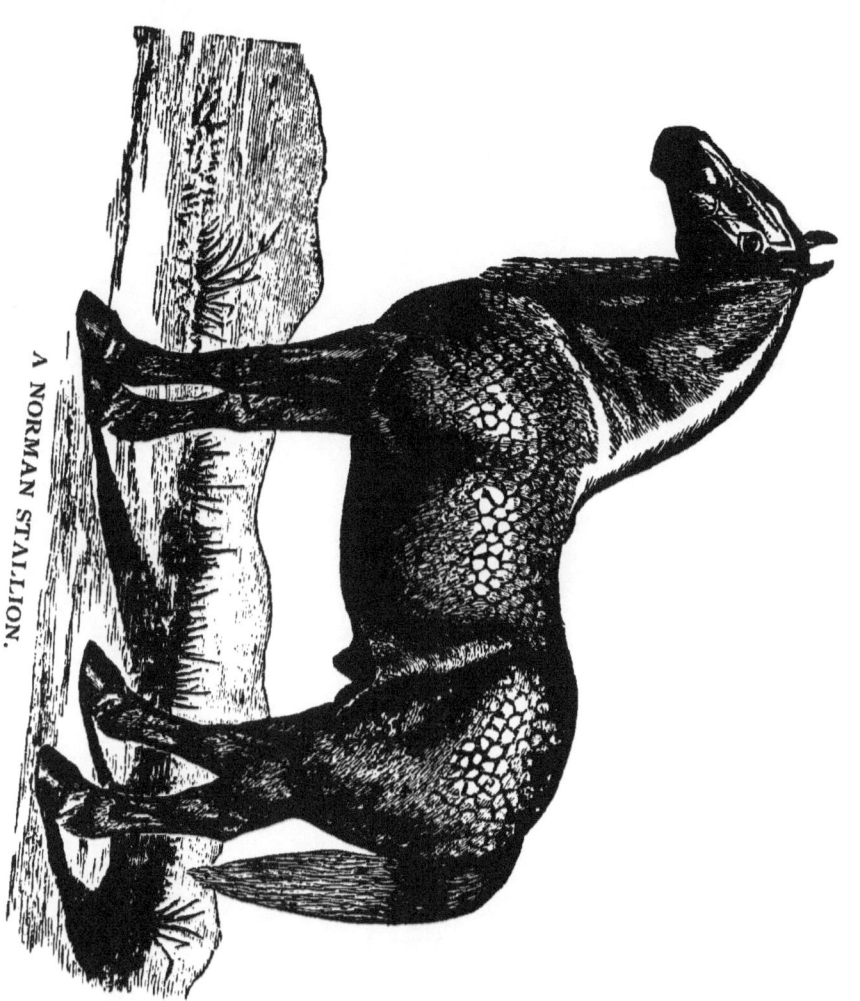

A NORMAN STALLION.

by the crossing of Pilot mares with Hambletonian stallions. Breeding of this kind produced Maud S. and Jay-Eye-See.

THE DRAFT FAMILIES.

The American Draft horse consists of a combination of the Norman, Clydesdale, English Cart and Shire, crossed with the native mares. The importation of these breeds from their native homes, of late years, has been very heavy, and pure bred ones of either kind or sex are now becoming very plentiful, and being bred pure in this country, as well as in their native country, and on account of the tempting prices offered for the best specimens of the respective breeds. America, no doubt, has now as good Draft horses, as well as running, trotting or pacing horses, as any other country known.

THE NORMAN.

The Norman is a native of France, and a descendent of the war horse used in that country in the early days. The improved Norman horse, known as the Percheron-Norman, as now bred, is from sixteen to sixteen and one-half hands high, and weighs from 1,600 to 2,000 pounds.

They are strongly built, with heavy shoulders and powerful hind quarters; big, sound, bony legs, and good feet. They are claimed to be a cross of the old Norman and the Arabian, by the use of the Arabian stallion with the heavy Norman mares, which, judging from their appearance, is no doubt true. They are a very active and quick moving horse for their size; good disposition, and generally of a gray color. In regard to the origin of the old Norman war horse, nothing is known. They have existed in France for centuries, and have a fixed type that must have been bred in the family for many generations, because it stamps its imprint so faithfully upon its offspring. The Normans have formed the basis of all the draft breeds that exist in Europe or America.

THE CLYDESDALE, THE ENGLISH CART AND SHIRE.

The Clydesdale horse is a native of Scotland, and a very superior breed of horses for draft purposes. Their color is generally bay or brown, with frequently white marks upon the legs or face. They are larger than the Norman horse, and more rangy. Their legs are large and heavy haired, bone very strong, and free of flesh, well set on to a good foot. As a breed of Draft horses, for vitality, power and endurance combined, they are unsurpassed.

The English Cart horse is a native of England, and about the largest breed of Draft horses known. In color and make up they resemble the Clydesdale very much, but generally show the white marks about the legs and face more, are heavier, more cumbersome and slower, but are valuable for heavy draft purposes about the cities.

The Shire horse is also a native of England, and also the Cleveland Bay. The Shires resemble the English Cart in color and form very much. The Cleveland Bay was formed by crossing the Thoroughbred stallion with Clydesdale or Shire mares. Then in-bred through themselves until a family was formed, resembling each other in color and form. They were about extinct at one time, but of late years they are being revived and brought to America. They are a bay horse, full sixteen hands, very rangy and fine in form in front, but often deficient in the hind quarters. Though an effort is now being made in the direction of their preservation and restoration as an acknowledged breed, the animals now being registered are selected rather for type than breeding.

THE ENGLISH CART HORSE.

CHAPTER XIX.

The Breeding of Horses a Science.

THE ART OR SCIENCE OF BREEDING.—RULES AND ERRORS IN BREEDING.—SPEED THE MAIN POINT.—A STANDARD BRED TROTTER.—POPULAR SIRES OF TROTTERS.—RECORDS OF 2:14, or less.—FAST RECORDS ALL DISTANCES.—THE GENERAL PURPOSE HORSE.

THE ART OR SCIENCE OF BREEDING.

Probably in the breeding of no other domestic animal, is the art or science of breeding called to as severe a test as in the breeding of horses, and especially of fast horses. In the breeding of all our other domestic animals, the art of feeding can be called upon to a great extent, to cover up defective points, but this is of little avail in the art of breeding fast horses of any kind. Here the science of combining the fast elements of blood, that have proven successful in producing the kind of horse wanted, has to be used with the best of judgment. The characteristics so derived in breeding, running, trotting, pacing and saddle horses, more so than in breeding any other animal, comes slow, and any mistake made, either by accident or otherwise, is hard to undo. Therefore, the inexperienced breeder, when contemplating starting in this business, should first give the subject careful study, as any mistake at this juncture may cause him to abandon the business in disgust. In the breeding of good horses of any kind, the desired qualities should be possessed, to some degree, by both stallion and mares, and the better the so derived blood lines are, running back through several generations, the more valuable it will be, and the more it can be relied upon when called into action. I will herein give a list of rules for the breeding of horses, as gathered from practical breeders, which may prove of value to those contemplating embarking, or already engaged in this business. If they are committed to memory, borne in mind, and adopted, they will save some serious mistakes in this most valuable business.

RULES FOR BREEDING.

First, determine exactly in your own mind the kind of horse you wish to produce, and never lose sight of it.

Second, avail yourself of any opportunity that offers to produce the finest animals and blood that will suit your purpose.

Third, avoid unhealthy animals at all times, and unsound animals, unless the blemish is caused by an accident. Ill-tempered or vicious animals are also dangerous. Never forget that if the good qualities are transmitted, the evil ones are sure to be.

Fourth, horses that are greatly dissimilar in their breed and shape, should not be mated to breed. For example, big stallions and very small mares should not be mated, or a large, rough Draft mare and a very small horse, as that cross would no doubt prove a failure.

Fifth, avoid the use of a course, loose-made stallion of any kind, or one that out-looks his size, or a half-bred one of any breed, if the use of a pure bred one can be obtained, and do not breed from mares and horses, which, having been mated once, produced bad colts. A brood mare that has produced a bad colt, if bred again should be bred to a well bred horse that is exceedingly good in the points that the colt was deficient in, and if that union proves successful she can be bred back again with safety. If the mare is deficient in any way, select a sound, well-bred horse which is good in the points where she is deficient, whether it be in endurance, body, limb or temper.

Sixth, to breed half-bred horses, select good native-bred mares. The better bred they are the more valuable they will be. They should be young, sound, well-shaped, with good temper, and good action, or a tried mare that has been a successful breeder.

These mares, coupled with a thoroughbred stallion, which is of good size, compact, well-shaped, sound, healthy and vigorous, with good temper and action, or one that is the sire of good running horses, capable of carrying heavy weight, will produce a good class of horses for the saddle, road or light work. The same mares bred to a pure-bred Draft horse of any breed, will produce a good class of horses for the farm, truck, omnibus or delivery wagon. Again, this same class of mares would be valuable to breed to a standard bred trotting stallion, to produce a good horse for the farm or road. Mares of this kind coupled with a good trotting stallion, which is sound and close to 16 hands high, strong and compactly made, of good color, action and disposition, and is so bred that he is capable of transmitting his good qualities to his progeny, when coupled with all classes of mares, would prove a valuable horse to use; as this breeding should produce a large stylish horse of good color, speed, action and disposition, that is eagerly sought after, and always commands a long price.

ERRORS IN BREEDING.

A great many valuable and well-bred mares are ruined every year by the thoughtlessness or carelessness of their owners in breeding them for the first time to a Jack or Draft horse. Mares thus bred the first time, invariably prove worthless from which to raise a fine bred trotting or running colt, for some years afterwards, as each colt, for at least five years afterwards, will show more or less of the characteristics of the horse to which they were first bred. Knowing this to be the fact, it shows how important it is to breed all well-bred trotting or running mares, or mares that are expected to be used to raise trotting or running colts, to a well-bred trotting or running horse the first time, and continue to do so as long as they are expected to be used for raising that class of horses. Afterwards, if they are used to raise draft horses, they will prove more valuable for that purpose, as the colts will show the characteristics of the well-bred horse in color or action to a great extent. Large native-bred mares or draft mares that are suitable for raising draft horses can be bred if so desired, the first time to a Draft horse, but should be a pure-bred horse of good color. When once mares of this kind have raised a draft colt, it is best to continue to raise that class of horses with them, for any attempt to raise a fine trotting or running colt from such mares, can only result in disappointment. And the same may be said of that class of mares, even if they have never been bred, when an attempt is made to raise a fast running horse from them, by using a Thoroughbred sire. The only way to raise a fast running horse is to breed a Thoroughbred, or at least a good half-breed mare, to a Thoroughbred horse. The same may be said in breeding fast trotting horses. The only successful way is to breed well-bred trotting or pacing mares to standard bred trotting horses.

SPEED AN ESSENTIAL POINT.

In breeding trotting horses, it is the speed and not the horse that brings the fancy price. There are hundreds of horses in the country that are as fine looking, have as good dispositions, and are worth as much money as any of the fastest trotters, for ordinary purposes, yet they do not bring a tenth of the money, because they have not the necessary speed. If you are breeding for trotters, breed for the best, but try to combine the speed with size and beauty.

The American people have a natural love of beauty, as well as speed, and the majority would rather have for road use high form, with good size, with a reasonable amount of speed, than the ungainly form, with a high rate of speed. The qualities of style, beauty and vitality will also commend the fillies or mares for the harem, and the young stallions for the stud. This is becoming more noticeable every day. The people who go out every pleasant day for recreation, are rapidly substituting the handsome, symmetrical horse of good size, for the smaller or plainer one. The horse that is to supply this demand, must be the well-bred trotting horse, bred for size, speed and beauty. He then has the instinct to trot, and the best ones of this breeding are as liable to go to the front as a more homely or smaller one. Whereas the breeding of trotting horses is now only begun, the breeders should try to avoid defective formation, and try to combine the speed with a larger and more symmetrical form. If they do this, the disasters and failures will not be so numerous in the future as they have been in the past.

A STANDARD-BRED TROTTER.

According to the rules, a standard bred trotter is one that has a record of 2:30, or better, and his sire or dam has a record of 2:30, or better, or traces direct to a sire or dam with a record of 2:30 or better. Again, the animal may not have a record of 2:30 or better, or its sire or dam, or even grandsire or grandam, but they have been the ancestors of horses that have records of 2:30, or better, and the animal would become standard under that rule.

What is termed a standard horse, is one whose breeding does not trace to a standard sire or dam, but has a record of 2:30 or better, or has produced a colt with a record of 2:30 or better. Fast horses never come by accident, but inherit the speed from their ancestors, and the more capable they are of transmitting great speed, combined with other good qualities, as color, size, beauty and disposition, the more valuable are they as breeders. "This particularly carries its lesson to young, or inexperienced breeders, and others who are looking for some lucky accidental wonder. Expected accidents do not happen, and would not be accidents if they did. But it is the famous blood lines coming together, through sire and dam for generations, that produce great and fast horses." Therefore, in order to raise a trotting horse, use a standard bred trotting stallion.

POPULAR SIRES OF TROTTERS.

As it may be interesting as well as profitable to the many readers of this book, I will give the names, description and breeding of horses that have sired ten or more two-thirty trotters, with the number they have in the two-thirty, two-twenty-five and two-twenty list.

I will commence with Blue Bull, who was without doubt one of the marvels of the age in siring speed, and who stands pre-eminently at the head of the list of all stallions as the sire of two-thirty trotters, of which he has fifty, twenty of which are in the two-twenty-five class, and one in the two-twenty class. He was fifteen years in the stud, served 1,380 mares, and got 900 living colts. He began his stud career as a teaser for a Jack, and died the king of sires. He was a s. h., 15¼ hands, foaled in Kentucky, in 1858. As to his sire, there is some doubt. He is credited to old Sam, as well as Pruden's Blue Bull, the sire of many fast pacers, he by Merring's Blue Bull. Dam by Blacknose, son of Modoc, out of Lucy, by Orphan; second dam, Lady Grey; third dam, Maria, by Melzar. Old Sam and Pruden's Blue Bull, as well as Blue Bull, were fast Pacers.

Rysdyk's Hambletonian, b. h., 15¾ hands, by Abdallah, by Mambrino, by imported Messenger, dam by imported Bellfounder, comes next to Blue Bull as a sire of two-thirty trotters, having 37 in the two-thirty list, 15 in the two-twenty-five and two in the two-twenty list. But Hambletonian's ability of transmitting to his descendents, running through successive generations, the ability to reproduce trotters, capable of the very best performances, far exceeds Blue Bull's.

George Wilkes, br. h., 15¼ hands, by Rysdyk's Hambletonian, dam Dolly Spaxker, by Henry Clay, comes next with 35 in the two-thirty list, 21 in the two-twenty-five list, and 7 in the two-twenty list.

Almont, b. h., 15 3-4 hands, by Alexander's Abdallah, by Rysdyk's Hambletonian. Dam, by Mambrino Chief;

second dam by Pilot Jr. This rich bred trotting horse is the sire of twenty-eight in the two-thirty list, thirteen of which are in the two-twenty-five list, and five in the two-twenty list.

Volunteer, b. h., 15¾ hands, foaled in 1854, by Rysdyk's Hambletonian, dam Lady Patriot, by Young Patriot, of Diomede and Messenger descent, ranks fifth in the list of great trotting sires, judged by the number of his get in the two-thirty list, of which he has 26, while he has 15 in the two-twenty-five list, and 5 in the 20 list. But judged by the quality of his sons and daughters, as shown by the total number of heats won by them in two-thirty, or better, he has eclipsed all other stallions, as his get has won six hundred and seventy-eight heats in two-thirty or better, an average of 26. Their average record is 2:23⅓.

Aberdeen, b. h., 15¾ hands, by Rysdyk's Hambletonian, dam Widow Machree, by Seely's American Star, has thirteen in the two-thirty list, seven in the two-twenty-five list, and three in the two-twenty list.

Belmont, b. h., 16 hands, by Alexander's Abdallah, by Rysdyk's Hambletonian, dam by Bellfounder, has ten in the two-thirty list, six in the two-twenty-five list, and two in the two-twenty list.

Green's Bashaw, bl. h., 15½ hands, by Veranl's Blackhawk, by Long Island Blackkawk. Dam, Belle, by Tom Thumb; second dam, the dam of Rysdyk's Hambletonian. Has fourteen in the two-thirty list, seven in the two-twenty-five list, and one in the two-twenty list.

Electioneerer, b. h., fifteen and three-fourths hands, by Rysdyk's Hambletonian. Dam, Green Mountain Maid, by Sayer's Henry Clay. This great sire has eleven in the two-thirty list, eight in the two-twenty-five list, and two in the two-twenty list. He was the sire of Hindo Rose, a horse which had the fastest record for a colt one or three years old; also of Wildflower, which had the best two-year-old record as a filly; and Fred Crocker, the noted two-year-old stallion, and of Albert W., a horse with the best four-year-old stallion record. This places him as a great sire of colts of early maturity.

Daniel Lambert, ch. h, 15½ hands, by Ethan Allen, by Hill's Blackhawk. Dam, by Fanny Cook, by Treadwell's Abdallah. This great sire has twenty-five trotters in the two-thirty list, 11 of which are in the two-twenty-five list, and one in the two-twenty list, which places him sixth in the list of great sires of trotters, judged by their two-thirty representatives.

Dictator, br. h., 15½ hands, by Rysdyk's Hambletonian. Dam, by Seely's American Star. Has only ten representatives in the two-thirty list, six of which are in the two-twenty-five list, and four in the two-twenty list, but this places him as one of the most popular horses of America as a sire of fast horses, being the sire of Jay-Eye-See, two-ten, and Phallas, two-thirteen and three-fourths, which is considered the fastest trotting stallion in America.

Edward Everett, b. h., by Rysdyk's Hambletonian. Dam, Fanny, by imported Margrave. Has eleven in the two-thirty list, nine of which are in the two-twenty-five list, and one in the two-twenty list.

General Knox, br. h., 15¾ hands, by Vermont Hero, by Sherman's Blackhawk. Dam, by Searcher. Has eleven in the two-thirty list, five in the two-twenty-five list, and two in the two-twenty list.

Whipple's Hambletonian, ch. h., 16 hands, by Guy Miller, by Rysdyk's Hambletonian. Dam, Martha Washington, by Washington, of Messenger descent. Has ten or more in the two-thirty list, three in the two-twenty-five list, and one of two-nineteen.

Wood's Hambletonian, ro. h., 15½ hands, by Alexander's Abdallah. Has ten in the two-thirty list, and six in the two-twenty-five list.

Happy Medium, b. h., 15¾ hands, by Rysdyk's Hambletonian. Dam, Princess, by Andrus' Hambletonian, by Bishop's Hambletonian, by imported Messenger. Has twenty-two in the two-thirty list, ten in the two-twenty-five, and two in the two-twenty list.

Strathmore, b. h., 16 hands, by Rysdyk's Hambletonian. Dam, Lady Waltermire, by North American; second dam, by Harris' Hambletonian. Has sixteen in the two-thirty list, seven in the two-twenty-five list, and two in the two-twenty list.

Woodford Mambrino, b. h., 15¾ hands, by Mambrino Chief. Dam, Woodbine, by Woodford (Thoroughbred). Has ten in the two-thirty list, four in the two-twenty-five list, and one in the two-twenty list.

Young Columbus, b. h., 15 3-4 hands, by Old Columbus. Dam, Black Maria, by Harris' Hambletonian, by Bishop's Hambletonian. Has eleven in the two-thirty list, and three in the two-tweny-five list.

Mambrino Patchen, (brother to Lady Thorn, two-eighteen and one-fourth) bl. h., 16 hands, by Mambrino Chief. Dam, by Gano, by American Eclipse. Has twelve in the two-thirty list, and three in the two-twenty-five list.

Tempest Jr., ch. h., by Tempest, by Red Bird. Has

THE BREEDING OF HORSES A SCIENCE. 375

ten pacers in the two-thirty list, five in the two-twenty-five list, and three in the two-twenty list.

Unless I have overlooked the list, these twenty stallions are all the sires that have ten or more two-thirty representatives, of which twelve belong to the Hambletonian family, three to the Morgan family, two to the Mambrino Chiefs, and three to the pacing element.

Following this I will give the names of all horses with records of two-fourteen, or less, trotting or pacing, one mile in harness, also the fastest records trotting or pacing, all distances, and all ways going.

RECORDS OF 2:14 OR LESS, TROTTING IN HARNESS ONE MILE.

Time, 2:09¾. Maud S., ch. m., 15¾ hands, Queen of the turf and Empress of all the trotters, was foaled in Kentucky in 1875. Sire, Harold, by Rysdyk's Hambletonian. Dam, Miss Russel, by Pilot Jr., by Old Pilot. At Lexington, Ky., Nov. 11, 1884.

Time, 2:10. Jay-Eye-See, bl. g., 14¾ hands. This celebrated gelding, which ranks next to Maud S., with a record only one quarter of a second slower, was foaled in Kentuckey in 1878. Sire, Dictator, by Rysdyk's Hambletonian. Dam, Midnight, by Pilot Jr. At Chicago, Illinois, July, 1884.

Time, 2:11¼. St. Julian, b. g., 16½ hands, foaled in New York in 1870. Sire, Volunteer, by Rysdyk's Hambletonian. Dam, by Sayer's Henry Clay. At Hartford, Connecticut, August 28, 1880.

Time, 2:13¼. Rarus, b. g., 16 hands, foaled in New York in 1869. Sire, Conklin's Abdallah, by Old Abdallah. Dam, by Telegraph. At Buffalo, New York, Aug. 3, 1878.

Time, 2:13¼. Maxy Cobb, b. s., 15½ hands, foaled

in Kentucky in 1877. Sire, Happy Medium, by Rysdyk's Hambletonian. Dam, by Clark Chief, by Mambrino Chief. At Providence, Rhoad Island, September 30, 1884. This is the best stallion record.

Time, 2:13 3-4. Phallas, b. s., 15 3-4 hands, foaled in Kentucky in 1877. Sire, Dictator, by Rysdyk's Hambletonian. Dam, by Clark Chief, by Mambrino Chief. At Chicago, Illinois, July, 1884.

Time, 2:14. Goldsmith Maid, b. m., 15¼ hands, for many years the Queen of the turf and Empress of all the trotters, was foaled in New York in 1857, and is still living. Sire, Alexanders's Abdallah. Dam, by Old Abdallah. Alexander's Addallah, by Rysdyk's Hambletonian. Dam, by Bay Roman.

PACERS WITH RECORDS OF 2:14 OR LESS, ONE MILE IN HARNESS.

Time, 2:06¼. Johnson, b. g., 15 3-4 hands, foaled in Michigan in 1879. Sire, Joe Basset, by Billy Bashaw. At Chicago, Illinois, in 1884.

Time, 2:11 3-4. Little Brown Jug, br. g., at Chicago, Ills., in 1881. Also the three fastest consecutive heats: 2:11 3-4, 2:11 3-4, 2:12 1-2.

2:12. 1-4 Sleepy Tom (Blind Tom), ch. g. At Chicago, Illinois, in 1879. This horse was considered the pacing wonder—being stone blind—and one of the sensational pacers of those days. He was foaled in Ohio in 1867. Sire, Tom Rolf. Dam, by Sam Hazard.

2:12 1-2. Buffalo Girl, b. m. Pitttsburgh, Pa.

2:12 1-2. Mattie Hunter, s. m. Pittsburgh, Pa.

2:12 1-2. Rich Ball, br. g., Pittsburgh, Pa.

2:13. Gem, b. m., Cleveland, Ohio.

2:13. Roudy Boy, bl. g., Rochester, N. Y.

THE BREEDING OF HORSES A SCIENCE. 377

2:13.   Flora Bell, bl. m., East Saganaw, Mich.
2:13¾. Fuller, b. g., Maysville, Ky.
2:13¾. Westmont, ch. g., Chicago, Ill.
2:14.   Billie S., b. g., at Buffalo, N. Y.
2:14.   Sorrel Dan, s. g., at Saganaw, Mich.
2:14.   Lucy, g. m., at Chicago, Ill.
2:14.   Sweetzer, g. g., in California.

FASTEST TROTTING AND PACING RECORDS—ALL DISTANCES AND ALL WAYS GOING.

One mile, by a yearling filly—Hinda Rose, San Francisco, Cal., Nov. 14, 1881, 2:36½.

One mile, by a yearling stallion—Nutbreaker, Lexington, Ky., Oct. 14, 1884, 2:42¼.

One mile, by a two-year-old filly—Wildflower, San Francisco, Oct. 22, 1881, 2:21.

One mile, by a two-year-old, stallion—Fred Crocker, San Francisco, Nov. 20, 1880, 2:25¼.

One mile, by a three-year-old filly—Hinda Rose, Lexington, Ky., Oct. 10, 1883, 2:19½.

One mile, by a three-year-old stallion—Steinway, Lexington, Ky., Aug. 28, 1879, 2:25¾.

One mile, by a four-year-old filly—Sallie Benton, San Fransisco, Dec. 13, 1884, 2:17¾.

One mile, by a four-year-old stallion—Albert W., Oakland, Cal., Sept. 5, 1882, 2:22.

One mile, by a four-year-old gelding, Jay Eye See, Chicago, Sept. 23, 1882, 2:19.

One mile, by a five-year-old filly—Trinket, Dover, Del., Sept. 30, 1880, 2:19¼.

One mile, by a five-year-old stallion,—Santa Claus, Sacramento, Cal., Sept. 11, 1879, 2:18.

One mile by a five-year-old gelding—Jay Eye See, Providence, R. I., Sept. 13, 1883, 2:10¾

One mile, over a half-mile track—Rarus, Toledo, O., July 20, 1878, 2:16.

Two miles, Monroe Chief, Lexington Ky., Oct. 21, 1882, 4:46.

Three miles—Huntress, Prospect Park, L. I., Sept. 21, 1872, 7:21¼.

Four miles—Trustee, Union Course, L. I., June 13, 1849, 11:06.

Five miles—Lady Mack, San Francisco, April 2, 1874, 13:00.

Ten miles—Controller, San Francisco, Nov. 23, 1878, 27:23¼.

Twenty miles—Captain McGowan, Boston, Mass., Oct. 31, 1865, 58:25.

Fifty miles—Ariel, Albany, N. Y., May 5, 1846, 3:55:40½.

One hundred miles—Conquerer, Centreville, L. I., Nov. 12, 1853, 8:55:53.

One hundred and one miles—Fanny Jenks, Albany, N. Y., May 5, 1845, 9:42:57.

TROTTING TO WAGON.

One mile—Hopeful, Chicago, Oct. 12, 1878, 2:16½.

One mile, drawing 1,000 lbs.—Mountain Maid, Long Island, 1865, 3:42½.

Two miles—General Butler, Fashion Course, L. I., June 18, 1863, 4:56¼, and Dexter, Fashion Course, L. I., Oct. 27, 1865, 4:56¼.

Three miles—Prince, Union Course, L. I., Sept. 15, 1857, 7:53½.

Five miles—Little Mac, Fashion Course, L. I., Oct. 29, 1863, 13:43½.

Ten miles—John Stuart, Boston, Mass, June 30, 1868, 28:02¼.

Twenty miles—Controller, San Francisco, April 20, 1878, 58:57.

Fifty miles—Spangle, Union Course, L. I., Oct. 15, 1855, 3:59:04.

TROTTING UNDER SADDLE.

One mile—Great Eastern, Fleetwood Park, N. Y., Sept. 22, 1871, 2:15¾.

Two miles—George M. Patchen, Fashion Course, L. I., July 1, 1863, 4:56.

Three miles—Dutchman, Beacon Course, N. J., Aug. 1, 1839, 7:32½.

Four miles—Dutchman, Centreville Course, L. I., May, 1836, 10:51.

TROTTING AND PACING, DOUBLE TEAMS.

One mile—Maxy Cobb and Neta Medium, New York, Nov. 13, 1884, 2:15¾.

Four in hand—W. J. Gordon's team, 2:40.

One hundred miles—Master Burke and Robin, 1834, 10:17:22.

TROTTER WITH RUNNING MATE.

One mile—H. B. Winship and Gabe Case, Providence, R. I., Aug. 1, 1884, 2:06.

Three miles—Ethan Allen and running mate, 1861, 7:03¾.

PACING IN HARNESS.

One mile—Johnston (gelding), Chicago, Oct., 3, 1884, 2:06¼.

One mile—Buffalo Girl, Pittsburgh, Pa., July 27, 1883, 2:12½.

One mile—Cohannet (stallion), Providence, R. I., Sept. 9, 1884, 2:18¾.

Two miles—Defiance and Longfellow, Sacramento, Cal., Sept. 26, 1872, 4:47¾.

Three miles—James K. Polk, Centreville, L. I., Sept. 13, 1847, 7:44.

Four miles—Longfellow, San Francisco, Dec. 31, 1869, 10:34½.

Five miles—Onward, San Francisco, Dec. 11, 1874, 12:54¾.

PACING UNDER SADDLE.

One mile—Billy Boice, Buffalo, N. Y., Aug. 1, 1868, 2:14½.

Two miles—James K. Polk, Philadelphia, June 20, 1850, 4:57¼.

Three miles—Oneida Chief, Beacon Course, N. J., Aug. 14, 1843, 7:44.

PACING TO WAGON.

One mile—Sweetzer, Chico, Cal., Nov. 21, 1878, 2:17¼.

One mile—Pocahontas, Union Course, L. I., June 21, 1855, drawing 265 lbs., 2:17½.

Two miles—Hero, Centreville, L. I., Oct. 17, 1855, 4:59.

PACING WITH RUNNING MATE.

Westmont, ch. g., by Almont, dam by Cattrill Morgan, with running mate, paced a mile at Chicago, Ill., Oct. 31, 1884, in 2:01¾. Minnie R., b. m., 2:03¾

BREEDING DRAFT HORSES.

The breeding of draft horses in America of late years

has become a very extensive one, and is a business that the farmer who has good, large mares, though only of ordinary blood, can safely invest in, for the breeding of such mares to pure bred draft horses, cannot fail to produce profitable results at once, whereas, to breed them to any other stallion, might prove a failure. The idea that a great many breeders have, that the breeding of draft horses will be overdone, and the market stocked so they cannot be sold, is an error. The demand for good horses of any kind, draft and road horses especially, will always exceed the supply, and that idea, like any other foolish one, the sooner it is abandoned the better, for the demand is all the time calling for more and better horses. The pet theory with some breeders—and especially the owners of draft horses, that the breeding of draft horses is a safer business, commanding surer profits than the breeding of road, coach and track horses, has caused a great growth of favoritism for mammoth horses, and the Norman, Clydesdale and others have added vastly to the wealth of the United States, but this theory, like others that are harped upon so much will not always hold good. The man who is breeding ordinary cold blooded farm horses or any other class of horses, on a hit or miss principle, who is not educated in the more modern art of breeding horses, and who is opposed to reading either books or papers upon the subject, cannot do better, and will certainly increase the earnings of his farm by the introduction of any pure draft blood, for when so doing he has taken a long step in advance. But the man who has standard trotting blood of approved families and is engaged in breeding trotting horses, or may possess a few, or even one well bred trotting mare of good action, does not take a forward step when he introduces the draft blood upon such mares, for the average price paid for good track horses, of any age, broke or unbroke, is above the price paid for good draft horses, and the average price paid for well-bred geldings, or mares, is far in advance of that paid for heavy geldings or mares, and for every "draft stallion that has been sold in the United States for $5,000, there has been five trotting stallions sold for $15,000," and as great a difference has been obtained for good brood mares. Again the price obtained for the service of a good standard bred trotting stallion, is always in advance of that obtained for a draft stallion. This has been one of the great drawbacks with the average farmer, who, slow to see, or rather omit, and adopt the use of a well bred horse, at a reasonable price, plods along in the same old rut, breeding scrubs, or else breeds his valuable trotting mare, to a draft horse or likely a jack. Again the average farmer seems to think—or at least such has come under my observation very often, that they cannot raise a good trotting colt, for if they do, they must have it educated to the road, and track, and probably have it trained to trot, and that is expensive, where if they raise a draft colt, they can work it themselves, or sell it unbroke. Now that is only an idea. It is no more trouble, nor expense, to raise or break a trotting colt, than it is a draft colt, if properly conducted. But on account of being of good blood—or at least ought to be—they will not stand the abuse that the cold blooded colt will, and if not properly handled are harder to control. But once educated to do what you wish them to do, let that be what

THE CLYDESDALE.

it will, do the work of the farm or road, they never forget it, and are always ready for whatever they are called upon to do, more willingly, more capable, and far more trusty, than the cold blooded horse, and because a farmer may raise a good trotting colt, is no reason that he should spend the worth of it with some professional trainer, unless desired. It will sell without track work for more than the average draft colt will, at the same age, and my experience and observations are, if properly conducted, the average farmer can raise both draft and trotting colts, providing he has suitable mares, and at a better profit than he can to confine himself to either one alone.

PACERS AS SADDLE HORSES.

The spirit of the farm says : "The impression prevails among those not familiar with the subject that any family of pacers are saddlers. This is a mistake. There is no animal of the equine race more abominable under saddle than a scrub pacer, in whose ancestry for a dozen years or more, nothing but cold blood can be found. A brute of this kind would require as much time and space to turn in as a cow, would stumble on a wax floor, and, if he failed to break his rider's neck in this way, would jolt the life out of him in a rough pace. From this family of pacers no good can ever come until they are crossed with some blood that will give them action. But there is another class of pacers that stand pre-eminently above all other species of the horse kind, from their loins have come the kings and queens of the trotting and pacing turf and the best saddle horses of the country. These show the clean limbs and supple action of the thoroughbred blood that has nicked so kindly with their pacing ancestors. It is from stallions of this kind, with two, three, or four pacing crosses on top of a thoroughbred foundation, that the best saddle horses will come when coupled with one-half or three-quarters thoroughbred running mares, so that the produce will have from 30 to 40 per cent. of thoroughbred blood in it. It is generally conceded that a thoroughbred can live longer and go further under the saddle, with weight up in proportion to his size, than any other horse. Nature seems to have intended him especially for this purpose. But in breeding the saddle horse as described, man has improved upon nature, and secured not only a more serviceable animal, but one that will stand more constant riding. As a rule a pure thoroughbred has no inclination to go any of the artificial saddle gaits, and when forced out of a walk goes into a trot, and out of this into a gallop. On the other hand a well-bred saddle horse will glide along five or seven miles an hour, in a smooth, frictionless running-walk, or fox-trot, without a jar to himself or rider; and at either of those gaits will go further with less fatigue to both horse and rider, than a thoronghbred carrying the same weight and moving at the said speed in a trot. The thoroughbred will last, and upon this line we rely for courage, activity, capacity, and willingness to go. But he is not inclined to the saddle gaits, and takes them with an effort when compelled to. When, however, his blood is mixed with that of a well-bred pacer the produce has a natural disposition to saddle, in addition to the valuable qualities of the runner. For this reason it is necessary to unite the two lines of blood n one animal, in order to get the best material that nature can give, and out of which a first-class saddle horse can be made."

"The memory of man extends to the day when the boys on the farm were proud to ride a fine young horse to church or to see the girls. They took pride in the colts, and taught them to move freely uuder the saddle, and above all, when the colt was broken he was taught to walk. Now the boys must have a fine buggy and harness, and the colt must show his style and speed all the time. The boy is in too great a hurry to allow the colt to walk. The colt, buggy and boy, are soon a used up set by fast driving.

If we could return to the fashion of riding on horseback, we would save millions to the farmers, and the boys and girls would develop better forms and have better health. Any lazy lout can ride in a buggy, but to be a graceful rider on horseback, one must have some energy and get up in their nature. There is life and health in riding on horseback. The whole system feels the invigorating effect of it. The rider and the horse catch the fire of sympathy and excitement in the run or fast paces, and every nerve and muscle of the body is brought into healthful, invigorating play. The farmer will find it to his interest to raise a class of colts that the boys would like to ride. He can raise three or four fine saddle colts for what one buggy and harness will cost, and a fair saddle horse will always sell at a good price."

THE GENERAL PURPOSE HORSE.

The diversity of opinion among horsemen, upon this question, as how the general purpose horse should be bred is as great, probably, as upon any other one question in the art of breeding horses. Some breeders claim that the best general purpose horse, is one produced by a cross of a high-bred racer, or trotter upon large cold blooded mares. Others claim right vis. vesra to this; while others claim that the only way to produce such a horse, is by the coupling of large trotting or pacing bred stallions, with mares of the same kind. And if ever a general purpose class of horses are produced, one that can be relied upon as to its characteristics, my opinion is that the last mentioned way is the best way, and the only way it will ever be done. That the general purpose horse should be composed of good blood, that will give him action and stamina as well as size, no intelligent breeder will dispute, for without this, how would anyone expect him to fill the numerous wants of man and serve him at home on the farm, in the plow or wagon, on the road, in the carriage or under the saddle. A general purpose horse, like a general purpose cow, may be classed under the handy kind of animals, suited for a great many purposes under divers circumstances; but to his value as a selling animal, he cannot be rated very high, for as a general thing the class of people that want him are not willing to pay a large price for a horse. Those that have the color, action and style combined with size enough for carriage use, full 16 hands high or more, are the horses of this class, that brings the best prices. Any intelligent breeder of these days need not be reminded of the value of breeding for some special purpose. What we need is not more horses so much as better ones. "A hint to the wise is sufficient."

CHAPTER XX.

General Information Upon the Horse.

MANAGEMENT OF THE STALLION.—BROOD MARES AND COLTS.—FEEDING, WATERING AND GROOMING.—SHOEING.—EDUCATION OF HORSES.

In speaking of the various subjects as to the general management of the horse, I shall endeavor to make it as brief as possible, and only give such information as I think may be of benefit to the mass of readers of this work.

Being an admirer of the horse, an extensive reader and close observer, with many years experience as to their management, if the rules as herein given are closely observed, they will be of great benefit to the experienced as well as the inexperienced horsemen.

MANAGEMENT OF THE STALLION.

First I will speak of the management of the stallion, which, if understood, is very often neglected by the owner and groom. His stable should be a box-stall not less than twelve feet square, well lined inside, with a box and manger snugly fit in one corner for the feed. The doors should be strong and securely fastened, ceiling high and the ventilators well up so as to prevent any strong draft of air upon the horse. In a stall of this kind, the horse should have perfect freedom and not tied unless during the day. The stable should be cleaned once, or oftener every day, and never allowed to become foul.

This is something that should be observed in every stable, if you wish healthy horses.

HOW TO FEED.

The food should be mainly good, sound oats—nothing is better; but this should be varied by an occasional ration of corn or barley; for horses, like men, are fond of variety in their food, and an occasional change of diet is conducive to health. Wheat bran is an invaluable adjunct to the grain ration, and can never be dispensed with. It is the cheapest, safest and best of all regulators for the bowels, and it is especially rich in some of the most important elements of nutrition. No specific directions as to the quantity of food can be given. Some horses will require nearly twice as much as others; and the quantity that may be safely given will depend somewhat upon the amount of exercise in any given case. Some horsemen recommend feeding three, and others five times a day; but in either case, no more should ever be given than will be promptly eaten up clean. If any food should be left in the box, it should be at once removed, and the quantity at the next time of feeding should be reduced accordingly. As a rule, it will be safe to feed as much as the horse will eat with apparent relish; and then with plenty of exercise, he will not become overloaded with fat. The hay, as the grain fed, should be sound, and free from mould and dust, and the stall should be kept clean, well lighted and perfectly ventilated.

The amount of exercise to be given will vary somewhat with the condition and habit of the horse. If he is thin in flesh, and it is thought best to fatten him up, the exercise should be lighter than it otherwise would be; and, on the other hand, if there is a tendency to become too fat that may be corrected by increasing the amount of exercise that is given. The exercise given the horse shoud be such as will be expected of his colts. Draft horses should not be led or driven faster than a walk in taking their exercise and they will require much less of it than the roadster or the runnig horse—three miles a day generally being sufficient, while the roadster and running horse may safely have five miles, which should in some cases be increased to eight and even ten, at a much more rapid gait than the draft horse.

The point to be aimed at in the stable management of the stallion, is to so feed, groom and exercise as to keep the horse to the very highest possible pitch of strength and vigor. The idea which prevails among many stable grooms that feeding this or that nostrum will increase the ability to get foals, is sheer nonsense. Anything that adds to the health, strength and vigor of the horse will increase his virility or sexual power, simply because the sexual organs will partake of the general tone of the system; and on the contrary, whatever tends to impair the health and vigor of the general system, will have a deleterous effect upon the sexual organs.

HIS EDUCATION.

While the temper and disposition of the stallion are largely matters of inheritance, yet much depends upon his education.

It is easier to spoil a horse than to cure him of bad habits when they are once formed. If there is any appearances of a disposition to be "headstrong" and unruly, he should never be led out except by a bridle that would enable the groom to exercise complete control over him.

It requires some skill and a good deal of patience to teach a stallion to behave himself properly when brought out to serve a mare. He should never be allowed to go on her with a rush; but should be led up on the near side of the mare, to within about ten feet of her, and made to stand with his head towards the mare, about opposite her head, and, when he is ready, he should be led towards her and made to commence the mount when at her side, instead of going a rod or so, with his fore feet sawing the air, as is often the case. By observing these directions, there will be but little danger of injury to the stallion by a kick from the mare when he is mounting, especially if a good man is at her head to prevent her from wheeling towards the horse when he approaches.

The danger to the horse is always the greatest when he is coming off, because many mares will kick then, that will stand perfectly still when he is mounting. To obviate this, it is always best for the groom who holds the horse to seize the mare by the bit with his left hand at this moment, and bring her head around towards him by a sudden jerk as the horse is coming off. But in most cases, indeed all cases where there is not absolute certainty that the mare will stand perfectly quiet, the hobbles should be used, and then there can be no danger.

WHEN THE MARE SHOULD BE TRIED.

A point upon which there is great diversity of opinion is, when and how often a mare should be tried after she has been served by the stallion. A mare will almost invariably be "in heat," on the ninth day after foaling, if she is healthy and has received no injury in giving berth to her foal; and in most cases it is best that she should receive the horse at that time, if it is desired that she should be kept for breeding purposes. We can remember when it was the almost universal custom to try mares every week after they had been served, but that is not the present practice of many experienced horsemen. The rule now that receives the most general sanction, is, not to try the mare again after service before the lapse of 14 days, then the eighteenth or twenty-second day after service, and then, if she refuses the horse, she should be tried every week for some four weeks; and then if she doesn't come within that time, it is reasonably certain that she is in foal. She ought to be closely watched, however, for some weeks afterwards, because in some cases mares will pass over a period of one or two months, or even longer, without any appearance of heat, and yet not to be pregnant. Again there are other mares, and they are more numerous than one would suppose, that will appear to be in heat and will freely receive the horse when they are in foal, and even up to almost the time of foaling. Such mares are always very annoying both to their owners and keepers of stallions.

Again mares that are uncertain breeders should be bred early in the spring, and carefully watched in the summer. If a mare is not with colt she will usually come in season again from 14, 18 or 22 days, and mares that receive the horse when taken to him but fail to catch after repeated trials, should be examined and operated upon. By examination, very often with mares of that kind, the mouth of the womb will be found closed, and unless it is opened they will not get in foal. This is contrary to some theoretical writings that I have read, but according to practical results that I have tried in my years of practice in the business. This is not a very hard operation to perform, and not a dangerous one. The hand should be well greased and the examination made with some caution. Another practice used with mares of that kind is, not to let the horse try them before service, if they are known to be in heat, but bring the horse out and allow him to mount at once, in this way she will be served before her amorous desires are arroused to so great a heat, and thus will be more apt to become pregnant. Again the practice of allowing two services only a few hours apart, or one in the evening and again in the morning, or vice versa, often proves successful, especially with young mares of nervous disposition. There are two other practices used by some horsemen, and which I have practiced with good results, upon uncertain and annoying mares. One is, when the mare is known to be in heat, give her a good brand mash with two ounces of sweet spirits of niter in it, in the evening, and early in the morning allow the horse to serve her. The other is by bleeding freely either from neck or mouth. Both practices are calculated to relax the system, and reduce their amorous desires. Any of the methods given here can be practiced by any practical horseman, and will prove successful, and are valuable to those owning uncertain and annoying brood mares.

THE NUMBER OF MARES TO BE SERVED.

The number of mares that a stallion may be permitted to serve during a season has long been a subject of discussion among horse breeders. It is generally held that the two-year-old stallion will be all the better for not serving any mares at all, that a three-year-old should be limited to fifteen or twenty services, and that a four-year-old should not go beyond twenty or thirty. It is very desirable, at the earliest possible stage in the life of a stallion, to ascertain what his qualities as a foal getter are likely to be, and with this object mainly in view I consider it wise to let the two-year-old serve a few choice mares, merely enough to show the character of his get. As a three-year-old, I should, with the same object in view, permit him to serve a larger number, which may thereafter be increased with each succeeding year until he is fully matured, when, if properly taken care of, with reference to food and exercise, eighty mares may safely be served during the year, but this number in my opinion should never be exceeded.

With the young stallion that is to serve but a few mares, I should prefer that these should all be served within the space of a few weeks—say two or three a week until his limit for the season has been reached—and then let him be withdrawn entirely from the breeding stud. He will soon forget all about it—will cease to fret after mares, and will have nothing to do but to grow until the next season. But when it comes to doing business with the stallion, he should rarely be permitted to serve more than twice a day; and even this should not be kept up for any great length of time. One a day during the season is better; but the groom cannot always do just as his judgement dictates in this matter.

Another thing is that people suppose that they can compensate for a great deal of service by an enormous quantity of stimulating food or drugs, and no exercise. This is an error. Good sound food, given regular in the right quantity, with some grass or green burdock—nature's own remedy—plenty of moderate exercise, and good grooming is the kind of treatment he wants to prove successful.

EFFECTS OF AGE UPON THE QUALITY AND FERTILITY OF THE GET OF THE STALLION.

Another point upon which there has been much discussion is, the effect which age has upon the fertility of a stallion ; and according to the information gathered from experienced breeders, it seems that the age of the stallion has nothing to do with his fertility. Hence the conclusion is that in the number of mares served, so in the matter of age, the reproductive powers of the stallion appear to be almost entirely a matter of condition, and that age has no effect whatever upon the percentage of foals from a given number of services. There has also been much speculation as to the comparative value of foals got by a stallion at different periods of life. The statistics of the trotting horse furnishes us with abundant evidence to prove that here also, the age of the sire has but little or no effect. If any difference is observable, it is in favor of the more aged stallion, generally those in the teens.

CARE OF BROOD MARES AND COLTS.

The next question to be considered is, how shall the mares be cared for while being bred, or while in their pregnant state? This I consider of as much importance as any other point in the art of breeding, for the following reasons:

First, upon the mare's condition when served, depends largely, as to whether she will become pregnant or not. For in poor health when served, she is not as apt to become

GENERAL INFORMATION UPON THE HORSE. 397

pregnant as if in good health and condition, but she should not be over fat. In the second place, it depends very much on the mental condition, when brought to the horse. If they have been rode or driven hard for a long distance, and are hot or excited, they are more liable to fail, than if cool and quiet. Again, mares that have been used for a long time on the road, and kept upon dry feed, are much harder to get with foal, than those that have run out and received all kinds of food, and the same may be said of quite young mares, two and three years old, or quite aged mares, as they are always more annoying than those of middle age. Last, but not least, is the manner in which the mare is kept while in her pregnant state, for upon her health and condition, while in foal, depends the growth, constitution and vigor of the colt.

RULES TO BE OBSERVED.

First, be sure the mare is in good health when bred, and give her such care and feed afterwards, as to keep her in good health, and a thriving condition. For this purpose there is nothing better than to turn her out in a good blue grass or timothy pasture, and let her run at leisure, or if in use, on the farm or road, with a reasonable amount of work, good feed and care she will do just as well, and will thus pay her way. Her feed should consist of oats, midlings and corn, and if possible a run at grass of nights, or when not in use, for by this means the digestive organs will be kept in a healthy condition.

Second, avoid heavy salting and clover pasture, especially in wet weather salt should be given twice or three times a week, and in small quantities, or what is better, keep rock salt where she can get it when wanted, or use soda in place of salt, a tablespoonful at a time. Clover pasture if used at all should be avoided in wet weather, as it is the cause of a great many mares failing to get in foal, or losing their colts when once pregnant. Again, avoid pulling, hard riding or driving. The last two months of pregnancy, she should be fed liberally with a bone and milk producing food, good oats, mill feed, oil cake, hay, if not dusty, and some corn, and should be used regular at slow light work, or else be turned out in a lot away from other horses during the day, and if in the winter or early spring provided with a box-stall sufficiently large and well secured to prevent accidents, to run in during nights and stormy days, but if during warm weather there is no place better than a grass lot or field well fenced, and then often several mares can be turned together without any danger. Mares treated in this way, rarely have any trouble at foaling time. But on account of the colt being born as it is, many times, with the head covered with the placental envelope, which will smother the colt in a few moments if not removed, safety demands that they be watched by some person of good judgement, and capable of rendering assistance if needed. A little attention at the proper time would save the lives of many valuable colts. A mare usually goes about eleven months, but the time varies considerably. By close attention, the time can be foretold quite accurately. A few days before foaling, there will be a perceptable shrinking of the muscles about the loin and back of the hips, the teats will fill out plump to the ends, and not unfrequently there will be a discharge of milk from the udder. As soon as these symptoms occur, the mare should be closely watched, as the foal may then be expected at any time, whether it be more or less than the usual period of eleven months.

THEIR CARE AFTER FOALING.

After the colt is foaled, the mare should receive for a week or more, light, easily digested food, as mentioned before, and if possible, a run at grass—or if in early spring turned on rye wheat for an hour or more at a time with a rest, free from work of any kind.

When the grass is poor, or the mare is not a good suckler, she should receive such food and in such quantities as will cause her to furnish milk as the age and growth of the colt may demand it. The first few weeks of a colt's life is the most critical time of its existence. It is then that it needs careful attention. The mare should receive such attention in the way of care and food that will promote good health. Her food should be so regulated that her bowels will be kept in a healthy condition, for if they become impaired, their condition is soon transmitted to the colt, which is the cause of the death of a great many, they should be closely watched in this respect, and if ailing, promptly treated according to the instructions as given upon this subject in the veterinary department.

If a rapid growth in the colt is desired, it is important that it should be full fed from birth, and in case the dam does not yield milk enough to give a strong and steady growth, this should be supplemented by cow's milk, and also by teaching it to eat oats and midlings. The colt can easily be taught to eat any kind of soft food, or sweet, warm skim milk, with occasionally a little oatmeal in it, will produce just as good a result.

When it becomes necessary to wean such a foal, it is only required to increase the amount of feed.

WEANING TIME.

The colt may be weaned at five or six months of age which is best done by keeping it from the dam for a few hours at a time, increasing the length of time at each separation. It will in this way learn to depend upon itself and be better for the mare.

No rules can be given for feeding, pasturing, stabling, grooming and handling colts. The breed, age, size and disposition of the colt, together with climate, locality and surrounding circumstances, and last but by no means least, the good practical common sense of the owner should govern in each case. A few suggestions may be made, not as a guide, but only as the result of some experience and observation, and a good deal of reading and thinking upon the subject of horse breeding.

Study nature, and conform to her laws as nearly as possible; but still bear in mind that you are rearing one of the most domestic of all animals. One of the first demands of nature is freedom in the open air. No course of exercises can do the colt or horse so much good. He will give full play to every muscle in his body, and expand every air-cell in his lungs. And not the least valuable part of this development is a good roll on mother earth. A horse that has been deprived of this privilege for most of his life cannot be said to be well developed. Another demand of nature is friendship. The well bred colt wants to be your friend. Treat him kindly and he will be one. Kindness will demand comfortable quarters, with abundance of sound food, and pure water. He should at all times have free access to salt. In case his appetite fails, smaller rations for a time, or change of feed, will likely be better than drugs; but if showing much illness should receive prompt medical treatment.

The horse colts if not castrated, should be put in a grass lot by themselves in due time to prevent accidents of any kind that may occur by leaving them run with brood mares or fillies. This should be attended to at the age of one and a half years, or before, as a well bred colt, or an early foal, often becomes troublesome during the second year.

WHEN TO CASTRATE COLTS.

The proper time to castrate colts, is something upon which there is great diversity of opinion, while some breeders prefer castrating them quite young, at the age of one year, and some even at six months or younger, others claim that they should be allowed to partly mature first. But practical results has proven that the castration of colts should be governed more by their development than age. If a colt has made a rapid growth at one year of age, and is well developed in front as to the head, neck and body, or if he shows a deficiency in the hind quarters, being light, he had better be castrated than allowed to go a year or two longer, as early castration with a colt, as with any other animal, refines the fore part and develops the hind part. When the colt is to be kept for a stallion, he should be kept the same as any other colt, allowed freedom in the open air at all times when the weather will permit, and not kept penned up like a lion. When two or three years of age he should be allowed to serve a few mares so as to test his breeding qualities, and when off duty should be used very much the same as any other horse when it can be done with safety. The heavy horse should be used on the farm, but the light horse should be used at just such work as his colts will be expected to perform. His feed should be just enough to keep him in good condition, but not fat.

Beware of over fat stallions, they are not sure breeders, and often some serious defects are hidden under superabundance of flesh.

It has already been suggested that no exercise is so good as freedom in a paddock, a pick of grass, a bite of earth, and a good out doors roll, and an opportunity to romp and play and be a colt again. Therefore every stallion owner should have a paddock, enclosed with a safe fence and large enough for a good run.

FEEDING, WATERING AND GROOMING HORSES.

There is probably no other work on the farm which the farmer will find so much difficulty in delegating to others as to the care of the horses.

The average work hand will over-feed with grain as well as with hay, but the watering of the horses and the cleaning of them, as well as the cleaning of the stables, and to the many little things looking to the health and good condition of the horses, are neglected with impunity. Unless the owner is convinced that his hand understands the management of horses better than he does himself, he should attend to the feeding of the horses, and see that the horses and the stable are kept perfectly clean.

A consideration of the anatomy of the horse's stomach affords useful indications regarding feeding and watering. When convenient, horses should be fed and watered at short rather than long intervals. This is an obvious indication, for the small size of the stomach precludes the horse from rapidly ingesting a quantity of food sufficient to serve for a long period. In the treatment of horses, the nearer we follow their natural inclinations the better. This is more forcibly brought to mind, when it is remembered that nature makes no mistakes.

The horse should be fed in proportion to his size, and the labor he is required to perform. And no more should be fed than it will readily digest. It is not what is eaten, but what is digested, that furnishes the strength and muscle. A horse that is not working hard every day does not require the amount of feed that one does that is kept busy. High feeding, unless the animal is heavily used, is a positive injury.

It is better to under-feed than to over-feed a horse. The first is only a temporary evil, but the last permanently injures the faithful animal. A fat horse is liable to indigestion, sun-stroke, cold, flatulence (colic), and ever so many other ills, which a horse in condition is not only free from, but if properly fed, cleaned, and worked, is not liable to get.

Night is the only time when hay should be fed heavy, especially to animals used for quick work. Even the slow plow teams should have but little hay at morning and noon feeds, but give them a generous supply at the evening meal. By doing this, your horse will keep in better spirits and condition, and be free from any tendency to "pot-belly" which horsemen so much dislike to see.

The best and cheapest way to salt horses, is to keep a piece of rock salt in the trough. They are then liable to get all they want, and when they want it without wasteing it.

VALUE OF GROOMING.

To all appearances a horse may be in good health and in a thriving condition, but little attention paid to him in the way of cleaning and rubbing, but it is evident that no horse can be in the best condition without a thorough grooming at least once a day. Don't think that you have properly groomed your horse, when you have succeeded in scraping the dirt off so that your neighbor cannot see it across the field and laugh at it. Too many curry their horses merely because others do, or because others might make fun of them if they did not make a pretension toward keeping them clean, and were they sure that no one would see them they would never use the comb or brush. They forget or never knew that while cleanliness is one of the objects of grooming, it is not the only or greatest one. The entire system of the horse is affected by the amount of rubbing it receives and the condition its skin is kept in. A beautiful coat of hair adds greatly to the value of a horse, and no one will doubt for a moment that grooming materially affects this part at least. Don't be afraid of killing your horses with cleanliness—many a horse has been unfitted for work a month or two from a sore shoulder caused by dirt under the collar that it would have taken but a few minutes to remove. The feet of many a horse have been completely ruined by the shoes becoming imbedded in them, that it would have taken less than a quarter of an hour to have removed. There are many little matters pertaining to the general welfare and comfort of horses on the farm that might be mentioned, but to the thinking man they will present themselves, and by the successful horseman they will be attended to.

SHOEING HORSES.

Upon this subject—the shoeing of the horse—is one that volumes of information could be written; but the author will confine himself to such information as he thinks will be of value, and shall offer only a few hints which he hopes may prove beneficial. Horse-shoeing, like any other profession, requires study and practice. If it is worth doing at all it is worth doing well, and if the horse-shoer be bent upon improvement, his practice will be worth more to him than all the written rules in the world. Let it be his aim to do what he does, well, and if he be suited to his profession, he will soon acquire that knowledge of horse-shoeing by reading and practice that will enable him to excel. Not all the fault of the bad or disordered feet of the horse lies with the horse-shoer, but owners of horses, and grooms are often responsible for many of the diseases which is found to lurk about the feet of horses, and they should see that their horses are properly cared for, and when necessary to be shod, that it is properly done.

The shoeing of the horse is a very necessary evil. In his natural state the horse possesses a foot answering to all his wants, its growth being equal to wear; but as soon as he is engaged as servant to man, there are but few horses, when in full work, whose feet will stand the wear and tear of road work; hence the necessity of protecting them with a shield of iron. The comfort and value of the horse very much depends on good or bad shoeing, in the same way as a man walking in good or bad-fitting boots. If at ease the horse will show his natural energy and buoyancy of spirit, in contrast to the sordid, and dejected appearance of one traveling in pain ; the one after work feeds with appetite and rest. the other is dejected, eats, and rests but little. These difficulties are discernable by those who are accustomed to horses and regard their welfare, whether he be master or groom, and any defect should at once be amended.

In shoeing the horse, as well as the man, the shoe should fit the foot, instead of trying to change the formation of the foot to fit the idea of a shoe.

One of the most important and least observed points in shoeing is the tread ; that is the proportion throw on different parts of the shoe. On a well-balanced foot the wear of the shoe is tolerably even all round, except the toe, where there is naturally an increased friction and wear. The shoe should be evenly worn and the farrier on taking off an old shoe should observe this and prepare the foot accordingly, for the chief thing to be accomplished is the manner in which a shoe is put on, rather than the pattern. In choosing a shoe the points to be aimed at are lightness and narrowness of iron, consistent with the class of horse and work ; it interferes less with the natural structure of the foot, and gives firmer foothold with less slip. A plain broad shoe without groove is the strongest, but allows free slip ; but is suitable for road use in summer, or for farm work and horses of heavy step.

HORSES WITHOUT SHOES.

The advice to allow horses to go barefoot during work on the farm is of paramount importance. It will do more good toward curing contracted feet than all other remedies. It will prevent contraction to a certain extent. Many severe cases of contraction by this simple and quite inexpensive process can be permanently cured.

Horses should be allowed a time to expand the hoof, and recoup by going barefoot. I mean all and every kind of horse, no matter how or where worked, if he can be spared for a few days where the work demands shoes. Let your horses go barefoot whenever you can ; at least two months a year they should be unshod.

SHOEING COLTS.

Colts should always be shod light at first, and if the roads are such as to permit it, with tips. That is a plain shoe running from the toe to front part of heel, and thicker and wider at the toe, than at the heel, Such a shoe comes nearer nature and is free from calks which may cause the colt to stumble or cut itself. Heavy shoes upon a colt and especially if they have calks, must feel cumbersome and cause a difference in its action, also makes its legs weary in traveling, causing it to forge, cut its quarters, etc., while if it be shod as directed, there will be little or no difference in its motion. All colts when first shod should be driven with care. If it be desirable the second set of shoes may be heavier than the first.

PARING THE FEET.

Before fitting the shoe the foot should be dressed properly, and made perfectly level ; this will best be made level with a rasp ; the shoe may then be fitted to the foot. This should be nicely done, so it has an even bearing upon the foot, the heels of the shoe should come close to the frog, but not so close as to touch it or interfere with it.

In shoeing the bars of the foot should not be cut out with the knife, or the frog interfered with, but let nature do her work with these.

The art of shoeing consists of fixing a shoe on the foot in such a manner as to preserve the natural tread whereby the freedom and elasticity of action will not be impeded. This skill is accomplished or not according to the skill with which the shoe is put on, more than to any particular style of shoe used, whether it be plain or with calks.

The suitability of either depends on the strength of foot, the nature of roads, and the kind of work required from the horse. So also with regard to the frog bearing on the ground. In a strong foot with strong, healthy frog, it may be allowed; but if the frog be soft or spongy it would be injurious, and lead to lameness. Under no circumstances should the frog be prominent beyond the surface of the shoe.

The frog is constructed of a very elastic material. It forms an elastic pad, diminishing concussion and allowing a limited expansion, giving some freedom to the action of the joints situated in the foot. Maintaining these parts of the insensitive foot in a healthy condition is of the utmost importance to insure a long life of usefulness.

Carelessness about horses feet produces much trouble. They should be closely looked after, and kept properly shod or trimmed, shoes should not be allowed to remain on to long, and when removed the clinches of the nails should be well cut and see that they are all removed and not allowed to remain in the foot to cause an injure.

EDUCATION OF HORSES.

Upon the education of the horse depends his value.

Therefore it is necessary that he should be thoroughly and properly educated, and the person who undertakes this calling should first learn to pay attention to the most important factor of a true horseman, namely,"self government."

Prof. York says: "The greatest study of mankind is man, and the greatest triumph is to obtain the mastery over ourselves. A hasty temper has permanently injured or absolutely ruined thousands of horses, man is superior to the horse only so far as he exercises that superiority of intelligence, and the moment he allows his passions to have full sway, his superiority ceases. Whenever the operator becomes heated and nervous, he should at once rest from his labors, and when he is cool and not excited, he will accomplish more in ten minutes, than he can in an hour of frenzied attempts at control. Strive from your first approach to obtain confidence of your subject, which once gained and never abused, will insure complete success.

REMEMBER THIS,

You can teach the horse only through two senses, sight and feeling, and he can learn but one thing at a time. Therefore teach that one act alone. Make sure by repetition that he unerstands you, and be careful that you remember how you taught him. It is the act in man that causes the act in the horse, and any change made by you in the manner in conveying to him a knowledge of your will, is sure to confuse, and he may fail to conform to your wishes from want of a conception of what you really mean, and not from a disposition to do wrong or rather not to do what you desire of him. Show your horse exactly what you want him to do, and endeavor to use the patience and reason in teaching and controling you would at least believe necessary for yourself to understand if placed in like circumstances. Make your horse a friend by kindness and good treatment. Be a kind master and not a tyrant."

CAREFUL TRAINING FOR HORSES.

The education of the colt should be commenced at an early age and thoroughly followed up until old enough for use. One of the most serious mistakes that farmers make in training their young horses is in not doing their work thoroughly. When once undertaken the work should be made complete. To stop and start at certain words, to turn to the right or left at other words, or signals, should not be enough, although many men who have the constant handling of horses are entirely satisfied with these results. The fact that horses are capable of learning these rudiments in training with as little teaching as they do only proves that they are capable of further training which may be carried to a considerable degree with profit as well as pleasure. It is not necessary to occupy the entire day with a colt, or give it a lesson every day, but an occasional lesson at not two long intervals, will go a long ways toward his education. The colt should be trained and developed to make him as nearly perfect in his class as possible. The heavy draft horse should be true and steady, and move off with his load at a square vigorous walk. The trotter, pacer or runner, should have a free honest gait, which is more valuable than a record, gained perhaps at too great a cost to his physical powers, or by being forced past an honest gait. One of the most

THE AMERICAN TROTTING HORSE.

important lessons now is for him to learn that he is becoming a horse, and that he should act like a good, sensible one, and not always be getting himself and master into trouble. And, above all, do not permit ignorant or brutal grooms to crush out that noble characteristic of every good horse, which Josh Billings calls "good horse sense."

Horses with high mettle are more easily educated than those of less or dull spirits, and are more susceptable to ill training, consequently may be good or bad according to the training they receive. If a colt is never allowed to get an advantage it will never know that it possesses a power that man cannot control ; and if made familiar with strange objects it will not be skittish and nervous. A gun may be fired from the back of a horse, an umbrella held over his head, a buffalo robe thrown over his neck, a railway engine pass close by, his heels bumped with sticks, and the animal take it all as a natural condition of things, if only taught by careful management that he will not be injured thereby. There is a great need of improvement in the management of this noble animal— less beating wanted and more education.

Timidity in a horse is a fault which usually can be cured, but only by a course of kind and patient treatment. Rough usage will never accomplish that end, but is only calcuated to make trouble more deep-seated. If he scares at any object, speak to him kindly and let him stop and look at it ; give him a few gentle strokes on the neck with your hand, speak kindly to him all the time, and gently urge him toward the object he scared at ; be careful not to urge him too hard at first ; above all do not whip him ; give him time to see that he is not going to be hurt ; when you can do so let him smell of the object, provided it is not some offensive carcass ; he will not scare at it again. When this has been done several times, he will have gained confidence in you and in himself. The timidity will soon wear off and your horse will be cured.

Avoid teaching bad habits for the reason that it costs more to correct one, and form a new one in its place than it does to teach ten good ones. So in the care and treatment of the horse that is sound and healthy, it is much less expensive to provide against accidents and disease, than to furnish medicines and treatment for repairing injuries or curing diseases. And I will invite your attention to some ounce packages of Preventitives as given by Prof. York and others:

To avoid accidents, educate your colts and aged horses as well, very thoroughly. Make your control absolute, and thus avoid many serious accidents, as they are termed, but are often the result of negligence, or, to be plain, laziness. All the theory in the wide world, without practical illustration thereof, is of no avail. Do not sit down and wish this or that done. Arise and do that which is needful, thereby increasing the value of your horse and adding to the safety of yourself and others. Take time to examine your harness and vehicle and keep them in perfect order. Many a life has been sacrificed and much property destroyed through negligence of this duty. Adjust your harness carefully to the horse, and avoid galls, soreness, and subsequent atrophy of muscles swelling. Ill-fitting collars often cause these affections.

Be sure that your horse is adapted to the work you

design him to perform, in size, form, and particularly as to disposition. Do not forget that the horse must go on foot while you ride, and avoid injuries from hard driving. Do not allow him to stand without covering when warm, in severe weather or in a draught of air, but cover him with a good blanket, and especially his front parts instead of his hind parts, and thus escape colds, pneumonia and rheumatic affections. Do not censure another person for neglect of something you ought to have attended to personally, namely, as to care, feeding, watering, or grooming, and discharge all help that neglects, or abuses your horses. Provide suitable shelter, food, and pure water. Allow but a small quantity of water at a time when your horse is heated. Feed but very little corn especially in hot weather. Fevers assume a more aggravated form in horses fed entirely upon corn. Oats, clean and bright, and good timothy hay are good enough for any horse." Give each horse twice a week, a tablespoonful of soda, and the chances are they will never be troubled with colic, worms or bots. Do not increase allowance of food in anticipation of a hard day's work or drive, also avoid change of food after such. Commence a long journey at a moderate rate of speed and increase it if necessary towards the end, and not stop the horse to cool out before reaching the stable, where you are sure of care. Attend personally to that care. Before you tie in stall examine its floors, and remove everything from the manger and see that there are no holes for the grain to escape. Do not let your pride overrule your judgement. I believe a strict observance of the foregoing rules will save many a person in a great measure, from the expense of surgical or veterinary aid and prolong the life of many a good horse. Retain the horse that is kind, and in which your family have confidence, and increase your care with his added years. Do not sell him, to suffer from neglect and hard usage in his old age. "A merciful man is merciful to his beast." And now having enumerated some of the most important preventives as to the care of the horse, I will give a treatise on their diseases, and also those of cattle and sheep. This I will make as plain and brief as possible, avoiding all superfluous or technical language so the average person may quickly find, plainly understand and adopt their use. In this department as in all my former writings, I shall not make use of any teachings except those that I know from practice, observation, or good authority, can be relied upon. This treatment, as well as the entire book, is intended to give the stock owner such information as will enable him to dispense with the unprofitable and perilous services of ignorant pretenders, and to apply rational means of cure when he happens to be beyond the reach of the accomplished veterinarian, and this, it is confidently hoped, it will accomplish, for all who will intelligently study its pages.

CHAPTER XXI.

Veterinary Department for Horses.

INTRODUCTION.—TREATMENT OF THE VARIOUS DISEASES, AND INJURIES TO WHICH THE HORSE IS SUBJECT.—FORMULAS FOR MEDICINES.—MISCELLANEOUS INFORMATION.

INTRODUCTION.

In discussing this subject I propose to depart from the usual method adopted by other works of this kind and instead of discussing at length the different treatments of stock, with a long article relative to pathology, symptoms and diagnosis of each case, which causes delay and tends to weary the reader without conferring any lasting benefit, to proceed, and give in as brief a way as possible the treatment for some of the most common and frequent ailments of stock, first among horses, and then cattle and sheep. In this part of the work, as well as in all other parts, it is my object to be useful rather than offend, or appear learned, and in offering to the public the information herein given, I shall do so with candor. I do not claim to be the originator of all the treatments given, but have in many instances tested the most of them, and know them to be of value. As medicines are only used to assist nature to effect a cure, those methods that will assist the most should be used, and my experience is that for internal treatment, the proper medicines administered in small doses, is far better than a heavy dose, and a proper application externally in most cases is far better than severe blistering or fireing. Kind treatment in the way of good nursing will do more toward restoration of a sick animal to health, than so much strong medicine.

Medicines, powerful in their nature, for good or evil, are often administered in large doses, when little or none is necessary, and such treatment is often prescribed by those not knowing what ails the animal, or without any knowledge whatever of the effect that such a mixture may produce upon the system, and strongly urge that it be administered, simply because somebody else had used the like, and the animal did not die. This is all wrong. The first business, when called to a patient is to ascertain the cause of trouble. Think for yourself, uninfluenced by the opinion of so many others, and give the patient prompt attention as is thought best, when such cases occur that are not properly understood and cannot be properly treated by the inexperienced, promptly employ some practical veterinary to attend to it.

HOW TO OBSERVE DISEASES.

The question is often asked: How to tell what the disease is that this or that animal is affected with, as it cannot speak. To this question I might repeat nature has but one set of weights and measures and these only should be used. Thus, if a horse or other animal has corns or an injured foot, they will be as sure to go lame as they would with an ordinary sprain. The uneasy eye, the anxious expression, and the sharp peculiar look, tell its tale of suffering, and the description is so plain and true, that every one should learn to interpret them. Often the suffering can be told by the pulse, which is felt on the inner angle of the lower jaw, as being the most convenient place, the state of the pulse tells the condition of the heart, whether the disease is of an exhalted or depressed character or whether sickness is at all present. The pulse is more frequent in the young than in old animals. In the full grown and healthy horse, it beats from 32 to 38 in a minute; in the ox or cow, 35 to 42; in the sheep, 70 to 75. For inflamation and fever the frequency of the pulse is increased, in the debility and depression it is slower, but sometimes quicker than natural. As the pulse varies so much it takes some practice to determine and understand it. A healthy horse breathes once to three of the pulse beats. When the breathing is not natural it indicates disease, but both the pulse and breathing can be quickened by exposure to heat, or the hot sun. Hence the advantage of placing animals in a cool and airy place when unwell, as it assists nature to cast off the disease.

TREATMENT OF DISEASED AND INJURED HORSES.

COLIC.—Spasmodic and Flatulent.—Colic with horses is not an uncommon thing, and most every person who is in the habit of handling them, is acquainted with the cause and symptoms of this disease. Cause—a change or excessive amount of food or water, or some similar unknown cause, which is the result of acute indigestion. Sympptoms—rapid breathing, uneasiness, pawing, lying down and rolling. With spasmodic colic the pain is more severe, and death occurs quicker than with flatulent colic, which is slow in its work, often the horse living for several days, and becoming partially or altogether blind.

Treatment: Take tincture of aconite, and belladonna in

equal parts, give on tongue from fifteen to thirty drops at a dose every twenty minutes, until relief is given. A colt will not require as much as a large horse. In a severe case when this dose does not give relief, the third dose, take sweet milk, one-half pint, turpentine, two tablespoonsful, and give as a drink. Give an injection of soap, salts, and warm water, and apply mustard and warm water to abdomen. The animal should never be urged out of a walk, and must be kept warm.

In case the aconite and belladonna cannot be procured, laudanum and ether, thirty to sixty drops at a dose, or twice the amount of spirits of camphor, in a small amount of water, or in one-half pint of whisky. Never resort to heavy drenching, puncture or violent exercise, such treatment has killed more horses than the disease. After the animal has recovered give him light food and avoid too much cold water at a time when recovering from a severe attack. Measures must be taken to tone the stomach, for this purpose use the condition powder.

NOTE.—Every farmer should keep a bottle of aconite and belladona in the house for immediate use, for you will see by this work that it is very valuable, not only for colic and other diseases with horses, but for milk fever with swine, cattle and sheep, and hoven or paralysis when used as prescribed.

BOTTS.—Symptoms and treatment the same as in colic.

DYSENTERY OR SCOURS.

This is something that occurs frequently with horses, and especially with road horses or colts.

Treatment: If where no other remedy can be procured, take wheat flour, one pint to a gallon of water and give it as a drink, where they will not drink use one-third the amount of water, to which add one fresh egg, and use as a drench, if it can be procured, to this add one tablespoonful of ginger, and from fifteen to thirty drops of laudanum, or a gill of whisky. Give every two hours until relieved, give light food, such as oats, bran, and sweet hay.

INFLAMMATION OF THE LUNGS.

PNEUMONIA.—This is a common and fatal disease with horses, and is caused very often by abuse and neglect which causes them to take cold. By riding or driving a horse until very warm and then stopping them in a cold draft to cool out, or by leaving a window open in the stable during a cold and sudden change, are some of the most fruitful causes.

Symptoms: The first attack is rather slow, the breathing is more or less laborious, and the patient dejected and down spirited. The coat is rough, the body and legs cold, and bowels constipated, the patient stands with head and ears drooped and legs apart as if to prevent falling. On examination, by placing the ear against the side of the patient, over the lungs, a grating or tearing noise can be heard as the patient breathes, then prompt treatment must be given.

Treatment: First make the patient as comfortable as possible in a good warm box-stall, well bedded, if in winter, and kept dry and clean if in the summer. Then give on tongue twenty drops of belladonna, which will regulate the pulse. Then make a thick solution of mustard and rub it well into the hair along the throat, chest, and over the lungs; cover with an old blanket and leave it on for some time, if in cool weather put a blanket over the patient to keep it warm, wash the legs in vinegar and salt as warm as can be applied, and rub vigorously with the hands until dry to get up a circulation, then bandage with flannel. If the patient commences to recover with first treatment discontinue the use of medicine, if not continue to give once or twice a day the aconite and belladonna, and keep the patient warm ; as soon as it can be induced to eat, give soft food with the condition powder in it twice a day, and give a tablespoonful of tincture of iron in the water once or twice a day. Care must be taken not to give too much food until recovery is complete.

OVER RIDING OR DRIVING

Very often brutal or thoughtless persons ride or drive a horse so hard as to cause congestion on the road. Often the horse will reel and fall in its tracks, or upon stopping a thumping noise can be heard several feet away and they can hardly stand.

Treatment: Bleed freely in the mouth or neck, a drop of blood now is worth a pint in an hour, give a small amount of salt water at first and as soon as possible thirty drops of aconite and belladonna, repeat until relief is given, bathe head with cold water and keep the body warm to prevent chilling. If any evil effect is observed afterwards, use cleansing powders in soft food and turn on grass.

INFLAMMATION OF BLADDER AND KIDNEYS. PROFUSE STALEING.

This is somthing that horses are troubled with considerably, and it is caused by bad food, or exposure to cold, rains, storms, etc.

Treatment: Use the cleansing or condition powder freely for some time, and give one ounce of sweet spirits of nitre or evacuate the bladder with catheter, or for horse press into the passage the pith of an onion, and for mares introduce a little black pepper—this will produce staleing in a few moments.

Foul sheath.—All horses are troubled more or less with foul sheaths, and they should be looked after and cleaned by washing in warm water and castile soap, then oiled with fresh lard or sweet oil. Either of these troubles can be told by the difficult staleing.

COLDS AND DISTEMPER.

These two diseases are of frequent occurrence with horses, but neither one at all dangerous if promptly attended to. Colds occur more with matured horses than colts, and are caused by exposure and neglect. Distemper is a colt disease, but frequently old horses are troubled with it.

Treatment: For colts give the condition powder in soft food twice a day, steam the patient well by placing a bag over the nose which has been filled with some hot hops and bran and then pour hot water in to keep up the heat, or put some tar in an old shoe that has a hole in the toe, set the tar on fire, and the smoke will come out of the toe of the shoe which can be held under the patient's nose, and in this way well smoked.

In bad cases bathe the throat well with mustard liniment, or distemper liniment, then smoke as directed.

For distemper: Give the same treatment, smoking or

steaming well every day, and using the distemper liniment until a free discharge from the nose is started, then occasionally to keep them running free, if they gather under jaw open with knife, as soon as ripe, which is as soon as the lump becomes soft. To hasten the gathering, apply under the jaw or throat a poultice of hops and bran. If this simple treatment is effectually carried out, using good sanitary means to keep the patient warm and dry in the winter, and feeding soft food with the condition powder, and in summer allowing free access to grass. The chances are that you will not lose one horse in a lifetime with these diseases.

EPIZOOTIC—PINKEYE.

This is a contagious disease. That occurs once in a while in an epidemic form through the country, and kills or injures a great many horses.

Symptoms: The attack is usually sudden and the horse soon drops its head and ears, and stands with back arched and braced legs as if to bring relief. These symptoms are always accompanied by a hoarse dry cough, rapid breathing, scanty, high colored urine, and hard muscus covered dung.

Treatment: Bathe the throat, chest and over the lungs well with mustard, and cover well with a cloth or blanket, give the condition or cleansing powder freely in soft food, smoke as in distemper once a day and take tincture of gentian root and tincture of iron in equal parts, give on tongue three times a day a teaspoonful, use moderately in warm weather or turn out for exercise, and place all feed on the ground, which will cause the horse to keep its head down thus giving relief. This disease being contagious, it is best not to bring the sick animal in close contact with the well, and by thoroughly cleaning the stable, using asafetida in the troughs, and feeding the condition or cleansing powders once a day to the well horses, it can be prevented from spreading.

HEAVES.

Heaves with the horse is similar to the asthma in the human family. It can be observed by difficult breathing, wheezing and frequently a cough. It is caused by feeding too much hay, especially dusty or clover hay. This statement has been confirmed, as it is seldom known in the West where clover is not used.

Treatment: Feed good sound grain, sweet timothy, or prairie hay, or corn fodder, and give twice or three times a week indigo water to drink. A piece of indigo the size of a large nut in one gallon of water, or use powdered alum, one pound; oil of origanum, two ounces; arsenic, half ounce; dose, teaspoonful twice a day, or smartweed juice, given as a drench, one-half pint at a time, twice a day for a few days.

GLANDERS.

The best treatment for this fatal disease, is to lead the patient to a suitable burial place and destroy it. Then thoroughly disenfect the entire premises by cleaning up every possible thing, and using whitewash and carbolic acid freely. No pains should be spared as this disease is highly contagious to both man and beast.

BRAIN FEVER—BLIND STAGGERS.

Treatment, the same as for congestion.

Paralysis: Bleed freely in the neck, and give three or

four doses, one hour apart, of aconite and belladonna.

FISTULA AND POLL-EVIL.

These terrible diseases of the horse are of frequent occurrence, and very annoying and hard to cure, but the treatment given here can be relied upon, or at least it has been successfully used in many instances, and highly recommended.

Fistula appears at the top of the shoulder blade, and on either side or both, at the same time, and also occasionally on the hips.

Poll-evil occurs on top of the neck just behind the ears. Both these diseases are caused by a bruise.

Treatment: When they first make their appearance they can be observed by a swelling and soreness, and up to the time that matter begins to form, the corrosive liniment will be found very effectual to drive it away. (See prescription, how to make it.) This is a powerful medicine, and in using it the horse must be fastened so he cannot rub or bite the afflicted parts, as it will burn for a minute or two. Apply every morning with a small mop, for some three days, and then take fine powdered gun powder, mix heavily in lard, grease the part well and let go three days, and repeat the treatment over again three times. If this fails to check it, the treatment will have to be changed and one used to cause heavy suppuration. For this purpose use May apple liniment. (see receipt.) A thin coating should be spread over the afflicted part every morning and carefully washed at night, and then greased. This treatment should be continued until matter forms, and as the pass begins to ooze out, increase the amount of liniment and the length of time between dressing up to twenty-four hours, but not longer. This treatment should continue for some three weeks, and always cleansing thoroughly with warm soap suds before dressing, but in using the corrosive liniment, never wash.

In some three weeks after using the May-apple liniment, omit its use and make a liniment as follows: Turpentine and ammonia each, one and a half ounces, croton oil, one-half ounce, mix, cleanse the wound thoroughly, and apply internally until healed.

BONE, BOG OR BLOOD SPAVIN AND THOROUGH-PINS.

These are ailments of the back and joints and are hard to do anything with, but with time and close attention they can be partially cured.

Treatment: Use the corrosive treatment as given for fistula, continue treatment for three or four weeks, and then let go for two weeks, and if necessary repeat, meantime feed soft light food and the condition powders occasionally and turn loose in a box-stall or use at slow moderate work. Where this treatment fails have it properly treated by fireing or fatten and trade off. Beware of bogus quacks offering to cure these blemishes.

RING-BONE AND CURBS.

Ring-bone is a bony substance or growth that appears just at the top of the hoof, and extends clear around. It is caused by a strain and if neglected makes the horse very lame, and soon becomes hard and hard to remove.

A curb is a long bony substance on the back part of of the leg just below the hock, and the same may be said of it as of ring-bone.

Treatment: For ring-bone the same as spavin. Another good preparation is corrosive sublimate, Spanish fly and venice turpentine in equal parts, to this add twice the amount of lard, apply once a day.

For a curb if the afflicted part is feverish, first reduce the fever by applying the cooling lotion, [see receipe,] then use the corrosive liniment, bathe once a day, then wash with soft soap and hot water, continue treatment for a week, then leave go a week, if necessary repeat. This same treatment will remove any splint or callous.

CRIBBING—WIND-SUCKING.

This strange habit of catching hold of some object with the mouth, and sucking wind is very common and no cause can be attributed for it, and no effectual cure. Some prevent it by buckling a strap tight around the neck, and others by running a fine saw between the front teeth, but a horse of this kind is frequently subject to colic and should be avoided.

LAMPASS.

This is something that horses and especially colts are troubled with a great deal, it is simply an inflammation of the muscles in the front part of the roof of the mouth, and have the appearance of ridges or bars.

Treatment: Puncture them well with a sharp knife, and apply copperas matter.

SCRATCHES AND GREASE HEEL.

These are two of the dreaded diseases of the American horsemen, although similar in their characteristics, grease heel is the most obstinate to cure. They appear on the back part of the leg, extending from the heel of the foot to the fetlock, and in extreme cases often reaches up to the knee or hock. The scratches begin with a scabby covering of the skin, coming in patches and continuing to spread until the leg is one mass of sores.

Grease heel commences by the flesh bursting open, and an offensive matter oozing out. If neglected it spreads rapidly and becomes very sore.

Treatment: Wash clean with soft soap and dampen afflicted parts with Dexter liniment for three days and grease with lard and gunpowder. This will cure any case if kept out of the water and mud. Dry snow makes no difference, it is good to help to reduce the fever. In all cases turn on grass or feed soft food, and the condition or cleansing powder, to cleanse the blood and system.

THRUSH.

This is a disease of the foot caused by neglect, damp filthy stables, and also by a bruise or injure of any kind. It often becomes very bad before the inattentive owner or groom notices it, which is observed by a very offensive smell.

Treatment: Clean out and pare away all the diseased part of the foot, then use the treatment as given for thrush. [See recipe.] Apply once a day for two or three days and keep the foot dry and clean while under treatment. This will soon effect a cure, or clean out and apply salt and wet blue clay as a stuffing.

DRESSING TO SOFTEN FEET.

Sliced onions, one pint; oat meal, one quart; charcoal, one half pint; boiling water, sufficient to form a stuffing; stuff the feet and fasten in with a cloth poke if you have no boots. This is excellent for feet either sound or unsound, is valuable in case of founder.

INJURED FEET.

In case an animal injures its foot with a nail or snag of

any kind, examine the foot carefully and if possible find and remove the article, then clean out the foot well and apply turpentine or sea salt to the wound, cover with a tarred rag, and be sure to cleanse and dress every day so as to keep the wound open, after two or three days use the Dexter liniment in place of the turpentine or salt. In case of graveled foot, keep the foot encased in a poultice made of oat-meal, bran and warm water in a sack until open, then cleanse with soap and water and apply the Dexter liniment until healed.

FOUNDER.

Bleed freely in the neck and in the small warts under the pastern joints. Take powdered alum, one-fourth pound; sunflower seed, two ounces; jimson seed, two ounces; mix, dose, one tablespoonful twice a day for two days. If the pastern joints become inflamed and swollen, use sweeting liniment. (See receipe.) Feed oats and bran mashes, with condition powders and new potatoes in absence of grass, and apply the onion dressing to the feet for a week or more.

For corns, pare out the foot well and apply the dressing or foot oil until all soreness is removed.

SWEENEY.

What is known as Sweeney, (atrophy) is located in the shoulder or hip, it is frequently caused by a strain or wrench, in some way injuring the muscular tissues, and sometimes by diseased feet, which causes the muscles of the shoulder to perish for want of exercise.

Treatment: Apply twice a day for several days some of the liniment made as follows: Oil origanum, four ounces; oil hemlock, four ounces; oil spike, two ounces;

oil sassafras, two ounces; chloroform, three ounces; powdered camphor gum, two ounces; olive oil, six ounces; alcohol, one quart. Mix, and shake well when using,

Give quiet work or turn out for exercise, and keep the skin loose by pulling at it every day. Some cure this by taking an old and well smoked hog joal, fry it out, and in the grease obtained mix gun powder, then grease with this.

SPRAINED TENDONS.

The horse is liable to sprains of the tendons, by accident or fast or reckless driving.

Treatment: Apply hot water to remove the fever. Then use the Dexter liniment.

SWELLED LEGS AND ANKLES.

This is caused by the feet being diseased, or by impoverished blood.

Treatment: Put the system in good order by the use of proper food and the condition powder, and bathe the legs with strong copperas water. If the feet are diseased treat them as for thrush, or apply the dressing.

SURFEIT AND MANGE.

These are skin diseases, caused by a weakened condition of the system, or blood.

Treatment: Use the condition powder with soft food, and moisten the parts where the spots or lumps appear with coal oil, one half pint; lard, one half pint; carbolic acid, one tablespoonful.

Water Farcey is another skin disease that appears under the belly, and frequently gathers, and water oozes out.

Treatment: The same as for mange, or bathe afflicted parts with strong hot salt water, or use the Dexter liniment.

LICE.—Treatment: The same as for mange, except omit the carbolic acid.

HIDE-BOUND.

This occurs when a horse becomes poor or neglected and system entirely deranged.

Treatment: Use freely in soft food the cleansing powder, and if possible give grass and special attention to grooming.

SADDLE OR HARNESS GALLS, OR BOILS.

These are so frequent and annoying to both horse and man that the proper treatment for them is of value.

Where the horse can be allowed to go idle it should be done until well, but where this can not be done, then other means must be resorted to. First, the saddle or harness should be so padded as to take the bearing off the afflicted parts. Then wash clean with warm salt water, and bathe with Dexter liniment and meat fryings or pudding grease, equal parts, which will heal any common gall, or paint over with white lead, or cover with a court plaster. Where a large collar boil has formed, cut it open and cleanse it out with warm water, then bathe it internally and externally with the Dexter liniment, by the use of a feather. A cheap application for bruises and galls, and to reduce external inflammation is a decoction of smart weed, two parts, and strong vinegar, one part. Make hot, pour over bran, and apply as a plaster, as hot as the horse will bear.

BLIND OR WOLF TEETH.

This is something that occurs with most all young horses, a small tooth that comes out by the side of the jaw tooth. Some people have great fear of them, thinking they cause week eyes. Some think not, but at any rate they are of no use and can be very easily removed, and are better out than in. But beware of the man that goes through the country pulling horse's teeth, and be sure the horse's tooth needs to be taken out before allowing it pulled. Occasionally a horse has a tooth that wants removing, as it is decayed or injured in such a way that it is annoying to the horse, and very frequently they need dressing, which any good veterinary surgeon can do, or you can do yourself by procuring a tooth rasp.

A VALUABLE EYE WASH.

Take three fresh hen eggs and break them in a quart of cold rain water. Stir until a thorough mixture is effected. Boil over a slow fire, stirring occasionally, adding one-half ounce of sulphate of zinz (white vitrol) to the mixture, remove and the curd will settle to the bottom, and the liquid rests on top. This liquid strained, makes a valuable eye wash for man or beast. The curd applied to the eye will draw the inflammation out. The liquid, if strained free of any sediment and bottled will last a long time. The curd can be applied to the eye of the horse by making a hood so it fits tight over the eyes, or one eye, and cut a hole for the other. Or take tincture of arnica, one ounce, laudanum one-half ounce, sugar of lead one-half ounce, bathe several times a day will remove inflammation or soreness caused by a blow or otherwise, or where the inflammation has caused the haw to appear, what a great many call hooks, and what ignorant pretenders cut out, claiming it is a disease. Use either of the washes and they will effect a cure. To remove slight inflammation take cold salt water and bathe the eye, or belladonna, one part, water three parts, make fresh each time, will soon remove it. If you wish to bleed, bleed below the eye. To remove dirt, etc., from the eye, insert flax seed. To remove film, finely powdered burnt alum, or equal parts honey and hen's oil, applied with a feather, is excellent.

CATARACT LINIMENT.

For a cataract of the eye, try the egg eye wash, or the honey and chicken grease, if these fail to effect a cure I would recommed the following liniment: Sweet spirits of niter, camphor gum and oil organum, each one-half ounce; ammonia, one ounce; alcohol, four ounces; rain water, four ounces; apply twice a day for two days with a soft eye brush or feather, and keep the horse quiet for the time. This was recommended to me by an old veterinarian to be a successful treatment, and is worth trying, for if neglected the horse is no better, if not worse, than a blind one, as it so effects the sight as to cause them to shy.

COOLING LOTION.

Chloroform, alcohol and Golard's Extract, each two ounces; mix, take one third the amount in a quart of rain water, bathe twice or three times a day. This is very cooling, and is used by a great many horsemen in rubbing out race horses, or on receiving a bruise to prevent callouses. Another good and cheap one is, copperas, one-half pound, rain water, one gallon; use twice a day. Will remove fever and soften the skin. White oak bark ooze is also good, made by boiling the bark until a strong liquid is obtained. To one-half gallon of the liquid add a hand full of salt, and apply twice or three times a day.

LEG OR BODY WASH.

Cider vinegar, three quarts; alcohol, 1 pint; ammonia,

VETERINARY DEPARTMENT FOR HORSES. 435

2 ounces; chloroform, 2 ounces; sal. moniac, 2 ounces; tincture of arnica, 2 ounces; shake and apply to the limbs, then bandage; when applied to the loins or shoulders, and cover with a blanket; will stimulate and remove all soreness.

FOOT OIL.

Oil of cedar, oil of hemlock and sweet oil, each 2 ounces; American oil, one gill; Neatsfoot oil, one gill; barbadoes tar, two gills; organum oil, one ounce; apply to frog and foot; will promote health and growth.

TO REMOVE CALLOUSES.

Strong hickory ash soft soap applied once a day, washing with hot water before each application will remove most any callous or splint. For a hard and long standing case, use the soap and corrosive liniment. Another good preparation is soft soap, four ounces; spirits of camphor, two ounces; aqua amonia, one ounce; apply daily. A good general liniment to remove callous is, Dexter liniment, 2 parts; spirits of camphor, one part; apply once or twice a day, and wash off with hot water and soap. The hotter the water the better, it softens the skin and opens the pores.

THRUSH.

Oil of cedar, oil of sassafras and gum of camphor, each one ounce; corrosive sublimate, one scruple; linseed oil, three ounces; keep the feet dry and apply once or twice a day.

MAY APPLE LINIMENT.

Make a strong syrup of May apple roots, while boiling add one-fourth as much strong lard as syrup, keep stirring all the time to prevent burning, cool and put away for use. This is used for poll evil or fistula in their second stage when matter has formed, it will draw it to the surface.

CORROSIVE LINIMENT.

Take one-half pint of turpentine, one ounce of finely pulverized corrosive sublimate, and one ounce of gum camphor. Let stand for a week, shaking every day, when it will be ready for use. Always shake well when using, pour in an earthen vessel and apply with a swab, never the finger, and keep it out of the way of children.

WORM POWDER.

Ginger, eight ounces; black antimony, six ounces; fenugreek, two ounces; worm seed, two ounces; capsicum, two ounces; mix; dose, one tablespoonful once a day. A change of diet is always desirable. Pin worms, which always inhabit the rectum, and occasion persistent rubbing of the tail, may be most effectually removed by the injection, every morning for a week, of three ounces of linseed oil and one-half ounce of spirits of turpentine, the agents to be thoroughly blended by shaking and injected into the rectum; or take salty lard and grease the inside of the anus.

FEVER POWDER.

Powdered gum camphor, two drachms; powdered opium, one-half drachm; powdered ipecac, one drachm; cream of tartar, one ounce; mix. Dose, one tablespoonful once or twice a day. This is excellent to abate fever.

COUGH POWDER.

Pulverized blood root, lobelia seed and licorice, each 4 ounces; nux vomica, 2 ounces; mix. Dose, teaspoonful on tongue three times a day. This is very valuable for any cough.

CONDITION POWDER.

For general use: Glauber salts, one pound; ginger, half pound; blood root, quarter pound; powdered golden seal, quarter pound; powdered licorice, quarter pound; sulphate of iron, quarter pound; mix thoroughly. Dose, one tablespoonful once or twice a day, as the condition may require. This is worth a bushel of the condition powders you buy.

CLEANSING POWDER.

For general use in all cases of blood disorder, hidebound, etc., it is worth its weight in gold: Spanish brown, 2 pounds; ginger, 1 pound; cream tartar, 1 pound; black antimonia, 1 pound; blood root, ½ pound; skunk cabbage, ½ pound; fenugreek, ½ pound; worm seed, ½ pound; indigo, ¼ pound; copperas, ¼ pound; salt-peter, ¼ pound; mix thoroughly. Dose, same as the condition powder.

DEXTER LINIMENT.

Oil of spike, oil of camphor, oil of stone, oil of British, oil of America, oil of opodeldoc, each one ounce; turpentine, one pint. This is the best general liniment I ever knew, either for man or beast, as it is invaluable for healing galls or sores, either fresh or chronic cases, removing collar boils, callouses, etc., with horses, and all cuts or bruises, chapped hands, burns, etc., with the human family. Will also remove the soreness of corns or chilblains, and a great benefit with rheumatism or weak back. In using it for chapped hands, burns or fresh cuts, take liniment one part, sweet cream, fresh butter or vaseline, three parts.

HEALING POWDER.

Burned alum, one-half ounce; powdered chalk, 1 ounce; pulverized gum camphor, one drachm; calomel, two drachms; mix. Sprinkle on sore, will heal quickly, and is good to remove proud flesh.

TO PRODUCE PRESPIRATION.

Tincture aconite, in ten to twenty drop doses every twenty minutes. Clothe warm.

STRAINED STIFLE OR WHIRLBONE.

Fine salt, one tea cup full; ground black pepper, two ounces; spirits of turpentine, two ounces; white of six eggs. Mix and apply, and heat with hot iron until dry.

TO STOP FLOW OF JOINT WATER.

Crocus martis, two ounces; sulphate zinc, one ounce; molasses, one pint. Use with a swab.

Capped hock—When first injured, apply the cooling lotion every hour for one day, then three times a day for one week. If of long standing, apply Dexter liniment. Blisters only aggravate the injury and thicken the skin.

CANKER, SORE MOUTH AND TONGUE.

Inject solution of pulverized borax, alum and strained honey, each one ounce; warm water, one pint, several times per day, and give condition powders on tongue twice per day. Another.—Sugar of lead, bole ammoniac, and burned alum, each four ounces; good cider vinegar, three quarts; use as a wash twice or three times a day, and keep the bit out of the mouth.

SWEATING LININENT.

Take two gallons of mullen leaves and one gallon of

water. Boil until half gallon of juice is obtained; strain, to this add one quart of cider vinegar, one half pint salt, two ounces oil organum, one large beef gall; apply hot. This is one of the best preparations for injured whirl bone, or deep seated strains I ever tried; also for caked bag (garget) with cattle or sheep. When applied, dry in with a hot iron, or cover with blanket. The mullen liquid, vinegar and salt alone is good for swelled or inflamed udders.

TONIC PREPARATION.

To make an old horse feel young and nimble, take tincture of asafetida, cantharides, oil of annis, oil of cloves, oil of cinnamon, fenugreek, each one ounce, and black antimony, two ounces, put this in two quarts of Brandy, let stand ten days. Shake well, and give ten drops to every pail of water. This is better than ginger, whip or spur.

Another good one is common soda, one pound; gun powder, one fourth pound; jimson seed, three ounces; mix. Dose, tablespoonful once a day for a week, in soft food. To prevent driving horses from chilling and contracting cold during the winter, feed them a tablespoonful of mustard seed twice or three times a week.

CARE OF TAIL AND MANE.

In order to thicken the mane or tail, wash well with soft water and castile soap, then dampen with common coal oil, one part, and whiskey two parts. This will prevent rubbing. Brush often with a soft brush, and see that the trouble is not caused by hen lice. To make the mane lay down smooth, or on either side, wet and brush it often, and plat, or weight it.

PARTURITION.

The natural presentation in birth of young animals, is

when both foreteet are presented at the same time, with the head lying extended between them, or when both hind feet are presented, thus forming a gradual wedge with an easy delivery, rarely needing any assistance from man. In some cases one fore foot only is presented, or the hind foot, or the forefeet may be presented, with the head turned on the side, over the back, or doubled on the breast. In cases of this kind assistance is necessary to save the life of the dam, or at least severe injury. To give assistance, oil the hand and insert it until the knee or hock is felt, then partially return, double closely, extracting the knee or hock, then the foot. When the head is missing, partially return, until the head can be straitened, then give assistance, always aiding when the animal strains, pulling downward as well as backwards. Very frequently it is necessary to attach a rope to the legs, or a hook in the eye socket or jaw, in order to give assistance, and may then take the force of two or three men. When it is necessary to cut away the limbs in order to save the dam, the amputation must be either at the hips or shoulders, strip away the skin, leaving it attached to the body, the dissected parts being taken away, the balance will follow easily. When it is necessary to turn the young, always turn down, not up. If flooding follows the delivery, apply cold water to the loins, and give injection of alum water. If the after birth is retained, oil and insert the hand and remove it with the fingers, when protrusion of the womb occurs generally, it turns wrong side out. Wash it off well in Castile soap and water slightly warm, oil it, then gently with your fingers, press from the center, constantly working from outside to center, and it will soon go back naturally, and in most cases, remain without any artificial restraint. Inflammation of the womb.—If this sets in it will cause shivering fits, and colicky pains, arching of the loins, vulva red and swollen, accompanied by a fetid discharge. In cases of this kind the womb is dilated with a fluid, and highly inflamed. This fluid must be drawn with a catheter, through which must be injected a wash of warm water, one quart, laudanum, one ounce. When much fever prevails give 15 drops of aconite at a dose every hour until relief is obtained.

DISEASES OR INJURIES OF COLTS.

Colts are troubled more or less with certain diseases, such as costiveness or diarrhoea, and those of the urinary organs, and very often prove fatal. Treatment: When colts are only a day or so old, they should be closely watched to see if their passages are natural. If constipated, take a piece of tallow candle two inches long, point it and carefully insert it in the anus, or give an injection of oil; if this fails to give relief give as a drench raw flax seed oil, one gill; croton oil, five drops. If the bowels are loose give as an injection, water ½ pint; laudanum, teaspoonful; charcoal, tablespoonful; for older colts increase the dose, give the mother good, sweet food, of the nature the colt requires. If they cannot pass water give one tablespoonful of sweet spirits of niter. In case of injury to the navel by the string being tore off, to close up, causing the water to leak out, cover the navel with cotton, over which pour collodion. This will form a coating, and can be kept in place by a wide muslin bandage being pinned around the colt, the bandage should be looked after every day and not be allowed to become very tight. Where the navel string is not torn off, to close up, tie a string around it.

WOUNDS OR CUTS.

All bad wounds or cuts should be immediately sewed up. This is very easy to do, by putting a twitch on the nose of the horse, also hobbles, or by throwing them, then taking a silk thread and a spaying needle, and thus close the wound, then take lard and sufficient turpentine to cut it well, take of this one part, Dexter liniment or coal oil one part, and keep oiled. This will cause the wound to slough off, and heal nicely without scarring. In a great many cases it can be quickly healed with a carbolic wash, water, one quart; carbolic acid, one tablespoonful, keep bathed. Or by the use of arnica, which is very valuable, or vaseline one ounce, carbolic acid, 30 drops.

CHAPTER XXII.

Veterinary Department for Cattle and Sheep.

SORE EYES.—MILK FEVER. — GARGET. — BLACK-LEG. — PLEURO PNEUMONIA, ETC.—GRUB.—SCAB.—FOOT ROT, ETC., WITH SHEEP.—REMARKS AND REFERENCE.

SORE EYES.

A disease called sore eyes has prevailed to some extent among the American cattle of late years. The disease attacks herds very suddenly and without apparent cause, and seems to be infectious or contagious, both eyes become very sore, and frequently they go blind in one or both. It, like the epizootic with horses, spreads throughout the country and causes considerable of trouble. To treat this, separate the sound from the unsound and from the building or yards where the disease has appeared. Give the affected a half pound of the Scotch powder at a feed in wet bran once a day, and bathe the eyes with the arnica wash for the eye. If possible keep the animal in a dark place during the day, or attach a cloth to the horns so it will hang down over the eyes. Some bleed below the eye, or apply a fly blister to the cheek, either, or both are beneficial. Great precaution should be used to prevent the spreading of this disease among the rest of the herd, or to the sheep. With common inflammation, or injure to the eye, with cattle or sheep, treat the same as with horses.

SCOTCH POWDER.

Epsom salts, 3 pounds; soda, 2 pounds; ginger, 1 pound; charcoal, 2 pounds; sulphate of iron, 1 pound; powdered resin, 1 pound; oil meal, 2 pounds; mix thoroughly. Dose, from one tablespoonful to one-half pound, as directed. This powder is very valuable to use with all kinds of stock, with the following diseases: With horses, for colds, distemper, epizootic, urinary trouble or loss of appetite. With cattle for hoven, dry or bloody murrain. With sheep for hoven, colds, catarrh, or in all cases of constipation or dysentary trouble. inflammation of the bowels or kidneys. Also all milk trouble, such as milk fever, garget, inflamed bag with any kind of stock, and good for swine or poultry as a tonic powder.

HOVEN.

For hoven with cattle, take a half pint of powdered charcoal; one tablespoonful of turpentine; and if at hand, 30 drops of aconite; stir in a quart of water and give as a drench. Hold the mouth open with the hand a minute and the wind will escape as from a bellows. In case the articles named can not be had immediately, give the Scotch powder, one pint, or the swine tonic powder, one pint, and the turpentine as directed. For sheep use the same treatment, only one fourth the amount.

MILK FEVER OR GARGET.

Garget, (caked bag) is one of the most common diseases among cattle, often occurring in the spring, just after calving, or it may be induced by high feeding at other times, or even when running on good grass later in the summer, and it may be induced by efforts to dry off a cow too rapidly. Symptoms and treatment:—The udder is hot, swollen and very tender. First one teat will become hard, then the others. The best remedy is to bathe the udder frequently with hot vinegar and salt, rubbing it gently with the hand, then make a fire with corn cobs or chips in an iron pot, take a large cloth, and put one end around the udder, letting the other end hang down around the pot, thus smoking it well. One or two applications will give relief. Give in soft food one half pint of Scotch or condition powder, or in absence of this, the same amount of epsom salts once or twice a day until the fever is reduced, then give less for a day or two as they may require it. The better plan is to adopt preventive measures. Examine the udder frequently before calving, and if it becomes filled with milk it should be drawn out. Feed the cow sparingly with fresh hay, and milk her frequently after calving.

Milk fever and its cause.—The conditions under which milk fever exists, or is caused, are various. The disease is seldom observed in the cow before the age of five years. It is more frequently found to attack animals in a plethoric condition. It more frequently affects the pure breeds than others, and is also more fatal with them. It seldom occurs subsequent to three days before calving, but always occurs, as a rule, after calving, and previous attacks favor its recurrence. Although the ewe is sometimes afflicted with the disease, and also the sow, and mare occasionally, it is more prevalent with the cow than any class of animals, and undoubtedly is a local inflammation of the womb, which rapidly extends to other parts until the entire system is affected, and true puerperal or milk fever ensues. The animal becomes restless and uneasy, the eyes are red, the horns and head hot; the cow is irritable, finally becomes weak in limbs and unable to rise, and dashes her head about, sometimes with such force as to break her horns. The disease is not to be trifled with, and as soon as the symptoms are noticed give one pound of epsom salts and a pint of raw linseed oil, as the bowels must be opened. Cover the entire body with a wet sheet or blanket, and give aconite and belladona, 30 drops at a dose every half hour until relief is given. If necessary repeat the dose of salts and oil in two hours until relief is obtained. Then feed soft food with the Scotch powder, as they may require it. If their bowels are loose and regular, it will require but little, if not, use it freely. Keep the milk drain off by milking often. A pint of raw linseed oil given the day before calving will prevent this dreaded disease. Another cure which Mr. William Hartley, of Wisconsin, says he has used with good success, is "one pint and a half of lard, one-half pint of coal oil given with new milk warm, and repeat in two or three hours. It has never failed to effect a cure in the ten cases which I have known it to be used." This, no doubt, is very good and worth trying, and especially where the other can not be adopted, as others, as well as Mr. Hartley, say they have used it with success.

ABORTION WITH COWS.

Abortion, or premature birth among cattle is considered a disease, but I do not consider it a contagious one. The calf is invariably lost, and not unfrequently the cow. If the cow survives, she is almost sure to drop her next calf at about the same period. Some have great faith in preventing this, and contagious diseases with horses and cattle by keeping a goat about the barn. I have more faith in asafetida given in doses of a teaspoonful once or twice a month. A month before the expected return time, and in case one cow loses her calf, it may be well to give other ones that are heavy with calf some attention, for where this occurs, very often it is on account of some local trouble, and calls for a change of food and care. The affected animal should be removed from the rest of the herd as soon as she slinks her calf, as well as should be all evidences of the trouble.

COW POX.

This disease may appear spontaneously among the cows on the farm or in a neighborhood, or may be communicated by the hands of the milkers from one cow to another. It seldom ends fatally; but, while it lasts, it may occasion considerable inconvenience, on account of the discharges and the inflammation of the bag and teats, which often occurs in this disease. In the beginning of the disease, it will be proper to give soft and cooling food and a laxative of half a pound of epsom salts, or the Scotch powder. Bathe the udder with warm vinegar and salt, and smoke as for garget. The milk should be drawn often, and, on account of the great soreness of the teats, as well as to avoid injuring or breaking the skin, the milk should be withdrawn by means of a milking tube, carefully inserted. After the milk is drawn bathe the sores with the Dexter liniment, one part, lard, one part, or with raw linseed oil, and to prevent it spreading, always milk the affected cows last, or wash the hands well before milking other cows. This is something that is more or less troublesome in every dairy, or with farmers that keep very many cows.

CHOKE.

When an animal is choked very frequently it can be told where the choke is, by its action. With high choke the animal holds its head very high and often strikes with its front feet, while with low choke it holds its head lower and keeps more quiet. Treatment: Give as a drench some oil, then if possible, get the animal to eat some soft wet food. This will cause it to swallow, and thus often remove it. If this fails for high choke; very often, if it is an apple, it can be felt, and mashed by holding some solid article against it on one side, and striking it with a mallet on the other side, or by taking the large end of a buggy whip and fastening a sponge to it, dip this in oil and push it down the throat. In fact, this is about the only remedy for low choke. To prevent choke, be careful in feeding apples, roots or pumpkins, and keep the cattle out of the apple orchard.

EGAT, SMUT POISON OR MURRAIN.

These diseases are of frequent occurrence with cattle, and often prove fatal, either by permanent injure or death. In the corn growing districts they occur more frequently in the fall of the year than any other season, and the probability is, that nineteen out of every twenty of such cattle so found dead, died from one or both of two prominent causes with which smut was not even remotely connected. One of these is the gorging of the animals' stomachs with an enormous quautity of highly stimulating food, much of it difficult of digestion, directly after their having been kept on meager, frost-bitten pasturage, or the scant nourishment of a straw stack, which was to tide them over from grass to such time as the corn would be out of the field. Such a sudden and violent change could scarcely do otherwise than demoralize the entire digestive system; and death, equally sudden, violent and unlooked for, ensues. The other prominent cause is the eating largely of dry frosted grass or forest leaves, or the woody, fibrous corn stalks and shucks—more especially the former—later in the season when the better portion of the food has been consumed, and but little else remains, and insufficient water is taken to soften and float it up as it must be before the processes of digestion can be completed; the mass comes to a stand-still, owing to impaction, forms a sort of blockade in the manifolds or third stomach, inflammation sets in and the animal becomes very sick and often past help.

Treatment: As soon as the trouble is observed, which can be told by the animal separating from the herd, becoming restless, lying down, then arising and moving slowly about, standing with a staring look, suddenly starting forward, and in doing so, often fall upon their knees. Something must be done immediately if you wish to save the animal. The first result to be obtained is a physic. This can be obtained by giving lard, one quart; raw oil, one pint; or brewers yeast, one quart, or epsom salts, one pint, dissolved in a quart of warm water. Then to this add one pint of raw linseed oil, and either preparation given as a drench. The latter I consider by far the best. If the animal seems to be suffering with much pain, give the usual dose of aconite and belladona or twice the amount of laudanum. In case there is any suspicion that the other cattle are affected, give the Scotch powder in soft wet feed twice a day for a day or two, to prevent any further trouble.

BLACK-LEG

Is a contagious disease that occurs among young cattle occasionally, and often destroys whole herds, and spreads over an entire neighborhood unless such means are used that will check it. One of the peculiarities of the disease is that it generally attacks the most thrifty animals first, and proves very fatal, the animals often being found dead in the field before notice has been had of them being sick. There is no doubt but what it is to some extent, caused the same cause as murrain.

Symptoms: High fever, lameness, excessive tenderness of the skin in spots, with deposits of black tar like blood, and gas among the tissues, which gives forth a crackling sound when the spot is pressed upon by the hand. The disease takes different forms, sometimes a bloody discharge oozes out of the sore, while again they dry up and crack open, or it may take an internal form, with bloody discharges from nostrils, dung or urine, the same as one form of the swine disease, and like it, soon proves fatal.

Treatment: Like swine fever, cholera in its worst form, but little can be done for it, except to treat the more mild cases, and adopt such measures that will prevent its spreading. Separate the sick from the well ones, and bury the discharges of the sick, and burn the carcasses of the dead. Give the well ones soft food twice a day, in which use the Scotch powder, and some recommend inserting a seton six inches long from the brisket upward, both treatments to be discontinued as soon as the danger is past. Give the affected ones the powder in larger doses, and also insert the seton wet with turpentine and bathe the sores or any swollen parts with any good stimulating liniment, and avoid the use of the milk or meat of all affected animals.

FOOT AND MOUTH DISEASES.

Frequently cattle are troubled with sore feet and mouths, and become very lame or weak, and, if allowed to go uncared for, soon depreciate in flesh, or milk, and in that way proves a loss to their owner. With sore feet, the animal is generally attacked in the hind feet first, and they become very sore between the hoofs, and can be observed by the animal shaking the feet and refusing to stand upon them.

Treatment: Clean and keep dry and apply the wash the same as for foot rot in sheep, or the Dexter liniment. Or run boiling hot tar into the sore, repeat every day until well.

Treatment for sore mouth, the same as for sore mouth with horses.

PLEURO-PNEUMONIA.

This terrible disease among cattle, which has caused millions of dollars of a loss among the cattle of some of the foreign countries, has begun to gain a foot-hold among the dairy districts of America, and is to be feared as much, or more, than the swine plague. It is caused by a paracite germ, the same as contagious diseases, and by damp, filthy stables and yards, and is very contagious, and certain death. There seems to be no mode of treatment yet discovered, that proves successful, except to kill the affected animals and disinfect the stables and premises thoroughly, then quarantine the farm or neighborhood to prevent any animals that may have been exposed to the disease from being sent abroad. This is a sensible, effectual and lawful way of contending with this dreaded disease, and one that should be thoroughly enforced by the American people before it has gained a strong hold, for then it may prove too late.

HIDE-BOUND.

With a poor and dilapidated, or hide-bound cow brute, treat same as for a horse in the same condition. Feed well with rich soft food, and use twice a day the condition powders to cleanse the blood, tone the system, and aid the digestive organs. If in the winter or early spring, a good warm dry stable will be found to be very beneficial.

URINARY TROUBLE.

Cows are just as much subject to urinary trouble as horses, and can be observed the same way, by their repeated efforts to stale, but unable to do so. To treat this give as a drench sweet spirits of niter, one ounce; water, one pint, and then use the condition powder in soft feed.

SCOURS WITH CALVES OR LAMBS.

To check this trouble, take sweet milk, put it over the fire long enough to come to a boiling heat. Let it cool, to one gallon of milk, add a cup of wheat flour, one tablespoonful of ginger, and one fresh egg. Give twice or three times in one day.

GRUB IN SHEEP.

An intelligent shepherd gives the treatment for this trouble, which he guarantees to work, if the sheep is not too far gone: Pour a few drops of turpentine in their ear, and to prevent this trouble, every year about the first week in June, tar their noses well, and give them a spoonful internally. Repeat the operation in July, August and September. If this advice is followed out, there will be no trouble with the grub. For catarrh, use the Scotch powder once a day for a short time, and give the sheep good dry quarters and good feed.

THE MAGGOT.

The maggot, so called, is a formidable enemy of the sheep. The eggs that form them are deposited by the common blue fly. When sheep are wounded by accident, or are allowed to become filthy when troubled with diarrhoea, the eggs or larva are deposited in vast numbers; the maggots soon become active, and spreading from their quarters and attack the skin, which they irritate and cause to secrete a serious fluid. In time the skin is pierced, and the flesh suppurates and wastes away, being devoured by the multitude of maggots which crawl upon it. In wet seasons the mischief is greatly increased. To prevent them it is necessary to carefully remove the wool from about the tail so that filth may not gather; to watch for any accidental wound; and in warm wet weather, for any dirty tags of wool upon which the flies may deposit eggs. In case any maggots are found, there is no better application than common crude petroleum and turpentine, both of which are repulsive and fatal to fly and maggot. A sheep that is "struck" with maggots will remain separate from the flock, and may be lost sight of unless the flock is counted and the straggler found. Weaning time, when the ewes may suffer from caked udder, is an especially critical period, and then extra watchfulness is called for, and the udder should be bathed with lard and camphor.

SCAB IN SHEEP.

Scab or itch with sheep is a contagious disease that shepherds have to contend with in all sheep growing districts. It can first be observed by the sheep rubbing against any projecting body within reach. As it becomes worse, the sheep bite and scratch themselves until they become raw in places. Upon examination, white or hard spots will be found, often from which a yellow substance oozes out, and adheres to the wool. There is no treatment that will prove effectual, except one that will destroy the parasite and its eggs, and the best treatment for this is a strong decoction of tobacco and sulphur, used as a dip or wash at blood heat. This, if thoroughly applied once or twice is an effectual remedy. And with small flocks where they can be handled, the mixture of lard, coal oil and carbolic acid as spoken of in this work, [page 431, Surfeit-Mange,] will effect a cure very quick.

In making the tobacco mixture, good tobacco should be used, either the stems or the entire plant, and the mixture should be made moderately strong, with both tobacco and sulphur. It is utterly needless for a carelesss sheep owner or superintendent to attempt to cure scab, or any other contagious disease with animals, but those however, who will take the necessary pains, can always exterminate most any disease. To rid the flock or herd of any contagious disease, the diseased, dead or dying should be destroyed by burying deep or burning them, and the premises as thoroughly renovated as possible. Ticks on sheep can be destroyed by the aforenamed treatments.

HOOF OR FOOT ROT.

Hoof or foot rot in sheep is another very contagious disease that sheep men have to contend with, and which is very hard to exterminate. It maintains itself year after year alike on wet or dry land, and cannot be eradicated except with considerable labor and skill. Anyone buying sheep should always be on guard for this annoying and contagious disease, and upon no consideration whatever, allow sheep brought upon the farm that are effected with it, or that shows lameness. To cure this disease, clean and pare the feet thoroughly, and apply the tobacco and vitrol treatment with a mop, or prepare a sufficient quantity in a long narrow trough and walk them through it. Keep the feet clean and dry, and repeat the operation once or twice within a week. The preparation of the foot is just as essential as the remedy, for if every part of the disease is not laid bare the remedy will not effect a cure. The solution of strong blue vitrol and tobacco made as hot as the hand can be born in, having the liquid three or four inches deep, or deep enough to cover all the affected parts; then hold the diseased foot in this liquid long enough to penetrate to all the diseased parts. Put the sheep on a dry barn floor a few hours to give it a chance to take effect. This remedy is said to be a dead shot when the foot is thoroughly prepared.

Fields that diseased sheep have been running in should not be used for sheep for some time, and are best cultivated before being used for that purpose again. Prevention is better than cure, and the diseases and parasites to which sheep are subject can be prevented more easily than they can be cured after they once commence their depredations on the flock. Want of care is the prolific cause of accident and disease among stock. The master's eye or the owner's solicitude are proverbially preventatives against trouble or waste; but if the master or the owner will not trouble themselves to exercise the watchful care needed, we may be sure no one else will.

In closing this work I respectfully invite all honest criticism, as well as correspondence and patronage, and will refer you to a few of the many I have worked for, or sold my work to as reference, and as **they** belong to the enterprising stock growing people of this country, they can be relied upon.

PRACTICAL EXPLANATIONS OF HOG CHOLERA—SWINE FEVER.

SPECIAL NOTES.

In order to more plainly explain what hog cholera—swine fever is, what causes it, how it is transmitted from one hog or place to another, and in support of my treatment, that I know to be correct, I will here give the answers to a few questions so frequently asked:

Question.—What is hog cholera?

Answer.—Hog cholera—swine fever is a lung, kidney, liver and intestinal disease.

Q.—What causes it? They are not all sick alike.

A.—It is caused by a parasitic germ, the same as Asiatic Cholera, or typhus or typhoid fever with the human family or epizootic and pneumonia with other stock. (See page 155.) These germs do not attack any particular part of the system, but only work upon the weak organs, hence the different stages of the disease. The lungs are invariably more or less affected. A diseased lung indicates a diseased liver or kidney, therefore the hog walks, as well as breathes, with difficulty. If the digestive organs are impaired, then the disease takes the intestinal form. which may cause constipation or diarrhoea, and inflammation and ulceration takes place which causes death. When these organs are diseased, that shows that the blood is impoverished, and then the disease may produce blood poison, scrofula, and in certain stages what is called measles.

Q.—How is it transmitted from one hog to another?

A.—Principally by the well hogs coming in contact with

the passages of the sick. The poisonous matter is in the urine, manure and where the hog vomits. There is also danger in allowing the well to sleep with the sick, as the poisonous matter is in the place inhabited; therefore the necessity of separating the well from the sick, and putting them in a clean place, and treating them in an open lot, instead of in a pen, or when the weather or circumstances are such that they have to be put in a pen, that the pen be kept clean, and disinfectants be used.

Q.—Can well hogs in one field take the disease from sick ones in another field, by breathing through the fence.

A.—No, the atmosphere takes up the germs and deposits them on the dew of the grass, or in some other way that they are taken into the system with the food or drink. This is why the disease breaks out in herds or localities where there is no accounting for it, and why herds often escape when thus located.

Q.—Why is it that a change of location will sometimes arrest the disease?

A.—Simple enough, the change gets the hogs away from the affected place, and the exercise and probable change of food they receive causes a greater discharge of the passages, thus working the poisonous matter out of the system. (See page 197.)

Q.--Can the disease be carried from one place to another on the boots or clothes of persons, as is claimed by some?

A.—Undoubtedly; also by dogs, buzzards, streams, etc., as explained in this work, page 156.

Q.—Why are hogs more subject to disease than other animals?

A.—The hog, according to its size, requires more oxygen, pure air, than any other animal. We know it carries its nose closer to the ground than any other domestic animal, inhabits more filthy quarters, eats all refuses, and therefore is more subject to malarial fever or contagious diseases. Often it is noticeable that with sick hogs the symptoms are very similar to those of ague with people, and that it occurs more in low or level, than in high lands.

Q.—Is there any difference in the swine disease in the Eastern and Western states?

A.—No, only in the West, on account of the country being newer and hogs more plentiful, being kept in larger herds and receiving less attention, the disease assumes a more malignant form, and spreads more rapidly. (See page 162.)

Q.—Does worms, lice or black-teeth cause cholera?

A.—No; worms only accumulate in a diseased organ. [See pages 163 and 204.] The accumulation of lice, or with sore teeth only, shows the system is otherwise impaired. [See pages 206-8.]

Q.—Will smut poison hogs?

A.—No. [See page 208.]

Q.—Did the Government or any state ever offer a reward for a cure for hog cholera?

A.—No, nor not likely to. [See page 214.]

Q.—Well, is there any cure that will save all the sick?

A.—No; nobody but frauds and quacks talk that; but it is as curable as any fatal disease with any other stock or the human family.

Q.—Are the hogs any account after they are cured?

A.—Yes, with my mode of treatment. I so thoroughly renovate the entire system that they are just as good as if they never were sick. But hogs that never receive no treatment when sick, are neither fit for meat nor breeders, as the disease is transmitted.

Q.—Is there any way to prevent this disease?

A.—Yes; study this book carefully and follow its instructions, and give the hogs every week, once or twice, the tonic powder as given in my recipe, and they will seldom die of any disease, and swine raising can be made a success.

This remedy acts as a stimulant to the entire system, keeps the organs healthy and the blood pure, prevents any clogging or souring of the stomach, stimulates the biliary organs and aids digestion, thus removing the prime causes of all diseases, and promoting perfect health. It will cause hogs to fatten much faster, saving time and feed, and also prevent their rooting, as it supplies the antidote that instinct teaches them to hunt. It thus rids the system of any parasite or disease, making the meat perfectly healthy for use.

This alone should induce every farmer to take care of his hogs, and not only produce healthy meat for his own use, but for that of his fellow men, for it has been practically demonstrated by eminent physicians, that diseased pork has caused consumption in the United States to increase ten-fold in the past ten years, and is also well known that there is at least one-third less pork consumed, than than there would be, on account of diseased hogs.

N. B.—The author, in publishing this work, intended to have the swine treatise in German as well as English, but upon further consideration, concluded it was not necessary, as there are but few families but what can read English.

PUBLISHERS.

ALPHABETICAL INDEX.

SWINE DEPARTMENT.

Author's Treatment—why it is a success	197
And special notes	457
Authors propositions	215
Berkshires	14
Best Breed	19
Boar—his care	24, 38 and 82
Breeding time	27
Buying breeders	77 to 79
Butchering	117 to 130
Breeds—cholera proof	149
Blind staggers	202
Blood poison	205
Black teeth	208
Chester whites	10
Chinese hog	17
Corn—its value as food	20 and 66
Cooking food	36 and 67
Castrating pigs	51
Commence feeding corn	63
Color—its value	81 and 97
Cross hogs	107
Cutting up hogs	124
Cutting and curing meats	126 to 130
Confining hogs	5 and 152
Cough	186
Cholera, what is it	457
Dead hogs	156
Disinfectants	169 and 170
Drenching	187 and 188
Durocks—Jersey Red	13
Essex	17
Errors in feeding	150
Exposure to disease	157
External application	189
Explanation of Cholera	155 and 457
First disease	5
Fattening swine	56 to 73
Fine stock breeding	84
Feed or swill for sick hogs	183
Founder	202
Frosted hogs	207
Germ—theory	6, 164 and 197
Government investigations	159 to 171
Grass for hogs	105
How many litters a year	28 to 37
How much pork will a bushel of corn make	66
How to form a breed	95
Houses or pens for hogs	131 to 145
Importations of swine	3
Improvement of swine	10
Improve your stock	90 to 97
Inbreeding	97
Injections	188
Incurable cases	195
Jersey Red—Durock	13
Judging hogs	25
Kidney disease	201
Killing hogs	117
Lungs—how effected	161 and 200
Local diseases	199
Lice	206
Magie hog	10
Mixed husbandry	37–59
Meats—how to cure	126
Medicine—see recipe or	185-6
Medicine—directions repeated	194
Mange	205
Poland China	10
Pigs, wintering them	32
Pigs—robbing each other	44
Pigs, their care	43 to 55
Pedigreed swine	74 and 97
Pools or streams	156
Pens—their objections	193
Practical explanation of cholera	457
Pneumonia—lung fever	200
Piles	203
Registers	76
Roots and Vegetables	99 to 106
Ringing hogs	106
Rack for hanging hogs	121
Rheumatism liniment	190

Rheumatism	202
Remarks	212
Suffolk	16
Swine breeding	21
Selecting breeders	22
Sows—breeders—their care	39 to 43
Sows—pure bred	85 to 87
Show pens	78 and 88
Stock catcher	108
Swine disease—prevailing causes	158 to 157
Straw—manure and dust	153
Swine disease—its infectious or contagious character	155 to 158
Swine disease—its treatment	174 to 198
Swine disease—explanation	457
Sort the hogs	181
Swill, how to prepare it	183
Sows with pig	162
Sore throat—diptheria	200
Snuffles with pigs	203
Sweating pigs	204
Scours	204
Trichinae	111 to 117
Troughs for hogs	146
Theoretical ideas	171
Tonic powder, see receipe, or	191
Thumps	199
Victorias	15
Vicious sows	107
Wintering pigs	32
Weaning pigs	54
Wheat for hogs	150
Worms—Intestine and lung	152, 163 and 204
Yorkshire	16

POULTRY DEPARTMENT.

Cholera	255
Dominicks	239
Ducks	249
Diseased poultry	254
Eggs, how to preserve them	245
Eggs, their weight	246
Feeding fowls	236
Fattening turkeys	253
Geese	251
Houses for poultry	242
Improve your fowls	226
Investments	230
Incubators	235
Improved fowls	225
Light Brahmas	227
Lice	246
Nests for hens	239
Plymouth Rock	229
Poultry in garden	241
Raising poultry	221 to 226
Roup	258
Selections of fowls	232
Sunflower seed	242
Sick fowls, how to tell them	255
Turkeys	252
Treatment of diseases—see recipe and page	157-8

SHEEP DEPARTMENT.

Breeding information	265
Breeding for profit	274
Coupling season	267
Cotswolds	271
Care and feed	275
Care—things to remember	278
Constipation	248
Ewes—their care	268
Feed and care	275
Foot rot	454
Garget	444
Grub	452
Hamshiredowns	271
Hoven	444
Lambs—their care	269
Lambs—weaning	270
Mutton Breeds	270
Merino	272
Milk fever	444
Maggots	453
Ram—his care	267
Ram, how to select him	268
Sheep husbandry	261
Southdowns	271
Scours	452
Scab	456
Wool growers	262

ALPHABETICAL INDEX

CATTLE DEPARTMENT.

Aberdeen---Angus	288
Alderney	291
Ayrshire	292
Abortion	446
Breeders, how to select	297
Bull, his care	310
Butter making	334
Butter packing	337
Blackleg	449
Cattle industry	284
Controling influence	298
Cows, noted milkers	292
Cows, their care	311
Cows, how to judge them	324
Cows, how to buy	326
Cows, how to feed and milk	331
Cows, stabled	327
Cow pox	447
Calves, removing	314
Calves, first year	315
Calves—scours	452
Choke	447
Dairying	321
Dairy cattle	322
Feeding cattle	305
Feet---Sore	451
Galloways	288
Gurnseys	291
Garget	444
Herefords	288
Holstein---Holland	291
Handling stock	299
Heifers, what age to calve	317
Hoven	444
Hide-bound	452
Influence of parents	298
Inbreeding	301
Jerseys	391-2 and 323
Milking, improper	313
Milkers, unruly	319
Milk fever	444
Murrain	448
Polled Angus	288
Pleuro-pneumonia	451
Shorthorns	284
Steers, large	296
Show herds	300
Sore eyes	443
Scotch powder	443
Stock raising	303
Scours	452
Urinary trouble	452
Water	309

HORSE DEPARTMENT.

Ancient horse	342
American trotter	348
Bellfounder, Imp	353
Bashaws	357
Breeding a science	365
Breeding rules	366
Breeding errors	368
Blue bull	371
Brain fever, blind staggers	425
Bone or bog spavin	427
Boils, collar, etc	432
Canadian Kanuck	342
Clays	357
Clydesdales	362
Colts	399
Colts, weaning	400
Colts, castrate	401
Care of horses	402
Colts, shoeing	407
Colts, education	410
Colic, spasmodic and Flatulent	419
Congestion	422
Colds, distemper	423
Curbs	427
Cribbing	428
Cooling lotion	434
Callouses	435
Colts, diseased or injured	441
Cuts--wounds	442
Draft horses	380
Diseases, how observe	418
Dysentry or scours	420
Distemper	423
English cart	362
Education of horses	408 and 414
Epizootic—Pinkeye	424
Eye wash	433
Eye, cataract	434
Feet, paring	407
Fistula	426
Feet, injured, dressing	429
Founder	430
Foot oil	435

ALPHABETICAL INDEX.

General purpose horse	387
Grooming horses	404
Glanders	425
Grease heel	428
Galls, harness, etc	432
Giving birth	439
Heaves	425
Hide-bound	432
Joint water	438
Kidneys—inflammation	422
Lungs—inflammation	421
Lampas	428
Legs, swelled	431
Lice	432
Leg or body wash	434
Liniment, cataract	434
Liniment, May apple	435
Liniment, corrosive	436
Liniment, Dexter	437
Messenger, imported	349
Messenger's sons, etc	350
Mamorino Chief	354
Mambrino Hambletonian	355
Morgan family	356
Messenger Durock	358
Mares, to be tried	392
Mares, uncertain breeders	393
Mares, number served	394
Mares, their care	396
Mange	431
Normans	361
Pilat	343
Patchers	357
Pacing element	358
Popular sires	370
Pacing in 2:14 or less	396
Pacing, all distances	377
Pacing, all ways	379
Preventives to avoid accidents	414
Pneumonia	421
Pinkeye	424
Poll evil	426
Powders, worm, cough and fever	436
Powders, condition and cleansing	437
Powder, healing	438
Perspiration, how produce	438
Parturition, giving birth	439
Rysdyks, Hambletonian	351
Ringbone	427
Shire horses	362
Speed necessary	369
Standard bred	370
Saddle horses	385
Stallion, management	389
Stallion, education	391
Stallion, effect ot age	396
Shoeing	405
Scours	420
Staleing, profuse	422
Spavin	427
Scratches	428
Sweeney	430
Sprained tendons	431
Surfeit	431
Sprained stifle or whale-bone	438
Sore mouth and tongue	438
Thoroughbred horse	344
Trotting in 2:14 or less	375
Trotting all distances	377
Trotting to wagon	378
Trotting double	379
Trotting, running mate	379
Timidity with horse	413
Thoroughpins	427
Thrush	429 and 435
Tonic preparation	439
Tail and mane care	439
Wind sucking	428
Wolf teeth	432
Whirlbone, sprained	438
Wounds, cuts	442

REMARKS AND REFERENCES.

I am aware that a few books and a great many recipes and medicines for the cure and prevention of hog cholera and then similar diseases, have been offered to to the public; but few of them any good, and some of them extensive frauds, out what more could we expect? The excessive demand itself would cause this. And then there are few who have made the diseases of swine a special study, and fewer yet who have made their treatment a profession, therefore we could not expect much else but failures.

In offering this work to the public, which contains my Swine Treatise in full, in its improved form, as well as the formulas for the medicines I sell to dealers, which are extensively sold and highly endorsed, I honestly believe it will give universal satisfaction and fill a long felt want, for the following reasons:

1st. It is the only treatise ever published by any one who has made the diseases of swine and poultry a special study, and their treatment a profession.

2d. It is not based on theory, but the work of many years of hard study, long experience and an extensive practice.

3d. It is a plain, practical common sense treatment, that the general farmer or stock handler can understand and successfully use.

4th. The drugs that I use are cheap and can be had at any common drug store, although I do not use any copperas, sulphur, ginger, pepper, arnica, saltpeter, lime, venetian red, tobacco, coal oil or caster oil, which constitute most all hog remedies.

5th. The explanations given in this work, as to what hog cholera is, what causes it, and how it is transmitted from one hog or place to another is based upon scientific principles, and I believe will be admitted to be correct when studied.

6th. That my method of treatment is correct and my remedies effectual, I will respectfully submit the following references, and can furnish hundreds of others if necessary. J. B. SHOOK.

REFERENCES.

JAMESTOWN, O., Aug. 21, 1884.

To whom it may concern:—This is to certify, that in addition to my law practice, I ran a large farm and have had considerable experience and observation in the use of Shook's Hog Cholera Remedy, and can say that if the directions are followed, it will do just what is claimed for it, and that Mr. J. B. Shook is a gentleman in every sense of the term.
W. A. PAXSON,
Attorney-at-Law.

JAMESTOWN, O., Aug. 20, 1884.

Mr. J. B. Shook, Circleville, O.: Dear Sir—Please send me some advertising matter; we are having a heavy trade with your medicine; have sold over 1,000 pounds in the last four months. Will be able to work up quite a trade now.
R. B. STRONG,
Druggist.

JAMESTOWN, O., Jan. 25, 1885.

Mr. J. B. Shook, Circleville, O.: Sir—Send me two dozen pamphlets and receipts as per contract. I sold 125 of your Swine Treatise last season in this, Green county, and have no trouble with them. They give good satisfaction and I can send you all the recommendations you want. I expect to do well this season, if I have time to look after it. If I can, I shall canvass the county this year, as I have never introduced the work very far from home, though I have sold 185 of your treatises in the county, and as to the medicine, I have kept no account, but the sales have been very large.
LISBON TURNER.

N. B.—Mr. Turner and Strong bought the right of Green county of me, and to say it paid them well is putting it in a mild form, and that my treatment has given satisfaction the sales and remarks will show, as while I was visiting the Jamestown fair, Mr. John W. Smith, a heavy feeder and shipper of hogs, said, "your remedy is all that is claimed of it. I have been using it over a year, and I not only keep my own hogs healthy with it, but I have frequently bought diseased hogs, taken them home and cured them without losing any, and made plenty of money on them. Every man should make use of it, then we would not be troubled with this hog disease." During the day a great many men spoke to me, as to my Swine treatise, and praised it highly, among whom was Mr. P. O. Johnson, Mr. Ryle Fornosdon, Mr. John Blakely, Mr. B. Rittenhouse, Creamer Bros. and others.

REFERENCES.

WICHITA, KAS., April 22, 1885.

Mr. J. B. Shook, Circleville, O.: Dear Sir— Your treatise for Swine received and given a trial. I am much pleased with it as it seems to be all you recommend it for sick hogs. ALFRED JOHNSON.

The following June Mr. Johnson writes, "we are using your preventative with great success." August 12th following he writes, "your remedy as a preventative or cure is a success. Please give me the price of this county, and what you will furnish the books for, as my son wishes to work it."

FLINT, MICH., Feb. 6, 1883.

Mr. J. B. Shook, Circleville, O.: Sir— Having thoroughly tested your medicine for hogs, as well as the treatise I bought of you for swine diseases and their prevention, I am satisfied you have a good work and I will now buy the right of this county of you.
Yours, J. W. FOSTER.

PLAINWELL, MICH., Jan. 24, 1883.

Mr. J. B. Shook, Circleville, O.: Dear Sir—Enclosed find $5.00 for which send me the worth of in your Hog Remedy.

January 29, 1883.—Medicine received and being used with good results. Enclosed find $5.00 again for which send me the worth of in medicine.

January 30.—Medicine is giving good satisfaction. Send me the recipe. LEVI ARNOLD.

PLAIN CITY, O., Aug. 20, 1883.

Mr. James Mitchell, in paying me for over 100 head of hogs I treated for him, and Mr. John Dodge for 40 or more, said : "We are well satisfied with your work, and that you understand your business." These gentlemen, as well as some of their neighbors, bought my treatment and have always spoke well of it.

ASHMORE, ILL., June 16, 1884.

Mr. J. B. Shook, Circleville, O.: Dear sir—Enclosed find ten ($10) dollars for which send me your treatise on diseased hogs. I have tried your medicine and consider it very reliable.
GEORGE W. OLMSTEAD.

PIPER CITY, ILL., Dec. 4, 1884.

To whom it may concern:—This is to certify that J. B. Shook, of Circleville, O., came here to look after our diseased hogs. He was highly recommended to me by responsible parties in Ohio, and any guarantee he makes I will be responsible for. I am using his treatment and am well satisfied with it. **JOHN A. MONTELIUS.**

PIPER CITY, ILL., Dec. 18, 1884.

Mr. J. B. Shook: Sir—After giving your Swine Remedy a fair trial I am satisfied it is the thing and will cure or prevent the diseases of swine. I had tried several high priced hog remedies, but yours excels them all. I want your treatment. **JOHN BURGER.**

PIPER CITY, ILL., Feb. 16, 1885.

Mr. J. B. Shook:—Your Swine Treatment is well liked here. Please send it to me for my brother. Enclosed find contract and money. The hogs you treated here done well, and I hear of no complaint. I think your work will sell well here now.

PETER MILLER.

SATER, O., Sept. 24, 1884.

Mr. J. B. Shook: Sir—My hogs are now all right. Out of the 150 I treated under your directions, I only lost two small pigs. Please call and see me before you leave Venice, as I want to purchase a right of you. **H. W. SCOTT.**

VENICE, BUTLER Co., O., Oct. 3, 1884.

To whom it may concern:—This is to certify that J. B. Shook, of Circleville, O., has been making his headquarters here for some three weeks, for the purpose of treating diseased hogs. He has been able to make his word good in doing all he claimed he could do, and myself and the people hereabout are well satisfied that he understands his business. **FRANK OCH.**

VENICE, O., Oct. 4, 1884.

Mr. J. B. Shook:—The 60 head of diseased hogs I treated under your advice are now all right. They recovered quick with the loss of but one. I beg pardon for talking to you as I did at first, for you know we have been abused so much that I was discouraged, but when you offered to do all that was right, I concluded a man must be very foolish to let his hogs die and not try your treatment, and I am glad I took your advice. If you ever come this way call and see me. **ORIN BROWN.**

CIRCLEVILLE, O., July 23, 1885.

Mr. J. B. Shook:—I have carefully read your book and can cheerfully recommend it to farmers and all breeders of swine, poultry and other stock. I would not do without it for twice what it costs. I used your receipt for hog cholera-swine fever in my herd of over 100 head, which were attacked during the last year, and it gave good satisfaction. Yours, very respectfully,

WILSON DRESBACH.